PATERNOSTER BIBLICAL MONOGRAPHS

THE WEAKNESS OF THE LAW

God's law and the Christian in New Testament perspective

PATERNOSTER BIBLICAL MONOGRAPHS

> A full listing of titles in both this series and
> Paternoster Theological Monographs
> appears at the end of this book

Series Preface

One of the major objectives of Paternoster is to serve biblical scholarship by providing a channel for the publication of theses and other monographs of high quality at affordable prices. Paternoster stands within the broad evangelical tradition of Christianity. Our authors would describe themselves as Christians who recognise the authority of the Bible, maintain the centrality of the gospel message and assent to the classical credal statements of Christian belief. There is diversity within this constituency; advances in scholarship are possible only if there is freedom for frank debate on controversial issues and for the publication of new and sometimes provocative proposals. What is offered in this series is the best of writing by committed Christians who are concerned to develop well-founded biblical scholarship in a spirit of loyalty to the historic faith.

Series Editors

I. Howard Marshall, Honorary Research Professor of New Testament, University of Aberdeen, Scotland, UK

Richard J. Bauckham, Professor of New Testament Studies and Bishop Wardlaw Professor, University of St Andrews, Scotland, UK

Craig Blomberg, Distinguished Professor of New Testament, Denver Seminary, Colorado, USA

Robert P. Gordon, Regius Professor of Hebrew, University of Cambridge, UK

Tremper Longman III, Robert H. Gundry Professor and Chair of the Department of Biblical Studies, Westmont College, Santa Barbara, California, USA

PATERNOSTER BIBLICAL MONOGRAPHS

The Weakness of the Law

God's law and the Christian in New Testament perspective

Jonathan F. Bayes

Foreword by James M.M. Francis

PUBLISHERS
Eugene, Oregon

Wipf and Stock Publishers
199 W 8th Ave, Suite 3
Eugene, OR 97401

The Weakness of the Law
God's Law and the Christian in New Testament Perspective
By Bayes, Jonathan F.
Copyright©2000 Paternoster
ISBN: 1-59752-745-9
Publication date 6/6/2006
Previously published by Paternoster, 2000

This Edition Published by Wipf and Stock Publishers
by arrangement with Paternoster

Paternoster
9 Holdom Avenue
Bletchley
Milton Keyes, MK1 1QR
Great Britain

All Scripture quotations, unless otherwise indicated, are taken from the
NEW KING JAMES VERSION.
Copyright © 1982 by Thomas Nelson, Inc.
Used by permission. All rights reserved.

Contents

Foreword ix
Acknowledgements xi

Part One: Setting the Scene 1

Chapter 1
Introduction 3

Chapter 2
Historical Survey 5
1   John Calvin 5
2   Antinomian Disputes amongst the English Puritans 8
        1   *The First English Puritan Debate* 9
                1   EATON: 'HONEY-COMBE OF FREE JUSTIFICATION' 9
                2   BOLTON: 'THE TRUE BOUNDS OF CHRISTIAN
                      FREEDOM' 12
        2   *The Second English Puritan Debate* 14
                1   CRISP: 'CHRIST ALONE EXALTED' 14
                2   WATSON: 'THE TEN COMMANDMENTS' 16
3   The Antinomian Controversy in Puritan New England 17
4   The 'Marrow Controversy' 19
        1   *'The Marrow of Modern Divinity, Part One'* 21
        2   *James Hadow: 'The Antinomianism of the Marrow
            Detected'* 23
        3   *Thomas Boston: 'Notes on "The Marrow of Modern
            Divinity"'* 25
5   Antinomianism amongst the Eighteenth-Century English
    Baptists 27
        1   *Brine: 'The Certain Efficacy of the Death of Christ'* 27
        2   *Hall: 'Helps to Zion's Travellers'* 29
6   Antinomian Conflicts within the Methodist Movement 30
        1   *Cudworth: Two Tracts* 32
        2   *Fletcher: 'Second Check to Antinomianism'* 33
7   The Law in the Nineteenth-Century American Holiness
    Movements 35

8	The Keswick Message and the Law		37
9	The Law in Dispensationalism		40
10	The Contemporary Debate		44
	1	*The American Controversy*	44
		1 JOHN REISINGER	44
		2 CHANTRY: 'GOD'S RIGHTEOUS KINGDOM'	46
	2	*The British Controversy*	47
		1 EATON: 'HOW TO LIVE A GODLY LIFE'	48
		2 ALDERSON: 'NO HOLINESS, NO HEAVEN'	49
	Summary		51

Part Two: New Testament Study 53

Introduction 55

Chapter 1
Acts 56

1	Introduction		56
2	Acts 13:39		59
	1	*The Meaning of 'Law'*	59
	2	*The Weakness of the Law*	61
	3	*The Ongoing Status of the Law*	64
		1 THE LAW AND THE JEWISH BELIEVER: THE TIME OF TRANSITION	65
		2 THE LAW AND THE GENTILE BELIEVER: THE TIME OF TRANSITION	67
		3 THE LAW AND THE BELIEVER: THE LONG-TERM VISION	71
		4 THE MORAL LAW AND THE BELIEVER	77
	Conclusion		79

Chapter 2
Romans 81

1	Introduction		81
2	Romans 8:3f		84
	1	*The Meaning of 'Law'*	88

		2	The Nature of the Law's Weakness 92
			1 WHAT IS THE LAW'S INABILITY? 93
			2 WHAT IS THE LAW'S WEAKNESS IN THE SPHERE OF THE FLESH? 95
			3 WHAT IS THE CONNECTION BETWEEN ἀδύνατον AND ἠσθένει? 99
		3	The Ongoing Status of the Law 101
			1 POSITIVE INDICATORS 103
			1 2:13-16 103
			2 2:25-29 107
			3 3:27,31 109
			4 6:19b 111
			5 13:8-10 112
			2 NEGATIVE INDICATORS 115
			1 6:14f 115
			2 7:4 117
			3 7:6 117
			4 10:4 119
		Conclusion 124

Chapter 3
Galatians 125

1 Introduction 125
    1   στοιχεῖα as Law 125
    2   The Background to Galatians 131
2 Galatians 3:21 and 4:9 135
    1   The Meaning of 'Law' 135
    2   The Nature of the Law's Weakness 137
    3   The Ongoing Status of the Law 165
    Conclusion 173

Chapter 4
Hebrews 175

1 Introduction 175
2 Hebrews 7:18f 177
    1   The Meaning of 'Law' 177
    2   The Nature of the Law's Weakness 181

	3 The Ongoing Status of the Law	190
	Conclusion	206

Summary 207
1   The Meaning of 'Law' 207
2   The Weakness of the Law 207
3   The Ongoing Status of the Law 208

Conclusion 210

Bibliography 215
1   Historical Sources (Introduction and Part One) 215
      1)   Primary Texts 215
      2)   Secondary Sources 217
2   Theological and Biblical Works (Part Two) 221

Index 235
1   Scripture References 235
2   Main Subjects 240

FOREWORD

This book by Jonathan Bayes is an important contribution to the fields both of moral theology and New Testament Studies. It is moreover one of those rare books these days which creates a careful interplay between theological and Biblical study and this is to be greatly welcomed. The subject of the law is one which almost from the beginning has had a prominent place in Christian reflection and debate. It was at the heart of Jesus' conflict with the Pharisees over patterns of observance. As the early church grew through the Gentile mission the question of the status of the law continued particularly in the controversy over circumcision and the relevance of *kashrut*. And as this book shows the subject of the law in its ongoing moral significance within the arena of doctrinal theology has continued to be debated. The conclusions reached at every point in this study are wise, measured and full of insight.

We are taken in the first part of the book through a fascinating study of how the third use of the law (i.e. its moral meaning as distinct from the ceremonial and the judicial) has been discussed within the particular context of Reformed theology. What is at stake is a discussion whether the law in relation to the indwelling of the Spirit has an ongoing ability to inform and shape the Christian life (advocacy of the third use of the law) as distinct from the power of the Spirit as the sole and sufficient means of sanctification (doctrinal antinomianism). This is no abstract question for on its outcome depends a Christian perspective on human nature, approaches to pastoral care and indeed the nature of revelation itself. The fact that it has been and continues to be debated so earnestly shows its continuing relevance. We are taken on a fascinating journey through a discussion which begins with Calvin and which traces important evidences of the debate in different traditions and settings, both historical and contemporary. This theological survey is of great value in and of itself, and it leaves the reader with a very sound grasp of the issues involved as the context for the ensuing exegetical task. The question of the weakness of the law is shown to be at the heart of the discussion. Dr Bayes carefully acknowledges this as a shared evaluation of the law which runs through all Reformed theology, and from the acknowledgement of that commonality he carefully identifies the key question not whether the law is weak but in what sense it is weak.

The exegetical journey parallels the preceding theological journey with a careful and balanced discussion of the five texts in the New Testament which speak of the weakness of the law. These texts are Acts 13.39; Romans 8.3-4; Galatians 3.21 and 4.9; Hebrews 7.18-19. Each is examined in careful detail and there is a clear commitment both to understanding the text in context and within the dynamic of the theology of the writer's own thinking. What emerges is an appreciation of the nuances and diversity of thought between the passages as they serve the respective writers' purposes, and a remarkable unanimity which encourages one to believe that a broad but coherent Biblical theology is to be found within the New Testament. The outcome of the exegetical study is not undertaken as a foregone conclusion (as can sometimes happen in doctrinal readings of texts), but patiently and skillfully we are shown that in diverse ways the sustained contribution of the law to sanctification is to be affirmed.

We are then returned to a dialogue with the various perspectives outlined in the initial theological survey. The insights of the exegetical findings are then applied to the range of arguments put forward by the advocates on both sides. In this concluding assessment we are shown with consummate skill how Biblical and doctrinal theology can interact, and we may reflect on the lesson that without such a dialogue both are actually impoverished.

The consistent understanding of "law" in these New Testament texts as the Law of Moses is in agreement with some recent reaffirmation in Pauline studies that *torah* can be an appropriate rendering of νόμος, and that what is in Paul's mind are indeed Israel's covenantal obligations. Dr. Bayes's study has the welcome outcome of showing that Paul, creative thinker though he is, stands within the broad faith outlook of the early church. Moreover it further confirms Christianity's place (as the only world religion which, to my knowledge, has the scriptures of another religion as part of its own canon) within the heritage of God's covenantal promise to His people. The affirmation of the validity of the third use of the law in the dispensation of Christ reminds the church through the Gospel that the work of the Spirit is the work of the selfsame God of Covenant whose blessings are signalled in their fulfilment in Christ. This study is indeed a work of the highest scholarship and which contains many creative insights. Its implications are profound for the life of the church in the modern world and for the ongoing formation of personal belief.

James M.M. Francis
Sunderland, 1999

Acknowledgements

I wish to express my gratitude to Dr. Francis, both for his help as my supervisor while this thesis was in preparation, and also for his generosity in contributing the foreword.

Thanks are due also to my wife, Cathy, for her constant encouragement, and also to my father-in-law, Mr. Raymond Eldred, who financed my studies.

Jonathan Bayes
Stockton-on-Tees, 1999

Part One

Setting the Scene

CHAPTER 1

Introduction

Naturally, since justification by faith had been joyfully rediscovered by the Reformation as the heart of the biblical message and since for that reason the revolt against Rome was a revolt against justification by the works of the law, it was inevitable that questions should be raised as to the function of the law in the life of believers.

So writes Professor Berkouwer. He observes that the function of the law to direct the life of believers "has been the subject of extended debate" within Reformed theology, and that 'the essential question' "whether the believer, because he is 'under grace,' has no further truck with the law" has "played a major role in the history of the church."[1]

The topic addressed by this work is the debate within the Reformed Evangelical constituency in the English-speaking world about what has become known as 'the third use of the law'. Three things must immediately be clarified.

(1) What is the meaning of 'Reformed Evangelical'? The Reformed tradition has been aptly defined as "that pattern of Protestant Christianity which has its roots in the sixteenth-century Reformation in Switzerland and Strasbourg".[2] The addition of the word 'Evangelical' narrows the focus to that section of the Reformed tradition which has continued to affirm the inspiration, inerrancy, sufficiency and authority of Scripture as the infallible Word of God, against the changing patterns of theology in the nineteenth and twentieth centuries.

(2) What is the meaning of 'law' in this context? The Reformed constituency has usually recognized the diversity of possible uses of this word, and has traditionally assumed the validity of the threefold division of the law into its moral, ceremonial and judicial parts, while also understanding the moral law to have primacy. There have, however, been some Reformed theologians who have rejected these distinctions.[3]

---

[1] G.C. Berkouwer, *Faith and Sanctification* (Eerdmans, 1952), pp. 163-5, 168.
[2] J.H. Leith, *Introduction to the Reformed Tradition* (St. Andrew Press, 1977), p. 8.
[3] E.g. J. Metcalfe, *Deliverance from the Law* (Metcalfe, 1992), p. 5.

(3) What is the purport of the phrase 'third use of the law'? The doctrine of the threefold use of the law, which applies particularly to its moral division, has been described as "a hallmark of Reformed theology".[1] The first two uses are the condemnation of unrighteousness in the sinner, and the social role of restraining those who are particularly unruly. The 'third use' refers to the function of the moral law as the pattern of life for the believer.

The third use of the law has been debated periodically since the Reformation, and the recent past has seen a recurrence of interest in the subject. The point at issue may be summarized as follows: does the moral element in the law of the Old Testament continue to have binding force and directing power in the life of the believer, such that it exercises a key role in sanctification when employed by the Holy Spirit, or does the Holy Spirit work directly, or, if He employs any means at all, is the Gospel of justification by grace through faith in Christ the sole and sufficient instrument of sanctification? This latter position has been called 'doctrinal antinomianism', and must be distinguished from 'practical antinomianism'. The issue is not whether Christians ought in practice to keep the law, but whether the law is itself a means to this end.

The purpose of this study is to contribute to the debate by assessing the implications for the question of the place of the law in the life of the Christian believer of the five New Testament allusions to the weakness of the law (Ac. 13:38f; Rom. 8:3f; Gal. 3:21; 4:9; Heb. 7:18f). The law's weakness has been asserted as an argument against the third use, and the debate sometimes involves analysis of the law in terms of weakness and power. That there is some sense in which the law is weak is universally acknowledged in Reformed theology: the matter in dispute is the precise area of its weakness.

Each of the five texts will be examined in the context of the book in which it occurs. The goal is to ascertain which of the two positions (advocacy of the third use of the law or doctrinal antinomianism) has the greater claim to New Testament support. Each position as here defined is a broad classification, akin to the sociologist's 'ideal-type': "one will find approximations to it and deviations from it, in varying degrees".[2]

The scene will be set for the Biblical study by an outline of the debate through reference to a selection of participants on each side. I shall focus, in approximate chronological order, on some of those periods when the issue of the law in the Christian life has surfaced in Evangelical history, concluding with the contemporary debate. Particular notice will be taken of the use of references to the law's weakness and power, and of the five New Testament texts mentioned above.

---

[1] I.J. Hesselink, *Calvin's Concept of the Law* (Pickwick, 1992), p. 218.
[2] P.L. Berger, *Invitation to Sociology* (Penguin, 1963), p. 27.

CHAPTER 2

Historical Survey

Although the parameters of this study have been set as the English-speaking world, the natural point of departure is nevertheless the theology of John Calvin, since it is to him that the English-speaking Reformed constituency traditionally looks back. The historical survey will therefore commence with an outline of the seminal teaching of Calvin's *Institutes* on the third use of the law.

1   John Calvin

Calvin accepts the threefold distinction between the moral law, the ceremonial law, and the judicial law.[1] The moral law is the most important as "the perfect rule of conduct".[2]

Great stress is placed both on human moral weakness and on the power of sin in human life. This underlies a recurrent emphasis on 'the weakness of the law'.[3] It is in II.7 that Calvin focuses particularly on the moral law. Our survey of his thought will, therefore, concentrate on this chapter.

First he argues that the Law, in the sense of "the whole system of religion delivered by the hand of Moses", was given to keep the Jews "in suspense" until the coming of Christ. The provisionality of the Law in this sense is stressed and Galatians 3:17-24 and Hebrews 7-10 are cited. At the end of the second paragraph Calvin admits that Paul sometimes speaks of the Law "in a more restricted sense, merely as law"; paragraph 3 then begins with an indication of his intention to speak, in these more specific terms, of the purpose of the Moral Law, which sets before us the perfect righteousness which is the prerequisite for eternal life; but, Calvin asks, "Of what use is it to see that the reward of eternal life depends on the observance of the law, unless it moreover appears whether it be in our power in that way to attain to eternal life?" The reality is that the law transcends our capacity, and therefore we cannot derive any benefit from

---

[1] J. Calvin, *Institutes of the Christian Religion* (MacDonald, 1559), e.g. IV.20:14.
[2] *Ibid.*, III.7:1.
[3] The precise phrase occurs at *ibid.* II.,7:3.

the promises which are annexed to the law. This is what constitutes the law's weakness. Hence, if we look merely to the law, despondency results,[1] because "the feebleness of our nature" makes obedience impossible. Romans 8:3 is cited.[2]

Calvin then proceeds to analyze the office of the law into three parts, indicating his own acceptance of the doctrine of the threefold use of the law. His comments on the first use are important for his understanding of the weakness of the law. He describes the law as a mirror of our impotence: "by itself it can do nothing but accuse, condemn and destroy" the sinner. It is the inability to justify which lies at the heart of Calvin's understanding of the law's weakness,[3] which is the concomitant of our lack of power to obey it. Consequently, part of the law's power is its ability to teach that the power to obey is derived from God's grace.

Paragraph 12 opens with these words: "The third use of the Law (being also its principal use and more closely connected with its proper end) has respect to believers in whose hearts the Spirit of God already flourishes and reigns."

In Calvin's view, the presence of the Holy Spirit in the regenerate human heart by no means implies that the law has become irrelevant. There are two ways in which believers "still profit in the law": (1) it enables them increasingly to learn what is the will of God; (2) it excites them to obedience: the law is pictured as "a whip to the flesh, urging it on as men do a lazy sluggish ass"; for the believer "the Law is a constant stimulus, pricking him forward when he would indulge in sloth".[4] The law is 'the positive expression' of fear and love of God and love for the neighbour.[5]

Calvin insists that this is not inconsistent with passages from Paul's letters on the inability of the law, which are applicable only when it is considered 'of itself', that is, in isolation from grace and the Spirit. The law is understood as part of the covenant, and the resulting ethic is one of gratitude.[6] Hence there is in Calvin's understanding of sanctification, an inextricable connection between the Holy Spirit and the law. The Spirit is the agent and the law the instrument. Employed by the Spirit, the law is, in the life of the believer, a power for exciting obedience. The law is "a peculiar organ of the Holy Spirit for renewing and reforming people in the image of God".[7]

---

[1] *Ibid.*, II.7:4.
[2] *Ibid.*, II.7:5.
[3] Cf. e.g. *ibid.*, II.2:8, 10, 22; 5:4, 6; 11:8; III.11:3.
[4] *Ibid*, II.7:12.
[5] T.H.L. Parker, *John Calvin* (Dent, 1975), p. 38.
[6] So Hesselink, e.g., pp. 87-94; cf. W. Niesel, *Reformed Symbolics* (Oliver & Boyd, 1962), pp. 219, 224.
[7] Hesselink, p. 251.

Although Calvin already stressed the third use of the law in his earliest writings,[1] it is apparent that his understanding developed in contrast to what he regarded as erroneous views. The expansion of the Institutes in successive editions bears witness to controversies in which he was engaged, and from the 1543 edition there are passages, including paragraphs 13-15 of II.7, which recall his struggles against the Spiritual Libertines.[2]

Although only fragmentary theological documentation of spiritual libertinism survives,[3] it seems that they stressed the direct work of the Spirit and freedom from all external norms, including the Scriptures and the law of God. The letter/Spirit distinction was absolutised.[4] According to Calvin, they "discard the whole law of Moses..., imagining it unchristian to adhere to a doctrine which contains the ministration of death". He retorts that, while the law can produce nothing but death in sinners, it ought to have a more excellent effect on the righteous, since it contains the perfect pattern of righteousness. This being so, "unless we ought not to have any proper rule of life, it must be impious to discard it. There are not various rules of life, but one perpetual and inflexible rule."[5]

The law is not to believers what it once was: it no longer condemns, and in that sense is indeed abrogated, because Christ was made a curse for us (Gal. 3:10-14). It is necessary, however, to "distinguish accurately what has been abrogated in the Law, and what still remains in force". The abrogation of the law's curse does not mean that it has lost any of its authority, and it "must always receive from us the same respect and obedience".[6]

The law's weakness, then, is both its incompleteness as a mere pointer to Christ, and its inability to justify because of human moral weakness, while its power lies in its ability to reveal the sinner's inability to obey. In the Christian life, the Holy Spirit works mediately, through the moral law. It was this position on the third use of the law which was thus established as Reformed orthodoxy.

---

[1] *Ibid.*, p. 8; *against* H. Höpfl, *The Christian Polity of John Calvin* (Cambridge University Press, 1982), p. 175.

[2] F. Wendel, *Calvin* (Harper, 1963), p. 119f; N. Cohn, *The Pursuit of the Millennium* (Paladin, 1970), p. 170, dates allusions to the Spiritual Libertines from 1539.

[3] G.H. Williams, *The Radical Reformation* (Westminster, 1962), p. 351.

[4] Cf. J.H.M. d'Aubigne, *History of the Reformation in Europe in the Time of Calvin*, Vol. III (Longman, 1864), p. 96; Cf. E. Doumergue, *Jean Calvin* (Editions de La Cause, 1926), p. 67; B.W. Farley, 'The Theology of Calvin's Tract Against the Libertines', in R.C. Gamble (ed.), *Articles on Calvin and Calvinism* (Garland, 1992), Vol. 5, pp. 209-17; Höpfl, p. 276, n. 20; J. Lecler, *Toleration and the Reformation* (Association Press, 1960), Vol. 1, pp. 165, 179; Vol. 2, pp. 9, 259; A. Verhey, 'Calvin's Treatise *"Against the Libertines"*, Introduction', in Gamble (ed.), Vol. 5, p. 222.

[5] Calvin, *Institutes*, II.7:13.

[6] *Ibid.*, II.7:14-15.

2 Antinomian Disputes amongst the English Puritans

The Puritans are linked to Calvin via the Heidelberg theologians, Ursinus, Olevianus and Zanchius.[1] Although it has been argued that the comments on the Sabbath in Q. 103 of the Heidleberg Catechism, indicate a different view of the law,[2] this is not the only possible reading of the section, which, arguably, does teach the third use of the law. The section concerned with the good works which are to be done by those who are redeemed through Christ defines good works as "those only which are done from true faith, according to the law of God". There follows an exposition of the law. It is admitted that, in this life, believers "have only a small beginning" of obedience to the law; nevertheless, "with earnest purpose they begin to live, not only according to some, but according to all the commandments of God."[3]

English Puritanism followed Calvin and Heidelberg in affirming the third use of the law. The Westminster Confession of Faith of 1646 includes the following statements on the Law:

> The moral law doth for ever bind all, as well justified persons as others, to the obedience thereof.... Although true believers be not under the law as a covenant of works, to be thereby justified...; yet it is of great use to them...; in that, as a rule of life, informing them of the will of God and their duty, it directs and binds them to walk accordingly.[4]

This section remained unaltered in the Savoy Declaration of 1658, and the Baptist Confession of 1689. Antinomianism was discussed in 1689 at the Particular Baptist Assembly, but was resisted.[5]

However, there was a group of preachers in this period, first led by John Eaton,[6] who taught doctrinal antinomianism as their theory of sanctification. The root of their teaching was probably the desire to allay the fears of Church members about their election,[7] and to solve the problem of assurance, a central pastoral issue for Calvinism.[8] The debate between the

---

[1] So R.T. Kendall, *Calvin and English Calvinism to 1649* (Oxford University Press, 1979), p. 38f.
[2] D. Carson, *School of Advanced Learning: Biblical Interpretation* (International Christian Communications, 1994), Tape 4.
[3] Heidelberg Catechism, Qs. 91-113.
[4] Westminster Confession of Faith (Free Presbyterian Publications, 1985), XIX:v-vi.
[5] R. Brown, *The English Baptists of the Eighteenth Century* (Baptist Historical Society, 1986), pp. 36, 73.
[6] So E. Pagitt, *Heresiography* (London, 1645), p. 89.
[7] So M.R. Watts, *The Dissenters* (Clarendon, 1978), p. 179f.
[8] Cf. D.W. Bebbington, *Evangelicalism in Modern Britain* (Unwin Hyman, 1989), pp. 43-5.

Historical Survey 9

'orthodox' puritans and the doctrinal antinomians has been documented by Ernest Kevan.[1]

The issue of antinomianism surfaced twice during the puritan period. The first dispute came to a head in the 1640's, though its origins can be traced back at least to the early 1630's.[2] When the Westminster Assembly met from 1643 its twin purposes were to guard against Arminianism and antinomianism;[3] the statement on the Law in the Westminster Confession was of directly polemical intent. The second controversy was occasioned by the republication in 1689 of the works of Tobias Crisp, one of the leading doctrinal antinomians[4] of the earlier generation.[5] The contest against antinomianism on this occasion was led by Richard Baxter and Daniel Williams.[6] Each debate will be illustrated by setting side-by-side one work from each party in the dispute about the law.

1   The First English Puritan Debate

The antinomians will be represented by John Eaton. From the side of the orthodox puritans who replied to the antinomian challenge I have selected Samuel Bolton.

1   EATON: 'HONEY-COMBE OF FREE JUSTIFICATION'

The thrust of this work, on Romans 3:21f, is that justification results, negatively, in God seeing no sin in believers, and, positively, in His seeing His people as perfectly holy and righteous. Eaton recognizes the weakness of the law as regards justification, and links this with human moral weakness: "The law of God it selfe containeth the perfect rule of righteousnesse, yet through our weaknesse it is unpossible that by it we can attaine unto righteousnesse."[7]

Hence, its function is to expose sin, and exercise its power of killing.[8] The "weaknesse and infirmitie" of man is answered by God's power,

---

[1] E.F. Kevan, *The Grace of Law* (Soli Deo Gloria, 1963, 1993), *passim*.

[2] S. Foster, 'New England and the Challenge of Heresy, 1630-1660: The Puritan Crisis in Transatlantic Perspective', in *William and Mary Quarterly* 38 (1981), p. 633.

[3] so D.Neal, *History of the Puritans* (Brown & Robinson, 1811), p. 65.

[4] So J.M. Kik, Notes to S. Bolton, *The True Bounds of Christian Freedom* (Banner of Truth, 1964), p. 152, n. 1.

[5] cf. R. Thomas, 'Parties in Nonconformity', in G.C. Bolam, J. Goring, H.L. Short, & R. Thomas, *The English Presbyterians* (Allen & Unwin, 1968), p. 107; *ibid*, 'The Break-up of Nonconformity', in G.F. Nuttall, R. Thomas, R.D. Whitehorn, & H.L. Short, *The Beginnings of Nonconformity* (James Clarke, 1962), p. 41.

[6] W.M. Lamont, *Richard Baxter and the Millennium* (Croom Helm, 1979), p. 266f; R. Thomas, 'Presbyterians in Transition', in Bolam, Goring, Short, & Thomas, p. 118.

[7] J. Eaton, *The Honey-Combe of Free Justification* (Lancaster, 1642), p. 21; cf. p. 33.

[8] *Ibid*, pp. 8f, 86; cf. pp. 11-17, 26, 124.

"mightily manifested" in the free justification which puts sin out of His sight.¹ Eaton refers on five occasions to Acts 13:38-40.² He also cites Romans 8:3f five times, understanding the fulfilling of the law's righteousness in us to be a statement of justification.³

That Eaton was fairly labelled a doctrinal antinomian is evident. He teaches that the joyful sense of free justification at the cost of the blood of the God's Son is the sufficient motive to holiness. At one point the marginal heading reads: "The mighty power of the Gospel, to true sanctification."⁴ Much use is made of Romans 8 in this context. Of the numerous statements on this theme, the following is typical:

> The laying out of the excellency of free Iustification worketh also this powerful effect; namely that it is the onely meanes to eradicate, and utterly root out that inbred originall corruption.... The true joyfull knowledge of [the benefit of Justification] is the only powerful meanes to regenerate, quicken, and sanctifie us, and to make us truly to love, feare, and trust in God, working in us the true Evangelicall repentance; in sincerity hating sin, because it is sin, and in truly loving all holinesse and righteousnesse: and thus it is Gods holy fire that enflameth his people with right thankfull zeale of Gods glory, in carefull and diligent walking in all Gods Commandements.⁵

It is correct to interpret this to mean that the believer does not need the law because he serves Christ spontaneously and thankfully.⁶ Indeed, Eaton stresses the hindrance to sanctification which results from the promulgation of the law: it causes a constrained, hypocritical sanctity. Works should flow in thankfulness from the assurance of justification.⁷

Underlying this view of sanctification is a radical disjunction between Law and Gospel, interwoven with a threefold understanding of the time of the Church, based, in part, on Hebrews 7:19, with references also to Galatians 3-4. (1) During the time of the Law Christ was veiled behind both the Ceremonial and the Moral Law, to show God's children that nothing pleased Him except the perfect righteousness revealed in the Law, and to make them groan for the coming of the Messiah. (2) With the coming of the Messiah the time of the Law expired, and with it the legal whippings of the

---

¹ *Ibid*, p. 96; cf. pp. 52, 58, 74, 89f, etc.
² *Ibid*, pp. 7, 74, 89f, and, as a marginal reference, pp. 146, 315f.
³ *Ibid*, pp. 88, 286f, 372, and, in the margin, pp. 59, 364.
⁴ *Ibid*, p. 466.
⁵ *Ibid*, p. 456f.
⁶ So D.D. Wallace, *Puritans and Predestination* (University of North Carolina Press, 1982), p. 116.
⁷ J. Eaton, p. 115; cf. pp. 404, 456.

people of God to obedience by fear. (3) At the time of the outpouring of Christ's blood on the cross, there commenced an era in which God no longer remembers His people's sins. They are free from the Law's schoolmaster-like government.[1] Eaton argues that this serves to give to each of the Law and the Gospel "its proper force, strength and power".[2]

This theory of sanctification is rigorously applied to the preacher.

> We Ministers of this glory of the Gospel, too many among us, doe not only limp in our practise, and lisp in our speech, but even halt downright;... that is, in not preaching and opening the glory of Free Iustification.... Wee slide back to the legall teaching of the Old Testament, from which we not understanding the intent of God in such high commending, and sharp exacting of works and legall righteousness, doe fetch our principall veine of preaching; and doe make it our common and chiefest manner of teaching, only a little as the old Prophets did, to glance at Free Iustification, mercy and grace in generall terms; but all our maine labour is to command things that are right, and to forbid wicked doings, to promise rewards to the followers of righteousnesse, and to threaten punishment to the transgressors.... But what comes hereof? truly we sow up againe (in respect of the former Pedagogie of the morall Law) the vaile that was rent in two pieces, from the top to the bottome: we shut up again the holy of holies: we hide & darken, if not put out the benefits of Christ, preaching, as if the children of God were not made perfectly holy and righteous from all spot of sinne in the sight of God freely. We confound the Old Testament with the New.

This challenge is underlined from Acts 13:38-42 and Galatians 4.[3] The Law alone in its killing power must be applied to the careless sinner until he is humbled, and then the Gospel alone to humbled ones. To fail in this involves "not feeling how powerfull the treasures of the Gospel alone are, both to abolish all sin from before God, and by joy and zeale thereof to mortifie all sin in ourselves."[4]

Whether this doctrinal antinomian position can in fact be consistently sustained may be questioned. Eaton suggests that the works of love and thankfulness will follow "in a manner of their own accord (with a little help of direction, and exhortation) flowing from a true, right, thankfull zeale of Gods glory, making them willing and ready to grow, and cheerfully to walk in all the holy duties of all his Commandements."[5]

---

[1] *Ibid*, pp. 98-111.
[2] *Ibid*, p. 85f.
[3] *Ibid*, p. 113f.
[4] *Ibid*, p. 135f.
[5] *Ibid*, p. 466.

The phrase in parenthesis is noteworthy: it is unclear how direction and exhortation differs from the preaching of the law.

2   BOLTON: 'THE TRUE BOUNDS OF CHRISTIAN FREEDOM'

Bolton distinguishes eight Scriptural uses of the word 'Law', and notes that controversy concerns the question "whether believers are freed from the moral law" as focussed in the Decalogue. He concludes that the law "remains as a rule of walking to the people of God".[1]

He makes frequent reference to the weakness of the law, like Eaton understanding this to be derived from human inability, a recurring theme in this book,[2] and a factor which makes it legitimate to say that "the law requires hard and impossible things."[3] The purpose of the giving of the law was "to show us our weakness and to stir up our hearts to seek Christ, who has fulfilled all righteousness for us."[4] However, the law is not to be described only as weak: as an instrument of the Spirit, with a view to the conversion of sinners, the law possesses enlightening, convincing and humbling power.[5]

It is the link between human weakness and the weakness of the law which explains a paradox in Bolton's work, in which he first asserts the abrogation of the law's power to justify, and then denies that it ever possessed this potential:

(1) For believers the law is abrogated in respect of its power to justify.

(2) If the law was given to show the full extent of sin, and the greatness of sin, then surely there is no possibility that man should be justified by it.[6]

This apparent contradiction is resolved by reference to the human condition. Considered in its own bare integrity, the law does, for Bolton, possess justifying power: any human being who did fulfil its requirements would be reckoned just in the sight of a righteous God. However, because of the fallenness of man, this logical possibility is never in fact enacted; this is a theoretical power which is absent in the context of a fallen world. In practice, therefore, within the given circumstances of life, the law has no power to justify sinful man, because he does not fully obey it. Rather, it possesses condemning, accusing, cursing and killing power.[7]

---

[1] Bolton, pp. 54-9.
[2] E.g., *ibid*, pp. 19, 213f.
[3] *Ibid*, p. 149; cf. p. 40.
[4] *Ibid*, p. 106f.
[5] *Ibid*, pp. 29f, 39, 72, 86, 96, 105f.
[6] *Ibid*, pp. 58, 103.
[7] *Ibid*, pp. 29-31, 38, 86, 103.

However, these aspects of the law's power relate only to the unbeliever, for in Christ the law is unable to condemn, accuse, curse and kill.[1] On the other hand, there is another aspect of the law's power under which the believer still remains, namely its commanding or directive power. As far as believers are concerned, "there is no further power left in the law than is for our good ..., and this is intended to lead to our futherance in grace."[2] "It still has power to direct us."[3]

Of the New Testament texts which are the theme of this study, Bolton refers most frequently (four times) to Romans 8:3, making the point that two impossibilities are taught simultaneously: we could not obey the law, and therefore the law could not help us; while the law is able to condemn, it cannot save.[4]

The inability of the law to impart strength to fallen man is another recurrent theme. Bolton notes that the law "lays heavy yokes upon us, but gives us not the least help or necessary strength for fulfilling its requirements."[5] However, on another occasion he writes: "The law shows us what is holy, but cannot make us holy, as long as it is a rule outside of us. It cannot make us holy, for that necessitates a rule within us."[6] The phrase 'as long as' is a very telling one. It implies that the law itself is able to become the 'rule within us', and so to acquire the power to make us holy. In the energy of the Spirit it is powerful as a means of the believer's transformation. Bolton's understanding of the interaction between Spirit and law is evident in the exhortation, "Let the righteousness of the law be fulfilled in us; let us walk not after the flesh, but after the Spirit (Rom. 8:4)."[7]

In one section Bolton attacks the Antinomians directly, accusing them of decrying the law for sanctification: "We claim to be free from the curses of the law; they would have us free from the guidance, from the commands of the law. We say we are free from the penalties, but they would abolish the precepts of the law." Bolton argues that a function of the law is to send sinners to the Gospel for justification, but that the Gospel then returns believers to the law for sanctification. He asserts that the law defines the eternal nature of good and evil, and cannot therefore be altered as the antinomians claim.[8]

---

[1] *Ibid*, pp. 28, 31-3, 38, 48, 58, 60, 65, 150.
[2] *Ibid*, p. 39; cf. p.65.
[3] *Ibid*, p. 58.
[4] *Ibid*, pp. 31, 92, 106, 107.
[5] *Ibid*, p. 40f (cf. pp. 97, 217).
[6] *Ibid*, p. 87.
[7] *Ibid*, p. 75.
[8] *Ibid*, p. 70f.

2   The Second English Puritan Debate

Because it was the republication of the works of Crisp which led to this controversy, he will represent the antinomians. His orthodox antagonists will be represented by Thomas Watson, the second part of whose 'Body of Practical Divinity' consists largely of an exposition of the Decalogue, but also includes material on the the third use of the law.

1   CRISP: 'CHRIST ALONE EXALTED'

This collection of sermons is concerned largely with justification. Crisp stresses that there is no justification through the law. He notes that the law's continual peal is 'cursed'. Herein lie both its power and its weakness: in respect of those who give the law power over themselves, it takes power and curses, while its weakness is explained in these words: "There cannot be a word of comfort heard.... There cannot come in the least glimmerings of light." His point is that the law is too weak to offer any hope at all: Christ does everything necessary to secure the justification of His 'free-men'.

The law's weakness is related to the weakness of sinful human nature: "There is no man, but in some respect or other, every act that he doth hath some infirmity or failing in it." Consequently, the law requires the impossible, and, however "weak and unable" we are, "will give no help at all". This constitutional human weakness is as true of the believer as the unregenerate: "the free-man of Christ ... is weak, poor, and unable to work." However, in this case the power of the law is redefined. It is still weak as regards justification, but it has lost its power to curse. Nevertheless, Crisp appears not to see the law as having sanctifying power in the believing life: the power for holy living comes directly from the Spirit of Christ.[1]

It was this which caused Crisp to be suspected of doctrinal antinomianism. One passage seized upon by the orthodox puritans reads: "If you be free-men of Christ, you may esteem all the curses of the law, as no more concerning you, than the laws of England concern Spain, or the laws of Turkey an Englishman."[2]

John Gill seeks to exonerate Crisp; he comments that Crisp's puritan antagonists misrepresented this passage as teaching that "a man under grace, hath no more to do with the law than an Englishman hath with the laws of Spain or Turkey". Correctly Gill points out that Crisp referred to "the curses of the law (not the law itself)".[3] However, it must be pointed out that Crisp's parallel is inexact, and therefore not surprisingly raised questions in the minds of the Westminster divines, and, in the next generation, of Baxter.

---

[1] T. Crisp, *Christ Alone Exalted*. 2 Vols. (Bennett, 1832), Vol. I, pp. 125-37.
[2] *Ibid*, p. 132.
[3] J. Gill, 'Notes Explantory of Several Passages in [the writings of Crisp]', in *ibid*, p. 132, n. 2.

Historical Survey

That Crisp was no practical antinomian is clear. In a sermon headed *'Revelation of Grace, no Encouragement to Sin'*,[1] he insists that "there is nothing that more establishes a restraint from sin" than the preaching of free grace. He quotes Romans 8:2f in support. He considers the objection that the preaching of the terrors of the law, the wrath of God, damnation, and hell-fire is "a safer way to take men off from sin, than to preach grace and forgiveness of sin beforehand." His main argument to the contrary is simply that to preach the terrors of the law to believers is untrue.

In the series of sermons, *'Free Grace the Teacher of Good Works'*,[2] the justified are exhorted to holy living. Crisp assumes that the end of God's love is our sanctification, answering to the two tables of the law.[3] The power of grace is the method, which is described as an immediate and internal act of God's Spirit.[4] Crisp acknowledges that legal and evangelical righteousness agree 'in matter'; the difference is that the law leaves a man without strength, whereas "our dear Lord and Saviour hath purchased our glorious liberty ....: that by grace we shall be taught and enabled the denial of ungodliness."[5] This seems to involve a confusing of justification and sanctification, another reason, perhaps, why the orthodox scented antinomianism.

As with Eaton, so with Crisp, it seems to be difficult to be a consistent doctrinal antinomian. This series of sermons includes the customary puritan list of 'Uses',[6] but it is hard to see a real difference between such exhortations and the teaching of the law. Indeed, that it is not Crisp's intention to dispense with the law totally is clear from a sermon based on Galatians 3:19 entitled *'The Use of the Law'*.[7] He suggests five uses of the law to believers. The latter four are a reiteration of earlier distinctions and contrasts between law and Gospel. However, the first use mentioned is "that in respect of the rules of righteousness, or the matter of obedience, we are under the law still, or else we are lawless." Crisp has been described as inconsistent, not a true antinomian, though betraying an antinomian tendency.[8]

Nevertheless, the orthodox puritans characterized Crisp a doctrinal antinomian, and with reason: Calvin's emphasis on the law as an instrument

---

[1] Crisp, Vol. I, pp. 159-77.
[2] Ibid, pp. 316-78.
[3] Ibid, pp. 317, 329-31, 339-41, 342-5, 363f.
[4] Ibid, pp. 327, 329, 337f, 341f; cf. pp. 347, 355.
[5] Ibid, p. 345.
[6] Ibid, esp. pp. 362-78.
[7] Ibid, pp. 396-403.
[8] K.M. Campbell, 'Living the Christian Life - The Antinomian Controversies of the 17th Century', in D. Bugden (ed.), *Living the Christian Life* (Westminster Conference, 1975), pp. 70, 74.

of the Spirit, invested with power for the sanctification of the Christian, is absent from Crisp's theology, and in proportion to this whole volume, there is truth in the comment that Crisp has in fact little to say about the moral law, and gives it little or no place in the life of the Christian.[1]

2   WATSON: 'THE TEN COMMANDMENTS'

Watson argues from the Preface to the Commandments, 'And God spake all these words', that Antinomians are condemned in denying the moral law to be a rule to a believer. A refutation of antinomianism includes the sentence: "We say not that it [the law] saves, but sanctifies."[2] In this context Watson gives no indication of how the law sanctifies. Later, in answering the question, 'What is the difference between the moral law and the gospel?', he writes: "The moral law requires obedience but gives no strength..., but the gospel gives strength."[3] He speaks of the need to implore the help of the Spirit, since it is He who "enables us to obey."[4]

Watson is clear that the fallen human being lacks the strength to render obedience to the law.[5] However, in the case of the believer, God enables obedience to His law: "Therefore, Christian, be not discouraged, though thou hast no strength of thine own. God will give thee strength."[6] Watson sees the power to fulfil the law as the personal power of God by His Spirit through the Gospel. The law cannot impart strength to obey its demands, and yet it is said to sanctify the believer. It is probably correct to interpret Watson as meaning, with Calvin, that the law has sanctifying power when taken up by God as the instrument of His Spirit and the channel of His power. Unlike Eaton, Watson does not perceive an absolute dichotomy between law and gospel: 'gospel' means that which is taken up by the Spirit as a channel for His power, and this may include the law.

Watson distinguishes a twofold power in the law: it has both condemning power and commanding power; Christians are under the latter, but not the former. The moral law forces the sinner to Christ, but, in Him, its curse is abolished for those who trust in Him, because He has suffered condemnation on their behalf. However, the law "remains as a perpetual rule to believers": its power to command remains, and, as such, it sanctifies them.[7]

Watson's position may be summarized in the following quotation: "The

---

[1] P. Toon, *The Emergence of Hyper-Calvinism in English Nonconformity*, (Olive Tree, 1967), p. 54.
[2] T. Watson, *The Ten Commandments* (Banner of Truth, 1692, 1965), p. 13.
[3] *Ibid*, p. 44.
[4] *Ibid*, p. 6.
[5] *Ibid*, pp. 44, 184-8.
[6] *Ibid*, p. 47.
[7] *Ibid*, p. 44.

moral law is unalterable; it remains still in force. Though the ceremonial and judicial laws are abrogated, the moral law delivered by God's own mouth is of perpetual use in the church. It was written in tables of stone, to show its perpetuity."[1]

3   The Antinomian Controversy in Puritan New England

"In contrast to European history, in that of the New World the phenomenon of antinomianism has won for itself a name and a significance of its own. It denotes the troubled period of Sir Henry Vane's governorship of the Massachusetts Bay colony in 1637, and the years immediately following."[2]

The complicated story of the antinomian controversy with its socio-political ramifications need not be recounted here.[3] Suffice it to say that it centred around the activities and somewhat idiosyncratic views of Mrs. Anne Hutchinson, who accused the majority of New England Congregational ministers of preaching a covenant of works rather than free grace. She had extrapolated to an extreme the teaching of John Cotton, who saw all good in the Christian life "as springing from union with Christ and the divine Spirit's direct leadership".[4]

Although the label 'antinomian' has become attached to Hutchinson's teaching, the question of the third use of the law hardly figured at all in the controversy, and references to the law's weakness and power are sought in vain in the literature. The real issue was how the believer may gain assurance of salvation.[5] Hutchinson's contention, in contradistinction to puritan orthodoxy, was that works of obedience to the law furnish no indisputable evidence of justification, and are, therefore, no basis for assurance, which must be sought in Christ alone through the direct witness of the Spirit.

Hutchinson's opponents, of whom the chief was John Winthrop, accused her of denying that the law is a rule of life to believers.[6] In her defence she rarely gave a direct answer to the questions put to her, and sometimes appears to use the same terms in a different sense from her opponents: hence it is difficult to be sure precisely what her theology was. She did,

---

[1] *Ibid*, p. 12f.

[2] G. Huehns, *Antinomianism in English History* (Cresset, 1960), p. 149.

[3] It is told in full by E. Battis, *Saints and Sectaries* (University of North Carolina Press, 1962), *passim*.

[4] M. Jinkins, 'John Cotton and the Antinomian Controversy, 1636-1638', in *Scot J Th* 43 (1990), p. 336f.

[5] cf. D.D. Hall, Preface to the Second Edition, p. xiv, and Introduction, pp. 15, 19, in D.D. Hall (ed.), *The Antinomian Controversy, 1636-1638* (Duke University Press, 1991); Jinkins, pp. 329, 333; Battis, p. 85.

[6] Cf. J. Winthrop, 'A Short Story of the Rise, reign, and ruine of the Antinomians, Familists & Libertines', in D.D. Hall (ed.), p. 203.

however, say: "I confess now the Law is a Rule of Life and I acknowledge the other to be a hateful error and that which openeth a Gap to all Licentiousness. And I believe the Law is a Rule of our Life and if we do anything contrary to it it is a grievous sin".[1]

However, in a Fast-Day sermon Hutchinson's closest ministerial sympathizer, John Wheelwright, does touch on the third use of the law, and appears to reject it. He acknowledges the absolute moral and spiritual weakness of fallen man, and finds the believer's sanctification not in the law, but in Christ. Although he does not use the word 'power', it is clear that the only power which he concedes to the law is that of killing.[2] However, he insists that believers who are under a covenant of grace are to live holy lives, and to "have a care that we give not occasion to others to say that we are libertines or antinomians."[3] Wheelwright is using the word 'antinomian' in its practical sense, but he would seem to be teaching doctrinal antinomianism as his theory of sanctification.

The alternative position may be represented by Thomas Shepard, one of the leaders of the New England establishment. He acknowledged that the law "begets terror", and so draws the sinner to Christ: obedience is not a condition of life.[4] However, the law has a vital place in sanctification, despite the fact that our sanctification is never complete, owing to our own weakness.[5] "We go to Christ", he writes, "poor, weak, and feeble, to enable us."[6] Just as the copy of a written text made by a child is less fair than the original, but is nevertheless accepted, Shepard suggests, so God accepts a weak and imperfect imitation of His law from those whom He has made His own.[7]

Chapter 3 of Shepard's *'The Sound Believer'* has the following title:

"All those that are translated into this blessed estate, are bound to live the life of love, in all fruitful and thankful obedience unto Him that hath called them, according to the rule of the moral law."[8]

Shepard considers the claim that the Spirit alone is the believer's rule. He acknowledges that the Spirit is the efficient cause of obedience, but denies that He is a rule. He refers to Romans 8:1-3, and notes that the Spirit does not free us from God's law: the two work together as the wind and the

---

[1] Report of the Trial of Mrs. Anne Hutchinson, in D.D. Hall (ed.), p. 376.
[2] J. Wheelwright, 'A Fast-Day Sermon', in D.D. Hall (ed.) pp. 160-6.
[3] *Ibid*, p. 168f.
[4] T. Shepard, *The Sound Believer*, (Young, 1812), p. 380; cf. p. 384f.
[5] *Ibid*, pp. 360, 363.
[6] *Ibid*, p. 382.
[7] *Ibid*, p. 385.
[8] *Ibid*, p. 379.

Historical Survey

compass. We are cleansed from dead works with a view to obedience. Shepard rejects the notion that the writing of the law on the heart of the believer removes the necessity for an external law, or collapses all the commandments into the single love-command. A consequence of the law within is delight in the whole law. Shepard argues that, love being the end and scope of the law, the abolition of the law amounts to the abolition of love.[1]

According to Jinkins, Shepard and his fellow Elders believed that God does not "in His free and gracious omnipotence, disregard or overpower man's created nature", but imparts to believers the power to obey the law.[2] They held, contrary to the antinomians, that the terrorizing power of the law, directed at man's moral weakness, is not its only power. It has also the power to direct the believing life, and this power answers to the new moral power which is imparted at conversion.

4 The 'Marrow Controversy'

From 1718 to 1722 a dispute took place within the Church of Scotland concerning the seventeenth-century English work by Edward Fisher, *'The Marrow of Modern Divinity'*, Part One of which had recently been republished in Scotland. Its detractors believed that it and its defenders taught antinomianism. The Marrow-men rejected both charges. Our concern is not the story of the controversy,[3] but the theological debate, which occurred against a background of hostility to antinomianism within the Scottish Church.

As early as 1560 the Scottish Reformers had drawn up their own Confession of Faith. This statement stresses the moral and spiritual weakness of human nature. such that good works require the power of the Spirit. In that justification is through faith in Christ, the believer's liberty from the law is taught, but not in the sense that we owe no obedience to the law. Practical antinomianism is rejected. it is the law which defines the works which please or displease God.[4] Thus, from its inauguration the reformed Church of Scotland implicitly upheld the third use of the law.

---

[1] *Ibid*, pp. 381-3; cf. p. 355.
[2] Jinkins, pp. 342, 347.
[3] For which, cf. T. Boston, *A General Account of My Life* (Hodder & Stoughton, 1908), pp. 245-61; D.C. Lachman, *The Marrow Controversy* (Rutherford House, 1988), pp. 201-460; T. M'Crie, *The Story of the Scottish Church From the Reformation to the Disruption* (Free Presbyterian Publications, 1874), pp. 453-60; A. Thomson, *Thomas Boston of Ettrick* (Nelson, 1895), pp. 200-4; H.F. Henderson, *The Religious Controversies of Scotland* (T. & T. Clark, 1905), pp. 24-42; S. Ferguson, *The Marrow Controversy* (Westminster Media, 1994), Tape 1.
[4] Scottish Confession, Arts. III, XII-XV (Schaff, pp.440f, 450-7).

Six years later the Scottish Church "cordially accepted the Second Helvetic Confession",[1] which teaches that the law was given not to bring justification, but to expose our weakness, and so drive us, despairing of our own strength, to Christ in faith. Romans 8:3 is cited. In so far as it no longer condemns us, the law is abrogated; however, the law is not therefore rejected: good works are born of a true faith through the Holy Spirit, and the law is said to prescribe for us the form of good works.[2] Here too is an allusion to the third use.

In 1647, in the interests of Reformed unity throughout Great Britain and Ireland, the General Assembly of the Church of Scotland adopted as its standard the Westminster Confession.[3] As a result the third use of the law was now more fully expounded as Scottish Church orthodoxy.

Macleod sees the Marrow Controversy as a 'secondary result' of the second puritan antinomian debate in England. Richard Baxter's reaction against antinomianism led him into Neonomianism, which regards the gospel as a new law with reduced requirements, namely faith in Christ and sincere obedience.[4] Baxter describes these as 'conditions',[5] thus introducing into the new covenant an element of conditionality which it is assumed that man has the ability to fulfil. At the end of the seventeenth-century, Baxterian Neonomian teaching began to creep into Scottish theology, which consequently "developed the legal strain which at a later stage showed itself as full-blown Moderatism".[6]

Macleod's judgement is that "the Marrow controversy brought to a head the conflict of two strains of teaching that could not be reconciled,"[7] namely the Evangelicalism of the Marrow-men and the legalistic Neonomianism of their opponents.[8]

Lachman, on the other hand, argues that the connection of their opponents with Neonomianism, though asserted by the Marrow-men, is difficult to make,[9] and in this I believe he is correct. It appears that the Marrow Controversy was not a battle between Evangelicalism and Neonomianism, but between two Evangelical groups each seeking a middle way between Antinomianism and Neonomianism. The Marrow-men claimed that Fisher's work represented true Evangelical Calvinism, and was

---

[1] J. Macleod, *Scottish Theology* (Banner of Truth, 1943), p. 21.
[2] Second Helvetic Confession, Caps. XII, XV (Schaff, pp. 259f, 266-8)
[3] Macleod, pp. 82f, 103.
[4] *Ibid*, p. 139.
[5] R. Baxter, 'A Call to the Unconverted', in Jenkyn (ed.), p. 146.
[6] Macleod, p. 111.
[7] *Ibid*, p. 154.
[8] cf. J.J. Murray, 'The Marrow Controversy', in J. Miller (ed.), *Preaching and Revival* (Westminster Conference, 1984), p. 34.
[9] Lachman, p. 488f.

a useful buffer against the Neonomian drift towards legalism. Their opponents, by contrast, perceived in 'The Marrow' incipient antinomianism, but their spokesman, James Hadow, was, as his writings show, a genuine Evangelical Calvinist. In my view the evidence seems to support Hadow.

I shall attempt to justify my conclusion by reference to one work each of Hadow and Thomas Boston, one of the leading Marrow-men. It will be well to begin with a glance at the theology of *'The Marrow'* itself in order to draw attention to its ambivalence on the role of the law in the believing life.

1 'The Marrow of Modern Divinity, Part One'

Originally published in 1645, when the first outbreak of puritan antinomianism was still a major concern,[1] the stated purpose of *'The Marrow'* was to find "the golden mean" between the two extremes of legalism and antinomianism. The question especially debated is whether or not "the Law ought to be a rule of life to a believer." The approach taken to resolve this issue is the threefold diversity of the law in the Scriptures, which Fisher calls "the law of works, the law of faith, and the law of Christ". The former two he terms alternatively the 'covenant of works' and the 'covenant of grace'. He insists that, as the law of works, the ten commandments ought not to be the believer's rule of life, but that they ought so to be as the law of Christ.[2]

The 'law of works' means the law as it offers life in return for obedience.[3] As such, owing to human moral inability, the law is "weak to justify and strong to condemn"; reference is made to Romans 8:3 and Hebrews 7:18f.[4] However, where the law was weak, Christ is mighty, and delivers the believer from the law as a covenant, as Acts 13:39 demonstrates.[5]

As well as its strength to condemn the law has pedagogical power: it drives the sinner, conscious of his own impotence, to Christ. This subject is treated under the 'law of faith' and related primarily to Israel.[6] Fisher describes the differences between the covenants as administrative rather than substantial: the way of salvation for sinners now is identical to that for Jews under the law.[7]

As he commences to expound the law of Christ, Fisher says: "The law

---

[1] E. Fisher, *The Marrow of Modern Divinity* (Calvert, 1645), p. 197.
[2] Cf. *ibid*, p. 12-14.
[3] *Ibid*, pp. 18, 47.
[4] *Ibid*, pp. 7, 26-32, 51-4, 74-9, 97-100, 109f, 119-21, 132, 153, 227f.
[5] *Ibid*, pp. 35f, 51, 68, 101-3, 106f, 111, 136, 139-41, 185f.
[6] *Ibid*, pp. 47-9, 51f, 54-7, 66, 70f, 73f.
[7] *Ibid*, p. 65.

of Christ in regard of substance and matter, is all one with the law of works." It is the moral law summarized in the ten commandments, which was "given of God to be a true and eternal rule of righteousness for all men of all nations and at all times. So that evangelical grace directs a man to no other obedience than that whereof the law of the Ten Commandments is to be the rule"[1]

Fisher insists that the Christian must receive the law at the hands of Christ and not at the hands of Moses. It then has a new form: it no longer says, 'Do and live', but, 'Live and do', and as such neither justifies nor condemns but is the rule of our life.[2]

On the basis of his distinction between the law of works and the law of Christ, Fisher lists 'six Gospel paradoxes'; all are true as the law is the law of works and false as it is the law of Christ. The first, the most relevant one in the present context, is "that a believer is not under the law, but is altogether delivered from it".[3]

It is clear that Fisher rejects practical antinomianism: he writes: "true faith, according to the measure of it, produceth holiness of life".[4] Good works are done by God's power,[5] and "he that is truly baptized is become a new man, and hath a new nature, and is endowed with new dispositions, and loveth, liveth, speaketh, and doth far otherwise than he was wont or could before."[6]

However, as regards doctrinal antinomianism, it seems that his position is ambivalent. He considers the following argument: "the Lord hath promised to write His law in a believer's heart, and to give him His Spirit to lead him into all truth, and therefore, he hath no need of the law written with paper and ink to be a rule of life to him, neither hath he any need to endeavour to be obedient thereto." On the one hand he replies that this is not true because we are not yet perfect, and therefore need the law for our instruction.[7] However, there are places where he seems to teach doctrinal antinomianism, as the following quotation illustrates.

> When a man through the hearing of faith, receives the Spirit of Christ, that Spirit... writes the lively law of love in his heart..., whereby he is enabled to work freely of his own accord, without the coaction or compulsion of the law. For that love wherewith Christ, or God in Christ, hath loved him... will constrain him to do so..., that is, it will make him to

---

[1] *Ibid*, p. 144.
[2] *Ibid*, pp. 145-53.
[3] *Ibid*, pp. 180-4.
[4] *Ibid*, p. 96; cf. pp. 161, 175.
[5] *Ibid*, p. 168f.
[6] *Ibid*, p. 155.
[7] *Ibid*, pp. 157-60.

Historical Survey

do so whether he will or no; he cannot but choose to do it.[1]

On another occasion Fisher says to the man who would grow in holiness,

> Let him not go about it as a moral man, that is, let him not consider what commandments there are, what the rectitude is which the law requires, and how to bring his heart to it; but let him go about it as a Christian, that is, let him believe the promise of pardon in the blood of Christ, and the very believing the promise will be able to cleanse his heart.[2]

He admits that the believer is to use means, but amongst those which he mentions the law does not appear.[3]

2 James Hadow: 'The Antinomianism of the Marrow Detected'

This work was published after the 1721 General Assembly in response to the Marrow-men's '*Representation*', which, Hadow contends, puts forward an antinomian scheme in the name of free grace; however, the Church's teaching, with which he concurred, was free grace, but "without Disparagement unto the Holiness and Authority of the Divine Law-giver; and the Honour and Obligation of his Law; and without Detriment unto personal Holiness in Heart and Life, and its Necessity unto salvation."[4]

That Hadow cannot justly be accused of legalism is clear. He insists on the moral and spiritual weakness of the sinner. This necessitates both the imputation without the law of the righteousness of Christ, who fully satisfied, in the place of sinners, the demands of the broken law, and the power of God's invincible grace to enable the sinner to answer the call to faith in Christ.[5]

This affirmation of human weakness and the power of grace leads Hadow to take issue with the teaching of '*The Marrow*' that repentance is impossible before faith. Hadow's response clears him of Neonomianism: "The Question is not, what a Man may do by his own natural Powers, but through the efficacious Grace of God".[6] In affirming the necessity of repentance as a condition of forgiveness he makes a statement of free grace in quite unequivocal terms: "This forsaking and returning are not Acts of Man's free Will, produced by his own natural Powers, nor a meer (*sic*)

---

[1] *Ibid*, p. 164.
[2] *Ibid*, p. 172.
[3] *Ibid*, p. 178f.
[4] J. Hadow, *The Antinomianism of The Marrow of Modern Divinity Detected* (Mosman, 1721), pp. i-iii.
[5] *Ibid*, pp. iv-vii, ix-x.
[6] *Ibid*, p. 45.

Law-work, but they are fruits of the renewing Spirit."[1]

Repeatedly Hadow voices his rejection of practical antinomianism.[2] However, he is equally opposed to doctrinal antinomianism. He acknowledges that the believer is not under the law for righteousness, but insists that he is still under "the commanding Power of the Law" as the will of the Lord.[3] He appears to see the law as itself having sanctifying power in the believing life: "So indispensible is the Obligation of the Moral Law upon Believers... that it constantly binds them to hate and avoid all Sin, to make Conscience of every Duty, and to follow Holiness in Heart and Life."[4]

It is at this point that Hadow's chief objection lies. He admits that '*The Marrow*' does not teach 'gross antinomianism', that it seeks a middle way between licence and legalism, and yet, Hadow perceives, Fisher identifies himself with antinomians, and might be described as a "sly antinomian", who mixes [doctrinal] antinomian tenets with free grace under the pretext of refuting [practical] antinomianism. Hadow also suggests that the Marrow-men are not themselves guilty of all these antinomian errors, and have misunderstood Fisher at various points.[5] This appears to be a correct assessment.

The heart of Hadow's complaint against the Marrow doctrine concerns the distinction between the law of works and the law of Christ, and the use made of the latter as the believer's eternal rule of righteousness in the doctrine of sanctification. He argues that the distinction is false because the matter of the two laws is identical: "Christ doth not divest [the law] of its original Authority, binding Power, and Penal Sanction, but admits it into his Gospel as the indispensible Law of God the Creator, and the perpetual binding Rule of Life unto all Men, Believers as well as others. The Law of Christ, in this Sense, is the very same with the Moral Law, or Ten Commandments."[6]

Moreover, the Law given at Sinai was given by Christ.[7] The difference during the age of the new covenant is that "there is, in the Dispensation of Grace, whereinto this Law is incorporated, an Ability and Power conveyed, whereby Sinners, impotent and averse... are enabled and inclined to give Obedience unto it."[8]

Hadow suspects that Fisher's understanding of the phrase 'eternal rule of

---

[1] *Ibid*, p. 50-3, 61; cf. J. Hadow, *The Record of God* (Mosman, 1719), pp. 7-23.
[2] *Ibid, Antinomianism*, e.g., pp. xi, 165f.
[3] *Ibid*, e.g., pp. 16, 69, 122, 160, 171.
[4] *Ibid*, p. xii.
[5] *Ibid*, pp. 5-8, 67f, 172.
[6] *Ibid*, p. 127f.
[7] *Ibid*, p. 106.
[8] *Ibid*, p. 75.

righteousness' is inadequate. He does not assert the law's "commanding Power and binding Force" on the Believer "by Virtue of the Authority of God"; rather, the law being simply a passive rule, the believer's obedience, whilst agreeable to the law, is offered without the compulsive or coactive power of the law. In that the power of the law is from God, '*The Marrow*', Hadow argues, leaves the believer effectively independent of God's authority.[1]

Hadow is deducing from '*The Marrow*' consequences which Fisher himself does not state; however, it is arguable that they are the logical conclusions of the Marrow doctrine. He is bewildered that Fisher cannot conceive of the conjoining in the believer's obedience of the motives of God's love in Christ and the compulsion of the law, but feels obliged to set them in opposition.[2]

3 Thomas Boston: 'Notes on "The Marrow of Modern Divinity"'

Boston's purpose is to defend '*The Marrow*' from the charge of antinomianism, which he perceives to arise from a position of Baxterian Neonomianism.[3] He emphasizes that to teach morality for the gospel is what in fact leads to practical antinomianism.[4] It is clear that Boston is familiar with Hadow's book. He defends Fisher's threefold use of the word 'law', and finds the difference between the law of works and the law of Christ to be one of form and not substance.[5] He insists on the weakness of the law as a covenant of works for justification and life, and links this with the "utter inability" of fallen man.[6] He cites Romans 8:3 several times to demonstrate the law's weakness, and notes that it was given for humbling sinners.[7] The law served for the Church in its minority as a schoolmaster to Christ. In this connection Galatians 3:21 is quoted.[8] The "great lesson taught by the ceremonial law" is "Christ's satisfying the law for sinners".[9] In Christ believers have satisfied divine justice, as Romans 8:4 teaches, and are changed by God's almighty power.[10] Believers are dead to the law as the law of works, and it has no more power over them.[11]

---

[1] *Ibid*, p. 68f.
[2] *Ibid*, p. 91.
[3] Cf. e.g., T. Boston, 'The Marrow of Modern Divinity', *with Notes* (Mair, 1789), pp. v, 144, 245.
[4] *Ibid*, p. iv.
[5] *Ibid*, p. 27f.
[6] *Ibid*, pp. 46, 64, 70, 83, 100, 113, 217, 266.
[7] *Ibid*, pp. 75, 82, 217.
[8] *Ibid*, pp. 77, 91, 104, 106.
[9] *Ibid*, p. 100.
[10] *Ibid*, p. 144, 154f.
[11] *Ibid*, pp. 28f, 32, 142, 150, 152f, 210f, 217f, 219, 221, 229, 249, 251, 303.

However, "the delivering of the ten commandments on mount Sinai, as the covenant of works, necessarily includes in it the delivering of them as a perfect rule of righteousness,"[1] and believers are under them as the law of Christ[2] "not for life and salvation, but from life and salvation received".[3] Boston insists that this is Fisher's teaching, and denies that his six paradoxes are essentially antinomian.[4] He takes issue with Hadow's claim that, for Fisher, the law's authority is merely passive,[5] and argues that it is groundless to say that the Marrow doctrine weakens the authority of God or the creature's obligation to His law.[6]

Boston stresses that sanctification is not by the law, but by faith and the Spirit, in virtue of the believer's union with Christ.[7] However, only "if... we were perfectly and altogether spiritual" would there be no need of the law. Once issued "in the channel of the covenant of grace", the law bears "a promise of help to obey".[8] Therefore, belief in the promise of sanctification "brings always along with it, the use of the means, that are of divine institution, for that end."[9]

Boston comments on the two passages from *The Marrow* quoted above as evidence of a doctrinal antinomian leaning. He equates coaction and compulsion with force, and claims to think it obvious that "the way how the law forceth men to work, is by the terror of the dreadful punishment, which it threatens, in the case of not working; that it doth but darken the matter, to say, the co-action or compulsion of the law consists in its commanding or binding power or force."[10]

He understands Fisher's distinction between the moral man and the Christian to mean simply "that no considerations, no endeavours will sanctify a man without faith." He then adds the comment: "Howbeit, such considerations and endeavours are necessary, to promote and advance the sanctification of the soul by faith".[11] This does seem like special pleading, and it appears that Hadow was right in his judgement that the Marrow-men, though not themselves doctrinal antinomians, had misunderstood Fisher.

---

[1] *Ibid*, p. 70.
[2] *Ibid*, pp. 29, 79, 235, 238f, 244, 249f.
[3] *Ibid*, p. 158.
[4] *Ibid*, pp. 33, 131, 214, 269f.
[5] *Ibid*, p. 233f.
[6] *Ibid*, pp. 30, 142, 146f.
[7] *Ibid*, pp. Iii-iv, 53, 116, 226, 228, 253f, 267.
[8] *Ibid*, p. 32.
[9] *Ibid*, p. 330.
[10] *Ibid*, p. 268.
[11] *Ibid*, p. 284.

5 Antinomianism amongst the Eighteenth-Century English Baptists

It is said that antinomianism was the dominant doctrine in eighteenth-century Particular Baptists circles.[1] This appears to have been a result of the republication of the works of Crisp at the end of the previous century.[2] Although the antinomianism of the Particular Baptist preachers was doctrinal, it brought the denomination into disrepute, as misinterpreted by some hearers as freedom to sin.[3]

Hoad claims that it was only in the eighteenth-century that antinomianism first appeared in these circles.[4] However, it is arguable that the seeds of this position were already latent in the Particular Baptists' First London Confession of Faith of 1644. Significantly, this document contains no chapter devoted to the subject of the law, and is ostensibly more sympathetic than the Westminster Confession to doctrinal antinomianism. It denies that any "terrors of the Law, or preceding Ministry of the Law" are necessary prior to conversion, and continues: "the same power that converts to faith in Christ, the same power carries on the soule still..., and continually whatever a Christian is, he is by grace, and by a constant renewed operation from God, without which he cannot performe any dutie to God."[5]

Clearly this is not an explicit contradiction of the Westminster doctrine. Nevertheless, the omission of reference to the directing power of the law in the life of the believer is noteworthy. This cannot fairly be denoted an antinomian confession, however, this omission would mean that a century later it would lack the power to stem the tide of antinomianism.

Particular Baptist doctrinal antinomianism will be represented here by John Brine. It appears to have held sway until soon after his death in 1765, when a new generation of leaders (foremost amongst whom was Robert Hall) emerged with a different emphasis.[6]

1 Brine: 'The Certain Efficacy of the Death of Christ'

Part III of this work is a response to Neonomianism, in which Brine makes some comments pertinent to the present theme. Human moral weakness is frequently stated. Brine writes

---

[1] W.T. Whitley, *A History of British Baptists* (Kingsgate, 1932), p. 229; cf. E.G. Rupp, *Religion in England*, 1688-1791 (Clarendon, 1986), p. 131.
[2] Cf. A.C. Bickley, 'Tobias Crisp', in Stephen & Lee (eds.), Vol. V, p. 100.
[3] A.C. Underwood, *A History of the English Baptists* (Baptist Union, 1947), pp. 128, 135.
[4] J. Hoad, *The Baptist* (Grace Publications, 1986), pp. 112, 133.
[5] London Confession, Arts. XXV-XXVI.
[6] Cf. Toon, pp. 66, 88, 97-101, 151; R. Brown, pp. 72-116.

The Will of Man is... strongly bent to Sin:.... Men unregenerate cannot chuse those Things that are pleasing to God.... They are without spiritual Ability, and have not Power to perform what is spiritually good. The sacred writer expressly affirms that we are without Strength, he doth not say, we are without great or sufficient Strength; but without Strength, which is exclusive of the least degree of Power.

The consequence of man's weakness is the impossibility of obtaining life by the law.[1] Brine alludes to Galatians 3:21: "There is no Law enacted, by which Righteousness, Justification, and Acceptance with God can be; and therefore there is no Law published, that can intitle Men to Life." He stresses that salvation is entirely by God's free grace. Hence the ability to obey God's law is dependent upon regeneration: "No Influences without the Infusion of gracious Habits, are sufficient to enable a Man, to chuse Holiness... because the Will without such principles cannot approve of that good." Moreover, when considered only as regards the flesh, the regenerate, as much as the unregenerate, is marked by weakness before the law: "according to the Flesh, he cannot but serve the Law of Sin"; however, in the regenerate "there is also a contrary Bent and Inclination": "according to the Spirit he cannot but hate Sin, and serve the Law of God."[2]

Brine is happy to say that the believer is under the law, not as a covenant, but as "a Rule of Conduct to God".[3] He insists that "Redemption from the Law's Curse, frees not from the Obligation to observe its Precepts,"[4] because the law of God is "the invariable and eternal Rule of Righteousness to Men", which is not made void, but established by the Gospel.[5]

Whether it is strictly accurate to describe Brine as a doctrinal antinomian, even of a mild type, is debatable. Nevertheless, it is clear why the next generation of Calvinists saw in his teaching the potential for antinomian inference. Brine lists five uses of the law to the saints: (1) it informs them what is good and what is sinful; (2) it teaches them their miserable natural state; (3) it reveals the necessity of placing their hope in Christ alone; (4) it excites adoration of the divine goodness which provided a Redeemer; (5) it teaches believers the knowledge of their duty.[6] However, it is noteworthy that Brine does not here mention the law as itself instrumental in the believer's sanctification.

His leading emphasis is on the power of Gospel motives. It is such truths as the remission of sin, our gracious acceptance by God in the righteousness

---

[1] J. Brine, *The Certain Efficacy of the Death of Christ* (Aaron Ward, 1743), p. 176f.
[2] *Ibid*, pp. 173f, 197; cf. p. 192.
[3] *Ibid*, pp. 155, 213.
[4] *Ibid*, p. 158.
[5] *Ibid*, p. 154f.
[6] *Ibid*, pp. 158-60.

of Christ, and our firm entitlement to eternal life in Him, which are "Incitements to Holiness, of a most persuasive Nature". Brine speaks of God's work of implanting in His people a holiness agreeable to the nature of His law.[1]

Brine was evidently not as rigorously antinomian as Eaton. Nonetheless, his stress was on the power of the Gospel doctrines upon the regenerate heart as the sole instrument of sanctification.

2 Hall: 'Helps to Zion's Travellers'

Hall was concerned that the teaching that believers are not in any sense under the law was preventing some from attending to practical religion.[2] While this teaching was not that of Brine, the need to refute it indicates that others had extrapolated their emphasis in this direction.

Hall acknowledges that believers are not under the law as a covenant of works. As such the law is weak because it was not given as a means to life, as is clear from Romans 8:3 and Galatians 3:21. This applies to both the ceremonial and the moral law. Hall says that the ceremonial law was "a shadow of the good things to come, and was done away in Christ, who was the substance which these laws tended to exhibit, and the end in which they terminated." There were two benefits to Israel of the ceremonial law for its time: it fostered their sense of guilt, and directed their hope to the promised Messiah. Hall goes on to depict the 'unprofitableness' of the ceremonies with the coming of Christ described in Hebrews 7:18; he quotes the phrase 'beggarly elements' (Gal. 4:9), which emphasizes their abrogation.[3]

Regarding the moral law, Hall notes its universality, and then says: "a title to life could not arise from, or spring out of, human obedience, because, according to the rule of righteousness, everyone is found culpable."[4]

The weakness of the law is thus linked with human moral weakness. Hall speaks of man's "utter inability", and concedes that God requires of His creatures that "which He knows and declares is not in their power to perform". Man's voluntary and culpable inability has brought him "under the sole power" of dispositions averse to the will of God. For sinners to be delivered from condemnation, they therefore need "the almighty operations of the Holy Spirit.... For till the sinner's disposition be changed, till he be born again, and become a new creature, he can have no true love to God, no spiritual delight in His law."[5]

---

[1] *Ibid*, p. 210.
[2] R. Hall, *Help to Zion's Travellers* (Caxton, 1781), p. 154f.
[3] *Ibid*, pp. 154-6, 158f, 172-5.
[4] *Ibid*, p. 160.
[5] *Ibid*, pp. 168f, 172, 175, 181f, 187-94, 196, 203, 205f.

However, even the believer, though "not under the sole dominion of sin", remains morally weak in himself: "he cannot do the things that he would. His resolutions are feeble..., being sanctified only in part." "Absolute dependence on the Lord" is needed for obedience, and "the gospel exhibits new motives to love and obedience, and graciously conveys new principles, in consequence of which saints yield to God new obedience."[1]

However, it does not follow that the law is irrelevant: "moral commands continue in full force." The apostle, being delivered from the law as a covenant, delighted to remain under it as an unalterable law.[2] Hall gives a number of reasons why the law remains binding on believers, including the following: "While the relation continues between the Creator and His creatures, their obligation to love Him... can never cease; the law, therefore, by which such love and obedience are enforced, cannot possibly vary."[3]

Hall exposes the absurdity of the "Antinomian tenet" that "believers are not under the law as a rule of life".[4] He implies that the law is a powerful means of sanctification in the lives of those in whom the power of grace is operative.

6   Antinomian Conflicts within the Methodist Movement

Concurrent with these developments amongst the Particular Baptists, the Evangelical Revival was making its impact upon the Established Church. Despite the "substantial theological disagreement between Wesley and the Reformed tradition",[5] it is to misunderstand early Methodism to equate it with its Wesleyan strand alone. While the Methodist Church which emerged from the Revival in England was Arminian, the Reformed wing of Methodism was more significant as long as it remained within the Established Church, and separated Methodism in Wales was to have an enduring Calvinist emphasis.[6]

Wesley had a "horror of antinomianism".[7] The first references in Wesley's works to antinomianism in Methodism are dated February, 1746.[8] Thereafter there are constant allusions until as late as October, 1790[9]

---

[1] *Ibid*, pp. 168, 175f, 206f.
[2] *Ibid*, p. 174.
[3] *Ibid*, p. 157; cf. p. 176.
[4] *Ibid*, p. 161f.
[5] Bebbington, p. 28.
[6] Cf. D.M. Lloyd-Jones, *The Puritans* (Banner of Truth, 1987), pp. 193ff, 304; A. Dallimore, *George Whitefield*. (Banner of Truth, 1970, 1980), Vol. I, pp. 83, 93, 242, 246, 382; Vol. II, p. 20f, 258.
[7] W.E. Sangster, *The Path to Perfection* (Hodder & Stoughton, 1943), p. 101; S. Baring-Gould, *The Evangelical Revival* (Methuen, 1920), p. 57.
[8] J. Wesley, *Journal*, Vol. III, p. 162; *Letters*, Vol. II, p. 196.
[9] *Ibid, Journal*, Vol. VIII, p. 105.

Historical Survey 31

evidencing his antipathy to the heresy. The subject was discussed in 1744 at Wesley's first Conference, and again a year later.[1] Wesley's eclecticism in his publications for his people has been noted; he drew the line only at antinomianism.[2]

Wesley's own position on the law in the life of the believer is evident from his teaching on perfect love, the essence of which is "obedience to the law of Christ".[3] Wesley recognizes that the perfect Christian is not free from weakness and infirmity, but yet manifests great confidence in the sanctifying power of the Spirit, who enables the believer to employ his own powers according to the Master's will.[4] Wesley refers to Romans 8:3f.[5] He evidently saw the law as itself having power in the believing life: he says that the law should be preached to believers so that they may draw fresh strength to run in the way of Christ's commandments.[6]

Sometimes Wesley describes the law of Christ as 'the law of faith' or 'the law of love'; this he distinguishes from 'the law of works', the Mosaic dispensation with its three parts ("the political, moral, and ceremonial"), which was terminated with the coming of Christ to which the believer is dead. The new law of faith is fulfilled by love: "faith animated or working by love is all that God now requires of man".[7] This is not doctrinal antinomianism, because Wesley understands that Christ "has adopted every point of the moral law, and grafted it into the law of love".[8] Schmidt is not quite right to say that, for Wesley, the law established by faith is the moral law.[9] It is rather the law of Christ, but into this law, the moral part of the law is adopted. However, Wesley is not totally consistent: elsewhere he says that Gospel liberty is not freedom from God's law, but from the law of sin.[10] On this basis he exhorts people to beware of antinomianism, which makes void the law through faith, warning specifically against the works of Crisp and Saltmarsh.[11]

Although Whitefield did not agree with Wesley on perfect love, he was one with him in opposition to antinomianism.[12] In 1739 he came across some people "who maintained antinomian principles". In response he

---

[1] A.C. Outler (ed.), *John Wesley* (Oxford University Press, 1964), pp. 139, 152.
[2] H. Abelove, *The Evangelist of Desire* (Stanford University Press, 1990), p. 83.
[3] J. Wesley, *A Plain Account of Christian Perfection* (Epworth, 1952), pp. 13, 53.
[4] *Ibid*, pp. 14, 16, 22, 24-7, 28, 42f, 56, 72, 75, 103.
[5] *Ibid*, p. 36, 61; *Letters*, Vol. V, p. 211f.
[6] Outler, p. 233.
[7] Wesley, *Plain*, pp. 69-72.
[8] *Ibid*, p. 91.
[9] M. Schmidt, *John Wesley* (Epworth, 1973), p. 54.
[10] Outler, p. 381.
[11] Wesley, *Plain*, p. 91.
[12] R. Elliot, 'A Summary of Gospel Doctrine taught by Mr. Whitefield', in G. Whitefield, *Select Sermons* (Banner of Truth, 1958), p. 42.

alludes to Article XII of the Church of England.

> For though (to use our Church Article) good works, which are the fruits of faith, cannot put away our sins, or endure the severity of God's judgement (that is, cannot justify us), yet they follow after justification, and do spring out necessarily of a true and lively faith, insomuch that by them a lively faith may be as evidently known as a tree discerned by the fruit.[1]

The following year, Whitefield found it necessary to clear himself of the suspicion that his own doctrine tended towards antinomianism.[2] He admits that "the prevailing power" of a person's heart is enmity against God, until removed by the Spirit.[3] However, he insists, against the Antinomians, that "though sanctification is not the cause, yet it is the effect of our acceptance with God", and that the law remains in force as a rule of life.[4]

I shall now set side-by-side one representative of each position in the debate about the law in eighteenth-century Methodism. The antinomian position will be represented by William Cudworth, and the other side by John Fletcher.

1   Cudworth: Two Tracts

Two of Cudworth's tracts, *'Some Reasons Against making Use of Marks and Evidences'*, and *'A Dialogue Between a Preacher of Inherent Righteousness, And a Preacher of God's Righteousness'* are relevant. The latter was written in answer to Wesley's *'Dialogue Between an Antinomian and his Friend'*. Although Cudworth resents being labelled antinomian,[5] it is clear why Wesley could so construe his teaching.

Although Cudworth does not refer to the law as weak, he insists that justification is not by the works of the law, but by faith only.[6] He objects to Wesley's view that faith without love is not true faith by demonstrating that it was precisely this aspect of Popery which Luther opposed in his commentary on Galatians. Indeed, Cudworth says more, arguing that the Christian is entirely free from the law, because "our Saviour has fulfilled every jot and tittle of the law in the body of his flesh, and has took it out of

---

[1] G. Whitefield, *Journals* (Banner of Truth, 1960), p. 323f.
[2] *Ibid*, p. 420.
[3] Whitefield, *Sermons*, p. 99.
[4] *Ibid*, pp. 66, 76.
[5] W. Cudworth, *A Dialogue Between a Preacher of Inherent Righteousness, And a Preacher of God's Righteousness* (Hart, 1745), p. 2.
[6] *Ibid, Some Reasons Against making Use of Marks and Evidences* (Hart, 1745), pp. 9-12.

the way, nailing it to His cross."[1]

Cudworth's objection to the use of evidences to support the assurance of faith is that this is a falling back to the righteousness of the law. He compares it to the doctrine of the Pharisees, who, he alleges, did not seek "to keep the law in their own strength", but made "acknowledgement of their own inability", but who nevertheless, even in seeking strength from the Lord, "went about to establish their own righteousness" as the ground of justification in the conscience.[2]

Cudworth refutes the charge that the liberty from the law which he proclaims is "a liberty to disobey God"; he retorts: "Our liberty is to walk in the Spirit, and not fulfil the desires of the flesh; we are at liberty both from the law and the flesh."[3]

Wesley feared that Cudworth's teaching would lead to practical antinomianism. Cudworth justly denies any such intention. However, his theology is a version of doctrinal antinomianism. Stressing the Spirit alone as the principle of sanctification, he makes this distinction: "The difference betwixt christian obedience and other obedience, consists in one's being the fruit of the Spirit through believing, and the other being the fruit of the law." Victory over sin, Cudworth insists, comes from "believing our perfection and compleatness in Christ".[4]

2 Fletcher: 'Second Check to Antinomianism'

A sharp controversy followed the publication of the Minutes of the Wesleyan Methodist Conference of 1770.[5] The Reformed constituency suspected the Minutes of teaching salvation by works, because they referred to salvation "not by the merit of works, but by works as a condition."[6] It was from this suspicion that Fletcher sought to exonerate Wesley in his vindication of the Minutes. However, he stated a second motive also: "to give some check to the Antinomianism, which is still spreading throughout the three kingdoms".[7] The continuation of the controversy evoked from Fletcher's pen the second, third, fourth, fifth and last Checks to Antinomianism. I have selected the second as the one with the most material of direct relevance to our topic. "Doctrinally, the Second Check set out to emphasize the necessity of good works after justification".[8]

---

[1] *Ibid, Dialogue*, pp. 6-8.
[2] *Ibid*, pp. 13f, 18.
[3] *Ibid*, p. 8.
[4] *Ibid, Reasons*, p. 7; *Dialogue*, p. 11.
[5] S. Ayling, *John Wesley* (Collins, 1979), p. 273.
[6] J. Fletcher, *A Vindication of the Rev. Mr. Wesley's Last Minutes* (Pine, 1771), p. 5.
[7] *Ibid*, p. 6.
[8] A. Brown-Lawson, *John Wesley and the Anglican Evangelicals of the Eighteenth*

Although Fletcher writes as an Arminian, he is confident that he speaks on behalf of many Calvinists.[1] His Arminianism is apparent when he speaks not of the moral weakness of the fallen human will, but of its "strong, self-determining power", which even resists the threatenings of the law, the entreaties of Christ, and the strivings of the Spirit.[2] Hence, failure to obey the law is portrayed as wilfulness only, and not also as inability. It may be that this is not exactly the meaning which Fletcher intended to convey, because later he quotes with approval part of an 'excellent discourse' by the Calvinistic Bishop Hopkins, which includes the statement, "we are impotent, but God is omnipotent", acknowledges that the sinner has no power without grace, and says: "Our impotency lies in the stubbornness of our wills.... It is impossible that men should stir without God's concurrence".

What Fletcher calls 'the rectified will' also has wonderful power derived from the Spirit.[3] Fletcher quotes again from Hopkins.

> God who finds us employment, will also find us strength.... And whence have [we] this ability? Is it not from the grace of God's Spirit?... One end of [Christ's] doing all that He did for us, was to enable us to do for ourselves.... He requires two things from us. (1) That we should put forth all the strength of nature in labouring after grace: and, (2) That we should put forth the power of grace in labouring for the salvation purchased for us.... It will not suffice you to say... that you had no power to do anything.[4]

Fletcher emphasizes the new covenant promise of the law written on the heart by the Spirit's power, and insists, with reference to Romans 8:4, that in Christ we find power for obedience to the law. However, this does not mean that believers do not need the written law. Fletcher describes it as a 'fair pretence' to insinuate that, because believers have the law written in their hearts,

> 'there is no need of preaching the law' to them, either to shew them more of God's purity, indear the atoning blood, regulate their conduct, or convince them of the necessity of perfecting holiness. But suppose these Objectors have, as they say, the law written in their inward parts,... is the writing so perfectly finished, that no one stroke needs be added to it? Is

---

Century (Pentland, 1994), p. 314.

[1] J. Fletcher, *A Second Check to Antinomianism* (Strahan, 1771), pp. 7f, 10 n., 32, 40, 42f, 60, 62, 66, 72, 78, 83, 86, 107.
[2] *Ibid*, pp. 36f, 72-4.
[3] *Ibid*, pp. 37, 83.
[4] *Ibid*, pp. 73, 75, 77f.

not the law an important part of the word of righteousness?

The law is "the perfect rule of right, and the moral picture of the God of love"; it is contained within the Gospel, and is the termination to which the Gospel leads. The law, disarmed of its curse, is the believer's delight, because it is no longer the yoke of bondage, but the law of Christ.[1]

To represent law-keeping as bondage Fletcher describes as "the very spirit of antinomianism". To clarify this claim he distinguishes the several meanings of 'Law' in Scripture: it is the ceremonial law which is represented as a yoke of bondage; it was the Galatians' attempt to secure justification by the observance of the ceremonial law which Paul described as a return "to the beggarly elements of this world" (Gal. 4:9).[2] The death of the believer to the law relates to the whole Mosaic dipensation: the believer is "dead to all that Christ has not adopted", namely the Levitical Law with its ceremonies and its curse, and the law as a supposed meritorious basis of justification. To make Paul mean more than this, Fletcher says, is to claim that the believer is unable to sin, and makes Paul contradict himself.[3]

Wesley's influence upon Fletcher is apparent in the phrase "all that Christ has not adopted". This implies its converse, that Christ has adopted into His law for His followers the requirements of the moral law as the essence of perfect love.

7 The Law in the Nineteenth-Century American Holiness Movements

Holiness teaching spread from Methodism into the Calvinist wing of American evangelicalism.[4] When they described 'perfection' in the 1830's the Oberlin Reformed holiness teachers, foremost amongst whom were Finney and Mahan, defined 'holiness' in terms of God's law, and so "kept the law functioning as a most important guide".[5]

This is evident from Finney's *'Views of Sanctification'*. He defines 'entire sanctification' as "that state of devotedness to God and His service, required by the moral law", which is the only standard of moral duty. While one function of the law is to "thunder death and terrible damnation against every kind and degree of iniquity," the law is not set aside in the case of the believer.[6] This is described, with reference to Romans 7-8, as the great error

---

[1] *Ibid*, pp. 52-6.
[2] *Ibid*, p. 17, 19f.
[3] *Ibid*, p. 53f.
[4] G.M. Marsden, *Fundamentalism and American Culture* (Oxford University Press, 1980), p. 72ff; cf. Bebbington, pp. 153-65.
[5] Marsden, p. 87.
[6] G.C. Finney, *Views of Sanctification* (Newman, 1843), pp. 8-11; 49, 87, 133-6, 144.

of antinomianism.¹ Mahan also interprets Romans 8:3f as referring to grace for sanctification.²

However, measured by traditional Reformed thought, Finney's view of the law is deficient. He lists some principles for the interpretation of the law, amongst which the following are the most noteworthy:

> Whatever is not consistent with the nature and regulations of moral beings... cannot be law. That which requires more than man has the natural ability to perform... is not law.... Laws are never to be so interpreted as to imply the possession of any attributes, or strength and perfection of attributes, which the subject does not possess.... Law must be so interpreted as that its claims shall always be restricted to the voluntary powers.... In the application of the law of God to human beings, we are to regard their powers and attributes as they really are, and not as they are not.³

Finney acknowledges that the fall has resulted in a diminution in human moral power (albeit not as absolutely as earlier Reformed theologians had maintained), but understands God's law to be adapted to human weakness.⁴ He insists that justification cannot be by the law.⁵ However, he does not see it as a role of the Spirit-empowered law to remake the Christian according to its own perfection, but simply to require the right use of such powers as the Christian has.⁶

Marsden notes that, despite the early acknowledgement of the law, the growing emphasis on a decisive anointing with the Holy Spirit led to the perception of a disjunction between the old and new covenants. He comments: "in the thirty years after Finney and Mahan first adopted their holiness views, the place of the law was drastically reduced in the writings of Reformed advocates of holiness." By the 1870's it was rare to find holiness teachers stressing the law. Their teaching encouraged a clear distinction between law and Spirit."⁷ It is arguable that the seeds of this development were already present in Finney's theology. Although he affirms the law as the standard of sanctification, he does not see sanctification as through the law: "The sanctification of the saints is effected only by renouncing all hope of justification or sanctification on the ground of the law and embracing Christ as our wisdom, righteousness,

---

¹ *Ibid*, pp. 164, 169.
² A. Mahan, *Life Thoughts on the Rest of Faith* (Longley, n.d.), pp. 12, 58f.
³ Finney, pp. 11-16; cf. p. 19.
⁴ *Ibid*, pp. 32, 48f (cf. p. 42f).
⁵ *Ibid*, eg, p. 205; cf. Mahan, p. 57f.
⁶ Finney, pp. 17, 71-3, 82f, 121.
⁷ Marsden, p. 87.

sanctification and redemption."[1]

That sanctification is by the strength and grace of Christ and the Spirit, and a fruit of the ability of God,[2] Finney holds in common with the Reformed tradition; his denial that the law has an instrumental role brings him close to the doctrinal antinomians, and, by lowering the demands of the law, he took a large step along the road towards the later position, where the law did not figure at all in perfectionism. Warfield points out that Oberlin Perfectionism soon died out, but left its mark in later movements, which were clearly forms of doctrinal antinomiansim.[3]

It may well have been in response to Oberlin that Horatius Bonar wrote '*God's Way of Holiness*'. Chapter six ('*The Saint and the Law*') is an answer to those who reject the law as the Christian's rule of life, which, in effect, Finney did by moderating its demands.

Bonar emphasizes the weakness of the law as regards justification, but denies that weakness is intrinsic to the law: it is the fact of sin which makes law and life incompatible, as Galatians 3:21 teaches. Bonar writes: "It is the very perfection of the law which makes life impossible under it."[4] However, through Christ, the believer stands on a different footing in relation to the law, which can no longer threaten and terrorize.[5] Nevertheless, the saint is still duty-bound to obey the law. Romans 8:4 teaches that condemnation is removed so that the righteousness of the law may be fulfilled in us. Since the law is the transcript of God's will, to argue that we have nothing to do with the law entails the conclusion that we have nothing to with God's will. Bonar sees it as a fallacy to replace law by love: love is not a rule, but a motive, and remains in the dark without the law. The ten commandments are a guiding rule which love enables us to follow.[6]

8 The Keswick Message and the Law

Holiness teaching came to the British Isles from America "both by books, such as Dr. Boardman's Higher Christian Life, and by the visits of teachers like Mr. and Mrs. Pearsall Smith".[7] Mrs. Pearsall Smith adopted such teaching after sensing her weakness; she learned that Christ delivers "from the power of sin".[8] In English Evangelicalism the Holiness Movement has

---

[1] Finney, p. 205.
[2] Cf. *ibid*, pp. 38, 52, 74, 106, 142-4, 207, 209f, 215f, 227.
[3] B.B. Warfield, *Studies in Perfectionism* (Presbyterian & Reformed, 1958), p. 213.
[4] H. Bonar, *God's Way of Holiness* (Nisbet, 1864), p. 134.
[5] *Ibid*, pp. 132, 135f.
[6] *Ibid*, pp. 137, 141, 143f, 153.
[7] E. Stock, 'Fifty Years Ago', in J.S. Holden (ed.), *The Story of the Convention's Fifty years' Ministry and Influence* (Marshall Brothers, 1925), p. 8.
[8] S. Barabas, *So Great Salvation* (Marshall, Morgan & Scott, 1952), pp. 16-19.

become associated with the town of Keswick, where the annual Convention 'for the deepening of the spiritual life' has been held since 1875. Keswick, though a distinctive tradition, can be placed broadly within the Reformed camp.[1]

The Keswick message was that believers, burdened by the power of sin in their lives and by their own weakness, might find this power broken and a new counteractive power imparted in a definite crisis experience.[2] 'Counteraction' is a technical term in Keswick vocabulary.[3] Writings on the Keswick message are, indeed, replete with allusions to power.

What place does the law have in this teaching? To answer this question I shall refer to *'The Law of Liberty in the Spiritual Life'*, by Evan Hopkins, one of the earliest Keswick leaders and speakers. This book describes itself as "the standard work of 'Keswick' teaching".

The role of the law in exposing sin is understood. Hopkins defines sin as 'violation of God's law'.[4] He strongly emphasizes the moral weakness of humanity, and the nature of sin as a power, which is stronger even than the renewed nature implanted at regeneration.[5] Perhaps it is because of this assessment of the relative power of sin and the new nature in the believer that the place of the law in the believing life appears to be minimized. Hopkins acknowledges that some people teach that, while pardon is obtained through the blood of Christ, sanctification is effected by the Word; he rejects this view, and finds the source of spiritual power in justification and sanctification alike in the blood of Christ.[6] Hopkins emphasizes the need for obedience and refers to God's law in defining obedience; the issue is not whether the law is to be obeyed, but how. He teaches that true obedience must be motivated by love, and that such obedience is an easy matter; hence he can speak of liberty not from the law, but in the law. The law is obeyed, not because it is empowered by the Holy Spirit, but almost incidentally, as the indwelling Christ fills the soul with divine love.[7] Acknowledgement of the importance of holiness is evident, but, Hopkins appears to separate holiness from the law: "God sent His Son, not only to be the 'Just One', who should fulfil all righteousness and meet all the claims of His righteous law, He sent Him to be the 'Holy One', who should

---

[1] Cf. Brown-Lawson, p. 351f; Lloyd-Jones, *Puritans*, p. 318.

[2] *The Message of Keswick and its Meaning* (Marshall, Morgan & Scott, 1957), pp. 19-21, 23, 32, 43; cf. B.G. Worrall, *The Making of the Modern Church* (SPCK, 1988), pp. 235-7.

[3] J.I. Packer, *Keep in Step with the Spirit* (IVP, 1984), p. 148.

[4] E.H. Hopkins, *The Law of Liberty in the Spiritual Life* (Marshall & Scott, 1952), pp. 12f, 32f, 49.

[5] *Ibid*, pp. 14, 12, 32f, 55, 76, 78, 85, 88, 91, 108.

[6] *Ibid*, p. 19.

[7] *Ibid*, pp. 48-50, 56, 60.

Historical Survey

satisfy all the desires of a Father's heart."[1]

Hopkins avers that the believer attains to holiness by his union with the indwelling Christ the Holy One, and explicitly denies that the Christian life is one of effort, discipline, struggle, or striving.[2]

It seems, therefore, that Kevan is justified in referring to "the evangelical Antinomianism of holiness movements".[3] Clearly Keswick has never taught practical antinomianism; quite the reverse: its stated aim was to promote practical and Scriptural holiness. However, its understanding of the means by which holiness is achieved may fairly be taken to imply doctrinal antinomianism.

The Keswick Convention no longer proclaims its original message. The preachers who now occupy the Keswick platform stand far more in the mainstream of traditional Evangelicalism.[4] To illustrate this we may glance at the third of John Stott's 1965 Bible Readings, entitled 'Freedom from the Law'. He depicts three possible attitudes to the law: the legalist, the libertine or antinomian, and the law-abiding believer. He summarizes as follows the burden of Paul's message in Romans 7:1-8:4 to each of the three:

> To the legalist, who is in bondage to the law, Paul emphasizes the death of Christ as the means by which we have been delivered from that bondage. To the antinomian, who blames the law, he emphasizes the flesh as being the prime cause of the law's failure, and of our consequent sin and death. To the law-abiding believer, who loves the law and longs to obey it, he emphasizes the indwelling of the Holy Spirit, as the God-appointed means by which alone the righteousness of the law can be fulfilled in us.

According to Stott, the antinomian does not understand the weakness of the law, "imagining that its weakness is inherent, when actually it is in us who cannot keep it".[5] He continues: "These antinomians who say our whole problem is the law are quite wrong,"[6] and emphasizes that salvation leads to obedience to the law.[7] Not that a Christian can keep the law by himself;[8] however, because of the indwelling Spirit, "he actually fulfils the law of

---

[1] *Ibid*, p. 69; cf. p. 36.
[2] *Ibid*, pp. 31, 34, 37, 71f, 76, 85.
[3] Kevan, p. 261.
[4] Cf. D.D. Sceats, *Perfectionism and the Keswick Convention, 1875-1900* (Unpublished M.A. Dissertation), p. 41.
[5] J.R.W. Stott, *Men Made New* (IVP, 1966), pp. 59-62.
[6] *Ibid*, p. 70.
[7] *Ibid*, p. 65f.
[8] *Ibid*, pp. 74, 76, 79.

God". Stott rejects the traditional Keswick tendency to separate and oppose the law on the one hand and the Spirit and holiness on the other. He cites Romans 8:4 as "of very great importance for our understanding of the Christian doctrine of holiness", which, he notes, consists in the righteousness of the law; thus this is an uncomfortable verse for those who say that the category of law is abolished for the Christian. While the means of holiness is the power of the Spirit, the nature of holiness is "conformity to God's will expressed in His law".[1]

9   The Law in Dispensationalism

Although Dispensationalism predates the holiness movements, it came to be much influenced by the Keswick teaching.[2] Nevertheless, it remains sufficiently distinctive to merit separate consideration. The justification for the inclusion of this section is that "historic Dispensationalism tends to view itself as an innovative and modified form of Reformed theology."[3]

Bass seems to be correct in regarding Dispensationalism as essentially a hermeneutical system[4] which has specific implications for a number of areas of doctrine. One chief implication of Dispensationalism is a radical divide between law and grace as separate, and even opposed, principles on which God may deal with people for salvation.[5] This radical disjunction affects the question of the third use of the law.

Cyrus I. Scofield explicitly rejects the third use in a passage in which he distances himself from orthodox Calvinism:

> Protestant theology is for the most part thoroughly Galatianized, in that neither law nor grace is given its distinct and separate place as in the counsels of God, but they are mingled together in one incoherent system. The law is no longer... a ministration... of cursing..., because we are taught that we must try to keep it, and that by divine help we may. Nor does grace, on the other hand, bring us blessed deliverance from the dominion of sin, for we are kept under the law as a rule of life.

Scofield describes "the notion that the believer, though assuredly justified

---

[1] *Ibid*, p. 81f.
[2] Cf. Bebbington, pp. 152, 192; J.H. Gerstner, *Wrongly Dividing the Word of Truth* (Wolgemuth and Hyatt, 1991), pp. 240, 245-7.
[3] R.C. Sproul, Foreword to Gerstner, p. x.
[4] C.B. Bass, *Backgrounds to Dispensationalism* (Baker, 1960), p. 19.
[5] Cf. *ibid*, p. 34f; F.R. Coad, *A History of the Brethren Movement* (Paternoster, 1968), p. 130; S. Osborne, 'The Christian and the Law', in *Bib Sac* (Jul-Sep, 1952), p. 240; R.L. Aldrich, 'Has the Mosaic Law Been Abolished?', in *Bib Sac* (Oct, 1959), p. 322f, 325, 331.

by faith through grace wholly without law-works, is after justification put under the law as a rule of life" as "the current form of the Galatian error". He reads Romans 6-8 and Galatians 4-5 as refuting this error. Justifying faith ends the rule of the pedagogue for the believer, so that he "is separated by death and resurrection from the Mosaic law": "one can never have deliverance from the dominion of sin, nor know the true blessedness and rest of the Gospel, and remain under the law.... Deliverance comes, not by self-effort under the law ..., but by the omnipotent Spirit", and not merely by the Spirit's help in the effort to keep the law, but by "the might of the indwelling Spirit alone".[1]

More recently Lewis Sperry Chafer has likewise argued that grace alone is the governing principle for Christian conduct. It is impossible for the unregenerate to be saved except by the Gospel of grace,[2] owing to man's universal failure in keeping the law. Chafer denies that this is due to any imperfection in the law itself: the problem is "the helplessness of man under the power of 'sin in the flesh'." He cites Romans 8:3 and Galatians 4:9, and insists that the law was not given as a means of justification: it was effective only as it drove the transgressor to Christ".[3]

Moreover, Christ represents the total termination of the law, including even its role as a rule for the believing life: "The Biblical appeal in grace never contemplates an observance of the law. Through the death of Christ, the law is not only disannulled; but, as a rule of life, it is never mentioned or included in the teachings of grace."[4] Chafer argues that, to impose the moral commandments of the Decalogue upon the Church is a form of legalism: the ten commandments are not the basis of divine government in daily life.[5]

Dispensationalism does not advocate practical antinomianism. Chafer puts great stress on the new degree of divine enablement in grace overagainst law: "The divine enablement provided under grace is nothing less than the infinite power of the indwelling Spirit."[6] It seems fair, however, to say that Dispensationalism, like the Keswick message which it follows at this point, teaches doctrinal antinomianism as an effective route to the overcoming of the flesh. Chafer recognizes that the sin-nature needs to be controlled, but this is achieved not by the law, but by the Spirit.[7]

In his critique of Dispensationalism John Gerstner argues that, whatever

---

[1] C.I. Scofield, 'The Grace of God', in R.A. Torrey et al. (eds), *The Fundamentals* (Kregel, 1958), pp. 403-7.
[2] L.S. Chafer, *Grace* (Bible Institute Colportage Association, 1928) pp. 81, 84f.
[3] *Ibid*, pp. 112-4.
[4] *Ibid*, p. 88.
[5] *Ibid*, pp. 88, 152f.
[6] *Ibid*, pp. 194-9; cf. Osborne, p. 244.
[7] Chafer, p. 341: cf. Aldrich, p. 344.

the intention, the logic of the system ought to push it into antinomianism, by which he clearly means practical antinomianism.[1] It is a weakness of Gerstner's work that he nowhere distinguishes between practical and doctrinal antinomianism. His argument is that Dispensationalism encourages antinomianism because it reinterprets the Reformed doctrine of the perseverance of the saint as the eternal security of the believer, and defines 'believer' in terms of a mere profession of faith. However, Dispensationalists do not intend to defend an empty profession, as Gerstner's own comments on the teaching of Ironside and De Haan make clear. They recognize human moral weakness; the only hope for its overcoming is the grace that brings victory through the Spirit, and His sanctification is seen as the fruit of the new life received at justification.[2] That Dispensationalists do look for sanctification, even though they give the law has no role to play in the process, is conceded in the following words of Gerstner's.

> Antinomianism springs from the dispensationalists' view of sanctification because it supposes sanctification to be merely the manifestation of the perfect, divine, new nature by the agency of the Holy Spirit. It is apparent that, if sanctification is but the manifestation of the divine nature within, there is no need of holding by the law, which is fundamentally negative. This new nature has no inclination to do the things forbidden in the law, therefore it is irrelevant for the new nature.[3]

Gerstner would be fairer to describe Dispensationalism as inconsistent doctrinal antinomianism, rather than to imply that it is practical antinomianism. Gerstner's own position, as a covenant theologian, is that law and grace both co-exist and must be distinguished in both Testaments.[4]

During the 1980's the 'Lordship controversy' arose within American Dispensationalism as a result of the teaching of Zane Hodges, that it is possible for faith to exist without works. In reply John MacArthur insists that practical antinomianism evidences the lack of genuine conversion: Jesus Christ is Lord as well as Saviour. MacArthur claims that the 'no-Lordship Gospel' stems from Chafer. Chafer himself was committed to practical holiness, but his system paved the way for legitimized carnality, because it taught that the Christian is not under law, but is to live Christ. The view that obedience to the law is not the pattern of the Christian life, was distorted to mean that justification might exist without sanctification. Thus Chafer's doctrinal antinomianism degenerated into practical

---

[1] Gerstner, pp. 1, 209-59.
[2] Ibid, pp. 142f, 215-7, 222, 234-6.
[3] Ibid, p. 248.
[4] Ibid, p. 249.

antinomianism.[1]

However, MacArthur questions Gerstner's view that this tendency is inherent in Dispensationalism,[2] and sets out his own 'Lordship salvation' position. He recognizes that there is no salvation through the law, because of human moral incapability; he quotes Galatians 3:21. MacArthur stresses the life-changing nature of real faith, which always produces righteous works. He insists that justification by faith leaves no room for antinomianism, and cites Romans 8:2-4. He interprets verse 4 as referring to sanctification.[3]

However, in warning against practical antinomianism, MacArthur seems to accept the doctrinal antinomian position. It is true that he says that God's commandments are precious to the believer, whose obedience is motivated by love, which fulfils the whole moral law.[4] However, his major emphasis is that the power to do what pleases God comes from grace (a view very similar to Chafer's), and that "sanctification is the continuous operation of the Holy Spirit in believers, making us holy, by conforming our character, affections, and behaviour to the image of Christ."[5]

What is interesting about this statement is less what it says (where there would be little disagreement amongst Reformed Evangelicals), than what it does not say: there is no mention of a role for the law in the Spirit's sanctifying work, and the image of Christ, rather than the law of God, is made the standard of behaviour. In the end it is the Lordship of Christ, rather than the law, which MacArthur stresses.

In Dispensationalism, the doctrinal antinomian tension remains. Chafer does not think that the believer is without a rule, but denies that the law of Christ is an adaptation of law. Yet, inconsistently, or at least by using extremely subtle distinctions, he can say: "However, no vital principle contained in the law is abandoned. It will be observed that these principles of the law are carried forward and are restated in the teachings of grace; not as law, but as principles which are revised adapted and newly incorporated in the issues of pure grace."[6]

Clearly it becomes impossible, in the effort to reject practical antinomianism, to avoid readmitting the law in some other guise. It is perhaps this tension which underlies Gerstner's objections.

---

[1] J.F. MacArthur, *Faith Works* (Word, 1993), pp. 27-9, 35, 95-7, 228, 231.
[2] *Ibid*, p. 224f.
[3] *Ibid*, pp. 40, 43, 50, 65, 98, 103, 106, 113, 117, 199, 202, 228.
[4] *Ibid*, p. 168f.
[5] *Ibid*, p. 109, 120.
[6] Chafer, pp. 88, 90; cf. pp. 153f, 156.

10 The Contemporary Debate

It is not only amongst Dispensationalists that debate about the law is raging today. In more orthodox Reformed Evangelical circles the question of the third use is again being discussed. This debate will be illustrated by reference to two controversies, one from America, and the other from the UK. In each case, one example will be selected from each side.

1   The American Controversy

In 1980 and 1981 the Council on Baptist Theology meeting in Dallas articulated a doctrinal antinomian position on the law in the life of the believer. This aroused opposition from other Reformed Baptists, and from the wider Reformed network in the USA.[1] The spokesman for the Dallas position will be John Reisinger. Its opponents will be represented by Walter Chantry.

1   JOHN REISINGER

Three of Reisinger's publications on the law will be synthesized. By 'law' he means the ten commandments as the document of the legal covenant given at Sinai to Israel, which Galatians 3-4 depicts as having had a historical beginning and ending.[2]

Reisinger speaks both of the law's inability, and of 'the mighty law'. Its inability pertains to the cleansing of the conscience, and is linked with our inability to render perfect obedience. The law is therefore "a yoke that is impossible to bear".[3] The power of 'the mighty law' is that of life and death, designed to administer death by blocking the way into God's presence against those who had failed to obey the law. The law was thus a preparation for the Gospel: its inability to cleanse the conscience was overcome by the sacrifice of Christ, who kept the old covenant, and earned blessing for us.[4]

Because Reisinger regards the law as "the God ordained instrument of condemnation... to bring lost sinners to see their need of faith in Christ,"[5] he rejects the view that the law was "a 'gracious covenant' given to a redeemed people for their sanctification". He suggests that the puritans "created confusion by trying to make the law serve as the mother of holiness in the believer's sanctification": the result was legalism, which

---

[1] Cf. E. Hulse, 'What it is to be Under the Law of Christ', in *Reformation Today* (Mar-Apr, 1984), p. 19.
[2] J.G. Reisinger, *Tablets of Stone* (Crowne, 1989), pp. 2f, 31, 33, 43, 46f, 48f, 80-83.
[3] *Ibid*, pp. 12f, 74f; *idem, The Law/Grace Controversy* (Grace Abounding Ministries, 1982), p. 7.
[4] *Idem, Tablets*, pp. 12f, 35, 37, 48, 51, 70, 76, 85.
[5] *Idem, Abraham's Four Seeds* (Sound of Grace, 1987), p. 51.

neither justifies nor sanctifies.¹ Reisinger speaks frequently of the nullification of the law covenant with the coming of Christ: the ten commandments are now obsolete. He rejects the view that the ten commandments are eternal moral law and as such the believer's rule of life.²

Reisinger is no advocate of practical antinomianism, and rejects the epithet 'antinomian'. He insists that law-keeping is not optional for the believer, that true love will fulfil the law, and that obedience is an essential mark of the genuine Christian.³ The ten commandments as a pedagogue have been replaced by the Holy Spirit who writes upon the heart of the believer the new covenant law, and works obedience in his life, as is clear from Romans 8:1-4.⁴

However, the key to assessing whether Reisinger is fairly described as a doctrinal antinomian lies in his answer to the question, how is obedience produced? Is the immediate work of the Spirit regarded as the sole factor, or is there a place for law as a tool of the Spirit? His answer is ambivalent.

On the one hand he is clear that there is a revealed will of God for the new covenant believer, and that "those clear commandments are our rule of life." The end of the ten commandments does not mean the end of the morality contained therein. This explains why there is so much in the New Testament about law, even though there is not one reference to the ten commandments.⁵ Moreover, Reisinger says: "The same moral rules that furnish our minds with help in pleasing our heavenly father functioned in the conscience of an Israelite as the condemning covenant of life and death."⁶ This seems to imply a sanctifying power addressed to the mind in the law of God, albeit that the law is not equated precisely with the ten commandments.

However, at other times Reisinger appears to teach that the Gospel alone is the sanctifying instrument used by the Spirit. He asks: "How and what do we preach in order to get the 'love that seeks to obey' into the heart of the listener in the first place [and] how do we protect and nurture that love, so that it will continue to grow and obey?"⁷ His answer is that "nothing can fill the heart with love to God except 'the preaching of the cross'."⁸ The experience of the indwelling Spirit is true liberty of conscience, and must be

---

¹ *Idem, Abraham's*, pp. 7, 53; *Law*, p. 22.
² *Idem, Abraham's*, pp. 24, 45f, 52, 71, 78; *Tablets*, pp. 14, 17, 39, 45f, 70-74; *Law*, pp. 17-21.
³ *Ibid*, pp. 5f, 8, 16, 19, 21f.
⁴ *Idem, Seeds*, p. 24; *Tablets*, pp. 50-53, 85.
⁵ *Idem, Law*, pp. 4, 15-21; cf. p. 83.
⁶ *Ibid*, p. 62.
⁷ *Ibid*; cf. p. 16; *Seeds*, p. 71f.
⁸ *Idem, Law*, p. 23; cf. p. 21f.

protected against legalism.[1]

The emphasis in the quotations in the previous paragraph suggests that Reisinger's theory of sanctification is indeed a version of doctrinal antinomianism. However, the quotations in the earlier paragraph suggest that it is impossible to carry through a doctrinal antinomian position consistently.

2 CHANTRY: 'GOD'S RIGHTEOUS KINGDOM'

Although Chantry wrote before Reisinger, he is responding to the earlier development of the position later articulated by Reisinger. He too is aware of the paradoxical nature of the law as both weak and powerful. Its weakness is seen in the fact that "no descendant of Adam can be approved by the Holy One on the basis of his own attempts to keep the moral law", because "that law cannot give us the strength to be holy."[2] However, "the fault does not lie with the moral law. It is weak only 'through the flesh' (Rom. 8:3)." The weakness of the law as a function of human moral weakness is linked with the power of the world and of sin.[3] On the other hand the law does possess the power to identify sin for the awakened conscience. Confronted in the law with God's holiness, the sinner is made aware that he falls short of God's glory. It is therefore only the power of God in the Gospel which can save the sinner.[4]

In the case of the justified sinner, the law acquires a new weakness ("the expression of God's righteous will for man can no longer condemn him"[5]), while the believer receives "a new infusion of spiritual power,"[6] which is variously attributed to the cross, to "the mighty grace of God", which imparts the love that "gives power and pleasure to the ways of law", and to "the mighty Spirit", who, in line with Romans 8:4, writes the law on believers' hearts.[7]

This raises the question whether faith makes void the law. In his reply Chantry discusses the relationship between the covenants. He insists on covenant unity: "there is but one covenant of grace (of promise) with varying administrations". He argues that Paul shows that the new covenant does not invalidate the old, and that the antinomian argument "creates a deep rift" between the Testaments.[8]

---

[1] *Idem, Seeds*, p. 71.
[2] W.J. Chantry, *God's Righteous Kingdom* (Banner of Truth, 1980), pp. 70, 73.
[3] *Ibid*, pp. 23, 45, 97.
[4] *Ibid*, pp. 26, 45, 66, 70f, 92.
[5] *Ibid*, p. 72.
[6] *Ibid*, p. 52.
[7] *Ibid*, pp. 54, 73, 93-7.
[8] *Ibid*, pp. 45, 71-3, 103.

Historical Survey

Not that there are no dissimilarities between the covenants.[1] The description of the old covenant as 'weak and beggarly elements' (Gal. 4:9) is connected with the transition from old covenant life as that of children, to the new covenant reality of "inward maturity of soul" through the Spirit. It follows that not all the Mosaic statutes apply to the believer. Chantry discusses Galatians 3:15-4:11, and demonstrates that 'law' in this context means the Mosaic economy, which, as the schoolmaster to bring God's people to Christ and to justification through faith in Him, has now passed away, along with its ceremonial and judicial regulations.

However, the change of covenants does not mean that the moral law is suspended. When God makes a new covenant with men, He does not utterly cancel the terms of former arrangements. His revelation is consistent, and the moral law, which finds its most succinct summary in the ten commandments, remains His revealed will for the human race. Hence, Chantry avers, "the New Testament binds the Ten Commandments upon Christian consciences:" "Without love in the soul..., the moral commandments cannot be kept.... But this does not mean that love is all that needs to be commanded. How is love to God and neighbour to express itself?... To answer this the apostles always return to the Ten Commandments."[2]

The indwelling Spirit empowers the saints to righteousness, but "it is that 'the righteousness of the law might be fulfilled in us' that we walk after the Spirit (Rom. 8:4)." Chantry therefore concludes: "We have returned to the moral law for direction in sanctification.... Nothing but the moral law can define for us what sanctified behaviour is."[3]

Moreover, the law itself has power in the life of the believer. Chantry describes the moral law as one of the "major instruments in the arsenal of the Spirit." The law must therefore be preached to Christians, who will discover it to be their delight.[4]

2   The British Controversy

Richard Alderson's study of contemporary antinomianism includes the following passage, in which he quotes Octavius Winslow:[5]

> 'Our Lord did not keep that law that His people might be lawless. He did not honour the law that they might dishonour its precepts. His obedience provided no licence for our disobedience.... Our faith does not make void

---

[1] *Ibid*, p. 48.
[2] *Ibid*, pp. 43f, 46, 49, 53, 73, 77-84, 96f, 101-18.
[3] *Ibid*, p. 72f.
[4] *Ibid*, pp. 90f, 94.
[5] O. Winslow, *No Condemnation in Christ Jesus* (Banner of Truth, 1853), p. 50f.

the law, but rather establishes the law....' Such words were once the universally accepted conviction of those who taught historic Christianity, but they have been challenged again in recent times. The Rev Michael Eaton, for example, is one who sees no need for Christians to honour the law.[1]

The British controvesy over the place of the law in the life of the believer will be illustrated by reference to one of Eaton's writings and to Alderson's advocacy of the third use in reply to the position which Eaton represents. Although Eaton's work referred to here was written later than Alderson's, it crystallizes the position which he has advocated since the early 1980's.

1   EATON: 'HOW TO LIVE A GODLY LIFE'

For Eaton the law is weak in respect of justification. This failure of the law is linked with the depth of our own weakness.[2] Eaton is no practical antinomian. He insists that holiness is necessary in the Christian life, and is, according to Romans 8:4, the purpose of salvation. However, he distinguishes holiness from both 'legalism' and morality, and offers fourteen definitions of holiness in which he refers not once to the law. He reads Galatians as a rejection of holiness through legalism, and defines sanctification as "the enlargement of what we already have in Christ".[3]

Eaton says that we need "some powerful drive" to make us holy, and that sanctification is "God working powerfully in us." However, "the Christian is not under the Mosaic law", and this includes the ten commandments: the power of the law was the fear of punishment, but God does not use this power towards new covenant believers. Rather, the power for a godly life comes from glimpsing the mercies of God: the Gospel, not the law, is God's means of sanctification. Hence, "we must get assurance of salvation before we start worrying about holiness."[4]

The power of the Gospel comes to the believer through the Spirit, whose leading is "more powerful than the Mosaic law." Recognition that the starting-point in Christian experience is justification by faith without the law leads to obedience, not to the law, but to the Spirit. Sanctification takes place because the Christian is united to Christ and indwelt by the Spirit, as Romans 8:4 shows. The believer looks to God for strength, and so proves His enabling.[5]

The outcome of a life of sensitivity to the Spirit is the fulfilling of the

---

[1] R. Alderson, *No Holiness, No Heaven!* (Banner of Truth, 1986), p. 23f.
[2] M.A. Eaton, *How to Live a Godly Life* (Sovereign World, 1993), pp. 19, 124.
[3] *Ibid*, pp. 13-17, 32f, 46.
[4] *Ibid*, p. 18, 20, 33f, 89, 93f, 119.
[5] *Ibid*, pp. 18, 28f, 36-9, 55-9, 61-5, 67-73, 94.

Mosaic law: "the life of love does not lead into sin".[1] However, that Eaton's position is justly described as doctrinal antinomianism is evident: "If you walk in the Spirit deliberately you will fulfil the Mosaic law accidentally."[2]

This raises the question whether there are any guidelines for the Christian in the way of holiness. Eaton replies that "there are many principles". However, "Christian holiness is more than just following rules", and, in the end, is reduced to one point, the law of love.[3] What, then is made of the instructions about Christian life found in the New Testament, and particularly the fact that "some verses from the law are picked out and applied to the Christian"? Eaton answers this question thus: Paul "was not expounding the Mosaic law! He was putting into his own words the kind of thing that he knows the Spirit will lead us into. Paul knew precisely how the Spirit would be leading," and sin is no part of the holy life.[4]

Eaton leaves us with the question whether consistent doctrinal antinomianism is possibile. His words raise several questions: how did Paul know what the leading of the Spirit would be in practice? If he was not expounding the law, why did he allude to 'some verses from the law'? If love does not lead to sin, and sin is no part of the holy life, how do we know what things are sinful? Surely we cannot avoid giving the law some place in the Christian life.

2   ALDERSON: 'NO HOLINESS, NO HEAVEN'

Alderson wrote to affirm that justification by faith will lead to a life of holiness.[5] Justification by faith is linked with the law's weakness: "the law cannot save," because it "supplies no power to fulfil its demands." The law's inability stems from the unbelieving man's incapability of complete obedience, hence the curse is on all who seek justification by the works of the law.[6] However, where the law cannot save, Christ can.[7]

This does not mean that the law is powerless absolutely. Several functions are mentioned which the law is able to perform. It defines, reveals, condemns, and restrains sin; it undermines human confidence that it is possible to meet God's requirements; it brings conviction of sin and enables God to impute guilt and enact wrath.[8]

However, Alderson, stresses the need for practical holiness in the life of the justified believer. He defines sanctification as the life "being changed to

---

[1] *Ibid*, p. 94.
[2] *Ibid*, p. 17; cf. pp. 46, 89, 93.
[3] *Ibid*, pp. 79-85, 89, 91, 119.
[4] *Ibid*, pp. 20, 92f, 104f, 122.
[5] Alderson, pp. 2-5.
[6] *Ibid*, pp. 12, 20, 22f, 25, 35, 41f, 52f.
[7] *Ibid*, p. 42f.
[8] *Ibid*, pp. 20, 30-32, 34f, 37, 49f.

bring it into conformity with the will of the Lawgiver." He notes that the faith which saves is that which expresses itself through love.[1] Alderson recognizes the distinction between practical and doctrinal antinomianism,[2] and so the question which arises is how is holiness produced in the believer?

Alderson acknowledges that it is the Holy Spirit who "enables the gospel believer to keep the law of God", but argues that the view that the moral law itself is therefore not binding on Christians leads in fact to practical antinomianism. He recognizes that the ceremonial and judicial laws have passed away.[3] However, he writes: "even where the New Testament does not explicitly quote the law of the Ten Commandments, it everywhere reflects its exact prohibitions.... The Father's very purpose in sending the Son to die for sin was 'that the righteous requirements of the law might be fully met in us (Christians)' (Rom. 8:4)."[4]

The moral law therefore continues; it is "God's blueprint for Christian living." Alderson lists reasons why this must be so:

> In the first place, the Moral Law reflects God's own essential attributes... God the Creator has imposed His Law on all created beings.... Obedience to God (because He is Creator) and to His Moral Law (because it reflects His sovereign will) lies at the heart of all true religion - and thus of sanctification. Becoming a Christian does not alter the fact that I am still a created being under obligation to obey. What conversion does is enable me to render to God that obedience of which I was incapable as an unbeliever.... The Ten Commandments were explicitly applied to God's redeemed people.[5]

Alderson addresses some particular mistakes made by antinomians. It is not true that the law can do nothing but curse. To oppose law to love is invalid and leads to subjectivism. To make a distinction between the law of Christ and the law of God is to misread Paul. Finally, to argue that, having love, "we do not need any external law to guide us", overlooks the fact that "the Moral Law is not external to the Christian", because God's new covenant promise is to write it on the heart.[6]

For Alderson, it is just because "the Holy Spirit can give life and power to law" that the believer is to keep the law:[7] It is the means of his

---

[1] *Ibid*, pp. 5f, 54f.
[2] *Ibid*, p. 13.
[3] *Ibid*, pp. 12, 17-19, 43f.
[4] *Ibid*, p. 22f.
[5] *Ibid*, p. 20.
[6] *Ibid*, pp. 25-30.
[7] *Ibid*, p. 12.

sanctification. It follows that the law should still be preached even to the saint. Alderson's conclusion tallies with that of the great reformer: "Take away the law, said Luther, and men in their ignorance will live carelessly, comfortable in their sin."[1]

Summary

Although there are differences of emphasis and detail, the main points which have emerged in this survey of the debate about the third use of the law may be summarized as follows. The weakness of the law has been understood primarily in terms of its inability to justify, and this is seen as a derivative of the moral weakness of fallen man. However, the law does have power to condemn sin and so to drive sinners to Christ for justification. Towards believers, though, the law has no condemning power. Both parties to the debate are agreed on these things. However, the doctrinal antinomians see the law's condemning and pedagogical power as its only power, and extend the idea of the weakness of the law, including the moral law, beyond the issue of justification in such a way as to deny it any significant role in the life of believers, a viewpoint with which the advocates of the third use would not agree.

Because of this disagreement, other differences emerge. Both parties are at one in their rejection of practical antinomianism. However, whereas the doctrinal antinomians conclude that sanctification is achieved by the direct work of the Spirit alone, the advocates of the third use, while acknowledging that the Spirit is the enabling cause of sanctification, also give the law a role when employed by the Spirit. While the description of the law as the believer's rule of life can be used by both sides, the doctrinal antinomians mean merely that the law defines holiness, whereas advocates of the third use understand the law as rule in an instrumental sense.

This theological difference leads on to differences in pastoral practice. Doctrinal antinomianism sees the preacher's responsibility as the extolling of free grace, and argues that the preaching of the law hinders sanctification. Those who teach the third use, on the other hand, are likely to regard the preaching of the law to believers as a source of strength.

It remains to highlight the uses made of our five key texts.

(1) ACTS 13:39. Calvin twice quotes this verse in defence of the view that what is imputed in Christ to believers is the righteousness of the law. It is used by Fisher to stress the contrast between the law's weakness and the power of Christ to deliver the believer from the law as a covenant. John Eaton cites it in the course of his plea for the preaching of free grace alone.

(2) ROMANS 8:3f. This text is quoted by several of our writers from both sides of the debate (Calvin, Bolton, Fisher, Boston, Hall, Chafer,

---

[1] *Ibid*, pp. 31, 84.

Chantry) in asserting the weakness of the law as a covenant unto life, owing to the impossibility of obedience on the part of the sinner. There is disagreement about whether verse 4 refers to justification (John Eaton, Boston) or sanctification (Bolton, Shepard, Wesley, Fletcher, Bonar, Stott, MacArthur, Reisinger, Chantry, Michael Eaton, Alderson), but this discrepancy cuts across the divide between the advocates of the third use and the doctrinal antinomians. On this Scripture Crisp bases an appeal for the preaching of free grace.

(3) GALATIANS 3:21. Brine and Bonar, from opposite sides of the debate take this verse to mean that life is impossible by the law because of sin. Bolton and Hall, both advocates of the third use, understand it to teach that the law was never given as a covenant of works for justification. The view of Calvin and Chantry, again defenders of the third use, is that 'the law' here means the entire Mosaic economy, which was a merely provisional arrangement pending the coming of Christ.

(4) GALATIANS 4:9. The doctrinal antinomians, Chafer and MacArthur, understand this verse also to teach the law's weakness for salvation owing to sin. From the other side, Hall, Fletcher and Chantry stress that the provisionality of the law is taught, and that the phrase 'beggarly elements' refers to the ceremonial law, now abrogated with the coming of Christ. The doctrinal antinomians Scofield and Michael Eaton understand this text to mean that the believer is not under the law as a rule of life.

(5) HEBREWS 7:18f. Fisher, from the doctrinal antinomian position, perceives in this text an allusion to human moral inability. John Eaton, also a doctrinal antinomian, uses it as part of his Scriptural evidence for the threefold time of the Church, and concludes that God's people in the present time are free from the law. Hall and Chafer, from opposite sides of the debate, are agreed that this verse teaches that the law was not given as a means to life, but to direct hope to the promised Messiah.

Part Two

New Testament Study

Introduction

This section will comprise four chapters, one on each of the four New Testament books from which our five texts come. Our aim is to assess which of the two broad positions documented above has more claim to New Testament support. The framework for the study of each text will be provided by the following three questions:

(1) What does 'law' mean in this text in the context of this book?

(2) In what sense(s) is the law held to be weak?

(3) What are the implications of this text in its context for the question of the place and power of the law (in the sense in which it must here be defined) in the life of the Christian believer?

The study will be pursued in canonical order.

CHAPTER 1

Acts

1   Introduction

It is reasonable to suppose that the purpose for which Luke wrote Acts is subsumed under that stated in the opening verses of his gospel:[1] his aim was to record a historically accurate narrative marked by complete fidelity to his sources (vv. 1-3), with a view to establishing the reliability of the faith which rests upon the historical facts (v. 4).[2]

It seems that Acts is composed with believers chiefly in mind.[3] Luke is writing to encourage the adherents of Christianity with the certainty of its truth. It has been suggested that the need for reassurance arising from the delay of the parousia called forth this work,[4] but this builds far too much on Acts 1:6f,[5] and overlooks Luke's hints at a long-term vision to which attention will be drawn below.

Luke's aim is probably twofold. First, he desires simply to celebrate the extension of the boundaries of the people of God to include the Gentiles. He writes as a Gentile Christian to Gentile Christians[6] out of profound

---

[1] Against J.V. Bartlet, *The Acts* (Caxton, n.d.), p. 6, E.F. Harrison, *Acts: The Expanding Church* (Moody Press, 1975), p. 16 [cf. L. Alexander, *The Preface to Luke's Gospel* (Cambridge University Press, 1993), p. 2, n. 2].

[2] Cf. I.H. Marshall, *Luke: Historian and Theologian* (Paternoster, 1970), p. 18f; W.W. Gasque, 'A Fruitful Field', in *Interp* 42 (1988), p. 129.

[3] So W.G. Kümmel, *Introduction to the New Testament* (SCM Press, 1975), p. 163; I.H. Marshall, *The Acts of the Apostles* (IVP, 1980), p. 20; P.F. Esler, *Community and Gospel in Luke-Acts* (Cambridge University Press, 1987), p. 25; against F.F. Bruce, 'The Acts of the Apostles', in D. Guthrie and J.A. Motyer (eds.), *The New Bible Commentary Revised* (IVP, 1970), p. 24, L.M. Wills, 'The Depiction of the Jews in Acts', in *JBL* 110 (1991), pp. 651-3, A.W.F. Blunt, *The Acts of the Apostles* (Clarendon, 1922), p. 12, J.B. Tyson, 'Jews and Judaism in Luke-Acts', in *NT St* 41 (1995), p. 38.

[4] Cf. Bartlet, pp. 13, 15-18; E. Haenchen, *The Acts of the Apostles* (Blackwell, 1971), pp. 94-8.

[5] Cf. Kümmel, p. 171; Marshall, *Acts*, p. 22.

[6] Against J. Jervell, 'The Acts of the Apostles and the History of Early Christianity', in *St Th* 37 (1983), p. 19; V.E. Vine, 'The Purpose and Date of Acts', in *Expos T* 96 (1984), p. 45f; E.P. Goodenough, 'The Perspective of Acts', in L.E. Keck and J.L

gratitude that salvation (a key word[1]) has been extended to them. Nothing could be more reassuring to first-century Gentile Christians than Scriptural proof that God's intention always was eventually to pour out His Spirit on all flesh (2:17; cf. 1:8; 3:25; 10:34f; 13:47; 15:16f; 22:15,21; 26:17f,20,23; 28:28). Second, building on this celebratory emphasis, Luke designs to demonstrate that the emerging Gentile Church is indeed the true offspring of the historic people of God, and is destined to become the people of God of the future.[2] As such, it was important that he should demonstrate the continuity of the Church of his own day, which included both Jews and Gentiles in significant numbers, with the people of God of the former dispensation.[3] However, he writes with a long-term vision and an acute insight. The flow of the movement which he depicts is away from Israel and towards a predominantly Gentile Church[4] which, while always rooted in the Jewish heritage, is nevertheless a new entity in Christ (Ac. 28:28), though not exactly a new religion: Luke views the Church as the new form of expression of the one people of God. To this extent Juel is correct to write: "Luke-Acts is not about the birth of a new religion",[5] though he fails to discern the newness of expression in Luke's concept of the Church.

Luke is writing during a time of transition when the Church included both Jews and Gentiles,[6] perhaps in approximately equal proportions, a time when it was necessary to cope with the tensions to which such a situation inevitably gave rise. However, he looks forward in anticipation to the day when the radical newness of the work of Christ will become as transparent as its historical continuity with Old Testament religion.[7] He foresees the coming day when the Jewish roots of the Church will be only roots, and when Jewish privilege will be a thing of the past. It is with the certainty of the new thing which God has done in Christ that Luke is concerned, and he writes to bolster that certainty for Gentile Christians, who, at the time of writing, may feel at times like the proverbial 'poor relation' in the ethnically mixed primitive Church.

Haenchen sees the real subject of Acts as the Word of God and its growth.[8] It is true that Luke discerns the growth of the Church as the fruit of

---

Martyn (eds.), *Studies in Luke-Acts* (Abingdon Press, 1966), p. 58.

[1] Cf. Marshall, *Historian*, pp. 92-215.

[2] Cf. J. Jervell, 'The Church of Jews and Godfearers', in J.B. Tyson (ed.), *Luke-Acts and the Jewish People* (Augsburg, 1988), p. 20, Gasque, *Fruitful Field*, pp. 120, 129.

[3] Marshall, *Acts*, p. 22; cf. B.S. Childs, *The New Testament as Canon* (SCM Press, 1984), p. 225.

[4] Against D. Juel, *Luke-Acts* (SCM Press, 1983), pp. 117-9.

[5] *Ibid*, p.109; cf. Vine, p. 48.

[6] Cf. Esler, *Community*, p. 31.

[7] Cf. J.D.G. Dunn, *The Partings of the Ways Between Christianity and Judaism* (SCM Press, 1991), p. 257.

[8] Haenchen, p. 49; cf. Childs, *NT*, p. 222.

the spread of the Word (cf. 6:7; 12:24; 13:49; 19:20), and it is through the description of the spread of the Word into and amongst the Gentiles that he celebrates Gentile salvation and calls for Gentile gratitude. The Word in question is the new Word of the Gospel of Christ, which nevertheless stands in essential continuity with the Word of the former dispensation. In the context of this movement away from the Jewish roots of the Word towards the radically new, predominantly Gentile, expression of faith in the Gospel (the Christian Church), the issue of the law acquires paramount importance.

In the transition period during which Luke was writing it was important that he should settle the question of the grounds of admission of Gentiles into the Church in such a way that the Gentiles did not become forgetful of the Jewish heritage into which they had been incorporated, but learned to appreciate their unity in the Church with Jews, whose customs were so different from their own. In such a context the issue of the law acquired strategic importance. The view stemming from Baur, that Acts is a conciliatory document to unite the Pauline and Judaistic factions in the Church[1] is now largely discredited (though recently revived in a modified form by Goulder[2]). Nevertheless, a careful reading does suggest that the law and the Church's unity in the light of the law's supersession are part of Luke's concern.

The Gentile Christians needed to be aware of the place of the law, both as regards their conversion to the faith and their membership of the Church, and in terms of their ongoing life as believers. The law revealed by God is a central theme in Acts.

However, Luke's long-term vision includes the perception that the day will come when the issue of the Jewish law will recede. At the time of writing the issue of Jewish-Gentile relations in the Church was pressing,[3] and it was necessary for the Gentile Christians humbly to accept the reality of the situation. It has been suggested that in 15:21 Luke wants to disprove the contention that the Gentile Christians did not care about the law;[4] it is perhaps more likely that, by reminding the Gentiles of the decree, he is implicitly calling them to remember the roots of their spiritual blessing. He indicates that "there were almost no lengths to which Paul was not prepared to go to demonstrate his respect for the Law as the divinely ordained way of life for those who bore the Jewish name."[5] In effect, he calls upon the

---

[1] F.J. Foakes-Jackson, *The Acts of the Apostles* (Hodder and Stoughton, 1931), p. xvif; J. Munck, *The Acts of the Apostles* (Doubleday, 1967), p. LV; Haenchen, pp. 15-17; Kümmel, p. 160; Childs, *NT*, p. 219.

[2] M. Goulder, *A Tale of Two Missions* (SCM Press, 1994), eg. p. 194f.

[3] Cf. Esler, *Community*, p. 71.

[4] Haenchen, p. 101.

[5] W. Neil, *The Acts of the Apostles* (Marshall, Morgan and Scott, 1973), p. 33.

Gentiles, for as long as it may be necessary, to follow the example of Paul, the missionary who, above all others, had championed their cause, and so to preserve harmony with those to whom, in the historical providence of God, they owe their entire salvation. Nevertheless, Luke is able to foresee the day when this expedient will no longer be necessary, when the newness of the Christian movement will have rendered the old ways obsolete. We shall observe in the course of this study how Luke conveys this long-term perspective.

2 Acts 13:39

Attending the synagogue on his first Sabbath day at Pisidian Antioch, Paul is invited to bring a 'word of exhortation' to the gathering. Having set the coming of Jesus in the context of God's dealings with Israel throughout history, Paul, as the goal of the speech,[1] announces,

> In Him everyone who believes is justified from all things from which you could not (οὐκ ἠδυνήθητε) be justified in (ἐν) the law of Moses.[2]

The weakness of the law is signalled by the negated verb δύνασθαι: there is something which the law lacked the power to accomplish.

1   The Meaning of 'Law'

The phrase 'the law of Moses' clearly restricts the concept νόμος to that body of legislation which was established for Israel by Moses under divine direction.[3] However, the precise import of the phrase in this verse is determined by the significance given to the preposition ἐν. It is frequently interpreted instrumentally, and thus translated 'by the law of Moses';[4] this has the effect of taking Paul's statement to mean that the law failed as a means or instrument of justification. It is then usually taken that Paul is implicitly challenging an approach to religion in which reliance was placed upon obedience to the law as the ground of hope.[5] However, Paul is here addressing Jews, and, while such a charge may well be true of certain

---

[1] J.J. Kilgallen, 'Acts 13:38-39: Culmination of Paul's Speech in Pisidia', in *Biblica* 69 (1988), pp. 480-5, 495.

[2] Original translation.

[3] Cf. A. Barnes, *The Acts of the Apostles* (Blackie, 1868), p. 211.

[4] So F.F. Bruce, *The Acts of the Apostles: The Greek Text with Introduction and Commentary Greek* (IVP, 1952), p. 271; Kilgallen, p. 480.

[5] cf. J.A. Alexander, *A Commentary on the Acts of the Apostles* (Banner of Truth, 1857), Vol. 2, p. 34.

groups within Judaism,[1] Paul does not appear in this sermon to be refuting a distortion of Old Testament faith: his point of departure is the sovereign electing grace of God (v. 17), and the emphasis is on Jesus as the fulfilment of promise and prophecy (vv. 23,27,29,33-35). It seems more likely, therefore, that the preposition should be given a locative sense, and translated 'in the law of Moses'; this has the effect of taking Paul's statement to mean that the law was not a sphere or environment in which justification was a reality. Consequently 'the law of Moses' refers to the entire way of life which was the defining feature of Jewish being.[2] This means that Calvin is probably correct to read these words as a reference primarily to the ceremonies of the law,[3] since it is in the ceremonial law that the Old Testament economy finds its heart and focus.

This means that 'law' has a different connotation in this verse from that in verse 15, where it refers to the Pentateuch as distinct from the Prophets. There is, however, a connection, in that it is in the books of Moses that the defining arrangements for the people of God are set down. If references to the law are traced through the Book of Acts as a whole, the fact that its normal meaning is the Jewish economy with its ceremonial basis is confirmed. The Jews' law is referred to in a somewhat uninterested tone by the representatives of Gentile authority on two occasions (18:15; 23:29), and with one exception (19:39), where the issue is Roman law, the word νόμος and its cognates in Acts has this specific meaning.[4]

In the latter half of Acts, where Paul is at the forefront of the Christian mission, the note which comes increasingly to dominate Luke's account is the dispute between Paul and the Jews over the law. The accusation against Paul is first voiced in 18:13 as the allegation that he "persuades men to worship God contrary to the law". This suggests that the Jews perceived their law as fundamentally stipulations for the proper regulation of worship. Later the dispute centres around the temple, the home of Jewish worship, which Paul was accused of having defiled (21:28; 24:6). Paul himself links law and temple on one occasion in the course of his defence (25:8). The temple was the focus of the economy within which the Jews lived,[5] and "everything against the law would be interpreted also as being against the temple, as most of the ceremonies required in the law were celebrated

---

[1] Cf. D.A. Carson, D.J. Moo, and L. Morris, *An Introduction to the New Testament* (Zondervan, 1992), p. 298; R.Y.K. Fung, *The Epistle to the Galatians* (Eerdmans, 1988), p. 207f, n. 29; K. Snodgrass, 'Justification by Grace - to the Doers', in *N T St* 32 (1986), p. 77; H. Räisänen, 'Paul's Conversion and the Development of his View of the Law', in *N T St* 33 (1987), p. 411.

[2] Cf. Dunn, *Partings*, pp. 255-31.

[3] J. Calvin, *Commentary upon the Acts of the Apostles* (Geneva, 1560), p. 541.

[4] Cf. 5:34; 7:53; 22:3.

[5] J.A. Alexander, Vol. 2, p. 281 (cf. Vol. 1, p. 253).

there".[1]

With worship at its centre the economy denominated 'the law of Moses' also contained other ceremonial requirements which were designed to protect the purity of worship. The issue of circumcision first surfaces in 15:1,5,24, where the Pharisaic Jews urge it as a matter of saving necessity. In 21:20, when the elders of the Jerusalem Church met Paul they pointed out to him that the Jewish Christians were "zealous for the law", which they still saw as "the expression of the divine will":[2] the following verse makes clear that this zeal was particularly concerned with circumcision, which is described as an ἔθος, a "usage prescribed by law",[3] and in verse 23f, Paul is persuaded to pay the expenses of four men who have taken a Nazirite vow, and to do so by participating in the preparatory rites of purification in order to be able to enter the temple with them on the expiry of their vow, so that his fellow Jews will realise that he keeps the law. The Jewish economy, then, with its ceremonial foundation, is the normal meaning of 'law' in Acts.

2 The Weakness of the Law

Paul's message to the Jews at Pisidian Antioch is that it is in Christ that justification is obtained from all things from which they could not be justified in the Mosaic economy. The weakness of that economy ('the law'), in other words, concerned justification: the law did not have the power to justify.

Calvin argues that the Jews stopped short at their ceremonies, thinking that there was righteousness for them in the sacrifices, and that Paul is attempting to draw them away from a false confidence in the law.[4] However, it seems a better reading of this sermon to understand Paul to be assuming common ground with his fellow Jews,[5] who, as long as they remained true to their own Scriptures, would have recognized that "man cannot set himself right with God by sacrifices or even by works",[6] and who cherished the hope of the securing of full atonement when Messiah should come. Larsson's comment that this is "Paul's most torah-critical statement in Acts",[7] is true only with reference to justification. The issue in Paul's preaching is not the way of salvation, but the identity of the Messiah.

---

[1] Barnes, *Acts*, p. 310; cf. Dunn, *Partings*, p. 63.
[2] Haenchen, p. 609.
[3] J.H. Thayer, *A Greek-English Lexicon of the New Testament* (T. & T. Clark, 1901), p. 168; cf. E.F. Harrison, p. 327.
[4] Calvin, *Acts*, p. 541.
[5] Cf. Munck, *Acts*, p. 123.
[6] Blunt, p. 192.
[7] E. Larsson, 'Paul: Law and Salvation', in *N T St* 31 (1985), p. 425.

His theme is that the promises are fulfilled in Jesus.

The basic question raised by this text involves the meaning of the verb 'to justify' (δικαιόω) in this context, and in particular its unusual use in conjunction with the preposition 'from' (ἀπό). Most commentators understand the verb in its forensic sense familiar in the Pauline epistles. Conzelmann, however, argues that its juxtaposition with 'the forgiveness of sins' (v. 38) modifies its meaning here,[1] although he does not make clear what he understands this modification to be. It seems unlikely that Conzelmann is right, because in the only other place in the Lucan writings where this verb is used in a comparable way, in the parable of the Pharisee and the tax-collector at prayer (Lk. 18:14), it is best read forensically.[2] The parable is preceded by a note to the effect that Jesus "spoke this parable to some who trusted in themselves that they were righteous (δίκαιοι)" [v. 9], and this must signal the meaning which is to be given to 'justified' (δεδικαιωμένος) in Jesus' final comment: the tax-collector went home righteous inasmuch as he, having recognized his own unworthiness, was a recipient of divine propitiousness (ἰλάσθητί) [v. 13]. He was accepted as righteous on account of his trust not in himself, but in a gracious God. Ludemann claims that Luke uses δικαιόω merely to give a feel of Pauline authenticity, but that he has not understood the doctrine of justification in a forensic sense. His quotation from Zeller ("Anyone who did not know the Pauline doctrine of justification and the law previously would certainly not perceive it from this fleeting intimation")[3] may well be true, but if such prior knowledge is assumed, then it becomes the most natural interpretation of this text.

The only other New Testament context where δικαιόω is used with ἀπό is Romans 6:7, where that from which justification is obtained is defined as sin. It is not necessary to allow the preposition to suggest an alternative translation of δικαιόο such as 'to free',[4] since it is sin which constitutes a

---

[1] H. Conzelmann, *Acts of the Apostles* (Fortress, 1987), p. 106; cf. P. Vielhauer, 'On the "Paulinism" of Acts', in Keck and Martyn (eds.), p. 41; E. Schweizer, 'Concerning the Speeches in Acts', in Tyson (ed.), p. 214.

[2] So J. Calvin, *Commentary on a Harmony of the Evangelists, Matthew, Mark, and Luke* (Geneva, 1555), Vol. 2, p. 206; A. Barnes, *Luke and John* (Blackie, 1868), p. 130; A. Plummer, *A Critical and Exegetical Commentary on the Gospel According to S. Luke* (T. & T. Clark, 1901), p. 419; W.F. Adeney, *Luke* (Caxton, n.d.), p. 325; N. Geldenhuys, *The Gospel of Luke* (Marshall, Morgan and Scott, 1951), pp. 451, 452f, n. 14; A.R.C. Leaney, *A Commentary on the Gospel According to St. Luke* (A. & C. Black, 1958), p. 236; L. Morris, *The Gospel According to St. Luke* (IVP, 1974), p. 265; W. Hendriksen, *The Gospel of Luke* (Banner of Truth, 1978), pp. 821, 824f (cf. J.M. Creed, *The Gospel According to St. Luke* (Macmillan, 1930), p. 224f).

[3] G. Ludemann, *Early Christianity according to the Traditions in Acts* (Fortress, 1989), p. 154.

[4] Against E.F. Harrison, p. 214; see Thayer, p. 150; R. Scroggs, 'Romans 6:7: ὁ γὰρ

person unrighteous in God's sight. Justification is God's gracious discharge from sin as guilt. While it is grammatically possible to read this verse as teaching the consummation in Christ of an incomplete justification in the law,[1] it is generally agreed that this is not the meaning:[2] Paul is insisting in Acts 13:39 on the absolute weakness of the law as regards justification.

The weakness of the law in this passage does not need to be explained by reference to the moral failure of sinful people;[3] the fact that it is the law as an economy with a ceremonial basis which is in view makes this explanation untenable. Paul's understanding is rather that the law's weakness is an aspect of its incompleteness:[4] it required fulfilment in the Messiah to whom it pointed forward, and in whom prophecy and promise were fulfilled.[5]

It does not, however, follow from this that it is strictly correct to say that, with the fulfilment of the promise in Jesus "the possibility opens of obtaining forgiveness of sins and justification, which the law of Moses did not offer".[6] The law of Moses certainly offered forgiveness,[7] but could not justify finally because the forgiveness was only provisional pending the fulfilment in Christ. It is to be noted that, in verse 38, Paul does not imply that forgiveness was not available under the law; his point is simply that now it is through Jesus that it is preached. Justification, however, had to wait absolutely for the coming of the age of fulfilment. The law was weak in this respect. Again, this does not mean that justification was unavailable to believers before Christ: we know that Abraham, for example, was accounted righteous (Gen. 15:6; Rom. 4:2ff; Gal. 3:6ff). However, his righteousness was obtained not through the law, but through faith in the Word of God's grace, and during the economy of the law that remained the only basis for justification: there were believers during the period of the law, who were justified by grace through faith, but the law itself had no power at all to justify.

It was the question of the power of the law for salvation which was addressed by the Jerusalem Conference. The teaching of the Jews who came down to the Gentile Churches was that without circumcision

---

ἀποθανὼν δεδικαίωται ἀπὸ τῆς ἁμαρτίας', in *N T St* 10 (1963), pp. 104, 107.

[1] So Vielhauer, p. 42; C.F. Evans, *Saint Luke* (Trinity Press International, 1990), p. 645; G. Bornkamm, 'The Missionary Stance of Paul', in Keck and Martyn (eds.), p. 198.

[2] Cf. F.F. Bruce, *Greek*, p. 271; Larsson, p. 427.

[3] Cf. J. Nolland, 'A Fresh Look at Acts 15:10', in *N T St* 27 (1981), p. 106; against J.A. Alexander, Vol. 2, p. 34f; R.B. Rackham, *The Acts of the Apostles*, (Methuen, 1910), p. 217; F.F. Bruce, *Greek*, p. 271; Marshall, *Acts*, p. 228.

[4] Cf. E.M. Blaiklock, *The Acts of the Apostles* (Tyndale, 1959), p. 105.

[5] Cf. Calvin, *Acts*, p. 541; Barnes, *Acts*, p. 211; Tyson, *Jews*, p. 30f; Kilgallen, p. 504f.

[6] Haenchen, p. 416.

[7] Cf. Lev. 4:20,26,31,35; 5:10,13,16,18; 6:7; etc.

according to the law 'you cannot be saved' [15:1]. It was this allegation of saving power in the law which Paul vehemently opposed, insisting that "there was no saving power in anything but the cross of Christ".[1]

This does not mean, however, that the law possessed no power at all. Speaking to the people in Jerusalem Paul indicates that the law did have the power to make him, and all the Jews, 'zealous towards God' (22:3). Nevertheless, at the end of the Book of Acts we find the law, in the narrower sense of the five books of Moses, pointing away from itself in its weakness to Jesus, the One in whom the kingdom comes with saving, justifying power (28:23; cf. 26:22). The Gospel is consistently portrayed in Acts as the fulfilment of the Jewish heritage of faith: the debate is not about the way of salvation, for that is not in dispute when Paul is engaging with authentic Old Testament religion;[2] the issue is "whether the facts concerning Jesus could be seen as the fulfilment of prophecy".[3] Paul's message was that Christ brings the secured justification towards which the Old Testament could only wistfully point. It is this element of incompleteness, imperfection, and unfulfilledness, which entails the absolute weakness of the law in respect of justification.[4]

3   The Ongoing Status of the Law

Esler rightly points out that tensions as to the place of the law burst to the surface with the account of the trial of Stephen.[5] It was clearly the perception of the Jews as early as Acts 6:13f that there was an opposition between the Christian faith and the law. Although Luke describes this as the testimony of false witnesses, the fact that such a charge could be concocted must indicate something about the Jews' perception. The tension was apparent to the non-Christian Jews quicker than to their Christian counterparts, and it is probably true to say that Stephen "saw more clearly the inevitability of a break" than did the apostles.[6] However, the suggestion that the opposition was in the nature of the two systems is inconsistent with Luke's theology.

A study of the ongoing status of the law for the Christian believer as far as Acts is concerned is best divided into four parts, considering the

---

[1] E.F. Harrison, p. 228 (cf. Tyson, *Jews*, p. 33; *ibid, Images of Judaism in Luke-Acts* (University of South Carolina Press, 1992), p. 147).
[2] Against C.S.C. Williams, *A Commentary on the Acts of the Apostles* (A. & C. Black, 1964), p. 243.
[3] Marshall, *Acts*, p. 424.
[4] Cf. Barnes, *Acts,* pp. 353, 373; Rackham, pp. 471, 504; Bartlet, p. 365; Blunt, p. 245; F.F. Bruce, *Greek*, p. 447; E.F. Harrison, p. 379f; Neil, pp. 245, 258.
[5] Esler, *Community*, p. 123.
[6] F.F. Bruce, *Greek*, p. 157; cf. Blaiklock, p. 75.

application of the law separately to Jewish and Gentile Christians respectively for the time of transition during which Luke writes, with a third sub-section returning to the question of the implications of Stephen's insight in the light of Luke's long-term vision. Fourthly, it will be necessary to consider the implications of Luke-Acts for the place of the moral law in the life of the Christian believer.

1   THE LAW AND THE JEWISH BELIEVER: THE TIME OF TRANSITION

According to 21:20 the myriads of Jewish believers were all zealous for the law. To describe this zeal as 'corrupt'[1] is surely anachronistic, and Barnes' list of six reasons why it need not seem remarkable that the earliest generation of Jewish Christians continued to observe the ceremonial law is full of insight: (1) the ceremonies were ordained of God, and they had been trained in their observance; (2) at the beginning the apostles had conformed to Jewish law at Jerusalem; (3) there had been no agitation at Jerusalem about the observance of the law; (4) the decree of Acts 15 had had reference only to Gentile converts; (5) as understanding grew the law could eventually be laid aside without agitation; (6) God in His providence would yet (in AD 70) secure the termination of the ceremonies.[2] Until that happened, it is understandable that Jewish Christians saw no need to abandon Jewish rites because they believed them to be fulfilled in Christ.[3]

Marshall writes on this verse as follows: "Paul himself had once been equally, if not more, 'zealous... for the traditions of (his) fathers' (Gal. 1:14), but had then met Jesus Christ and abandoned the law as a means of obtaining a righteous relation to God (Phil. 3:8f). Other Jews found it less easy to abandon their previous life-style and continued to follow out the cultural expressions of Judaism."[4]

However, this statement involves an invalid contrast: Marshall's words imply two things which are not in fact true.

(1) He implies that other Jews had not abandoned the law as a means of obtaining a right relation to God. This is not true, and it is necessary to make two comments.

[a] The implication that authentic Jewish faith regarded the law as a means of righteousness Paul denies: his ancestral faith taught justification on the basis of the sovereign electing grace of God. Where a right understanding of the place of the law prevailed, it was not possible, therefore, to abandon it as a way of righteousness, since it had never held such a position.

---

[1] Calvin, *Acts*, p. 277; cf. J.T. Sanders, 'Who is a Jew and Who is a Gentile in the Book of Acts?', in *N T St* 37 (1991), p. 452.
[2] Barnes, *Acts*, p. 306.
[3] Cf. Blaiklock, p. 171.
[4] Marshall, *Acts*, p. 343.

[b] On the basis of this understanding of the Old Testament, Paul believes that certain Jewish groups, pre-eminently the Pharisees, to whom he himself once belonged, did distort the faith by interpreting it in terms of law-righteousness. However, he would have been insistent that all Jewish Christians must abandon the idea (in those cases where they had subscribed to it) of the law as a means of obtaining a righteous relation to God: to continue to perpetuate such a distortion of true Biblical faith, was essentially incompatible with a profession of Christian faith (cf. 11:18; 15:11).

(2) Marshall appears to assume that Paul himself abandoned his previous lifestyle and did not continue to follow out the cultural expressions of Judaism. This also is not true. It was perfectly possible, both for Paul, and for the rest of the Jews who had become Christians, to continue to follow 'the cultural expressions of Judaism' without the slightest sense that they were thereby obtaining righteousness.

Bruce notes that "Paul himself, so far as we can tell, continued to observe the law throughout his life, especially in Jewish company", and sees his consent to the elders' request to be purified and pay the expenses of the four Nazirite men as "entirely in keeping with his settled principle".[1] It is indeed evident from the purpose for which the elders made this request ("that all may know that ... you yourself also walk orderly and keep the law" [21:24]) that the keeping of the law was Paul's regular way of life. The alternative is to conclude that he and the elders were hatching a piece of hypocrisy, an unlikely scenario.[2] Neither is it appropriate to portray this event as a pragmatic compromise.[3] On two subsequent occasions Paul gives his own testimony as to his attitude to the law: his belief in the law (in the sense of the written torah) is total (24:14), and he has not sinned against the law (in its ceremonial requirements) in anything (25:8).[4] Paul himself also commends Ananias as a man who, after his conversion, was still "a devout man according to the law" (22:12). It is, then, true that "To the last Paul moves within Judaism. He is never guilty of any transgression of the law"[5]

One further issue remains. We learn from the elders' words to Paul in 21:21 that it was rumoured that, although in a Jerusalem situation he was happy, along with his fellow Jewish believers, to continue to observe the law, in the context of the Diaspora he advocated the cessation of Jewish

---

[1] F.F. Bruce, *Acts*, p. 1002.

[2] Juel, p. 84.

[3] Blaiklock, p. 171f; W.D. Davies, *Paul and Rabbinic Judaism* (Fortress Press, 1980), pp. 70, 74f, 321.

[4] Cf. A. Ehrhardt, *The Acts of the Apostles* (Manchester University Press, 1969), p. 108f.

[5] Ludemann, p. 232 (cf. M. Salmon, 'Insider or Outsider?', in Tyson (ed.), p. 79; Vielhauer, p. 37f; Esler, *Community*, p. 125).

law-keeping. Most commentators rightly recognize that these rumours were false, and were at best an incorrect inference from Paul's teaching that the law provided no basis at all for justification.

The exception to this general agreement is Calvin, who, having quoted the charge stated in verse 21, begins his comment with the declaration: "It was so indeed". He then proceeds to cite texts from the Pauline Epistles (1 Cor. 7:19; 10:25; Gal. 5:1; Col. 2:11,14,16) which allegedly prove that Paul taught that Jews were to be free from the law.[1] However, an examination of these texts shows that they do not necessarily sustain such a reading. The most that they demonstrate is why such a false accusation could be levelled against the apostle. Apart from the first, all Calvin's verses are directed towards a Gentile environment, and therefore are strictly beside the point in the present context. However, 1 Corinthians 7:19 makes the point that both circumcision and uncircumcision are equally irrelevant in the matter of Christian calling.

This is precisely the same viewpoint as that expressed by Luke as common to all the apostles and elders of the primitive Church. The reason why the Jewish believers go on in the observance of the ceremonial law is that the whole issue is a total irrelevance in the debate about justification and salvation: for the Jews at that time to break with their tradition might well have conveyed the impression that there was saving merit in emancipation from the law, a theory just as heretical as the view that there was righteousness in the law. As regards the Jews, therefore, the ceremonial requirements of the law continue to be observed for the duration of the period chronicled in Acts.[2]

2   THE LAW AND THE GENTILE BELIEVER: THE TIME OF TRANSITION

The Jerusalem Conference assembled in order to settle the question of the applicability of the ceremonial law to Gentile Christians. The basic issue was whether Gentiles had to come into the Jewish economy in order to be saved. The conclusion was that such a notion had to be opposed.

Though it might be quite appropriate for Jewish Christians to continue with their ethnic customs, while recognizing that neither now nor at any previous time did they possess justifying power, as far as Gentiles were concerned, the ceremonial law had no ongoing status because it had never had any status in their past. To imply that Gentile believers should now begin to observe the law in order to be justified was at odds with the purpose of the law as revealed in the Hebrew Scriptures themselves. The emphases in the speeches of Peter and James at the Conference are the sovereignty of God in giving the Holy Spirit to circumcised and uncircumcised alike (v. 8), salvation by grace (v. 11), and the fulfilment of

---

[1] Calvin, *Acts*, p. 279.
[2] Cf. Jervell, *Acts*, p. 20.

prophecy (vv.15-17), and "there is not a shred of evidence that circumcision of the Gentiles was ever demanded by the Church after the Jerusalem council".[1]

In this connection it is important to consider the significance of the modest demands which were made of the Gentiles in 15:20,29 (reiterated in 21:25). In 15:28f these requirements are described as 'necessary things', in the observing of which the Gentile Christians 'will do well'. These are: to refrain from things offered to idols, from things strangled, from blood, and from πορνεία, usually translated 'sexual immorality'.

There is no doubt that the Jewish view of the 'sinful' Gentile world is reflected in the stipulations of the decree. However, the first question which must be raised is whether Gentile 'sin' is perceived essentially in moral or ceremonial terms, and hence whether the four requirements are taken from the ceremonial law, the moral law, or not from the law at all. The last possibility is suggested by Rackham, who describes the requirements as "certain Gentile practices which were the chief causes of offence to the Jews".[2] However, this explanation is bound to lead back to the law, in that the things which were offensive to Jews were things contrary to their law. Another way of separating these demands from the law as here defined is to refer to the Noachite food-laws.[3] However, while this may account for the reference to abstention from blood, it does not do justice to the remaining three requirements. We must conclude that the law lies behind the decree, which requires of Gentiles "observance of certain features of the torah".[4] The question then remains whether the demands are drawn from the ceremonial or moral law.

This issue arises because of the presence in a list of otherwise seemingly ceremonial requirements of one matter (πορνεία) which appears to be essentially moral, and which can be seen as the only one of the list which is not a merely temporary expedient.[5]

One explanation which has been offered is that our tendency to make a sharp division between moral and ceremonial laws in the quest for an accurate explanation of the decree merely reflects a Gentile inability fully to understand Jewish ethical thought-patterns, in which no firm differentiation between the moral and the ceremonial is recognized.[6] This, however, is not

---

[1] Ehrhardt, p. 107.
[2] Rackham, p. 254.
[3] Eg. Ehrhardt, p. 88; F.F. Bruce, *The New London Commentary on the New Testament: Commentary on the Book of Acts* (Marshall, Morgan and Scott, 1962), p. 312; J.D.G. Dunn, 'The Incident at Antioch (Gal. 2:11-18)', in *J St N T* 18 (1983), pp. 25, 38; J.T. Sanders, p. 452.
[4] Juel, p. 78.
[5] So J.A. Alexander, Vol. 2, p. 92.
[6] So Foakes-Jackson, p. 142; E.F. Harrison, p. 235; E.P. Sanders, *Paul* (Oxford

entirely true: not infrequently the Old Testament depicts the LORD as reminding His people that "to obey is better than sacrifice" (1 Sam. 15:22),[1] and thus affirms both the distinction between the moral and the ceremonial law, and the primacy of the former. Thielman has documented the presence of this emphasis in extra-cacnonical Jewish literature also.[2] Moreover, this distinction between the ceremonial and the moral aspects of the law begins, arguably, to become clearer still in the New Testament (cf. 1 Cor. 7:19), and it would not therefore be surprising if the Jewish Christians were able to understand such a differentiation already by the time of Acts 15.

It seems necessary to maintain that the four requirements are intended to be regarded as ceremonial rather than moral. If the stipulations of the decree were intended to include moral requirements, it is hard to see why they should have stopped short at these four. This is not to deny that ceremonial requirements may frequently have had moral associations, and even a moral rationale; it is simply to argue that the emphasis in this context lies on the ceremonial aspect. It is this contextual argument which seems decisive: in the context of Acts 15, where the major issue is circumcision, the introduction of moral demands would be out of place.[3] The necessity laid upon the Gentiles is for the sake of the unity of a racially mixed Church: the decree is concerned about Gentile behaviour within the Church, but the Gentiles are being requested to make a concession for the sake of their Jewish brethren,[4] who still have to live with the scruples which the ceremonial law has ingrained into them.

What then is to be made of the presence in the list of πορνεία? It has been pointed out that sexual immorality was associated in Gentile worship with idolatry.[5] However, this comment assumes that "things polluted by idols" means idolatry itself, and implies that the practice of idolatry has a polluting effect on its participants. However, there are two reasons for rejecting this interpretation of the phrase. First, to read here a reference to idolatry itself would intrude moral presuppositions alien to the context. Second the context itself defines "things polluted by idols": in verse 29 (cf. 21:25) the meaning is clarified as "things offered to idols".[6] The point is

---

University Press, 1991), p. 86.

[1] Cf. Pss. 40:6-8; 51:16f; Prov. 15:8; Isa. 1:11-17; 66:3f; Jer. 6:19f; 14:10-12; Hos. 6:6; Am. 5:22-4; Mic. 6:6-8.

[2] F. Thielman, *From Plight to Solution* (Brill, 1989), pp. 54-7.

[3] Cf. M.A. Seifrid, 'Jesus and the Law in Acts', in *J St N T* 30 (1987), p. 50; Tyson, *Images*, p. 148.

[4] Cf. Seifrid, *Jesus*, p. 51; against M. Dibelius, *Studies in the Acts of the Apostles* (SCM Press, 1956), pp. 97, 99, Haenchen, p. 449, Conzelmann, p. 118.

[5] Rackham, p. 265.

[6] Cf. Thayer, p. 174; H.G. Liddell & R. Scott, *A Lexicon, Abridged from Liddell and Scott's Greek-English Lexicon* (Clarendon, 1909), p. 196; H.K. Moulton (ed.), *The Analytical Greek Lexicon Revised* (Zondervan, 1978), p. 117.

that, from a Jewish viewpoint, the use of meat in idol-worship has a polluting effect on the meat, and the Gentiles are being invited to respect that sensitivity.

Most commentators suggest that πορνεία has a specific meaning here, and must be interpreted in the light of the Old Testament marriage law, regarding prohibited degrees (Lev. 18).[1] This interpretation has the advantage of drawing the requirement from Old Testament law, and of recognizing that the primary emphasis in Leviticus 18 is on avoiding ritual defilement (cf. vv. 23-30). It has also been pointed out that the marriage laws occur in close proximity to regulations about the eating of blood, suggesting that all four of the demands made of the Gentiles may have been prompted by this single section of the torah.[2]

On the other hand, as Seifrid observes, this is not a particularly convincing explanation, especially since there is nothing in the context to suggest this meaning of πορνεία. He argues that it is a sufficient explanation of the presence of this term to say that the common concern with ritual defilement ties together the four elements in the decree. He argues, to my mind persuasively, that "polluted" is the interpretive key, signalling that this matter of ceremonial defilement underlies all four requirements.[3] This interpretation still bases the decree on the torah, though without focussing on any particular text.[4]

In the specific context of Jewish-Gentile relationships in the early Church during the transition period, there was therefore a need for the Gentiles to make a concession to the Jews in order to protect the unity of the New Testament people of God. It was recognized that there was, for the Gentile believers, a burdensome aspect to this (15:28);[5] however, the Church was unanimous in its recognition that the ceremonial law ought not to be imposed as a matter of course on believers from amongst the Gentiles, that it had no ongoing application to them.[6] This was made concrete by the refusal to require from the Gentiles circumcision, the rite which was the entrance into the entire economy now superseded by the era of fulfilment in Christ.

Moreover, even in the time of transition the decree was drafted only for a

---

[1] Cf. F.F. Bruce, *Greek*, p. 300; *New London*, p. 315, Guthrie and Motyer (eds.), p. 992; Haenchen, p. 449; R.P.C. Hanson, *The Acts* (Clarendon, 1967), p. 163; E.F. Harrison, p. 235; Neil, p. 173.

[2] Marshall, *Acts*, p. 246; C.S.C. Williams, p. 183; Conzelmann, p. 118.

[3] Seifrid, *Jesus*, p. 48f.

[4] Cf. T. Callan, 'The Background of the Apostolic Decree (Ac. 15:20,29; 21:25)', in *C B Q* 55 (1993), pp. 285-7.

[5] So Marshall, *Acts*, p. 255 (cf. Tyson, *Images*, p. 149), against Haenchen, p. 450, n. 1; Conzelmann, p. 120.

[6] So Larsson, p. 430f.

specific geographical area. This is the unanimous understanding of Luke, Paul and the apostles and elders at Jerusalem. It was not imposed upon Gentile believers where there was no necessity for it. This explains why it is not mentioned in Paul's letter to the Galatians, which, as I argue elsewhere, was addressed to a different set of people. Paul was happy to agree to the requirements of the decree as a temporary expedient for dealing with the specific problem of relationships between Jews and Gentiles in the Churches of Antioch, Syria and Cilicia. His basic understanding, however, like that of Luke, was that the ceremonial law, whose purpose was to regulate the worship of God by His people in the age before the coming of Christ, had no application to Gentile believers who lived in the new age after Christ had come, and who were to worship Him in the Spirit.[1]

3   THE LAW AND THE BELIEVER: THE LONG-TERM VISION

Mention has already been made of Luke's long-term vision of a movement away from Israel towards a predominantly Gentile Church. Actually, the predominantly Gentile composition of the Church of the future is rather incidental.[2] Luke's main insight for the years to come is that the newness of the movement which looks back and upwards to Jesus of Nazareth as the Christ will render the old ways obsolete for Jewish and Gentile Christians alike, that the ceremonial law is destined, in the nature of things, to pass into disuse by all Christians.[3]

It has been noticed that, during the transition period described in Acts, the Jewish Christians continued to observe the requirements of their ceremonial law. Nevertheless, there are hints already that this situation will not continue indefinitely, since the economy of the law has been effectively terminated by the crucifixion of Christ, in whom Old Testament prophecy finds its authentic fulfilment: "the work of Christ logically involved the abrogation of the whole temple order. ... The Gospel meant the end of the sacrificial cultus and all the ceremonial law".[4]

Luke lays great stress on the fact that the Jews were not satisfied with Paul's stance in agreeing to fulfil the request of the Jerusalem elders in chapter 21. His consent did not avert his arrest and trial. Conzelmann makes the shrewd comment: "Paul's fate is settled precisely as he fulfils obligations of Jewish Law".[5] This fact may well be Luke's way of

---

[1] Cf. Vielhauer, p. 42.

[2] Cf. Gasque, *Fruitful Field*, p. 129; V. Fusco, 'Luke-Acts and the Future of Israel', in *Nov Test* 38 (1996), p. 6; against J.T. Sanders, p. 455 (cf. Wills, pp. 632-44, 653).

[3] Against M. Pettem, 'Luke's Great Omission and His View of the Law', in *N T St* 42 (1996), p. 37 (cf. p. 47).

[4] F.F. Bruce, *New London*, p. 135f; cf. Marshall, *Historian*, p. 183; D.R. Schwartz, 'The Futility of Preaching Moses (Acts 15,21)', in *Biblica* 67 (1986), p. 280.

[5] Conzelmann, p. 180.

indicating that, though the Jewish believers may persist with the customs of the law for a season, nevertheless the law as an economy is really at an end: it has lost its moral credibility, and must eventually disappear from the scene. Part of the reason for this is that the crucifixion of Jesus of Nazareth, the One in whom the economy of the law is fulfilled in accordance with God's prophetic promise, was an act of lawlessness (2:23).

The key to this eventual separation of the young Church from continuing Judaism is found in the question of the identity of the Messiah. Luke's account of Paul's preaching and that of the Jerusalem apostles does not centre on the issue of the way of salvation. On that Christianity agreed with the Jewish Scriptures; the law does not enter into consideration at this point: salvation was on the basis of the sovereign grace of God enacted in the Christ. The fundamental question was whether or not Jesus was the Christ.[1] The answer given by both Paul and Apollos was that "Jesus is the Christ" (18:5,28; cf. 9:22), and in this they are in agreement with all the apostles, who 'did not cease from teaching and preaching Jesus as the Christ' (5:42; cf. 2:36), and as such as 'the hope of Israel' (28:20). If this conclusion was to carry any conviction at all with the Jews, it was vital that the early Christian preachers should emphasize from the Old Testament Scriptures that the fact of Jesus' Passion was not incompatible with His status as the Christ (17:3).[2]

There are indications already in Luke's Gospel that the coming of Jesus as the Christ who must suffer (Lk. 9:20,22), heralds the displacement of the ceremonial law by the new reality of fulfilment in Him. It is noteworthy that five references to the law are clustered in 2:22-39, but the word occurs only four times in the Gospel thereafter.[3] For this reason the authenticity of Luke 1-2 has been doubted, but this view has been compellingly refuted.[4] More likely, the phenomenon is symbolic of the fact that a transition to something new has begun with the event described in chapter 2. Luke notes that, for the angels, it was more important that the One who had been born was the Christ than that His name was Jesus (2:11). Later, Jesus twice pronounces 'Woe' on the lawyers (11:46,52): this again may be an indication of the approaching demise of the law. In 22:37, in connection with the fulfilment in Him of the Scripture prophesying His identification with the transgressors (ἀνόμων), Jesus says: 'The things concerning Me have an end (τέλος)'. Perhaps there is a deliberate *double entendre* here: the τέλος (goal) of what was prophesied about Jesus, and of the life which

---

[1] Cf. Blunt, p. 156.
[2] Cf. Marshall, *Acts*, p. 277; J.A. Alexander, Vol. 2, p. 135.
[3] Lk. 10:26; 16:16f; 24:44.
[4] P.S. Minear, 'Luke's Use of the Birth Stories', in Keck and Martyn (eds), *passim*; J.B. Chance, *Jerusalem, the Temple, and the New Age in Luke-Acts* (Mercer University Press, 1988), p. 47.

He lived, was this identification in His death with the lawless, but that very death spells the τέλος (termination) of the law which thus pointed forward to Him.

Because Jesus is the Christ, His coming, and particularly His death have rendered the old ceremonies unnecessary, since He is their fulfilment. Without Him, the law was incomplete; now that He has come the law is obsolete,[1] and the time would come when that would be recognized and the ceremonies would cease.

A few verses from the end of Acts we find the law pointing away from itself to Jesus, the One in whom the kingdom comes (28:23). Paul is emphasizing the fact that the Gospel is the fulfilment of the Jewish heritage of faith: his message was that, without Christ, the law was unavoidably incomplete, imperfect, and unfulfilled. With this understanding highlighted at the point of climax, it is not surprising that Luke's long-term vision is of a day when even the Jews will cease to perform the ceremonies of the law.

It is not necessary, with Goulder, to conclude that Luke describes the progress towards victory of the Pauline gospel without the law over its Petrine rival.[2] He suggests that the real leader of the Jerusalem Christians (the Petrines), James, "stood out for principle, where Peter was weak-kneed; the Law was God's Law and must be obeyed, however inconvenient."[3] The problem with this thesis is that Luke makes it clear that the incipient break with the law took place even before Paul's conversion. As we have seen, as early as Acts 6, Stephen set the direction for the future. In chapter 10 Peter is the first to take the Gospel to the Gentiles as the result of a vision through which he learnt, in effect, that the food laws were obsolete in Christ.[4] Even James is responsible for the judgement that 'we should not trouble those from the Gentiles who are turning to God' (15:19). His proposal of the four ritual requirements is soleley for the purpose of maintaining unity in the Church.

Goulder depicts Luke as an irenic character, a Pauline who nonetheless tries to bridge the gap between the two missions.[5] However, given Luke's stated commitment to historical accuracy, it is safer to conclude that he documented the facts as he believed them to be, and, given his proximity to the events, that his understanding of the facts was correct. It follows that there was no rivalry between Paul and the Jerusalem apostles: the supersession of the law which Luke could foresee once the Church had become established was the end result of a logical and constant process of development stretching back at least as far as Stephen.

---

[1] Cf. Seifrid, *Jesus,* p. 41; Larsson, pp. 427, 434.
[2] Goulder, p. 182f; cf. Dunn, *Partings*, p. 134.
[3] Goulder, p. 188.
[4] Cf. Seifrid, *Jesus,* p. 43.
[5] Goulder, pp. 12, 15.

Dunn suggests that it is too readily assumed that Stephen criticized the law as such, arguing that his martyrdom had more to do with his attitude to the temple and that the Hellenistic Jewish Christians did not question the law independently of their questioning of the temple. He claims that the wider question of the law is raised only during the mission of Peter to Cornelius. However, to speak in such vein overlooks the fact that νόμος in Acts consistently means the ceremonial law, and therefore is, for practical purposes, indistinguishable from temple and cult. Dunn thinks that the theology of Jesus' death as the sacrifice to end all sacrifices first emerged with Stephen and the Hellenists.[1] Whether this is factually correct or not, it does amount to saying that Stephen and the Hellenists first foresaw the abrogation of the law, in the sense in which Luke chiefly uses the word. In any case Dunn appears to be right in seeing the Stephen episode as the first 'parting of the ways'.[2]

Ultimately, however, Luke traces this long-tem vision back to Jesus Himself.[3] It is worth noting that his Gospel ends with an emphasis similar to the end of Acts, this time from the lips of Jesus, with the law (in the sense of the textbook for the ceremonies) pointing away from itself to the new reality in Christ (Lk. 24:44; cf. 24:27). However, in his Gospel too Luke recognizes that the break with the law does not come immediately: in 24:53 he tells how the disciples continued at the temple; there is to be a transition phase.

Esler claims that Luke wants to portray the law as continuing into the Christian epoch: Jesus' coming fulfils the law, but does not result in its abrogation. He argues, however, that Luke's desire to depict Christian fidelity to the law conflicts with the facts, and that this conflict arises from the influence on his theology of the socio-ethnic pressures of the community.[4] However, it seems more accurate to argue that Luke does faithfully describe the facts current at the time of writing, but hints at the future development, the beginnings of which he already discerns. He foresees a Christianity which is the genuine fulfilment of Jewish traditions,[5] and will therefore supersede those imperfect traditions and continue without them into the long-term future. The weakness of Esler's thesis is that he overlooks the fact that Luke is writing during a stage of transition.

Dunn's claim that the separation of Christianity from Judaism was also

---

[1] Dunn, *Partings*, pp. 63-71, 119f, 294, n. 36 (cf. Juel, p. 74f).
[2] Dunn, *Partings*, pp. 68,70; cf. D.P. Moessner, '"The Christ Must Suffer": New Light on the Jesus - Peter, Stephen, Paul Parallels in Luke-Acts', in *Nov Test* 28 (1986), p. 227.
[3] Dunn, *Partings*, p. 230.
[4] Esler, *Community*, pp. 128-30.
[5] Cf. *ibid*, p. 221.

something of a schism within earliest Christianity[1] does not appear to do justice to the history as told in Acts. Luke makes it clear that there was general agreement as to the long-term direction, even though the transition period may have been marked by tensions which demanded some expediency. Even if Dunn is right to say that the parting of the ways was not so much between Christianity and Judaism as between mainstream Christianity and that Jewish Christianity which the early fathers portray as a group of heretical sects,[2] fairness to Luke's account demands the inclusion of Peter and James, and the other Jerusalem leaders, in the mainstream.

Juel notes that the interpretation of Luke's perspective which I am proposing (namely that the Church "understands itself as distinct from the synagogue", the exclusive Jewishness of its roots becoming a thing of the past) is the traditional one, but that it has been challenged in recent years; Juel himself would endorse the challenge. He denies that Luke has a theology of 'replacement', where the Church supersedes Israel, and claims that he is more concerned with the continuity than the discontinuity between Israel and the Church: torah adherence is not past. Juel opposes those who claim that the first two chapters of Luke's Gospel display an interest in Jewish piety which is uncommon elsewhere in Luke-Acts, and points out the importance to Luke of the fact that the initiator of the Gentile mission was Peter, whose Jewish credentials were beyond question. Juel suggests that the decree of Acts 15 imposes torah obligations on Gentile Christians and testifies to the continuing validity of the law as a guide central to the life of believers, both Jew and Gentile. Luke-Acts is, therefore, not about the birth of a new religion.[3]

In response to this seven points may be made. (1) While at the time of writing torah-adherence was still a present reality, Juel misses Luke's hints concerning the long-term direction. (2) Despite Luke's interest in Jewish piety throughout his two volumes, the possibility must not be discounted that the concentration of occurrences of νόμος in Luke 2 is significant. (3) The fact that Luke stresses Peter's seminal part in the bringing of the Gospel to Gentiles need not be read as a statement of the continuing Jewishness of the Church: it might stand as an indication of the recognition, even by the Jewish Christian leaders, of the element of newness in the future Church. (4) In his comments on the decree Juel overlooks both the explicit geographical limitation of its scope, and the implicit temporal limitation of its expedient necessity. (5) Juel comes close to contradicting himself when he later writes: "The future of Israel lies with the Gentiles".[4] Even though he rightly stresses the continuity between Israel and the

---

[1] Dunn, *Partings*, pp. 95f, 135.
[2] *Ibid*, p. 239.
[3] Juel, pp. 102-9 (cf. Bornkamm, p. 201).
[4] Juel, p. 111; (cf. pp. 63, 68f).

Church, this sentence indicates that he cannot avoid recognizing that there is also a major factor of newness. (6) Juel is correct in denying that Christianity is, for Luke, a new religion. However, he fails to see that Luke is setting out to describe the emergence of a new form of expression of the one Biblical faith. The place of the law is a key issue as regards the emergent new entity in Christ. (7) It seems that an important reason why Juel distorts Luke's perspective is that he nowhere defines the word 'law', and consequently introduces confusion into the term. He treats the subject uniformly, but it is not clear that he always means precisely the same thing by 'law'. Had he distinguished more carefully between the moral and ceremonial aspects of the law, he may well have recognized the validity of 'the traditional reading'.

The thesis of J. Bradley Chance is worthy of note. His summary of Luke's theology is that "with the arrival of Jesus, the New Age, in its fullest eschatological sense, has dawned."[1] He sees the Gentile mission as intrinsically eschatological,[2] and recognizes that Luke believed that the time in which he lived was "predominantly Gentile-time".[3] Nevertheless he questions the interpretation of Acts which sees Luke as portraying Christianity as a religion which is becoming increasingly independent of Judaism, and challenges the view that Luke's theology advocated the transferral of salvation to the Gentiles.[4] Chance believes that Luke's ultimate eschatological vision embraces a restored Israel, and finds evidence for this in the prominent place given to Jerusalem and the temple, including the fact that Paul is depicted as an extension of the Jerusalem Church.[5]

Three comments may be made. (1) Chance's work is a healthy corrective to those interpretations which attempt to drive a wedge between Paul and the Jerusalem authorities. We have already observed that all the early missionaries were agreed as to the long-term direction. (2) The eschatological emphasis is to be welcomed: Luke does indeed understand the coming of Jesus as the dawn of the 'new age'. However, Chance fails to recognize that this inevitably means the obsolescence of the ancient ceremonies which served as provisional pointers to Him. (3) The fact that Luke's time and the future were predominantly Gentile is clear. It has already been noted, however, that this is really quite incidental for Luke. The possibility of the restoration of Israel therefore remains open, although it seems that Chance builds his argument at this point on a rather flimsy foundation: Luke's concern with Jerusalem and the temple is to be read not

---

[1] Chance, p. 140 (cf. p. 56).
[2] Ibid, p. 99.
[3] Ibid, p. 141.
[4] Ibid, pp. 100f, 128f.
[5] Ibid, pp. 56-72, 83-5, 108, 141, etc.

so much as an insistence on the continuing Jewishness of the Church, but rather as an affirmation of the continuity of the Church with its Jewish roots. Within that continuity, however, there is a measure of newness of form even for the Jewish believers.

Perhaps it is because Luke was a Gentile that he was able to see so clearly that in the course of time the ceremonial law must cease to be observed even by the Jews. He could understand the logic of the Christian faith, and of the explanation of it offered by the Jerusalem authorities as much as by Paul: since the Christ had come in the Person of Jesus, it was inevitable that the ceremonies should pass into obsolescence, because they had attained their fulfilment in Him.

4   The Moral Law and the Believer

As we have seen, in Luke-Acts νόμος means the ceremonial law. However, the status of the ceremonial law is not of direct relevance to the question addressed by this thesis. It is necessary, therefore to raise the question whether there is anything in Luke's history regarding the issue of the permanent validity of the moral law. It has to be said that this issue is of slender concern for Luke. The sole instance where the word 'law' may be used with a moral sense is Luke 16:17. If this is the correct interpretation, then this is the only explicit word in Luke's writings on the permanence of the moral law. However, while Jesus' teaching of His disciples in Luke largely concerns Christian service and the cost of Christian commitment, there are some places where He can be read as implying the continuing relevance of the law of God.

Luke's version of the Sermon on the Mount (6:20-49) has points of contact with the law. These are noted by Hendriksen.[1] However, it is an interesting question why Luke has not recorded in this context the words which form Matthew 5:17-20, and which make explicit the fact that the Sermon is intended as an exposition of the law. Does the absence of this passage mean that Luke is a moral antinomian? I think not. The omission is probably sufficiently explained by the fact that Luke (unlike Matthew) writes for Gentiles who would be less familiar with the Old Testament moral law. It is enough for such an audience that their Lord's authoritative interpretation of the law be quoted, without the citation of chapter and verse from the Hebrew Scriptures.

That Luke saw an ongoing role for the moral law in the life of disciples is indicated by his selection of a number of other dominical sayings. Jesus redefines His family as 'those who hear the word of God and do (ποιοῦντες) it' (8:21), and later pronounces a blessing on 'those who hear the word of God and keep (φυλάσσοντες) it' (11:28). Both these verbs

---

[1] Hendriksen, *Luke*, pp. 348-57 (cf. Geldenhuys, p. 211; Morris, *Luke*, p. 130).

appear frequently in the LXX in conjunction with νόμος.[1] Although 'the word of God' can here be understood as "the teaching of Jesus",[2] it is arguable that this amounts to the true interpretation of the law, and that Jesus' emphasis is on the duty of obeying the law of God.[3] The note of duty reappears at 17:10, where Christ speaks "of an entire observance of the law".[4]

As far as Jesus is concerned the evidence that Zacchaeus is a recipient of salvation is his giving to the poor and his fourfold restitution of unjust acquisitions (19:8f). The immediate result of Zacchaeus' experience of salvation was thus that he obeyed the law (cf. Ex. 22:1; 2 Sam. 12:6). Indeed, he went beyond the minimal requirement of the law; Luke, like Matthew (cf. Matt. 5:20), is aware that the righteousness of Jesus' disciples must exceed that of the scribes and Pharisees.

Luke's second volume opens with the observation that the risen Christ spent the time until His ascension giving commandments to the apostles (Ac. 1:2). The content of Jesus' commanding is variously interpreted. Most commentators take it to be the commission to preach the Gospel,[5] while others understand it as a reference to the command of verse 4.[6] Calvin understands it as directions about the manner in which the commission was to be fulfilled,[7] while Munck defines it rather vaguely as instruction "concerning the kingdom of God".[8] The possibility, however, seems worthy of consideration that the commandments concerned the Christian way of life which the apostles were to live out and in which they were to instruct their converts. In other words, Jesus used the forty day period to give His authoritative exposition of the law, so elaborating on what He had earlier said in the Sermon on the Mount. The form of life of the primitive Jerusalem Church (2:44f; 4:34f) may well then reflect this exposition of the law: the duty of providing for the needy within the covenant community is certainly enshrined in the Old Testament legislation.[9] Peter's rebuke of Ananias for lying (5:3f), and of Sapphira for testing the Spirit of the Lord (5:9), presupposes that obedience to the law, which prohibited such lying

---

[1] Eg: Ex. 12:49f; 13:10; 18:20; Lev. 19:37; Num. 5:30; 9:3,12,14; Deut. 17:10f; 24:10; 27:26; 28:58; 29:29; 30:10; 31:12; 32:46.
[2] I.H. Marshall, 'Luke', in D. Guthrie, & J.A. Motyer (eds.), *The New Bible Commentary Revised* (IVP, 1970), p. 901.
[3] Cf. Barnes, *luke*, p. 75.
[4] Calvin, *Evangelists*, Vol. 2, p. 197 (cf. Morris, *Luke*, p. 257).
[5] Cf. J.A. Alexander, Vol. 1, p. 4; Barnes, *Acts*, p. 2; Rackham, p. 4; Haenchen, p. 139; E.F. Harrison, p. 36; Neil, p. 63f.
[6] Blunt, p. 131; F.F. Bruce, *Greek*, p. 67.
[7] Calvin, *Acts*, p. 34f.
[8] Munck, *Acts*, p. 5.
[9] Cf. Ex. 23:11; Lev. 19:9f; 23:22; Deut. 24:21; Job 29:12; Ps. 72; Prov. 31:9; Isa 58:7; Zech 7:10; etc.

and testing,[1] is expected within the Christian community.

The fullest account which we have in Acts of Paul's ministry to believers is his address to the Ephesian elders (20:17-38). In the course of his speech he offers his own life as an example of Christian living. Two elements are worthy of note. First, his claim to humility (ταπεινοφροσύνη) [v. 19] uses a noun found in the LXX Codex Ephraemi of Proverbs 16:19, and commended by its equivalent cognate verb in Psalm 130(131):2. Second, verse 33 is an obvious allusion to the tenth commandment. Paul also instructs the elders in Christian living, and verse 35a should be noted. The phrase, 'you must (δεῖ) support the weak', echoes Leviticus 25:35, where the same verb (ἀντιλαμβάνομαι) is used, and Paul's word ἀσθενούντων replaces the LXX's ἀδυνατήσῃ, a functional synonym. Moreover, the word δεῖ is sometimes used in the LXX for the obligation to obey the law of the LORD (Lev. 4:2; Ruth 4:5; Prov. 22:14). It seems, then, that Alexander falls short of a full explanation of this verse when he describes it as "a general fact or principle of duty":[2] it is emphatically a duty drawn from the moral law of God.

Finally we may note Paul's own testimony in 24:16, where he takes the fact of resurrection as a chief motive for striving to maintain 'a conscience without offence (ἀπρόσκοπον) towards God and men'. The cognate verb προσκόπτω, is used in a metaphorical sense in Proverbs 3:23 and 4:19 of those who fail to walk in the ways of wisdom; within the same passage (Prov. 3:16) wisdom is associated with νόμος. Paul's striving, therefore, is to observe the law.[3]

This evidence of a concern with the ongoing role of the law in a moral sense is, admittedly, slender. The reason for this is that the issue was not central to Luke's primary purpose of undergirding the believer's confidence. However, the few references cited may indicate that a concern with the moral law was not totally lacking in Luke's writings, and that Christian obedience to the law in its moral aspect was anticipated.

Conclusion

The Book of Acts makes it clear that, if νόμος is defined as the Old Testament economy as focussed in its ceremonial requirements, then it has no ongoing status in the life of the Christian believer. This applies unequivocally to Gentile Christians, some of whom were simply invited for a time to accept some constraints drawn from the ceremonial law out of love for their Jewish brethren. In the course of his celebration of Gentile

---

[1] Cf. Ex. 17:2,7; Lev. 6:2f; 19:11; Num. 14:22; Deut. 33:8; Josh. 24:27; Ps. 77(78):41,56; 94(95):9; 105(106):14; etc.

[2] J.A. Alexander, Vol. 2, p. 255.

[3] Cf. Marshall, *Acts*, p. 378.

salvation, therefore, Luke is facing up to what was, for the Jews, the perplexing problem of "the obsolescence of what had been revealed under Divine sanctions",[1] in order to dissuade the Gentile believers from any sense of superiority towards their Jewish brethren.

Although Luke portrays a situation in which the Jewish believers continued to observe the law's ceremonial requirements, to which they were accustomed, there are hints in his work that, this is only for a transitional phase. The perception, both of the Jerusalem apostles and of Paul is that the ceremonial law is destined for oblivion, because, with the coming of Christ, who is its fulfilment, it is effectively finished as an economy. The time is bound to come when it will cease to be observed even by Jewish Christians: "the break in principle has been made when the Gentiles are no longer required to keep it."[2]

As regards the moral law, Luke has almost nothing to say, and what he thinks has to be pieced together from slender hints. However, it appears that he understands Jesus, the Jerusalem Church, and Paul, to be unanimous in affirming the continuing validity of the moral law of God. Obedience to these requirements has not been rendered obsolete by the dawn of the age of newness.

---

[1] Bartlet, p. 30.
[2] Marshall, *Historian*, p. 191.

CHAPTER 2

Romans

1   Introduction

Despite his constant intention, Paul had been 'hindered' (1:13) from visiting the Roman Church. This had given rise to some suspicion. It seems that he had been accused of an unreadiness to preach in Rome, and even of being ashamed to evangelize in the imperial capital (1:15-16a).[1] A first purpose behind the writing of this Epistle was therefore to clear up any misunderstanding, and to give a proper explanation of why he had been hindered, namely that his policy had been to preach the Gospel in pioneering situations (15:20-22), and Rome was not in this category.

At the time of writing Paul is about to set out for Jerusalem conveying the contribution made by the Churches of Macedonia and Achaia for the Jewish Christians who were afflicted by poverty (15:25-27). He is aware that a journey to Jerusalem will involve him in potential danger, and therefore a second purpose in writing is to enlist the prayer support of the Roman Christians (15:30f).

This departure for Jerusalem marks the completion of Paul's work in the east (15:23a), and his future plans include a mission to Spain; his hope is to take in a visit to Rome en route, and so to realise his longstanding ambition (15:23b-24a,28). His wish is to enjoy fellowship with the Roman Christians for a while before proceeding to Spain with their support (15:24b; cf. 1:10-12). A third purpose in writing is to prepare the way for this intended visit.

The above-mentioned three reasons for the writing of Romans are clear. A problem, however, arises in seeking to relate the bulk of the Epistle (1:16b-15:16) to these stated purposes. The point has been well made that, were these Paul's only reasons for writing, "the means would be quite out of proportion to the end."[2]

The chief question in trying to assess the purpose of Romans is whether

---

[1] So M. Barth et al., *Foi et Salut selon S. Paul* (Institut Biblique Pontifical, 1970), p. 45f.

[2] A.E. Garvie, *Romans* (Caxton, n.d.), p. 19; cf. G. Smiga, 'Romans 12:1-2 and 15:30-32 and the Occasion of the Letter to the Romans', in *C B Q* 53 (1991), p. 258.

or not Paul is intending to address a concrete situation at Rome. Traditionally it was held that Romans was simply Paul's summing up of his many years of reflection upon the Gospel to the preaching of which he had devoted his life.[1] On this understanding, the condition of the Roman Church is more or less irrelevant. There are, however, problems with this view. It has been well pointed out that "important aspects of Pauline doctrine ... are not touched on at all."[2] Romans is not therefore a full statement of Paul's theology.

In 1977 a symposium on 'The Romans Debate' was published. It grew out of the gradually developing restlessness amongst scholars with this treatment of Romans, as a result of which "the question of the concrete *Sitz im Leben* of Romans emerged more frequently."[3] It is noted[4] that, once the theory is rejected that Romans is a timeless dogmatic treatise, two approaches remain. The first is to see the letter as arising out of Paul's preoccupation with his own concerns,[5] and the second to see the Roman situation as decisive for the nature of the letter. Both approaches were represented in the symposium.

By 1991, however, when 'The Romans Debate' was revised and expanded Donfried observes an emerging consensus which includes the view that Romans is addressed to the particular situation of the Christian community in Rome.[6] It seems right to conclude that "Paul knew a great deal about the church in Rome, and his knowledge controlled his writing."[7] It appears that Paul had heard about a problem in this Church, which he set out to address by bringing the heart of the Gospel message to bear upon it. What, then, can we infer about the Church at Rome from the internal evidence of the Epistle?

At first sight it might seem that the major issue was interracial tension between Jews and Gentiles.[8] The composition of the Church is often discussed. It is probably correct to describe it as "of Jewish origin but of

---

[1] Cf. (e.g.) R. Haldane, *An Exposition of the Epistle to the Romans* (MacDonald, 1958).

[2] Kümmel, p. 312; cf. Sandmel, *Understanding*, p. 90.

[3] K.P. Donfried (ed.), *The Romans Debate* (Hendrickson, 1977, 1991), pp. xli-xlii.

[4] G. Klein, 'Paul's Purpose in Writing the Epistle to the Romans', in Donfried (ed.), p. 30.

[5] So, e.g., J.A. Crafton, 'Paul's Rhetorical Vision and the Purpose of Romans: towards a new understanding', in *Nov Test* 32 (1990), pp. 325-8; K.E. Kirk, *The Epistle to the Romans* (Clarendon, 1937), p. 25.

[6] Donfried, pp. lxix-lxx.

[7] Garvie, p. 21.

[8] So J. Marcus, 'The Circumcision and the Uncircumcision in Rome', in *N T St* 35 (1989), pp. 68-70; M.B. Thompson, 'Strong and Weak', in G.F. Hawthorne & R.P. Martin (eds.), *Dictionary of Paul and His Letters* (Leicester: IVP, 1993), p. 917.

Gentile growth",[1] but it is "impossible to decide with anything like absolute certainty whether at the time Paul wrote to them the majority of the Roman Christians were Gentiles or Jews".[2] Immediately after his introduction, Paul insists that the Gospel is applicable to both Jew and Gentile (1:16b), and sets out to charge both Jews and Greeks that they are all under sin (3:9). Sometimes he seems to be addressing Jews particularly - at least primarily (eg. 2:14-29; 3:10-19; 3:27-4:25; 7:1-25), and at other times he appears to be addressing Gentiles specifically - at least primarily (eg. 3:1-9; 6:1-23; chs. 9-11; 14:1-15:13). It appears that Paul was waging battle on two fronts simultaneously, and that his main aim was to foster unity between opposing parties.

However, to couch the problem at Rome in the terms of interracial tension between Jew and Gentile is probably to oversimplify.[3] The major issue appears to have been the place of the law. Friction had arisen within the Church because of a diversity of views on this question. Not that there is any hint of systematic Judaizing at Rome as at Galatia.[4] Perhaps chapters 14-15 give us a glimpse of the problem at Rome,[5] with respect to one particular aspect of the question of the law. There were some within the Church who believed the revealed law of God to retain its authoritative status in such a way that it was, in every particular, absolutely binding upon believers. There were others who believed the message of the Gospel to be one of liberty from at least some elements of the law. It is not necessarily the case that all in the former category were Jews: it is quite likely that some of the Gentile Christians were tending to become enthralled with the law to a degree which Paul perceived to be unhealthy. Nor is it necessarily the case that the latter group was composed entirely of Gentiles: it is quite possible to imagine Jews who understood the Gospel to proclaim so complete an emancipation from the law that Paul felt obliged to sound a warning against the danger of antinomian tendencies and practices.

It is not likely that the Roman Christian community divided neatly into these two clearcut groups.[6] It is more probable that Paul has singled out two

---

[1] M. Black, *Romans* (Oliphants, 1973), p. 23.

[2] C.E.B. Cranfield, *A Critical and Exegetical Commentary on the Epistle to the Romans* (T. & T. Clark, 1975, 1979), p. 21.

[3] Cf. F. Watson, 'The Two Roman Congregations: Romans 14:1-15:13', in Donfried (ed.), p. 203 (cf. W.A. Meeks, 'Judgement and the Brother: Romans 14:1-15:13', in G.F. Hawthorne & O. Betz (eds.), *Tradition and Interpretation in the New Testament* (Eerdmans, 1987), p. 292.

[4] Cf. C. Hodge, *A Commentary on Romans* (Banner of Truth, 1835), p. 7.

[5] So J.C. Beker, 'The faithfulness of God and the Priority of Israel in Paul's Letter to the Romans', in *Harv Th R* 79 (1986), p. 15, A.J.M. Wedderburn, *The Reasons for Romans* (T. & T. Clark, 1988), p. 59f; against R.J. Karris, 'Rom. 14:1-15:13 and the Occasion of Romans', in *C B Q* 35 (1973), pp. 156-78.

[6] Against F. Watson, p. 206.

representatives of a broad spectrum of opinion about the place and function of the law in the life of the Christian believer.[1] As we shall see later, Paul's overriding concern is not with the laws concerning food and festivals, but with the moral heart of the law. In that sense chapters 14-15 are dealing with an issue somewhat tangential to Paul's chief interest. A major purpose of the Epistle is to define the place and role of the law in relation to the salvation which God has provided in Jesus Christ.[2]

2   Romans 8:3f

The first phrase of 8:3 is very difficult to translate. It reads: τὸ γὰρ ἀδύνατον τοῦ νόμου ἐν ᾧ ἠσθένει διὰ τῆς σαρκός. There are several grammatical problems which need to be addressed before a satisfactory exegesis can be made. It will probably be clearest to begin by proposing a translation, and then to argue backwards from there, indicating, over against other possible interpretations of the linguistic intricacies, the conclusions which have led me to the preferred rendering.

It is commonly alleged that verse 3 forms an anacolouthon.[3] In my view this is not correct. There is at least one way of translating this verse on the basis of the assumption that it is a grammatically complete sentence.

The translation of the two verses which I would therefore propose is

For this being the law's inability while it used to be weak in the sphere of the flesh, God, having sent His own Son in the likeness of sinful flesh and for sin, condemned sin in the flesh, in order that the law's righteous requirement might be fulfilled in us who do not walk according to the flesh but according to the Spirit.

Alternatively, verse 3 could be rendered

For since this was the law's inability while it used to be weak in the sphere of the flesh, God sent His own Son in the likeness of sinful flesh and for sin, and condemned sin in the flesh.

There are seven grammatical points which need to be discussed here.
(1) I am reading τό as equivalent in this context to the demonstrative

---

[1] So F.F. Bruce, 'The Romans Debate - Continued', in Donfried (ed.), p. 186 (cf. P. Lampe, 'The Roman Christians of Romans 16', in Donfried (ed.), p. 229f.
[2] Cf. J.D.G. Dunn, *Romans* (Word, 1988), p. lxvi.
[3] So (e.g.) V.P. Branick, 'The Sinful Flesh of the Son of God (Rom. 8:3): A Key Image of Pauline Theology', in *C B Q* 47 (1985), p. 247; M.D. Greene, 'A Note on Romans 8:3', in *Bib Z* 35 (1991), p. 103.

pronoun τοῦτο.¹

(2) In the former of my two proposed translations I have inserted the present participle, 'being', thereby understanding the first phrase of the verse as a clause whose meaning is complete in itself. The alternative translation serves to clarify the causative sense of the present participle and to give an easier flow in English. In conjunction with γάρ, to understand the verb 'to be' has the effect of making τό refer backwards, so that verse 3f becomes an explanation of verse 1f.

The expedient of understanding an unexpressed verb at this point is one which is followed by many commentators. Most, however, prefer the verb 'to do', reading τὸ γὰρ ἀδύνατον τοῦ νόμου, *God has done*. However, it seems preferable to understand the verb 'to be', rather than a stronger verb, since the verb 'to be' is frequently omitted in Greek, whereas to speculate regarding the omission of some other verb is inevitably more tentative.

The possibility of understanding the verb 'to be' has been mentioned by Cranfield, along with an interpretation of the phrase τὸ γὰρ ἀδύνατον τοῦ νόμου as a nominative absolute: 'the impotence of the law being this that it was weak through the flesh...'. Cranfield rightly implies that this makes for an unclear sense and an awkward construction.² I would argue that the insertion of the verb 'to be' in the form in which I have done so makes clear sense, suits the context, and avoids a clumsy construction.

Another common understanding of the construction of this phrase takes it as an accusative absolute in apposition to the later part of verse 3.³ This has the effect of making verse 3b define the law's ἀδύνατον, namely to condemn sin in the flesh. There are, however, two problems with this view. First, an accusative absolute would be more likely to come at the end of the sentence than at the beginning.⁴ Second, Paul's teaching is that the judicial condemnation of sin was within the power of the law.⁵

(3) I have chosen to take the genitive τοῦ νόμου at face value. In so doing I am parting company from most modern commentators, who, arguing from the view that ἀδύνατον has a passive sense, conclude, almost inevitably that τοῦ νόμου must here be equivalent to the dative τῷ νομῷ. As Cranfield has pointed out,⁶ however, the Greek fathers appear to have

---

[1] Cf. H.G. Liddell & R. Scott, *A Greek-English Lexicon* (Clarendon, 1940), pp. 1193f; W.F. Arndt & F.W. Gingrich, *A Greek-English Lexicon* (Cambridge University Press, 1957), p. 552; Thayer, p. 433.
[2] Cranfield, *Romans*, p. 378f, n. 3.
[3] So (e.g.) W. Sanday & A.C. Headlam, *A Critical and Exegetical Comentary on the Epistle to the Romans* (T. & T. Clark, 1902), p. 191.
[4] So C.J. Vaughan, *St. Paul's Epistle to the Romans* (Macmillan, 1885), p. 148.
[5] Hodge, p. 252.
[6] Cranfield, *Romans*, p. 378, n. 3.

read the genitive literally without even considering other possibilities.[1]

(4) I have opted for the active sense of ἀδύνατον, which I have translated as 'inability'; perhaps the best rendering might have been 'disability',[2] in order to convey the idea which Paul proceeds to stress, namely that the law is not intrinsically unable or powerless, but has been or become disabled through other factors.

Most modern commentators prefer to take ἀδύνατον in a passive sense, 'impossible', and therefore treat τοῦ νόμου as equivalent to the dative, the latter following almost inevitably from the former.[3] However, I find myself influenced by the words of Sanday and Headlam when they write: "It must be confessed that the balance of ancient authority is strongly in favour of this way of taking the words [as active with the genitive understood literally and subjectively], and that on a point - the natural interpretation of language - where ancient authority is especially valuable." Although Sanday and Headlam proceed to adduce evidence that in the LXX and the New Testament ἀδύνατος is active when masculine or feminine and passive when neuter,[4] it does not seem inappropriate to argue that this particular use might be a unique exception, especially in view of the fact that the word occurs only ten times in the New Testament, and a mere twice in Paul. The fact that the patristic authors could read the word actively here must count against the absolute conclusiveness of otherwise normal Biblical usage.

(5) I am proposing that ἐν ᾧ be understood temporally as meaning 'when, while, for as long as'.[5] Most commentators prefer to read it either modally ('in which, wherein')[6] or causally ('because').[7] However, according to Owen, Beza refers to Mark 2:19 and Luke 5:34 as instances where ἐν ᾧ means 'while', designating either a certain time or a certain state and condition.[8] Given Paul's use of the imperfect tense ἠσθένει, which would appear to be significant, a temporal understanding of ἐν ᾧ seems appropriate.

---

[1] Cf. Origen, 'Commentary on the Epistle to the Romans', in *J Th St* 14 (1912-13), p. 17.

[2] Cf. H.G. Liddell & R. Scott, *A Lexicon Abridged from Liddell and Scott's Greek-English Lexicon* (Clarendon, 1909), p. 13.

[3] Cf. D.E.H. Whiteley, 'Hard Sayings [Romans 8:3]' in *Th* 67 (1964), pp. 114-6.

[4] Sanday & Headlam, p. 192.

[5] Cf. K. Aland, *Vollständige Konkordanz zum Griechischen Neuen Testament* (Walter de Gruyter, 1983), Band 1, Teil 1, pp. 382-409, Band 1 Teil 2, pp. 998-1011; ibid, *Komputer Konkordanz zum Neuen Testamentum Graecae*, (Walter de Gruyter, 1977), Z-Ω, Appendix, p. 45f.

[6] So, e.g., E. Käsemann, *Commentary on Romans* (SCM Press, 1980), p. 216.

[7] J. Calvin, *Commentaries on the Epistle of Paul the Apostle to the Romans* (Geneva, 1539), p. 278, J.A. Fitzmyer, *Romans* (Geoffrey Chapman, 1993), p. 484.

[8] J. Owen, *Calvin's Commentaries on the Epistle of Paul the Apostle to the Romans, Translated and Edited* (Baker, 1849), p. 278, n. 1.

(6) I have attempted to bring out the force of the imperfect tense ἠσθένει by translating 'used to be weak'. I am reading it as an Iterative Imperfect.[1] The significance of the tense is largely overlooked by commentators. The result is that the time element implicit in the imperfect is concealed, and the impression is given that Paul is stating a timeless truth. However, it seems to me that Paul's use of the imperfect tense is very significant, as implying that there is a time when, or a state in which, the law is no longer weak. This implication will be taken up later in the course of the theological study.

The only commentator whom I have read who appears to do any justice at all to the imperfect tense is Karl Barth, when he refers to "that which was not possible to the Law in its perverted form, in its infirmity,"[2] although I would not wish to endorse this statement precisely as Barth means it.

(7) The final point of grammatical debate concerns the significance of διὰ τῆς σαρκός. This is often translated simply as 'through the flesh'; this, however, is vague. Sometimes the phrase is taken as an instrumental clause, and Käsemann argues that, in spite of the genitive, διὰ should be understood as 'on account of' or 'in virtue of'.[3] Dunn, however, argues that the genitive is significant, and I agree that this is so. He understands the genitive in terms of the interaction between the law and the flesh.[4] I have arrived at my proposed translation by considering διὰ plus genitive here as expressing attendant circumstances or environment.[5] It was in the environment, the sphere, of the flesh that the law used to be weak. I am intrigued also by Winer's comment that the primary meaning of διὰ ('going through'): "in a local sense, always has attached to it that of coming 'forth' or 'out'."[6] It is likely that the transferred sense of passing through a metaphorical environment (the flesh) will also contain the idea of emerging therefrom, and thus it seems again that this construction, διὰ plus genitive, is closely related to the imperfect tense of the verb, ἠσθένει.

Having isolated these seven key grammatical points which affect the exegesis of this clause, it is necessary next to address the meaning of the clause as a whole in the context of the entire epistle.

---

[1] C.F.D. Moule, *An Idiom Book of New Testament Greek* (Cambridge University Press, 1953), p. 9; cf. F. Blass, *Grammar of New Testament Greek* (Macmillan, 1905), p. 319.

[2] K. Barth, *A Shorter Commentary on Romans* (SCM Press, 1959), p. 90.

[3] Käsemann, *Romans*, p. 216.

[4] Dunn, *Romans*, p. 420.

[5] Cf. Turner, p. 267, C.F.D. Moule, p. 57.

[6] G.B. Winer, *A Treatise on the Grammar of New Testament Greek* (T. & T. Clark, 1882), p. 472.

1   The Meaning of 'Law'

It will be well to begin by stating that I am taking for a working hypothesis the assumption that Paul uses the word νόμος (law) consistently throughout Romans. It is necessary to stress this point for two reasons. First, since Origen, it has sometimes been claimed that when it occurs without the article it is used of law in general, and not the Jewish law in particular;[1] this distinction is, however, difficult to carry through consistently. Second, sometimes the word occurs qualified by a genitive phrase: it appears in this form twice in 8:2, the verse preceding that under consideration, the same form having already occurred a number of times towards the end of chapter 7, as well as twice in 3:27, and again later in 9:31; it is frequently alleged that Paul uses the word differently in these contexts.

However, given that the issue of the law is the chief problem for the Church at Rome, and is a central theme of this Epistle, it seems extremely unlikely that the apostle would use the key word with varied meaning. Such a policy would amount to an invitation to be misunderstood. It seems reasonable, therefore, to assume consistency of usage.

That the word νόμος in 8:3 refers to the law of God, the law of Moses is, as Dunn notes,[2] usually taken for granted by commentators. The one partial exception which I have discovered is Morris, who is prepared to consider the possibility that Paul, while speaking primarily of the law of Moses, may also be making a general statement about any law.[3] This is most unlikely however: three times in the passage surrounding 8:3 Paul explicitly uses the phrase 'the law of God' (7:22,25; 8:7), and this theme is central to the Book of Romans; it seems necessary therefore thus to limit this reference. However, it is necessary to clarify what Paul means by the law of God: what is the precise content of the term in this Epistle?

The word νόμος first occurs in 2:12 in contrast with ἄνομος (without the law), a term descriptive of the Gentiles, whereas the Jews are ἐν νομῷ (in the law). Up to this point Paul has been exposing the universal sinfulness of humankind, and stressing the impartiality of divine judgement. In 1:18-32 he states the general principle that all people are liable to the wrath of God, making a personal application in 2:1-5 to any who may seek to exonerate themselves. This is followed by a statement of the criterion, the consequences, and the basis of divine judgement (2:6-11). Paul then introduces the subject of the law in order to demonstrate the equality with which all human beings stand before their Maker and Judge. His aim in this passage is to undermine the false security of the Jews which they derived from the mere fact of having received the law.[4]

---

[1] Cf. (e.g.) Haldane, p. 88f, Sanday & Headlam, p. 58, M. Black, p. 57.
[2] *Dunn, Romans* p. 419.
[3] L. Morris, *The Epistle to the Romans* (Eerdmans, 1988), p. 302.
[4] Cf. (e.g.) C.K. Barrett, *A Commentary on the Epistle to the Romans* (A. & C. Black,

The phrase ἐν νομῷ in contrast with ἄνομος immediately identifies 'the law' decisively as the torah in the fullest sense of the word, in its completeness. As such it was given to the Jews, and formed the demarcation[1] of their sphere of being as a people. The torah as a coherent system was that on which the Jews rested (verse 17), the basis of their instruction (verse 18), and the object of their legitimate[2] boast (verse 23): in it the Jews possessed the one authentic revelation of knowledge and truth (verse 20). By contrast, the Gentiles exist without the gift of that special revelation of God; their situation is further defined in verse 14 as 'not having the law' (τὰ μὴ νόμον ἔχοντα, νόμον μὴ ἔχοντες). These phrases do not have pejorative connotations.[3] Paul is simply stating the fact that the Jews were entrusted with God's revelation while the Gentiles were not.[4]

That νόμος refers to the torah as a whole is borne out by the use of the similar phrase ἐν τῷ νομῷ in 3:19, which may be translated, "Now we know that whatever the law says, it says to those who are in the law". In the first part of chapter 3, after admitting the advantages of the Jews, Paul has sought to emphasize the fact that the Jews are in no way exempt from the universal condemnation of God. He has driven this point home by means of a catena of quotations from the Old Testament, and then comes the statement containing the twofold reference to the law. The natural reading of this statement identifies the preceding catena as the law, thus equating it with the entire Hebrew Bible, and makes the point that the Jewish law addresses specifically those whose sphere of being it demarcates, whom it identifies as one subsection of 'all the world', and it is read as such by most commentators.

These two instances of ἐν (τῷ) νομῷ serve to fix the meaning for the contexts in which they occur, and the first is really programmatic for the whole Epistle. In the light of 2:12 and 3:19, all the occurrences of νόμος in these chapters can be assumed to refer to the torah as a whole,[5] and the probability that any instance of νόμος in Romans will bear this meaning is established. There is, of course, "a major turning point"[6] in Paul's argument at 3:21, as he begins to expound the righteousness of God 'apart from the law' and concludes that justification is through faith in Jesus Christ. Nevertheless, the references to the law in 3:19f form the essential

---

1957), p. 49; J. Philip, *The Epistle to the Romans* (Didasko Press, n.d.), p. 36.

[1] Dunn, *Romans* pp. lxix, 95.
[2] Against (e.g.) F.J. Leenhardt, *The Epistle to the Romans* (Lutterworth, 1961), p. 85.
[3] Against, e.g., E. Brunner, *The Letter to the Romans* (Lutterworth, 1959), p. 21.
[4] Cf. Garvie, p. 108.
[5] Cf. (e.g.) J. Murray, *The Epistle to the Romans* (Eerdmans, 1959, 1965), Vol. 1, p. 73; against (e.g.) A. Nygren, *Commentary on Romans* (SCM Press, 1952), p. 124.
[6] J. Ziesler, *Paul's Letter to the Romans* (Trinity Press International, 1989), p. 106.

background for this new departure,[1] and serve to elucidate the meaning of νόμος in the latter verses of chapter 3.

A slightly different phrase, ἐκ τοῦ νόμου, is used to describe the Jews,[2] the genetic descendants of Abraham, in 4:14,16. The point of chapter 4 is to illustrate the fact that God's method of justifying the ungodly has always been on the basis of grace through faith in His word, and not through works,[3] and that the promise of the word consequently extends to all who believe, whether or not they are 'of the law'. Here again 'law' must be read as a reference to the torah as a complete system; not only is the law the sphere of Jewish being, it is also the source of their identity as a people, the defining factor in their national character.[4] Paul uses this phrase to distinguish the Jews as one subsection of 'all the seed'; the emphasis is on the universality of God's promise: the Jews, whose life grows out of the law, are included, but not only they.

A slightly different, though closely related, nuance in the definition of νόμος as the torah as a whole is found in 5:13a, 5:20 and 9:4. In the last of these texts the cognate term νομοθεσία is used, emphasizing that the law was given at a specific moment.[5] Each of these represents 'the law' as denominating a phase in God's dealings with humanity. The first part of chapter 5 explains that the prime result of justification is an overwhelming assurance of the love of God, and then from verse 12 Paul shows how, in the face of abounding sin in Adam, because of which the law was given to bring sin to clarity of definition, God's grace in Christ abounded even more, that His coming inaugurated a new epoch and constituted a new humanity of the redeemed who reign in life. The dispensation of law refers to that period in salvation history during which God revealed Himself to His people through the torah considered as an integrated system: even where Paul gives the word 'law' a dispensational sense, therefore, the recognition that 'the law' means the torah in its entirety is strongly implicit.

However, it appears to be true that Paul's concern in Romans is with the moral aspects of the law primarily,[6] notwithstanding Käsemann's insistence that "the apostle does not restrict the Torah to the moral law and thereby dilute it".[7] Paul uses 'law' of the torah as a whole, but finds the heart of the

---

[1] Cf. *Dunn, Romans* p. 176.
[2] Against W. Hendriksen, *Romans* (Banner of Truth, 1980, 1981), p. 156.
[3] Cf. D.M. Lloyd-Jones, *Romans, An Exposition of Chapter 1* (Banner of Truth, 1985), p. 25.
[4] Cf. *Dunn, Romans* pp. 213, 234.
[5] So E.J. Epp, 'Jewish-Gentile Continuity in Paul: Torah and/or Faith', in G. Nicklesburg & G. MacRae (eds.), *Christians Among Jews and Gentiles* (Fortress, 1986), p. 89.
[6] Cf. Haldane, p. 103; Ziesler, *Romans*, p. 87.
[7] Käsemann, *Romans*, p. 64.

torah in its moral requirements. In chapters 6 to 8 he shows how the very fact of God's abounding grace in Christ, in whom the believer has died to sin, implies the daily reality of the resurrection life of obedience to God. 'Law' in 6:14f and 7:1-4 is clearly to be understood in moral terms within such a context.

This becomes especially clear in 7:7-13, where 'commandment' (ἐντολή) serves as the practical equivalent of νόμος,[1] the tenth commandment in particular being seen as epitomizing the law.[2] This apparent limitation of the scope of 'law' as torah provides the definition of the word for 7:5-8:7, the passage which includes our key verse.

Even before this point there have been indications that Paul's especial concern is with the moral heart of the law. In the section prior to the first occurrence of the word νόμος (from 1:18), he has stressed the wrath of God against sin, applying it to all people regardless of ethnicity. This already points towards an understanding of the torah in which moral requirement has the primacy. The details of 2:12-29 also lead in this direction: Paul's starting-point is that the law, which includes commandments (2:21f), is the standard (though not the ground[3]) of eschatological righteousness: "the doers of the law will be justified" (2:13). This statement appears to be basic to his understanding of the function of the law, and the phrase is echoed by the second use of νόμος in 2:14 which also sees the law as containing things which must be done. These statements, together with the references to the breaking (2:23,25,27), the keeping (2:25,26), and the fulfilling (2:27) of the law imply that its moral demands are in view. The phrase τὰ τοῦ νόμου (2:14) also appears to have moral implications.[4] The converse of this is that the law becomes the criterion for the judgement of Jews who sinned (2:12): not only does the law define righteousness, it also identifies its opposite - sin.

Similarly, the references to the works of the law (3:20,28), and to the revelation of God's righteousness apart from the law (3:21), are most naturally read, with the older exegetes,[5] as a rejection of the tendency to seek one's own righteousness on the basis of enacting the morality which the law requires.[6]

---

[1] Cf. Dunn, *Romans*, p. 380; Morris, *Romans*, p. 283.

[2] So Fitzmyer, *Romans*, p. 466; cf. R.G. Hammerton-Kelly, 'Sacred Violence and Sinful Desire: Paul's Interpretation of Adam's Sin in the Letter to the Romans', in R.T. Fortna & B.R. Gaventa (eds.), *The Conversation Continues* (Nashville: Abingdon, 1990), p. 47.

[3] Cf. C.H. Cosgrove, 'Justification in Paul: A Linguistic and Theological Reflection', in *J B L* 106 (1987), pp. 653-70.

[4] *Pace* Barrett, *Romans*, p. 51, Murray, Vol. 1, p. 85, Morris, *Romans*, p. 140.

[5] Cf. Calvin, *Romans*, p. 149; Haldane, p. 124; Hodge, p. 100.

[6] So C. E. B. Cranfield, 'The Works of the Law in the Epistle to the Romans', in *J St N T* 43 (1991), pp. 93-6, against Dunn, *Romans*, p. 158f - and *passim*.

The law's function of identifying sin is one to which Paul gives great prominence in this letter. Having hinted at this in 2:12, it is at 3:20 that he first makes the point explicitly: "by the law is the knowledge of sin". This indicates that Paul understands sin to exist independently of the law, but the law serves to make sin known. This may be understood in three senses.

(1) The law defines what sin is, so transforming it into recordable transgressions. This seems to be the point of 4:15b ("where there is no law there is no transgression") and 5:13b ("sin is not imputed when there is no law").[1] When Paul says further in 5:20a, "the law entered that the offense might abound", the abundance in view is probably one of clarification or definition.[2] This means that when Paul uses νόμος dispensationally, he acknowledges that this was a dispensation in which moral demand was at the forefront.

(2) The law exposes how sinful human beings are, in that sin latches on to the law's definitions to arouse the passions of sinfulness (7:5,8f), and so to bring the person to self-awareness as a sinner;[3] the statement in 7:7, "I would not have known sin except by the law", appears to refer to the knowledge of oneself as a sinner.[4]

(3) The law demonstrates just how sinful sin is, in that it is by means of a law which is good that sin stimulates transgression, and through a law which was intended to bring life that sin produces death (7:10-13).

It is apparent from the above summary that Paul gradually builds up his teaching on the function of the law to make sin known: the three aspects are introduced and developed in turn in the order here given. The main point to reiterate for the present is that this, the most prominent function which Paul accords to the law in this letter, highlights the fact that it is with the moral centre of the torah that he is especially concerned.

Coming as it does within the section of Romans where the moral element in the law is particularly to the fore, the probability is confirmed that νόμος in 8:3 means the torah but with its central aspect of moral demand uppermost.

2   The Nature of the Law's Weakness

This section must be divided into three parts, because of the presence in the text of two closely related concepts, expressed in the words ἀδύνατον and ἠσθένει. First, the phrase τὸ ἀδύνατον τοῦ νόμου must be exegeted, and then the phrase ἠσθένει διὰ τῆς σαρκός must be explained. Finally the

---

[1] So, e.g., J.A.D. Weima, 'The Function of the Law in Relation to Sin: an evaluation of the view of H. Räisänen', in *Nov Test* 32 (1990), pp. 227-31.
[2] Cf. Ziesler, *Romans*, p. 152.
[3] So Murray, Vol. 1, p. 250.
[4] So (e.g.) F.F. Bruce, *The Epistle of Paul to the Romans* (Tyndale, 1963), p. 149.

relation between the two must be explored.

1 WHAT IS THE LAW'S INABILITY?

The precise understanding of this phrase is linked with the construction which is preferred. If my construction of τὸ γὰρ ἀδύνατον τοῦ νόμου is correct (τὸ as equivalent to τοῦτο, and γὰρ connecting it backwards, with ἀδύνατον understood actively and the genitive τοῦ νόμου taken at face value), then this phrase is not, as most commentators argue (reading ἀδύνατον passively and τοῦ νόμου as equivalent to τῷ νομῷ), declaring that there is something which the law could not do, but rather is describing its inability. The emphasis is not on the object which was impossible for the law, but on the inability itself, which was the mark of the disabled law.

Thus understood, the opening words of the phrase, τὸ γὰρ, point to the law's inability in the preceding phrase, "the law of sin and death", which is contrasted with "the law of the Spirit of life in Christ Jesus". The law is disabled because it has become 'the law of sin and death'; it is sin and death which have disabled the law.

By this phrase I understand 'the law of God as employed by sin so leading to death'.[1] The two instances of νόμος in 8:2 with a qualifying genitive phrase are the last of several such constructions since 7:21. It is my contention that νόμος is to be understood throughout this passage as the torah, with its moral heart in the forefront, and that the genitives are to be taken as possessive, defining in the possession of what or whom the law is in each instance.[2]

However, it is often alleged that Paul is here using the word νόμος in a more general way, and not of the law of God. Most comentators take the references to 'the law of God' in 7:23,25 to mean the torah; however, the use of νόμος in verse 21, the reference to "another law" (v. 23), and νόμος when its qualifying genitive phrase is (τῆς) ἁμαρτίας [of sin] (vv. 23,25), are deemed decisive for a transferred sense of the word. 'Law' is then interpreted in the sense of a regular principle of operation with imperative and authoritative force. The 'law of sin' is then defined in terms of the power which sin exercises over us.[3]

Some have interpreted νόμος as the torah in some of these instances, but as a general determining principle in others; the fact that there is disagreement as to which instances are to be interpreted in which way[4]

---

[1] Cf. Dunn, *Romans*, p. 409.

[2] Cf. K. Snodgrass, 'Spheres of Influence: A Possible Solution to the Problem of Paul and the Law', in *J St N T* 32 (1988), p. 99.

[3] So St. John Chrysostom, 'Homilies on the Epistle to the Romans', in P. Schaff (ed.), *The Nicene and Post-Nicene Fathers*, Vol. 11 (Christian Literature Company, 1889), p. 429f.

[4] E.g. compare Chrysostom, p. 429f, with Barrett, *Romans*, p. 149.

suggests that such a procedure is somewhat haphazard. Apart from the fact that Paul is unlikely to use a key term so flexibly as to risk indeterminacy of meaning, there would seem to be greater objectivity in the interpretation of the present passage in assuming the identical reference for νόμος in each of its occurrences. That νόμος should be understood consistently in these verses as the torah has been argued by a few writers,[1] and this seems right.

As regards 8:2 also most commentators do not read the two instances of νόμος as references to the torah, but as the authority or power of the Spirit on the one hand, and of sin on the other. Dunn, however, argues cogently for understanding both occurrences as the torah,[2] and finds his case strengthened by the linking word gar in verse 3, where, as was noted earlier, it is generally taken for granted that νόμος refers to the Jewish law.

If it is correct to read these genitive phrases as possessive, then the main point to be made in the present context is that the law's inability consists in its possession by sin and death. In other words, it is in its relationship with sin, which it serves to define, thus producing death, that the law is disabled. Paul is not saying that anything is impossible for the law, per se. Paul's point is that it is the law as the law of sin and death, not the law in its essential, intrinsic nature, which is disabled. He is not passing judgement upon the law in itself; indeed, he appears not to be able to view the law in isolation from that which possesses it: in itself it is a good entity (7:12,14a); its possession by sin and death was its disablement.

In this phrase I understand Paul to be saying in summary form the same thing as he has worked out in greater detail in 7:7-13.[3] Throughout 7:7-8:2 (with the exception of 8:1) he writes in the first person singular. This stylistic device points to the need to treat this passage as one coherent whole. In the first section Paul is addressing the question whether the law is sin. The question arises because some of his earlier statements, especially 6:14 and 7:5f, could be read as tying the law and sin together inextricably. Paul's concern now is to obviate such a misinterpretation of his language.

Reference has already been made to this passage in connection with the law's function of defining, and so exposing and stimulating sin. At this point it is necessary to examine the passage in order to see how Paul understands the law to become the law of sin and death.

The key phrases in this respect are found in verses 8a and 11; they are very similar in vocabulary and sense. Verse 8a reads: "sin, taking opportunity (ἀφορμήν) by the commandment, produced in me all manner of covetousness (ἐπιθυμίαν)", and verse 11: "sin, taking opportunity

---

[1] So Dunn, *Romans,* pp. 392-5; H. Hübner, *Law in Paul's Thought* (T. & T. Clark, 1984), p. 144; Snodgrass, *Spheres,* pp. 100-7; P.W. Meyer, 'The Worm at the Core of the Apple: Exegetical Reflections on Romans 7', in Fortna & Gaventa (eds.), p. 79.

[2] Dunn, *Romans,* p. 416f.

[3] Cf. K. Barth, *Romans,* p. 81.

(ἀφορμήν) by the commandment, deceived me, and by it killed me".[1]

The word ἀφορμή means literally a base for military operations,[2] hence a starting-point, and so that which provides opportunity. Sin is "personified as a powerful enemy."[3] It seizes opportunistically upon the law, using it as its entry point into human life. In verse 8b Paul describes sin as dead until the law caused it to spring into life (v. 9).[4]

The way in which sin utilized the law was threefold. The first is stated in verse 8: almost certainly this means that sin employed the law to stimulate precisely that which the law forbade.[5] Paul has in mind the Jewish agony[6] that the torah not only clarified what was forbidden and so gave it definition as sin, but actually increased the sins which it forbade, by causing the covetousness which was deep-seated in the human heart, though repressed, to surface with intensity.

The second and third ways in which sin used the law are stated in verse 11: it deceived, and it killed. These last two actions of sin by the law are closely connected, and are clarified by what Paul has already said in verse 10.[7] Whereas the law's true purpose was to bring life, in fact it achieved the opposite: it brought death (vv. 10,11,13), the reason being that it was opportunistically taken possession of by sin. The deceptiveness of sin was that it caused the promise held out by the law to fail, by giving the objects of covetousness a sham attractiveness, and resulted in the law achieving exactly the reverse of its promise. Thus it is that the law was disabled as the law of sin and death: sin took possession of the law as its opportunity for total conquest in human life, and so the law lost its ability to confer life.

2 WHAT IS THE LAW'S WEAKNESS IN THE SPHERE OF THE FLESH?

In his comments on this phrase Dunn speaks of "the law weakened in its divine purpose by being identified too closely with Israel as a national and physical entity marked out particularly by circumcision." He continues: "It was precisely their engagement with the law too much at the level of the flesh which was Israel's and the law's undoing!"[8] However, such an interpretation of 'flesh' (σάρξ) seems rather remote from the context.

It is necessary now, therefore, to seek to define 'flesh' as used by Paul in

---

[1] Original translations.
[2] Cf. D.J. Moo, 'Israel and Paul in Romans 7:7-12', in *N T St* 32 (1986), p. 122.
[3] F.F. Bruce, *Romans,* p. 149; cf. Käsemann, *Romans,* p. 198.
[4] Cf. J. Ziesler, 'The Role of the Tenth Commandment in Romans 7', in *J St N T 33* (1988), p. 42; *ibid, Romans,* p. 187.
[5] Against Ziesler, *Romans,* p. 176f.
[6] Cf. P. Trudinger, 'An Autobiographical Digression? A Note on Romans 7:7-25', in *Expos T* 107 (1996), p. 173; Moo, pp. 122f, 127, 129f.
[7] Cf. Murray, Vol. 1, p. 252.
[8] Dunn, *Romans,* p. 420.

this Epistle, in order to illluminate the meaning of ἠσθένει διὰ τῆς σαρκός.

It has been suggested that "Paul's uses of the noun σάρξ present a bewildering variety of nuances."[1] However this is to exaggerate. Paul can use the word to denote ordinary human descent (1:3;[2] 4:1; 9:3,5,8; 11:14), and the external, physical part of the human constitution (2:28). When he speaks of 'the things of the flesh' [τὰ τῆς σαρκὸς] (8:5) and 'fleshly things' [τοῖς σαρκικοῖς] (15:27) he appears to mean the things pertaining to the present creation.[3] The reference to all flesh (πᾶσα σὰρξ) in 3:20 similarly means humankind as a whole in its creaturely reality.[4] The common feature of all these references is that they focus on the present created order. It seems right to say that this understanding of σάρξ is basic to Paul's use of the term in Romans.[5]

However, his major use of the word is a development from this basic concept. He speaks of being 'in the flesh' [ἐν (τῇ) σαρκί] (7:5; 8:8f) or 'fleshly' [σάρκινος] (7:14), of walking or living 'according to the flesh' [κατὰ σάρκα] (8:4f) and of 'the mind of the flesh' [τὸ φρόνημα τῆς σαρκὸς] (8:6f). As such the flesh is characterized as the place where nothing good is located (7:18), and as the impetus for serving the law of sin (7:25; cf. 7:14). It is enmity to God, such that the subjection to God's law which pleases God is impossible (8:7f); it is indeed the exact antithesis to life in the Spirit (8:4f), and so leads to death (8:6).

In this developed sense of the word the flesh is a sphere of existence, a realm of being. The significance of this development from the basic idea is that to live according to the flesh or in the flesh is to idolize the present created order: it is precisely the condition which Paul has described in other words in 1:25. The basic and developed meanings of the term are therefore closely associated. The characteristic of life in the sphere of the flesh is that flesh is accorded ultimate significance, "the creature, not the Creator, is our point of orientation."[6]

A crucial verse for the understanding of the weakness of the law in the sphere of the flesh is 7:5, which reads: "For when we were in the flesh (ἐν τῇ σαρκί) the passions of sins (τὰ παθήματα τῶν ἁμαρτιῶν) which were

---

[1] Cranfield, *Romans*, p. 59.
[2] R. Jewett, 'The Redaction and Use of an Early Christian Confession in Romans 1:3-4', in D. Groh & R. Jewett (eds.), *The Living Text* University Press of America, 1985), p. 116, and J.D.G. Dunn, 'Jesus - Flesh and Spirit: An Exposition of Romans 1:3-4', in *J Th St* ns 24 (1973), p. 44, detect (wrongly in my view) negative associations in the use of σάρξ here.
[3] So (e.g.) Calvin, *Romans,* p. 285; Barrett, *Romans,* p. 157; Morris, *Romans,* p. 305.
[4] Cf. Käsemann, *Romans,* p. 188.
[5] Against Branick, p. 251.
[6] Brunner, p. 69.

through the law (τὰ διὰ τοῦ νόμου) worked in our members to bear fruit to death (τῷ θανάτῳ)."[1] There are four key words which are shared in common by 7:5 and 8:2b-3a: σάρξ, ἁμαρτία, νόμος and θάνατος. It is therefore necessary to look more closely at this verse.

The first phrase which must be observed is 'which were through the law'. Many commentators read this, surely correctly, as an alternative way of expressing the opportunism of the law which Paul is shortly to go on to explain in verses 7-11. The passions of sins were by the law, in the sense that the law aroused them from their slumbers. Paul mentions the subject in passing here, before going on to develop it in greater detail.

The key thing to notice is that what Paul proceeds to say in 7:5 applies 'in the flesh'. Leenhardt claims that ἐν here is not locative but instrumental, representing a way of life rather than a place.[2] He appears (rightly) to be concerned to avoid the implication that Paul believed material reality to be by definition evil. Nevertheless, Paul's use of ἐν seems to be more than merely instrumental, and Leenhardt seems not to have taken full account of either the difference, or the connection, between the basic and extrapolated meanings of 'flesh'. Certainly Paul does not intend 'flesh' to be understood as a literal, physical place, but it does seem to denote a sphere of existence, and as such ἐν may be said to be at least quasi-locative. Dunn makes reference to Wilckens' description of σάρξ as 'Machtsphäre', and suggests as possible translations which also do justice to Paul's meaning, 'conditioning context' or 'determining condition'.[3] It must be stressed that this sphere of existence is not the created world, but, in the extrapolated sense of 'flesh', that way of life in which the created world is accorded ultimate significance.

Taylor defines those who are in the flesh as "the earth-bound".[4] Morris expresses more precisely the meaning of being in the flesh, when he refers to "those whose interests are earth-bound", and goes on to speak of being "wholly involved in this life".[5] This rightly implies that to be 'in the flesh' is to be not merely physically bound to earth, but bound to earth in the orientation of one's life. For Paul to be 'in the flesh' is to live in the (metaphorical) sphere of existence where the motivating goals, driving ambitions, and dominating interests are all bound up with σάρξ, that is, with the present creation, such that creation is offered the devotion which is properly due to the Creator alone.

It is necessary now to clarify how the function of the law in the sphere of the flesh, as that which defines and thereby exposes sin, represents the

---

[1] Original translation.
[2] Leenhardt, p. 207.
[3] Dunn, *Romans*, p. 364 (cf. Branick, p. 251; Snodgrass, *Spheres*, p. 99).
[4] V. Taylor, *The Epistle to the Romans* (Epworth, 1955), p. 50.
[5] Morris, *Romans*, p. 307.

law's weakness in that sphere.

This question is really answered in 8:5-8. Verse 5 is connected to verse 4 by γάρ, which indicates that verses 5-11 are explanatory of the final phrase of verse 4, where 'according to the flesh' is contrasted with 'according to the Spirit'. The three phrases 'being in the flesh' [ἐν σαρκὶ ὄντες] (v. 8f), 'being according to the flesh' [κατὰ σάρκα ὄντες] (v. 5) and 'walking according to the flesh' [κατὰ σάρκα περιπατοῦσιν] (v. 4) may be taken as synonymous. For those of whom such a state of being is a valid description Paul sees it as true by definition that they set their minds on the things of the flesh [τὰ τῆς σαρκός φρονοῦσιν] (v. 5): that is to say, their mindset is upon earthly realities, their motivating ambitions are entirely this-worldly, their determining intentions are centred upon the things of this creation.[1] The inevitable end-result is death (v. 6; cf. v. 13), since fleshly reality is by definition transient and temporal; hence, to identify one's being so entirely with such passing entities is to submit oneself to the same fate as is theirs.[2] The reason why this is so has to do with divine judgement,[3] because the fleshly mindset entails opposition to God (v. 7a): this again is true by definition, since to choose this-worldly aspirations is to accord to the created order the ultimate loyalty which rightly belongs to God alone. As a result the fleshly mindset neither does, nor indeed can, obey God's law (v. 7b), and, *ipso facto*, because "'the law of God' enunciates what is well-pleasing to God",[4] cannot please Him (v.8).

It is interesting that on the one occasion when Paul seeks to epitomize the law of God in a single commandment (7:7), the one which he selects is the prohibition of covetousness, οὐκ επιθυμήσεις being an exact quotation of Exodus 20:17a and Deuteronomy 5:21a in the LXX. This is no doubt a significant selection, but the significance has been variously interpreted. The various interpretations are not necessarily mutually exclusive.

Paul may intend to imply that the tenth commandment is a summary of the inner, essential meaning of the whole Decalogue and of the entire law of God.[5] As such, covetousness may be seen as the root of all sin,[6] and therefore as a universal sin,[7] in which case the suggestion that Paul may be speaking strictly autobiographically, highlighting the one commandment

---

[1] Cf. (e.g.) Calvin, *Romans*, p. 285; E.F. Scott, *Paul's Epistle to the Romans* (SCM Press, 1947), p. 50; J.A.T. Robinson, *Wrestling with Romans* (SCM Press, 1979), p. 97.

[2] Cf. Bultmann, p. 247.

[3] So (e.g.) Cranfield, *Romans*, p. 394; Dunn, *Romans*, p. 448.

[4] Murray, Vol. 1, p. 287.

[5] So Augustine (cited by Calvin, *Romans*, p. 252); Leenhardt, p. 185, notes that Philo "singles out this commandment as typical of the law".

[6] Dunn, *Romans*, p. 388; Ziesler, *Commandment*, p. 47.

[7] E. Best, *The Letter of Paul to the Romans* (Cambridge University Press, 1967), p. 81.

with which he personally struggled,[1] becomes true by definition. The reason for all this is that the prohibition of covetousness deals with hidden motives, rather than with outward action.[2]

However, at its heart covetousness may be defined as the craving for σάρξ, for fleshly, this-worldly realities; elsewhere in the Pauline literature (Eph. 5:5; Col. 3:5) covetousness is identified with idolatry, and in the light of Romans 8:5-8 it is clear why such an identification is possible. Covetousness, essentially, represents a life whose sphere is entirely flesh, a life whose ambitions are contained within the created order, a life in which creaturely things are served as objects of worship (cf. 1:25), and hence involve disobedience to God's law and enmity towards God Himself. Those who are in the flesh cannot, therefore, please God (8:8), since they are setting up in rivalry to Him an alternative object of devotion.[3]

The weakness of the law in the sphere of the flesh, therefore, is that it is not possible for it to be obeyed, because in that sphere the covetousness which the law prohibits is the defining feature: all the aspirations of the fleshly mindset are directed towards created things as giving them quasi-divine significance. In such a context the law is weak as to its life-giving purpose: it arouses passions which are directed to the sinful objective of covetousness, and so leads to death, because the fleshly objects of covetousness are transient.

3   WHAT IS THE CONNECTION BETWEEN ἀδύνατον AND ἠσθένει?

This may be briefly stated. The law is weak just because of its disablement, and it is in the sphere of the flesh that this disablement takes place. The final phrase of chapter 7 sums it up: the law is weak in the sphere of the flesh because the flesh is enslaved (δουλεύω) by the law of sin, that is, the disabled form of the law (7:25).

These words, together with the preceding phrase, 'with the mind I myself serve the law of God', are rightly seen as a summary of the foregoing section,[4] particularly from verse 14, where Paul defines σάρκινος as 'sold under sin', and then proceeds to express the typical Jewish dilemma: the Jew delights in the law of God according to the inward man, endorsing it with his mind, but with his flesh he serves the disabled law of sin, the law opportunistically seized on by sin to stimulate covetousness.

It is this disabled law which, because of its conjunction with the flesh which is destined for death, is weak as regards its purpose of bringing life. It is interesting to note the frequency with which the verb ἀσθενέω is used

---

[1] Murray, Vol. 1, p. 249; Hendriksen, *Romans*, p. 220.
[2] So (e.g.) R. Bowen, *A Guide to Romans* (SPCK, 1975), p. 95; Cranfield, *Romans*, p. 349; Morris, *Romans*, p. 279.
[3] Cf. Leenhardt, p. 185f; F.F. Bruce, *Romans*, p. 148.
[4] Best, p. 84.

in the LXX to translate the Hebrew word meaning 'to stumble', 'to fall' or 'to stagger'.[1] It is possible that this meaning of weakness was in Paul's mind as he wrote these verses. The condition of disability is the occasion for stumbling, and is a specific and heightened expression of weakness. The disabled law merely stumbles along, marked by constant failure, as long as it remains in the sphere of the flesh, that is as long as it is addressed to those whose ultimate commitment is directed towards created reality.

This failure, as has already been noted, involves the miscarriage of the law's promise of life. In this epistle Paul links life with righteousness (1:17; 5:17f,21; 8:10): the attainment of eternal life presupposes the possession of eschatological righteousness (2:7,13). This brings us to the heart of the law's weakness and disability as far as Romans is concerned. In 3:20a Paul says that by the works of the law "no flesh will be justified". The word 'flesh' is used here primarily in its basic sense: no human being will attain righteousness by the works of the law. Both the entire preceding context from 1:18 and the future tense of the verb indicate that Paul still has eschatological justification in mind: he is looking on to the final verdict when God comes as Judge. That no Gentile will be justified at the last judgement on the basis of works of the law Paul could take for granted; the preceding context has established that the same will be true also of the Jews. However, it is likely that Paul intends a *double entendre* in his use of σάρξ here: of course no flesh will receive eschatological acquittal on the basis of obedience to the law, because flesh, by its very nature, fails to be a doer of the law; it lives for the present created order, and confers upon it the honour which should be reserved for God alone.[2] Bruce is quite right to make the point that 3:20b gives the reason for 3:20a:[3] the reason why no flesh will be justified by works of law is that in the sphere of the flesh, the law serves to define sin, and is therefore weak, because, by definition, it cannot be obeyed in that sphere, where covetousness (the this-worldly orientation) predominates. Even though the law is the standard of righteousness (2:13), nevertheless, its disablement and weakness in the sphere of the flesh mean that it cannot make good its promise of life to those who pursue righteousness on the basis of works of the law. This is a route which is doomed to failure. In 3:20b Paul is applying his basic premise that the law is the standard of eschatological righteousness to the condition where universal sin prevails, in the sphere of the flesh. God has therefore provided the grace-gift of righteousness apart from works of the

---

[1] 1 Kgs(1 Sam): 2:4; 2 Chr. 28:15; Job 4:4; Ps. 9:3; 26(27):2; 30(31):10; 104(105):37; 106(107):12; 108(109):24; Prov. 24:16; Jer. 6:21; 10:15; 26(46):6,12,16; 27(50):32; Lam. 1:14; 5:13; Ezek. 21:15; Dan. 11:14,19,33-5,41; Hos. 4:5; 5:5; 14:2(1),10(9); Nah 2:5; 3:3; Zeph. 1:3; Zech. 12:8; Mal. 2:8.

[2] Cf. A. Ito, 'Romans 2: A Deuteronomistic Reading', in *J St N T* 59 (1995), p. 29.

[3] F.F. Bruce, *Romans*, p. 99.

law to those who have faith in Jesus Christ (3:21,28; 4:2,6; 10:5f), and faith lifts the orientation of being out of this world to God.

3 The Ongoing Status of the Law

The implication of the imperfect tense ἠσθένει is that the law is weak no longer, and, if my favoured translation of ἐν ᾧ as 'while' is correct, this implication is strengthened. From this it may be inferred that, other than in the sphere of the flesh, Paul considered the law to be neither weak nor disabled. The use of 'now' in verse 1 similarly suggests that a contrast is being drawn between a state of affairs which used to obtain and that which is the present situation. The contrast is that, whereas the law was disabled as the law of sin and death, as the law of the Spirit of life, on the other hand, the law is now for the believer a powerful reality.

For Paul the Spirit is an alternative 'sphere of existence' which is absolutely antithetical to that of the flesh.[1] In 7:5 he writes: "when we were in the flesh..." The implication is that this is a state which is no longer applicable to 'us'. Thus Paul can write in 8:9: "But you are not in the flesh but in the Spirit". Whereas the sphere of the flesh denotes that way of life in which the creation is given quasi-divine status, the sphere of the Spirit is that in which God is rightly acknowledged, worshipped and served as God: this is the believing way of life. In the sphere of the Spirit the law is no longer weak as it used to be in the sphere of the flesh. Interwoven, therefore, with our basic question as to the place of the law in the life of the believer is a second question regarding the relationship between the law and the Spirit according to this Epistle.

Verse 4 is Paul's immediate answer: since the law was disabled by sin and death for as long as it was weak in the sphere of the flesh, God sent His Son in the likeness of sinful flesh and with reference to sin,[2] and condemned sin in His flesh (reading τῇ demonstratively[3]), with the following purpose: "that the righteous requirement of the law might be fulfilled in us who do not walk according to the flesh but according to the Spirit" (ἵνα τὸ δικαίωμα τοῦ νόμου πληρωθῇ ἐν ἡμῖν τοῖς μὴ κατὰ σάρκα περιπατοῦσιν ἀλλὰ κατὰ πνεῦμα).

There is general agreement that the final phrase of this verse describes the new sphere of life which follows upon justification, but the precise meaning of the former phrase is debated. Some have taken δικαίωμα as equivalent to δικαιοσύνη, and so read verse 4a as a further statement of

---

[1] Cf. Käsemann, *Romans,* p. 189; B.A. Hedin, 'Romans 8:6-11', in *Interp* 50 (1996), p. 56.
[2] This general meaning seems best [against T.C.G. Thornton, 'The Meaning of καὶ περὶ ἁμαρτίας in Romans viii.3', in *J Th St* ns 22 (1971), pp. 515-7].
[3] Cf. (e.g.) F.F. Bruce, *Romans,* p. 161; Cranfield, *Romans,* p. 382.

forensic justification.¹ It seems better, however to read verse 4a as already a description of the practical living of the justified, verse 4b further defining the same reality.² On this reading the fulfilment of the law's δικαίωμα is the outworking in the life of the believer of the law's righteous demand. The singular may be read as representing the unity of the law's requirements, "the plurality of commandments being not a confused and confusing conglomeration but a recognizable and intelligible whole."³ However, Ziesler's theory that the singular refers to one particular requirement, and that it is "overwhelmingly probable" that this is the tenth commandment which has been discussed in the immediately preceding context,⁴ merits serious consideration. If correct, this would mean that the work of Christ is with a view to the radical re-orientation of being in the justified believer from the creation to the Creator. This seems indeed a likely interpretation of this verse. It is sometimes objected that πληρωθῇ is too strong a description of the achievement of the sanctified life. However, this objection falls if it is recognized that the believer's intended perfection will be completed only eschatologically, and that meanwhile the fulfilment of the law is progressive and always incomplete in this life, though nonetheless real as a process.⁵ It has been well pointed out that the passive voice indicates that the fulfilment is not the personal achievement of the believer, but the work within him of the Spirit of God.⁶ It is in the sphere of the Spirit that the law becomes a liberating power which leads to life (verse 2).⁷ Where justification through faith is already a reality, the law in the possession of the Spirit liberates the man in Christ from the same law as taken possession of by sin; in the possession of sin the law weakly leads the sinner along the road of its own disablement to death, whereas in the possession of the Spirit its pristine energy as a life-giving power is restored.

Here, then, we have a declaration of the ongoing relevance of the law to the believer. The believing life, it appears, is not a life in which the law has no place; rather, through the Spirit, the law acquires a new power towards the believer's sanctification. A few verses later Paul says that the mindset of the flesh neither is, nor can be, obedient to God's law, with the result that it is impossible for those who are in the flesh to please God; immediately he

---

¹ So, (e.g.) Calvin, *Romans*, p. 283; Haldane, p. 326f; Hodge, p. 254; Nygren, pp. 316-20; cf. M.A. Seifrid, 'The Subject of Rom. 7:14-25', in *Nov Test* 34 (1992), p. 332.
² So, (e.g.) Brunner, p. 68; F.F. Bruce, *Romans*, p. 161; Murray, Vol. 2, p. 283; Cranfield, *Romans*, p. 384f; Morris, *Romans*, p. 304; Fitzmyer, *Romans*, p. 487; H. Räisänen, *The Torah and Christ* (Finnish Exegetical Society, 1986), p. 11.
³ Cranfield, *Romans*, p. 384.
⁴ Ziesler, *Commandment*, p. 50; cf. *ibid*, *Romans*, p. 207.
⁵ Cf. Murray, Vol. 2, p. 283; Cranfield, *Romans*, p. 384, n. 1.
⁶ E.g. Morris, *Romans*, p. 304, Ziesler, *Romans*, p. 208, Fitzmyer, *Romans*, p. 487.
⁷ Cf. Snodgrass, *Spheres*, p. 107.

continues with an adversative[1] clause: "but you are not in the flesh but in the Spirit" (8:7-9). The implication is that the mindset of the Spirit (v. 6) both can, and does, obey God's law: "the spiritual man delights in the law of God, and loves His commandments."[2]

It is necessary now to seek to verify this explanation of 8:2-9 by reference to the wider teaching of Romans as a whole. It is possible to divide into two groups the texts in Romans which pertain to the place of the law in the life of the justified believer. On the one hand there is a set of texts which appear *prima facie* to accord the law no status whatsoever in the believing life. On the other hand, there are further texts which, like 8:4, seem to teach that the law has a vital place. Our task now must be to try to understand how these two sets of texts hold together. I shall deal with the latter group first, seeking to demonstrate that, for Paul, the law retains a strategic place in the life of the Christian believer. I shall then turn to the texts which might appear to pose a problem for this theory, and aim to explain them consistently with this conclusion. In each case I shall work through the relevant passages in order.

1   Positive Indicators

1) 2:13-16

Paul's earliest discussion of the law in Romans is, arguably, designed to prepare the way for this conclusion. In 2:13 he states that the law is the criterion of eschatological righteousness, but that it is not the mere having of the law which will lead to justification, but doing it. His aim at this point is to demonstrate to the Jews that they cannot assume that they are the only people who are doers of the law. To this end, he announces in verse 14f that there are Gentiles, who do not have the law, who nevertheless 'do the things of the law'. Paul depicts them as being the law to themselves, and writes: these "show the work of the law written in their hearts" (ἐνδείκνυνται τό ἔργον τοῦ νόμου γραπτόν ἐν ταῖς καρδίαις αὐτῶν). The fact that this is so is sufficient to establish the point, but the question, which Paul does not imediately answer, arises: And who precisely are these Gentiles?

The most common interpretation is that these are Gentiles in general, and Paul is observing that the practices even of Gentiles do sometimes coincide with the requirements of God's law.[3] However, such a theory leads to

---

[1] So Morris, *Romans*, p. 307.

[2] Haldane, p. 338f.

[3] So (e.g.) Calvin, *Romans*, p. 98; Murray, Vol. 1, p. 73; Best, p. 28; Dunn, *Romans*, p. 98; G.P. Carras, 'Romans 2:1-29: A Dialogue on Jewish Ideals', in *Biblica* 73 (1992), p. 197f; T.H. Tobin, 'Controversy and Continuity in Romans 1:18-3:20', in *C B Q* 55 (1993), p. 309f; J.W. Martens, 'Romans 2:14-16: A Stoic Reading', in *N T St* 40 (1994), pp. 64-6.

several insuperable problems, most notably that such a positive view of Gentile life is hardly consistent with the sweeping indictment of the world in the previous chapter. It has been suggested that the earlier passage may have been misunderstood, and is not asserting the irretrievable sinfulness of everybody.[1] However, 1:18-32 is best read as a universal indictment; it is more likely 2:14f which has been misunderstood. Even conceding that Gentile practices do occasionally coincide with the requirements of God's law, it is quite unthinkable that Paul could use that fact as evidence that there are non-Jewish doers of the law who will be eschatologically justified.[2]

The most satisfactory reading of these verses is made on the basis of the view that Paul, without specifying the fact, has in mind Gentile Christians. He is inviting the Jewish members of the Roman Church to look around their own congregation for the evidence that what he says is true.

This interpretation of this passage was put forward by Ambrosiaster[3] and Augustine[4] in the fourth and fifth centuries respectively, and has been reaffirmed by Barth,[5] Cranfield,[6] and Ito.[7] In explanation and defence of this interpretation, the following points must be made.

(1) It is grammatically possible to take 'by nature' (φύσει) (v. 14) with the preceding clause: Paul is not saying, as most commentators assume, that Gentiles who do not have the law, do the things of the law by nature, but that there are Gentiles, who do not have the law by nature, who nevertheless do the things of the law.[8] Thus constructed, the phrase τὰ μὴ νόμον ἔχοντα φύσει avers that it is not part of the nature of Gentileness to have the law; it depicts all the Gentiles as those who were not born into the sphere of being demarcated by the torah. However, Paul insists, there are some Gentiles who now do the things of the law (and they do so by means of a special dispensation of God's grace: they have become Christians).

(2) This dispensation of God's grace he describes as having "the work of

---

[1] Ziesler, *Romans*, p. 85.

[2] Against C.H. Dodd, *The Epistle of Paul to the Romans* (Hodder and Stoughton, 1932), p. 37.

[3] Ambrosiaster, *Commentarius in Epistulas Paulinas, Pars 1: In Epistulam ad Romanos*, in *Corpus Scriptorum Ecclesiaticorum Latinorum*, Vol. 81. (Hoelder-Pichler-Tempsky, 1966), pp. 74-9.

[4] Augustine, 'Against Julian', in *The Fathers of the Chuch*, Vol. 35 (Catholic University of America Press, 1957), p. 189; *ibid*, 'The Spirit and the Letter', in J. Burnaby (ed), *The Library of Christian Classics*, Vol. 8. *Augustine: Later Works* (SCM Press, 1955), p. 229f.

[5] K. Barth, *Romans*, p. 36f.

[6] Cranfield, *Romans*, pp. 156-62.

[7] Ito, pp. 33-6.

[8] So Cranfield, *Romans*, Vol. 1, p. 156f; R.B. Hays, *Echoes of Scripture in the Letters of Paul* (Yale University Press, 1989), p. 44.

the law written in their hearts" (v. 15a). There is a clear allusion here to Jeremiah 31:33f, but the question must be raised as to the meaning of 'the work of the law' and its relationship to 'the law'. It is my contention that the two phrases are synonymous; Paul is making no distinction between them,[1] but uses the subtle phrase to underline the point that it is the moral requirements of the law of God which are uppermost in his concern. He is emphasizing the distinction between merely having the law and actually doing the work which it requires. Gentile Christians have God's law written on their hearts, and therefore do the work which it requires; they may therefore equally validly be said to have its work written in their hearts. The Jews, by contrast, Paul contends, have the law as 'letter' [γράμμα] (v. 27), but fail to keep it.

(3) Although most commentators argue that verses 13 (or 14) to 15 are a parenthesis, it is my view that verses 15b-16 should be read together, despite the difficulties which must be faced. Cranfield has worked hard at interpreting the section consistently, though there are points at which I disagree with his interpretation. I agree with him that the prefix συν- in συμμαρτυρούσης has at most the effect of intensifying the sense of the verb.[2] However, it does not seem to do full justice to Paul's words to see the witness of conscience as operating on judgement day and the next phrase as explanatory of the witness of conscience.[3] It is indeed necessary, in order to maintain the connection with verse 16 to read the latter phrase as an event which occurs at the last judgement, but it is more natural to understand the witness of the conscience as a present reality for the Gentile believer. Cranfield is right not to equate conscience with the work of the law written on the heart;[4] it is rather the effect of the writing of the law upon the hearts of Christian Gentiles that their conscience is stimulated to bear witness: the law activates the conscience. How then is the phrase "and between themselves the thoughts (τῶν λογισμῶν) accusing or even (ἢ καὶ) excusing"[5] to be explained? First, καὶ should in this case be seen as indicative of something additional, rather than as continuing the previous thought. It is best to take "between themselves" to mean between the various λογισμῶν, rather than between various people.[6] To do justice to what Paul says it seems necessary to interpret the λογισμοὶ not as thoughts within the Gentile, but as the judgements passed by God on that day. The

---

[1] Against Barrett, *Romans*, p. 52, Ziesler, *Romans*, p. 88.
[2] Cranfield, *Romans*, p. 162.
[3] Against *ibid*, p. 162.
[4] *ibid*, p. 160.
[5] Original translation.
[6] So (e.g.) Calvin, *Romans*, p. 98; Hendriksen, *Romans*, p. 98, n. 60; Fitzmyer, *Romans*, p. 311; against (e.g.) Murray, Vol. 1, p. 76, n. 30; M. Black, p. 58.

LXX can use this word of the thoughts of God.¹ This may depict the fact that even the life of the believer remains a mixture of law-keeping and sin, and even their law-keeping is sin-tainted,² so that there will be much that will come under accusation when they have to give account; however, the surprising thing (ἢ καὶ) is that, despite their sin, they will receive God's defence.

Before moving on from this passage, it is necessary to consider the objections which have been raised against the Christian Gentile interpretation, and to seek to offer satisfactory answers to them. Five objections must be considered. The answer to the first has already been anticipated; the other four must be considered now.

I. Hendriksen, Käsemann, and Snodgrass all make the point that φύσει τὰ τοῦ νόμου ποιῇ is an improbable way of describing the activity of the Holy Spirit and must mean before conversion, and Hendriksen and Snodgrass note further that to describe Christian Gentiles as τὰ μὴ νόμον ἔχοντα, is hardly appropriate.³

This argument proceeds on the assumption that φύσει is to be connected with what follows. It is certainly a valid criticism of Ambrosiaster and Augustine (who did not connect φύσει backwards), and one made already by Luther.⁴ However, I have already questioned this construction.

II. Sanday and Headlam note that the general Gentile interpretation of this verse was "liberal doctrine" both for Jews in Paul's day and for Christians since. They see the Christian Gentile interpretation as, in effect, a device for evading this liberal doctrine.⁵

This objection, however, fails to face up to the genuine difficulty of harmonizing 2:14f with 1:18-32 and 3:9-19. Unless we accuse Paul of inconsistency, we must assert either that his indictment of the world is not as absolute as a *prima facie* reading of the latter passages inevitably concludes, or that 2:14f cannot be referring to Gentiles in general.

III. Leenhardt points out that to interpret 2:14f of occasional and incidental right behaviour by Gentiles in general does not in fact conflict with 1:18-32, and that Paul indicates in 1:32 that the Gentiles do know what is morally right. Leenhardt insists that the evidence of the facts of Gentile life are consonant with the general interpretation.⁶

While there is little reason to object to anything that Leenhardt actually

---

¹ Ps. 32(33):11; Jer. 18:11; 27:45; 28:29; 36:11; Mic. 4:12.
² Cf. Cranfield, *Romans*, p. 162.
³ Hendriksen, *Romans*, p. 99, n. 61; Käsemann, *Romans*, p. 65 Snodgrass, *Justification*, p. 75.
⁴ M. Luther, 'Lectures on Romans', in H.C. Oswald (ed), *Luther's Works*, Vol. 25 (St. Louis: Concordia, 1972), p. 186.
⁵ Sanday and Headlam, p. 59f.
⁶ Leenhardt, p. 83, n.

says, the problem is to relate such an interpretation to the context: if verse 14f is Paul's evidence of the truth of verse 13 - which is the most natural connection - then Leenhardt's interpretation is hardly defensible. Similarly, Fitzmyer's claim that "the thrust of Paul's argument demands that it be understood of Gentiles as such"[1] is not obviously true.

IV. Morris argues that "it is not easy to see in the simple ἔθνη Gentile Christians", and proceeds to reject any alleged parallel with 11:13 and 15:9, because "the context there indicates that believers are in mind", which is not the case in chapter 2.[2]

The answer to this is that Paul is deliberately leaving the term unspecific as yet, as he builds up his case gradually. However, he himself has Gentile Christians in mind.

V. Käsemann makes the point that the word ἀνόμως and the phrase "a law to themselves" are unlikely designations for Gentile Christians.[3]

The reference to ἀνόμως is strictly irrelevant, since Paul uses that word before he cites the example of Gentiles who do obey the law. There is more weight to the objection based on the other phrase, but the next phrase, "who show the work of the law written in their hearts", must be read as elucidating these words. Paul could say of Christian Gentiles that they are a law to themselves just because the law has been written on their hearts, and therefore comes to them from within themselves.

It remains to note the significance of this passage for the question of the ongoing status of the law in the Christian life. Paul clearly sees a place for the law in the life of the Gentile believer. However, at this stage he seems to imply that it is encountered by the Gentile believer in a different way than by the Jew: it is written on the heart, so that the Gentile Christian becomes in a sense the law for himself. How the law written on the heart relates to the torah of Israel, as focussed in its moral requirements, but as a written document must await a later stage in the development of Paul's argument.

2) 2:25-29

In these verses Paul is particularly addressing the Jew, and his initial concern is the relationship between the law and circumcision, both of which were Jewish distinctives. He insists that there is value in circumcision (that is, in being an ethnic Jew) only if the law is practised. It was circumcision which gave the Jew his identity as a member of God's covenant community, but if he was a transgressor of the law this Jewish identity became meaningless. Paul sees true circumcision not merely as the physical act, but as the way of life in obedience to the law: the validity of the sign

---

[1] Fitzmyer, *Romans*, p. 310.
[2] Morris, *Romans*, p. 125, n. 84.
[3] Käsemann, *Romans*, p. 65.

and seal of the covenant presupposes a covenant lifestyle.[1] In verse 25 Paul drives a wedge between two things which the Jews united, in order soon to bind them inextricably together in a redefined sense.

Verses 26-27 state the converse of verse 25, and contemplate again the possibility of a man, uncircumcised by nature (ἐκ φύσεως) - in other words a Gentile - keeping the law's righteous requirements, and fulfilling the law. In this case his uncircumcision will be reckoned as circumcision; in other words he will truly belong to the people of God. Once again Paul is stressing the true nature of circumcision, which is located not in the physical act, but in the way of life as law-keeping which it symbolizes, such that the way of life may stand alone without the symbol.[2] The very way of life of the Gentile who is reckoned as circumcised will stand as a judgement[3] on the Jew who, despite possessing the law in written form (γράμματος)[4] and prizing circumcision, is nevertheless a transgressor. Gentile Christians are again in mind.[5]

In verse 28, Paul shows how his definition of true circumcision relates to the question of authentic Jewishness. There is a threefold contrast: 'visibly' (ἐν τῷ φανερῷ) contrasts with 'invisibly' (ἐν τῷ κρυπτῷ), 'in the flesh' (ἐν σαρκὶ) with 'of the heart' (καρδίας), and 'in the letter' (ἐν γράμματι) with 'in the Spirit' (ἐν πνεύματι).

Paul's point is that, on the day of judgement, it is not the factors which manifest Jewish descent to human eyes, such as circumcision of the flesh and possession of God's law in written mode, which will count. It is rather a matter of the hidden realities which are open to the scrutiny of God alone (cf. v. 16).[6] After mentioning in parenthesis that the true circumcision (obedience to the law) of which he has already spoken is a matter of the heart, Paul defines authentic Jewishness as being a Jew in the Spirit as distinct from the written form. The point of this further contrast is that there are two ways of embracing the law:[7] it may stand simply in its written form as that which demarcates the boundaries of Jewry, but as such, while it may well serve to make manifest a particular ethnic community, it is of no profit (cf. v. 25), since the law embraced only in its written givenness is precisely the disabled entity which is weak in the sphere of the flesh; it is only when the law is empowered by the Spirit that the Jew is able to keep it, because it is by the Spirit that the law is written on the heart. There is an echo here of

---

[1] Cf. Calvin, *Romans*, p. 108f; Haldane, p. 101f.
[2] Cf. Carras, p. 202f.
[3] So Vaughan, p. 47 (cf. K. Barth, *Romans*, p. 38).
[4] So Owen, *Romans*, p. 111, n. 2.
[5] So (e.g.) Murray, Vol. 1, p. 86; Dunn, *Romans*, p. 122; Käsemann, *Romans*, p. 75.
[6] Cf. Fitzmyer, *Romans*, p. 322; J.D.G. Dunn, 'Works of the Law and the Curse of the Law (Galatians 3:10-14)', in *N T St* 31 (1985), p. 530.
[7] Cf. Käsemann, *Romans*, p. 77; Dunn, *Romans*, p. 124.

verse 15, where the writing of the law on the heart of Gentile Christians is in view; here Paul's point is that precisely the same invisible writing of the law on the heart is necessary for the attaining of authentic Jewishness, and that this is a work of the Spirit. Although the fact is not here specified, it is a clear implication that it is by the same Spirit that the work of the law must be written upon the heart of Gentile believers.

The fact that authentic Jewishness is a matter of the Spirit in the heart, a reality accessible only to the all-searching eye of God, does not mean that there is no outward expression of that authentic life. Paul has already insisted that true circumcision is a life of obedience to the law, and while that includes inner obedience, the motives and thoughts of the mind being brought into conformity with the law, it does not exclude outward obedience. The point is that the seed of the sanctified life of the believer which follows upon justification through faith is the Holy Spirit in the heart, which is the same as the writing of the law upon the heart.

Verse 29 is a key to the understanding of Paul's view of the law. His basic premise is that it is doing the law which leads to eschatological justification (v. 13). However, that is only a possibility for Gentile Christians if the law is written on their hearts, and that inscription is the work of the Spirit. Similarly, it has always been the case for the Jews that true heart-obedience to the law is impossible except in the power of the Spirit, for it is His presence and work which transforms the disabled law which is weak in the sphere of the flesh into a power for sanctification in the sphere where the Spirit defines the orientation of being. It is therefore true that, on Paul's definition, the true Christian is the true Jew.[1] Paul is therefore saying only implicitly at this early point in his Epistle exactly what he later says explicitly in 8:2,4,8 and 9, and his words imply that the Gentile Christian, who lives in the sphere of the Spirit and so keeps the law, is at heart what the true Jew ought to be, and will be judged accordingly by the impartial God. It is the doing of the law which ends in eschatological justification, but that is a possibility only for those who have been initially justified by faith, who are now living in the Spirit.

3) 3:27,31

In 3:21ff Paul expounds the doctrine of justification through faith apart from the law. Verse 28 sums up the preceding discussion: "We conclude that a man is justified by faith apart from works of law". Immediately before this summary statement Paul makes the point that this doctrine rules out boasting, and asks, "By what law? Of works?" His answer is, "No, but by the law of faith (διὰ νόμου πίστεως)". The chapter concludes by facing up to what, to a Jewish objector, must seem the logical conclusion to draw

---

[1] W.S. Campbell, 'Did Paul Advocate Separation from the Synagogue?', in *Scot J Th* 42 (1989), p. 466.

from this gospel: "Do we then make void the law through faith?" After registering a strong objection to this deduction Paul finishes with the statement, "we establish (ἱστάνομεν) the law". It is necessary therefore to understand (1) in what sense the doctrine of justification by faith apart from the law establishes the law, and (2) what is meant by 'the law of faith'?

(1) A number of improbable theories as to how the law is established by faith must be cited. That which sees chapter 4 as the explanation[1] is quite popular, but verse 31 seems to belong more with chapter 3 than chapter 4. Dunn's theory that the law's proper function is confirmed in its universalization, which brings all God's creatures under His rule, rather than Israel exclusively,[2] likewise seems to overlook the emphasis in Romans on the moral focus of the law, and hence renders verse 31 a rather trivial conclusion to the grand passage on justification by faith. Nygren's attempt to link verse 31 directly with verse 27, by saying that both the law (according to 3:10-20) and also the doctrine of justification by faith sound the death-knell to human boasting[3] is difficult, given the introduction of a new theme in verse 29f. The following words of E.F. Scott could hardly be more adrift from Paul's meaning: "The gospel, resting as it does on faith,... does not oppose itself to any endeavour by which men have sincerely sought to find salvation. All that it has done is to bring clearly to light the hidden truth which lies at the heart of all religion."[4]

Worthy of greater consideration are two related theories. The first understands the establishment of the law in terms of atonement, justification, and imputation: the law is established in that it was, for believers, fulfilled in the Person of their substitute, who faced its penalty on their behalf, and whose righteous fulfilment of the law's demands is reckoned to them through faith.[5] The other sees the establishment of the law as its culmination in the Gospel to which it pointed forward.[6] Views such as these may contain part of Paul's meaning.

However, it seems most probable that the imaginary objector's question of verse 31a entails the allegation that the doctrine of justification by faith implies moral antinomianism, and that Paul is intent on denying precisely that charge. When he says that the law is established by the Gospel he means that, by the Holy Spirit, the law is empowered and becomes a force for sanctification in the life of the one who is justified through faith; far

---

[1] Refuted by Hodge, p. 102, Murray, Vol. 1, p. 125.
[2] Dunn, *Romans*, p. 191.
[3] Nygren, p. 166.
[4] Scott, *Romans*, p. 39.
[5] Cf. Haldane, p. 157f; S. Olyott, *The Gospel as it Really is, Paul's Epistle to the Romans Simply Explained* (Evangelical Press, 1979), p. 34.
[6] Cf. (e.g.) K. Barth, *Romans*, p. 48; Barrett, *Romans*, p. 84; F. Davidson & R.P. Martin, 'Romans', in Guthrie & Motyer (eds.), p. 1022; Cranfield, *Romans*, p. 223f.

from rejecting the law because he is justified apart from law, the Christian is transformed into one who truly desires to obey the law and progressively grows in that obedience. In verse 31b Paul is serving notice of a subject which he will develop later; here he makes the point cryptically and in passing.[1] Verse 31 is therefore, if this understanding is correct, an important indication of the ongoing relevance of the law in the life of the believer.

(2) By 'the law of faith' I understand Paul to mean the law as embraced by faith to become, in the power of the Holy Spirit, a force for sanctification in the believing life. From the perspective of the gospel of justification by faith, there are no grounds for boasting about obedience, since holiness is the result of the translocation of being from the sphere of the flesh to that of the Spirit, and this is not the achievement of the believer, but a miracle of God's grace. The transfer from the one sphere to the other does not come about by works of the law, but through faith, and the work of the law written upon the heart, the experience of life in the Holy Spirit, is the fruit and result of the transfer. Paul uses the phrase 'law of faith', therefore, of the law in its ongoing function as the pattern and power for the believing life.

4) 6:19b

Here Paul is contrasting the life of the believer with the pre-conversion state. In each case he compares life with slavery, speaking of "a life deeply and irrevocably committed one way or the other".[2] The former life of the Roman Christians entailed slavery to "uncleanness and to lawlessness, leading to lawlessness", while the Christian life is slavery to "righteousness leading to holiness". Here Paul uses ἀνομία (lawlessness) to describe both the fundamental nature of the unconverted human being, and the outworking of that nature in practical life. In both cases, the law of God is the standard against which human life is assessed.

The repetition of ἀνομία means that it is contrasted, in the second clause, with both righteousness (as the fundamental nature of the person) and holiness (in the sense of concrete acts). This implies that Paul is using 'righteousness' in its normal sense for this letter of the that which is imputed for faith in Jesus Christ,[3] and that righteousness is the fundamental description of the believer's being, out of which flows the sanctified life. Righteousness as an imputed state contrasts with lawlessness, because the law is the standard of righteousness, and, in Christ, the believer is credited with the perfect law-abiding achievement of his Saviour. Holiness as the believer's way of life contrasts with lawlessness, because it involves

---

[1] Cf. (e.g.) Hodge, p. 102; Morris, *Romans*, p. 189; Fitzmyer, *Romans*, p. 367.
[2] Dodd, *Romans*, p. 98.
[3] So Barrett, *Romans*, p. 133, against Calvin, *Romans*, p. 239; Fitzmyer, *Romans*, p. 451.

actually living in obedience to the law of God.

This brings us to the major issue: the implication of this text is that the law does have ongoing status in the believing life, not only in that the Lord has obeyed the law on behalf of His people, but also in that the sanctified life of the Christian may legitimately be defined as a life of law-keeping. The authentic Christian life takes its description from the moral law of God, and finds expression in a ready and deliberate obedience to that law.[1]

5) 13:8-10

That the believing life entails obedience to the law is finally made explicit in Paul's last references to law in Romans. Verse 8 insists that no debt is to be outstanding except that of love. The reason for this is that the person who loves the other has fulfilled the law (νόμον πεπλήρωκε). In verse 9 Paul lists some of the commandments from the second table of the law, indicating that they are summed up (ἀνακεφαλαιοῦται) in the saying, "You shall love your neighbour as yourself". It is to be noted that ἐντολή and νόμος are here to be distinguished from each other. They are not being used as practical equivalents as in 7:8-13. The commandments are the constituent parts of the law, its concrete expressions. Verse 10 argues that it is because love does no evil to the neighbour, which is probably to be read as a litotes, implying a strong affirmation of the benefit that love will seek to bring to the neighbour,[2] that love is the πλήρωμα of the law.

The word πλήρωμα has been the subject of much debate. Some have taken it in its normal Biblical sense of fulness; that is, love is that by which the law is completed or brought to full measure.[3] The problem with this interpretation is that it appears to imply that there is a deficiency in the law; it is hard to believe that Paul would agree to that: while he sees the law as weak in the sphere of the flesh, in the sphere of the Spirit, he sees it as a transforming power, and in itself it is holy, just and good (7:12,14). An alternative interpretation translates πλήρωμα 'fulfilling', in the sense that love is the doing of the law, and that the one who loves obeys the law;[4] this would be a unique use of the word in Biblical Greek, and would make it similar to the use of πλήρωσις in the LXX translation of Jeremiah 5:24. It has the *prima facie* attraction of making verses 8 and 10 say the same thing, but the disadvantage of translating the word inexactly.

A third possibility may be ventured. Etymologically πλήρωμα has a

---

[1] Cf. Calvin, *Romans*, p. 239; J.C. O'Neill, *Paul's Letter to the Romans* (Penguin, 1975), p. 117; Dunn, *Romans*, p. 347.
[2] So Hendriksen, *Romans*, p. 440.
[3] So, eg, Murray, Vol. 2, p. 163f.
[4] So (e.g.) R. Schippers, 'Pleroō', in C. Brown (ed.), *New International Dictionary of New Testament Theology* (Paternoster, 1975, 1976 & 1978), Vol. 1, p. 738.

passive sense which may be rendered 'that which is filled'.[1] It is possible, therefore, to translate the phrase, 'Love is that which is filled with/full of the law', and therefore, perhaps, 'Love is that which is filled out by the law'. If this is the meaning, then Paul would not only be saying that love fulfils the law (v. 8), but also stating the converse, that the law expounds the full meaning and content of true love. Such an interpretation would appear to be consonant with Paul's total positive understanding of the law.

This leads on to the issue of the overall meaning of this passage. To say that the law "requires nothing but what is implied in love"[2] is clearly a valid inference from these verses, but it fails to address the crucial question. It is evident that Paul does not deny the need, in some sense, for Christians to obey the law, but the interpretative puzzle is this: does Paul mean that where there is true love the law will in fact be kept, or is he saying that love is all that accomplishes the law, so that love may be said to have superseded the law? To put the question another way: is Paul looking for obedience to all the commandments as the authentic expression of love, or is he saying, 'be directed by love, and you have fully done your duty', so that the law becomes an irrelevance for the believer?

It will already be apparent from comments made in passing above that I think that the former understanding is correct. Before returning to an exposition of this interpretation, however, I shall make reference to those who adopt the other reading.

This view is put forward in expressions such as the following: "ἀγάπη takes the place of definite legal relations",[3] and "the one who expresses love does not really need the prescriptions and proscriptions of the Mosaic law".[4] It is suggested that what the law aims to compel happens spontaneously where there is love,[5] and so the purpose of the law, "which can never be perfectly carried out by mere external conformity to positive commands of the law" is realized.[6]

This interpretation is most forcibly represented by Dodd. He argues that Paul sees ἀγάπη as the sentiment which is the principle of all moral action, out of which arises a sense of duty towards all men. However, the obligations imposed by love "can never be defined or limited by any code of behaviour; they arise out of the varying situations in which one is

---

[1] Thayer, p. 518; R.P. Martin, 'Fullness', in J.D. Douglas & N. Hillyer (eds.), *Illustrated Bible Dictionary* (IVP, 1980), Part 1, p. 529, notes the passive meaning as the first connotation of πλήρωμα, but argues, wrongly in my view, that this connotation "does not seem to be relevant in the Scriptures".
[2] Haldane, p. 588.
[3] Sanday and Headlam, p. 373.
[4] Fitzmyer, *Romans*, p. 678.
[5] Scott, *Romans*, p. 69.
[6] Garvie, p. 271.

involved with other people, and are felt as duties in so far as love for men is a dominant sentiment." The whole law can be summarized as love for the neighbour, not in the sense that a scheme of Christian ethics can be deduced from this command; rather, Paul "begins with the grace of God, which implants in men who accept it a new life of the Spirit, renewing the mind, transforming the nature, and bringing about a dedication of the whole personality to the will of God, which is sovereign love." Dodd sees Paul as "true to the spirit of the teaching of Jesus", and as "a safer guide to the mind of Christ than those who made of His teaching a new Law".[1]

It seems, however, that such statements are founded upon a false dichotomy. While it may well be true that the purpose of the law is more than mere external conformity, such conformity is nonetheless necessary, for true external conformity is the reflection of an inner spirit, and the inner spirit will inevitably have an external effect. The inner reality of love can be measured only by its outward effects, and the law serves to define what these should be. This theory fails to give due weight to the fact of sin, even in the believer: we cannot simply assume that spontaneous impulses will inevitably come to proper expression unless that expression is given definitive guidelines in the law. If my proposed understanding of πλήρωμα is correct, then it implies that the imprecise concept 'love' must be filled out by the details of the law.

I therefore side with that group of commentators who read Paul as teaching that it remains the duty of the believer consciously and deliberately to obey the law of God, and who maintain that this is the only way in which true interpersonal love can be expressed and proved. As Bowen well puts it: "Christians need detailed explanations to help them to know how to love God and their neighbour."[2]

The fullest exposition of this line of interpretation has been given by Murray, and I can do little better than to quote him.

> We are not to regard love as dispensing with law or as displacing law as if what has misleadingly been called 'the law of love' has been substituted under the gospel for the law of commandments and precepts. Paul does not say that the law is love but that love fulfils the law and the law has not in the least been depreciated or deprived of its sanction.... It is the law that love fulfils.

Murray argues that Paul's appeal to the Decalogue in verse 9 demonstrates four propositions: "(1) The decalogue is of permanent and abiding relevance. (2) It exemplifies the law that love fulfils and is therefore correlative with love. (3) The commandments and their binding obligation

---

[1] Dodd, *Romans*, pp. 205-8.
[2] Bowen, p. 179.

do not interfere with the exercise of love; there is no incompatibility. (4) The commandments are the norms in accordance with which love operates."[1]

This is the more satisfactory way of understanding the overall thrust of this passage, not least because it accords with the unity of God's entire revelation. To see love as the replacement of law is to drive a wedge between parts of God's revelation which Paul is keen to hold together. The law does have an ongoing role as a binding authority in the life of the Christian believer.

2 NEGATIVE INDICATORS

It is necessary now to consider those texts which might seem to pose a problem for the view that Paul asserts the ongoing relevance of the law for the believer.

1) 6:14f

Paul states as a reason for sin's loss of lordship in the life of the believer the fact that the believer is not under law but under grace. An imaginary objector, evidently interpreting these words to mean that the law's demands have no further relevance at all for the Christian, asks whether this implies that we are given a licence to sin. Paul strongly denies that this is so, and proceeds to explain that the believer is now a slave of righteousness, who must live a holy life.

The question therefore arises as to the meaning of the phrase 'not under law'. Dunn's claim that it refers to the social identity of Israel as a national entity and characterizes "life under the old aeon as it has been experienced within Judaism"[2] is inappropriate to the context, where the moral aspects of the law are to the fore.[3]

It is often said that Paul is referring to the law as a way of salvation, a system of justification and acceptance with God: the believer is not under law in that sense, since Christ has fulfilled its demands and its curse on his behalf, and he is justified by grace.[4] This is not, however, a satisfactory explanation, since the law is not portrayed in the Bible as a way of salvation, except as a distorted understanding. To this extent E.P. Sanders is right in his emphasis on 'covenantal nomism'.[5] The Old Testament, at least, did not teach law-keeping as a means of earning salvation. It is, however, necessary to make some qualification to the new scholarly consensus which says the same about the Jews of Paul's day. Some Jewish teaching saw

---

[1] Murray, Vol. 2, pp. 160-2.
[2] Dunn, *Romans*, pp. 339f, 352.
[3] Cf. Haldane, p. 258.
[4] So (e.g.) Hodge, p. 205f; Leenhardt, p. 169; Hendriksen, *Romans*, p. 203.
[5] E.P. Sanders, *Paul and Palestinian Judaism* (SCM Press, 1977), *passim*.

righteousness as obtaining reward:[1] "The Law implied that it was the ultimate, and that man, in using it, could help himself".[2] Paul himself found it necessary to re-evaluate, in the light of his experience of Christ, the Pharisaism which he had known, and to make a critical evaluation of its subconscious motivation to seek to win God's favour by law-based works (cf. Philip. 3:4-9). Nevertheless, this is not his concern in Romans.

Calvin sees verse 14 as a word of consolation to Christians in their weakness, assuring them that, because they are justified by faith, they are no longer under the law as requiring perfect obedience, because God is merciful.[3] However, Paul teaches, at least as the ideal, that the law remains the unaltered standard of righteousness, even for the believing life.

To understand the significance of 'you are not under law' it is necessary to read the phrase in the light of Paul's teaching about the law in this Epistle up to this point. He has shown that it is those who obey the law who will be acquitted at the final judgement (2:12-24), and that their obedience is possible only in the power of the Spirit (2:25-29). Hence, they will not be justified on the basis of their law-obedience, because the function of the law in the sphere of the flesh is to define what sin is; justification is therefore on the basis of faith, and obedience is the result (3:19-31). From this follows the universality of God's grace; His promise is not restricted to those who are of the law, because the function of the law before the coming of Christ is to activate wrath through clarifying the meaning of sin (4:13-16). The major point thus far, that the law gives sin abundant definition, and so makes it recordable, is repeated in 5:13 and 20.

The next reference to the law in 6:14f must be read in the light of this emphasis on the function of the law when its existence is independent of the Spirit in the sphere of the flesh. It is the law in its sin-defining function that the believer is not under. In the life of the believer the role of the law is not to clarify sin.[4] The believer is under grace as the defining feature of his life, affirming his acceptance and forgiveness. It is clear from Paul's answer to the objection voiced in verse 15 that this does not imply that the believer has no relation at all to the law. The law is precisely the will and word of God Himself; to be subject to the one is inevitably to be subject to the other also. The law does have ongoing relevance for the believer, though no longer in its function as the definer of sin, for that applies only in the sphere of the flesh. In the sphere of the Spirit, the law stands before the believer as

---

[1] Cf. Davies, p. 268; Carson, Moo and Morris, p. 298.

[2] Sandmel, *Understanding*, p. 69 (cf. W.H. Brownlee, *The Meaning of the Qumran Scrolls for the Bible* (Oxford University Press, 1964), p. 150; D. Cohn-Sherbok, *A Dictionary of Judaism and Christianity* (SPCK, 1991), p. 83f; R.H. Eisenman & M. Wise, *The Dead Sea Scrolls Uncovered* (Element Books, 1992), pp. 184f, 200).

[3] Calvin, *Romans*, p. 233f.

[4] Cf. (e.g.) K. Barth, *Romans*, p. 71; Cranfield, *Romans*, p. 320.

the definition of holiness, and becomes, in the Spirit's power, a force in the believing life for the reproduction of its own demands.

2) 7:4

Paul reminds the Romans that they were put to death with respect to the law through the body of Christ. In the preceding three verses Paul has first stated the principle that the law has applicability to a person only for the duration of his lifetime, and then illustrates this by reference to the law of marriage: it is only when her husband dies that a woman is free to remarry without becoming guilty of adultery. However, it seems that the sole point which Paul intends to make is that the law is applicable only to the living, and that death brings release from the obligation to law.[1] Paul's point is that there is a sense in which the law is irrelevant to believers because of the death of Christ. In what sense, then, is this so?

That this is substantially the same point as that made in 6:14 is widely recognized. Older commentators often, therefore, understood this to mean that believers are dead to the law as a way of salvation and justification.[2] The difficulty with this theory is that Paul believes that the law never had such a function, and it is therefore hard to see how he can speak of believers having died in Christ to such a role of the law. Dunn speaks of the believer's death to the law as exercising authority over the life of the old epoch;[3] however, as the symbol of God's authority, the law retains this status even in the new age.

It seems better, therefore, as in the case of 6:14, to interpret these words in the light of the teaching on the law in Romans so far. Paul's main point has been that in the sphere of the flesh the law has a sin-defining function. It is to this function of the law that the believer has been put to death, because his sphere of existence is no longer the flesh but the Spirit.

Does this mean that the law has no further relevance to the Christian? Clearly not. In the previous chapter Paul has insisted that death with Christ implies also participation in His resurrection, this being a present reality, which involves walking in newness of life (6:4). As 6:19 has shown, it is the role of the law in the sphere of the Spirit to give concrete definition to that new walk.

3) 7:6

The first part of this verse reads: "But now we have been delievered ἀπὸ τοῦ νόμου, having died ἐν ᾧ κατειχόμεθας. I leave untranslated for the

---

[1] So A. Barnes, *Romans* (Blackie, 1868), p. 169; Nygren, pp. 270, 273; against Sanday and Headlam, p. 172, J.D. Earnshaw, 'Reconsidering Paul's Marriage Analogy in Romans 7:1-4', in *N T St* 40 (1994), p. 72.

[2] Haldane, p. 279; Hodge, p. 216; Barnes, *Romans*, p. 160.

[3] Dunn, *Romans*, p. 362.

moment two phrases of which the proper translation will be an important part of the ensuing discussion.

Commentators generally interpret verse 6 in the light of verse 4, and so read "we have been delievered ἀπὸ τοῦ νόμους as equivalent to 'we have died to the law', translating the phrase: 'we have been delivered from the law'. The next phrase is then regarded as an amplification of the same idea, and is translated, 'having died to what we were held by'.

However, it seems to make better sense to regard verse 5 as the beginning of a new section, which looks forward to the discussion of the law's opportunism in verses 7-11. I would therefore propose a rather different translation of verse 6a: "But now we have been delivered from that law, having died while we were held captive." It is necessary to comment on three elements of this translation.

(1) I am reading the article demonstratively, as taking up the reference to the law in verse 5: it is only from THAT law that believers have been delivered, that is, from the law as arousing the passions of sins, or, in other words, from the law of sin, which is the law as taken possession of by sin.

(2) As in 8:3 I am understanding ἐν ᾧ temporally. Paul speaks of the law as a killer in verses 9-11 and 13. However, that is true only in the sphere of the flesh, where sin latches on to the law to stimulate that covetousness which entails a fundamental orientation of life to the things of this world. However, such a state of being is, for the Christian, a thing of the past (7:5), and he now lives again in Christ. This reading has the advantage of tying verse 6 closely to verse 5, where fruit-bearing to death is seen as an aspect of life in the sphere of the flesh; it is likely that this next reference to death should be understood in the same terms.

(3) This raises the question as to what it is which holds the unbeliever captive, and results in his death. Although most commentators think that Paul is referring to the law, it seems more probable in the light of verses 8-11 that the answer is in fact sin. It was because sin seized opportunistically upon the law that the law proved to be the death of the pre-Christian Jew. In verse 14 Paul speaks of being 'sold under sin'. The imagery of slavery found there is already present in verse 6.

This verse then continues by stating the purpose[1] of our deliverance from the law of sin which killed us while sin held us captive: it is that we might serve in the newness of the Spirit and not in the oldness of the letter. This contrast between the Spirit and the letter has been interpreted broadly in two ways. Some commentators speak in terms of the Christian life as "maintained and controlled by the Holy Spirit" in contrast with "life under the commandments of the law of Moses".[2] However, Paul's distinction is emphatically not between the Spirit and the law, but between the Spirit and

---

[1] So *ibid*, p. 366.
[2] Garvie, p. 173; cf. Sanday and Headlam, p. 176; O'Neill, p. 126.

the letter, which are to be seen as two antithetical approaches to the law.

It is not as if the law has no further relevance for the Christian believer: it is the law as letter, as a mere piece of writing viewed in independence from the Spirit[1] which is old and obsolete, and which, according to 2:29, never was of any value. Such is the law in its disability and weakness in the sphere of the flesh. However, in the sphere of the Spirit where the believing life is lived, the law is taken up by the Spirit to be the definition and empowering for authentic Christian existence. "The Christian is not exempt from service to God.... Obedience is central in Christian freedom."[2]

4) 10:4

This verse reads: τέλος γὰρ νόμου Χριστὸς εἰς δικαιοσύνην παντὶ τῷ πιστεύοντι. The word τέλος has been understood in three different ways: (i) as goal, in the sense that it is to Christ that the law points forward;[3] (ii) as fulfilment, in the sense that in Christ the law was in fact fulfillled;[4] (iii) as termination, in that Christ, in some sense at least, abrogated the law.[5] Some commentators attempt to combine meaning (iii) with one or both of the other two. If meaning (iii) is correct, this verse becomes a negative indicator for the ongoing status of the law.

It has been pointed out that, under the influence of Luther, Protestant theology had, by the nineteenth-century, come almost unanimously to the opinion that Romans 10:4 teaches the abrogation of the law with the coming of Christ.[6] This meaning is defended from two considerations, the first linguistic and the second contextual. The linguistic argument is that it is the normal usage of τέλος in the Bible. Although Badenas has adduced much evidence for the meaning 'goal' in extra-Biblical Greek,[7] Murray

---

[1] So Cranfield, *Romans*, p. 340.

[2] Barrett, *Romans*, p. 138.

[3] So (e.g.) G.E. Howard, 'Christ the End of the Law', in *J B L* 88 (1969), p. 336; R. Bring, 'Paul and the Old Testament', in *St Th* 25 (1971), p. 47; C.T. Rhyne, 'Νόμος δικαιοσύνης and the Meaning of Romans 10:4', in *C B Q* 47 (1985), p. 493; S.R. Bechtler, 'Christ the Telos of the Law', in CBQ 56 (1994), pp. 289,298-302; J.V. Hills, 'Christ was the Goal of the Law...', in *J Th St* ns 44 (1993), p. 590; R. Badenas, *Christ the End of the Law* (JSOT Press, 1985), pp. 38-80, 114f.

[4] So Owen, *Romans*, p. 384, n. 1; cf. W.S. Campbell, 'Christ the End of the Law: Romans 10:4', in E.A. Livingstone (ed.), *Studia Biblica 1978*, Vol. 3 (JSOT Press, 1980), p. 77.

[5] So (e.g.) A.M. Hunter, *The Epistle to the Romans* (SCM Press, 1955), p. 95; J.D.G. Dunn, '"Righteousness from the Law" and "Righteousness from Faith"', in Hawthorne & Betz (eds.), p. 222; E.P. Sanders, *Paul, the Law, and the Jewish People* (Fortress Press, 1983), p. 39; Räisänen, *Torah*, p. 11.

[6] Cf. Howard, *Christ*, p. 331; Bring, pp. 24, 51; Badenas, pp. 25-34.

[7] Badenas, pp. 38-80, supported by R. Jewett, 'The Law and the Coexistence of Jews and Gentiles in Romans', in *Interp* 39 (1985), p. 353f.

points out that, for Biblical usage, though the word can mean aim or purpose, "preponderantly, and particularly in Paul, it means termination."[1]

Second, the context is judged conclusive for meaning (iii). Verse 3 teaches that Israel proved to be ignorant of the righteousness of God, and therefore sought to establish their own righteousness, and so did not submit to the righteousness of God. Our verse is connected to verse 3 by the word 'for'. This implies that verse 4 is designed to explain why Israel erred in seeking to establish their own righteousness on the basis of the works of the law;[2] namely, because Christ is the τέλος of the law εἰς δικαιοσύνην. This qualifying phrase is taken to mean that it is as a route to righteousness (justification) that Christ brings the law to a termination. The surrounding verses 9:30-32 and 10:5-9 are read as again contrasting the righteousness which is on the basis of the law with the righteousness which is on the basis of faith in Jesus as Lord and Saviour. The radical nature of this contrast points, it is claimed, to 'termination' as the proper translation of τέλος in this context.

However, both these arguments may be answered. As regards the linguistic argument, it must be admitted that Murray's claim seems to hold good both for the canonical LXX[3] and in the New Testament.[4] Nevertheless, in neither case is this true invariably.[5] Moreover, Murray appears to be wrong in claiming that it applies particularly for Paul, and in that the two other relevant uses of τέλος within Romans (6:21f) could be given meaning (i), it might be argued that the probability of the meaning 'goal' at 10:4 is increased.

As for the contextual argument, it seems necessary to reconsider what Paul is saying in this context, in view of the fact that there is one obstacle to the meaning of τέλος as 'end' which seems insuperable. As Murray rightly notes, the Old Testament never taught a way of justification by the works of the law, and Paul has stressed in Romans the Old Testament basis for his

---

[1] Murray, Vol. 2, p. 49.

[2] So Sanday and Headlam, p. 284; Morris, *Romans,* p. 379.

[3] The meaning 'termination' is best in Gen. 46:4; Deut. 31:24; 32:1; Josh. 8:24; 10:13; Jg. 11:39; 2 Sam. 15:7; 24:8; 2 Kgs. 8:3; 18:10; 1 Chr. 28:9; 2 Chr. 18:2; 31:1; Neh. 13:6; Job 14:20; 23:3,7; Ps. 9:7,18,31; 12:2; 15:11; 17:35; 37:7; 43:23; 48:9; 51:5; 67:16; 73:1,3,10,11,19; 76:8; 78:5; 88:46; 102:9; Eccl. 3:11; 7:3; Isa. 19:15; 62:6; Ezek. 20:40; 36:10; Dan. 1:15,18; 4:31; 6:26; 9:26; 11:13.

[4] The meaning 'termination' seems to be required in Matt. 10:22; 24:6,13,14; 26:58; Mk. 3:26; 13:7,13; Lk. 1:33; 18:5; 21:9; Jn. 13:1; 1 Cor. 1:8; 10:11; 15:24; 2 Cor. 1:13; 3;13; 11:15; Philip. 3:19; Heb. 3:6,14; 6:8,11; 7:3; 1 Pet. 3:8; 4:7,17; Rev. 1:8; 2:26; 21:6; 22:13.

[5] A different translation is more suitable in Lev. 27:23; Num. 17:13; Josh. 3:16; 10:20; 1 Chr. 29:19; 2 Chr. 12:12; Job 6:9; 20:7; Eccl. 12:13; Ezek. 15:4,5; 22:30; Dan. 2:34; 3:19; 7:26; Am. 9:8; Hab. 1:4; Lk. 22:37; Rom. 6:21,22; 1 Thess. 2:16; 1 Tim. 1:5; Jas. 5:11; 1 Pet. 1:9.

gospel.[1] The response on the part of those who adopt meaning (iii), would be that Paul is rejecting the law misunderstood as a way of earning righteousness. As has been noted, there is evidence, notwothstanding Dunn's claim to the contrary,[2] that such a misunderstanding of the law was present in some strands of the Judaism of the day. The coming of Christ, therefore, sounds for Paul the ultimate death-knell to such a misunderstanding and abuse of God's law.[3]

However, it seems to be a mistake to understand verse 4 to be referring to that misunderstanding, even if it is the theme of 9:30-32 and 10:5-9. The statement in verse 4 is made without qualification: it reads as a proposition true of the law itself,[4] and, moreover, objection can be raised to meaning (iii) on the grounds of the larger context of the Epistle as a whole: the idea that Christ has brought the law to an end would be contrary to Paul's general teaching in this Epistle.[5]

This suggests that Paul's point is not that Christ has terminated the law as a route to righteousness, for that it never was, but that the law always had as its goal Christ as the believer's righteousness. It seems necessary to opt for meaning (i) on both linguistic and contextual grounds.[6]

To establish the contextual point it is necessary to take a closer look at 9:30-10:9. Throughout chapters 9-11 Paul's concern is the perplexity of the rejection of Christ by the Israel of his generation. In his observations here he moves from an assessment of the different practices of Gentiles and Israel as timeless ideal entities to a specific comment on two particular events in his own generation.

The timeless truths, shown by the present participles, are (1) that Gentiles are not pursuers of righteousness (μὴ διώκοντα δικαιοσύνην), whereas (2) Israel is in constant pursuit of the law of righteousness (διώκων νόμον δικαιοσύνης). The specific events, indicated by the aorist verbs, are (1) that Gentiles obtained righteousness (κατέλαβε δικαιοσύνην), while (2) Israel did not attain to the law of righteousness (εἰς νόμον δικαιοσύνης οὐκ ἔφτηασε).

The apparent symmetry of 9:30f is disturbed by the appearance of νόμος,[7] and it is important to determine the meaning of 'law of righteousness', and its relationship to 'righteousness' *tout simple*. The presence of 'law' probably serves to emphasize the distinct advantage that

---

[1] Murray, Vol. 2, p. 50f.
[2] Dunn, *Romans*, p. 597.
[3] Cf. (e.g.) Dodd, *Romans*, p. 165; Murray, Vol. 2, p. 50; Olyott, p. 91.
[4] So Bring, p. 49.
[5] Cranfield, *Romans*, p. 519; Hendriksen, *Romans*, p. 342, n. 293.
[6] Cf. W. Elliger, 'εἰς', in H. Balz & G. Schneider (eds), *Exegetical Dictionary of the New Testament*, Vol. 1 (Eerdmans, 1990), p. 398.
[7] So Rhyne, p. 488.

Israel had, in that for them, unlike the Gentiles, righteousness was clearly and explicitly defined. The genitive phrase can be understood to mean 'the law which demands or promises righteousness'.[1] It is perhaps better, however, to understand it as 'the law which defines righteousness'.[2] The result of the juxtaposition is that righteousness and 'the law of righteousness' are almost equated: the law is recognized to be the true definition of authentic righteousness (cf. 2:20), and the surprising thing is that those who had had righteousness defined for them failed to attain, while Gentiles obtained (by grace) a righteousness not previously defined for them.

Verse 32f is designed to answer the question why Israel failed to attain to the law of righteousness. The answer is the elliptical phrase, which, translated literally, reads 'because not by faith, but as by works of the law (ὅτι οὐκ ἐκ πίστεως, ἀλλ' ὡς ἐξ ἔργων νόμου)'. A verb must be understood here, and it is usual to supply 'to pursue' from the previous verse. However, the verb 'to be' may well be implied: Israel defined her being not on the basis of faith, but as if it were on the basis of works of the law.[3] That is to say, Israel's error was to give her own works done in obedience to the law[4] the fundamental position in the constitution of her life, which rightly belongs to faith. Israel turned the law into a quest[5] for self-righteousness, instead of looking in faith to the grace of God which justifies the ungodly (cf. 4:5). Paul is here caricaturing Israel in general in the light of what he knows to be the fundamental error of the Pharisees. The evidence offered for this error in their basic approach to righteousness is their rejection of Christ, who was the embodiment of God's righteousness. This was the end result of a misconstruction of being; it was this rejection of Christ which was Israel's single, specific failure to attain the law of righteousness.[6]

This theme is resumed in 10:3: Paul now reverts to the use of present participles (ἀγνοοῦντες/ζητοῦντες). He is again considering Israel in a timeless sense. They are habitually ignorant of God's righteousness, and hence it is their perpetual quest to establish a righteousness of their own on the basis of the works of the law.

Thus far there is little difference between my understanding of the problem which Paul identifies in these verses and that of those interpreters who adopt meaning (iii) for τέλος in verse 4. However, my reading of this passage leads me to meaning (i), as I shall now show.

---

[1] *Ibid*, p. 489 (cf. Bechtler, p. 293; Badenas, p. 104).
[2] So Dunn, *Romans*, p. 581.
[3] Cf. Käsemann, *Romans*, p. 277.
[4] Cf. Cranfield, *Works*, p. 92, against Dunn, *Works*, pp. 524-8.
[5] Against Dunn, *Romans*, p. 590, *ibid, Righteousness*, p. 221f.
[6] Cf. Bechtler, p. 295.

It is generally taken for granted that 'Christ' is the subject of verse 4, and that the predicate, τέλος νόμου, is "thrown forward for the sake of emphasis".[1] However, this does not seem to be the best construction. The phrase makes excellent sense if translated in the order in which the words appear,[2] with τέλος νόμου as the subject and Χριστὸς εἰς δικαιοσύνην as the predicate. Further, a convincing case can be made for understanding the absent verb as in the past tense. 'The goal of the law was[3] Christ unto righteousness for all believers.'

Paul's point is that Israel's misunderstanding of the law as a route to righteousness was itself the outcome of a deeper misunderstanding: they failed to to see the law as leading to Christ, in whom the righteousness defined by the law was to be granted as gift. The word νόμος is here used in its widest possible sense:[4] the whole of God's revelation had Christ as its culminating point; recognizing that in Romans the moral heart of the law is to the fore, even its sin-defining, exposing, and stimulating functions were designed to lead Israel at last to the Messiah, to find in Him God's gift of righteousness. It was the failure to understand the Christological thrust of the law which resulted in a pursuit of self-righteousness on the part of Israel, and so blinded their eyes to the recognition of Jesus as the Messiah.

In that verse 5 is an explanation of verse 4, it seems necessary to understand it Christologically:[5] Christ alone is the Man who has attained life by doing the things of the law; He is the only One who is not condemned by the law in its sin-exposing role. The law is the standard of eschatological righteousness, and Christ is the eschatological embodiment of righteousness. Verses 6-13 then expound the contrasting route to righteousness which is the only one available to sinners, whether Jews or Gentiles: that is, righteousness through faith in Christ.

Thus my reading of this passage agrees with those who adopt meaning (iii) that the problem which Paul is confronting is Israel's habitual pursuit of righteousness by the works of the law – a hopeless quest in the sphere of the flesh. However, Christ, and righteousness in Him, is held up as the goal to which the law had always pointed.

What then is the significance of 10:4 for the question of the ongoing status of the law in the believing life? The answer is: very little. The subject of this passage is justification: to this end the goal of the law was Christ. That, however, leaves open the question whether the law has any other function, and the answer must be supplied from elsewhere. As we have seen, Paul's teaching is that, in the context where righteousness is first

---

[1] Cranfield, *Romans*, p. 515; Rhyne, p. 486.
[2] Against Murray, p. 50.
[3] Hills, pp. 585-8.
[4] So Badenas, p. 103.
[5] Cf. the comments by Bring, p. 49; W.S. Campbell, *End*, p. 77.

given to faith, the law does indeed have an ongoing role as the Spirit-empowered rule of the believer's life.

Conclusion

In the foregoing pages I have sought to expound Paul's teaching on the law by letting Romans speak for itself. The reconstruction of the situation in the Roman Church proposed in the Introduction to this section can be no more than a tentative inference arising out of the internal evidence. If it is correct, then Paul's account of the ongoing status of the law in the life of the believer spoke powerfully to a real dilemma in the Roman Church, with its spectrum of attitudes ranging from total bondage to the Jewish law in all its aspects to complete antinomianism. Even if this reconstruction is not correct, the exposition of Paul's theology does, I submit, still stand.

According to this Epistle, the law does have an ongoing place in Christian life, because, though it was disabled for as long as it used to be weak in the sphere of the flesh, in the sphere of the Spirit (where the believer now has his being), the law is empowered as a means of sanctification.

CHAPTER 3

Galatians

1 Introduction

1 Στοιχεῖα as Law

The inclusion of Galatians 4:9 amongst our five key texts is based on the view that the word στοιχεῖα, first used in 4:3 followed by the genitive phrase "of the world" [τοῦ κόσμου] (cf. Col. 2:8,20), and then again in 4:9 qualified by the adjectives "weak and beggarly" [ἀσθενῆ καὶ πτωχὰ], refers to the law. Since this is not the only interpretation, it is necessary to present the arguments which have led me to the conclusion that this is the correct interpretation.

The most popular view amongst modern exegetes understands τὰ στοιχεῖα in the sense of personal cosmic powers. Hatch has demonstrated, by reference to a Syriac work, that this was a recognized meaning of the word by the end of the second century; he argues "that Paul in writing to the Galatians and Colossians meant by τὰ στοιχεῖα τοῦ κόσμου personal powers or elemental spirits similar to those mentioned in 'The Book of the Laws of the Countries', and that the recipients of his letters understood the words in this sense."[1] This argument is, however, tenuous, given that Paul was writing over a century earlier than the work cited, although evidence has been adduced for a first-century background to this use of the term.[2]

The fundamental meaning of the word is the members of a series (from στοῖχος - a row), but from the time of Plato it came to be used of the elements, or constituent parts, of any organism, and then more specifically of the primary elements of the universe, which, from the time of Empedocles, had been numbered as four: earth, air, fire, and water.[3] In later Greek thought the στοιχεῖα came to be identified with the planets and

---

[1] W.H.P. Hatch, 'Τα στοιχεῖα in Paul and Bardaisan', in *J Th St* 28 (1927), p. 181f.

[2] C.E. Arnold, 'Returning to the Domain of the Powers: στοιχεῖα as Evil Spirits in Galatians 4:3,9', in *Nov Test* 38 (1996), pp. 57-9.

[3] E. Schweizer, 'Slaves of the Elements and Worshippers of Angels: Gal 4:3,9 and Col. 2:8,18,20', in *J B L* 107 (1988), pp. 456, 466, defends this view.

stars, and then with the astrological signs of the zodiac: "every element has its god; so also every star", and it was these personified elements which became the normal referent of στοιχεῖα.¹ Reid thinks that the gods in view are local, tribal deities.²

That this is the meaning in the Pauline letters is argued by many. Sometimes the reference to the angelic mediation of the law in Galatians 3:19 is used as evidence,³ although this seems forced, because "the angels are not powers who tyrannize men, but those who add even greater lustre to the law":⁴ Paul's sole point appears to be that the law was a provisional arrangement, in contrast to the covenant, which is an eternally unalterable divine dispensation. The weak and poor στοιχεῖα are sometimes identified with 'those which by nature are not gods' of verse 8.⁵

The alternative interpretation takes account of the use of the word in Hebrews 5:12, and understands its use in Galatians (and possibly in Colossians too⁶) in a similar sense as first principles, or basic, rudimentary knowledge. In the section beginning at 3:23 Paul has depicted the law as a feature of the infancy stage of religious life: it is described as a tutor (παιδαγωγὸς) (3:24f). Paul then uses an illustration: he points to the way in which in a normal household the heir, for the duration of his minority, is under guardians and stewards (4:1f). Verse 3 forms the application of the comparison: "So we, when we were children, were enslaved under the στοιχεῖα of the world". The parallelism between 'under guardians and stewards' and 'under the στοιχεῖα of the world' makes it clear that Paul sees the στοιχεῖα as that to which the guardians and stewards appointed by the father are equivalent, namely the law, the παιδαγωγὸς appointed by God. It is noteworthy, furthermore, that these two phrases are bracketed by two instances of the similar phrase 'under law' [ὑπὸ νόμον] (3:23; 4:5).

This interpretation was favoured by many of the older commentators.⁷

---

¹ G.A. Deissmann, 'Elements', in T.K. Cheyne & J.S. Black (eds.), *Encyclopaedia Biblica*, Vol. 2 (A. & C. Black, 1901), cols. 1258-61.

² D.G. Reid, 'Elements/Elemental Spirits of the World', in Hawthorne & Martin (eds.), p. 232.

³ So Deissmann, col. 1261; B. Reicke, 'The Law and this World according to Paul', in *J B L* 70 (1951), p. 262; F.F. Bruce, *Paul: Apostle of the Free Spirit* (Paternoster, 1977), p. 192; cf. H. Maccoby, *Paul and Hellenism* (SCM Press, 1991), p. 46.

⁴ H.N. Ridderbos, *The Epistle to the Galatians* (Marshall, Morgan and Scott, 1961), p. 153, n. 5.

⁵ So (e.g.) F.F. Bruce, *The Epistle to the Galatians* (Paternoster, 1982), p. 203; H.D. Betz, *Galatians* (Fortress, 1979), p. 205.

⁶ Cf. H.C.G. Moule, *Colossian Studies* (Hodder & Stoughton, 1903), p. 141f; W. Hendriksen, *Colossians and Philemon* (Banner of Truth, 1971), p.109f.

⁷ E.g. M. Luther, 'Lectures on Galatians, 1535, Chapters 5-6; Lectures on Galatians, 1519, Chapters 1-6', in J. Pelikan (ed.), *Luther's Works*, Vol. 27 (Concordia, 1964), p. 285; *ibid*, 'Lectures on Galatians, 1535, Chapters 1-4', in J. Pelikan (ed.), *Luther's*

"'In Christ', so the Apostle seems to say, 'you have attained the liberty and intelligence of manhood; do not submit yourselves again to a rudimentary discipline fit only for children.'"[1] A few more recent writers also defend this interpretation, with various differences of emphasis.[2]

Each of these two interpretations must adequately explain the difficulties it faces if it is to be given serious consideration. The difficulty faced by the first interpretation is the unavoidable stress on the law throughout the passage which forms the context for the two occurrences of στοιχεῖα. The other interpretation faces two difficulties. First, Paul is writing to Gentiles: in what sense then can submission to Jewish law be represented as a 'turning again' to the στοιχεῖα and the desire to be in bondage to them again, since as Gentiles they were never subject to the Jewish law? Second, how can Paul describe the law of God as the στοιχεῖα of the world?

Three different ways will be mentioned in which the advocates of the theory that Paul is referring to cosmic spiritual forces have incorporated into their arguments Paul's undeniable emphasis in the context on the place of the law in the pre-Christian infant stage of experience.

(1) Lietzmann argues that the Jews could be said to be slaves to the στοιχεῖα because the observance of days, months, seasons and years (4:10), in other words, the timing of the major ceremonies prescribed by Jewish law, was derived from the course of the stars, and thus Jewish religion, like Gentile paganism, could be portrayed as a nature religion.[3]

(2) Ebeling speculates that the religious background in Galatia was an atmosphere of polytheistic syncretism which incorporated some aspects of Judaism into an astrological scheme in a predominantly nature-orientated piety. The law had therefore become identified in popular superstition with the spiritual powers.[4]

(3) Schlier notes the parallel between ὑπὸ τὰ στοιχεῖα and ὑπὸ νόμον (4:5), and argues that Gentile slavery to the elements was analogous to Jewish slavery to the law, and indeed, that, in their slavery to the elements,

---

Works, Vol. 26 (Concordia, 1963), p. 326f; J. Calvin, *Commentaries on the Epistles of Paul to the Galatians and Ephesians* (Geneva, 1548), p. 123; J. Brown, *An Exposition of Galatians* (Christian Classics, n.d.), p. 79; J.B. Lightfoot, *The Epistle of St. Paul to the Galatians* (Zondervan, 1865, 1957), p. 167.

[1] J.B. Lightfoot, *Saint Paul's Epistles to the Colossians and Philemon* (Macmillan, 1892), p. 178.

[2] So (e.g.) M.-J. Lagrange, *Saint Paul Épitre aux Galates* (Libraire Lecoffre, 1950), pp. 99-101; G. Delling, 'Στοιχεῖα', in G. Kittel (ed.) *Theologoical Dictionary of the New Testament,* Vol. 7, nn. 95-108 (cited by H-H. Esser, 'stoicheia', in C. Brown (ed.), p. 452f); L.L. Belleville, 'Under Law: Structural Analysis and the Pauline Concept of Law in Galatians 3:21-4:11', in *J St N T* 26 (1986), p. 67f; B. Witherington, 'The Influence of Galatians on Hebrews', in *N T St* 37 (1991), p. 148.

[3] H. Lietzmann, *An die Galater* (J.C.B. Mohr, 1971), pp. 24-6.

[4] G. Ebeling, *Die Wahrheit des Evangeliums* (J.C.B. Mohr, 1981), p. 296.

the Gentiles were in bondage to law, while, in their slavery to the law, the Jews were in bondage to the elements. In other words, his claim seems to be that pre-Christian Gentile religion was demonic, and that it expressed itself in the pressure to conform to certain norms, while the Jewish commitment to the torah had also become a demonic bondage.[1]

The following comments may be made by way of critique of these explanations.

(1) While Lietzmann is undoubtedly correct to hold verses 9 and 10 closely together, recognizing that Paul identifies enslavement to the στοιχεῖα with observance of daily, monthly, seasonal, and annual festivals, and sees a close connection between the στοιχεῖα and law or rules, it seems very unlikely that Paul would deduce from the annual cycle of Jewish feasts, as prescribed by God Himself, a link with astral orbits, or would disparage Judaism as a nature religion subject to spirit powers.

(2) Ebeling's theorizing about the religious situation in Galatia is risky. Lietzmann claims that it must remain an open question whether Paul is simply dealing in an apologetic theory, or whether the Galatians were really involved in a cult of the elements and stars.[2] However, it seems probable that the alleged link between a form of gnostic Judaism and astrology has no basis in fact. Even if it were an element in the Galatian environment, it seems remote from the issues addressed by Paul in this letter.

(3) Schlier's theory, which is the most credible of the three, is based upon the commonly held assumption that Paul sees enslavement to the στοιχεῖα as a characteristic of both Jews and Gentiles in the pre-Christian era 'before the coming of faith' (3:23). Ebeling also expresses this viewpoint when he says that Paul unites the Jewish and Gentile Christians into a 'We', not only as a consequence of the wonder of their uniting by the Holy Spirit, but also in the situation where their separation from each other was sharpest, in their former lives as Jews and Gentiles.[3] However, as I shall argue later, this is not the most likely reading of this passage.

The strength of this interpretation of στοιχεῖα in all three forms is that it attempts to do justice to the fact that Paul is linking the Jewish law with the 'elements' when writing to Gentiles. It is at this point that the alternative interpretation faces its strongest challenge. If στοιχεῖα means law, then how can Paul write as he does in verse 9 to Gentile Christians?

One way of solving this difficulty is to understand Paul to be describing in this passage the religious state before the coming of Christ of the world as a whole. That state can be depicted as one of fear and servitude because

---

[1] H. Schlier, *Die Brief an die Galater* (Vandenhoeck und Ruprecht, 1962), p. 193f [cf. L. Gaston, 'Angels and Gentiles in Early Judaism and in Paul', in *S R* 11 (1982), p. 73f].

[2] Lietzmann, p. 26.

[3] Ebeling, p. 297.

of bondage to religious principles and laws, and is applicable equally to Jews and Gentiles, though each group was enslaved by a different law. For the Gentile Galatians to submit to Jewish law after having been liberated by Christ was, therefore, to return again to a bondage exactly equivalent to that from which they had been emancipated.

However, this does not appear to be a satisfactory reading of the text. The theme of Galatians is (as will be argued later) the law which God revealed to the Jewish people. The word 'law' is not used in a generic sense any more than in Romans, and therefore, if στοιχεῖα does indeed mean the law, it must be restricted specifically to the revealed law of God.[1]

The nature of the Galatians' return to bondage is better represented by those who read the connection between verses 8 and 9 as follows: verse 8 refers to the pre-Christian past of the Gentiles, when they were involved in idolatry, and, in verse 9, Paul is expressing astonishment that those released from such a bondage should now submit to a very different bondage, this time to the law.[2] This means that 'those which by nature are not gods' are not to be equated with the στοιχεῖα.[3] The list of regulations in verse 10 is a set of examples of the sort of things to which the Galatians are now submitting as a matter of alleged religious necessity.[4]

The word πάλιν (again) requires explanation in the light of this interpretation; it may be understood in either of two ways. (1) Its use may be figurative, to underline the height of the Galatians' folly.[5] (2) It may be better translated 'back' or 'on the other hand',[6] indicating that the Galatians are turning back from their true knowledge of God to an alternative which is a bondage, but not necessarily implying that they are turning back to precisely the same bondage as before;[7] if ἐπιστρέφετε is translated 'you turn back' rather than simply 'you turn',[8] and πάλιν is read in close connection with the verb, rather than with the subsequent phrase, 'to the weak and beggarly στοιχεῖα', the possibility of this interpretation is strengthened; moreover, the phrase πάλιν ἄνωθεν should perhaps be connected with 'you wish to be in bondage' rather than with 'to which': this has the effect of making it clear that the Galatian error is a resumption of

---

[1] Against L. Gaston, 'Paul and the Law in Galatians 2-3', in P. Richardson & D. Granskou (eds.), *Anti-Judaism in Early Christianity*. Vol. 1: *Paul and the Gospels* (Wilfrid Laurier University Press, 1986), p. 52.

[2] So, e.g., Calvin, *Galatians,* p. 122; Lightfoot, *Galatians,* p. 170; Belleville, p. 69.

[3] E.D. Burton, *A Critical and Exegetical Commentary on the Epistle to the Galatians* (T. & T. Clark, 1921), p. 517.

[4] Cf. J.D.G. Dunn, 'Echoes of Intra-Jewish Polemic in Paul's Letter to the Galatians', in *JBL* 112 (1993), p. 470.

[5] So Calvin, *Galatians,* p. 123.

[6] Thayer, p. 475.

[7] Cf. Burton, p. 527.

[8] Cf. Thayer, p. 243f.

bondage, but avoids suggesting that their desire is to be enslaved again by the identical bondage.¹

The key to understanding this passage is to pay careful regard to Paul's alternation between the first and second person plural. 'We' does not mean the human race as a whole,² but the Jews, of whom Paul was one, and therefore speaks representatively. 'You' refers to the Gentile Galatian Christians. This means that the passage beginning at 3:23 has four movements. In 3:23-25 Paul points out the function of the law within Jewish life preceding the arrival of the Messiah, which was to lead them through their infancy to maturity in Christ, and the consequent change which His coming has now introduced. In 3:26-29 he ackowledges that the mature sonship into which the coming of Christ has brought Jewish Christians is shared also by Gentile Christians: Jews and Gentiles in the Church form one community in Christ, the (spiritual) descendants of Abraham. In 4:1-5 the Jews are again the theme: the Jews before Christ were enslaved under the στοιχεῖα of the world, just as a minor is 'under guardians and stewards until the time appointed by the father'; when God's appointed time had come, He sent His Son to redeem the Jews from that slavery, which is now further defined as being to the law, and to bring them to maturity as (adult) sons. Then from 4:6 Paul again turns to the Gentiles of Galatia, repeating his earlier statement that they too are adult sons and heirs; the crucial question comes in verse 8f: having been set free from slavery to idols, why do you now simply exchange one slavery for another, as you turn to the στοιχεῖα, the law, from which even the Jews have recently been redeemed?

The second problem faced by the interpretation of στοιχεῖα as the law is the qualifying genitive phrase 'of the world'. In what sense could Paul apply such an epithet to God's inspired revelation? In verse 3, where Paul uses this phrase, he seems, on the whole to be making a positive assessment of the law. It was, indeed, enslaving, but this slavery was purposive, designed to guard the Jews during their religious minority, and to bring them to the Messiah in whom they should find their spiritual adulthood. The only other place in Galatians where the word κόσμος occurs is in 6:14, where Paul affirms that, through the cross of Christ, the believer's intercourse with this world has been terminated, but this tells us nothing about the relationship between the world and the law. The implication of 6:14 is that, even for the devout Jew, pre-Christian life was confined within the boundaries of earthly life; the coming of Christ has resulted in enlarged horizons, and indeed, in a transformed perspective. The law, however, being a factor in the infancy phase of Jewish life, is contained within the

---

¹ Against T. Martin, 'Apostasy to Paganism: The Rhetorical Stasis of the Galatian Controversy', in *J B L* 114 (1995), pp. 441-6.

² Cf. G.W. Hansen, *Galatians* (IVP, 1994), pp. 110, 120.

material world, and lacks the heavenly dimension which Christ has brought. The genitive in 4:3 is probably best interpreted to mean that the στοιχεῖα belong exclusively to this present world.

Enough has been said, I believe, to verify my conclusion that στοιχεῖα in Galatians 4:3 and 9 refers to God's law.

2 The Background to Galatians

The letter to the Churches of Galatia was probably written from Ephesus during Paul's third apostolic tour. This conclusion arises from the view that the North Galatian hypothesis for the recipients of the letter is the more weighty,[1] and that the two visits to the territory implied by Paul's phrase 'at first' (4:13) are those referred to by Luke in Acts 16:6 and 18:23. It seems likely that Luke's description of the apostolic team as 'passing through' the region of Phrygia and Galatia (16:6) implies evangelistic activity rather than mere transit,[2] and thus that the disciples whom they 'strengthened (ἐπιστηρίζων)' on their second visit (18:23) were their own converts from the previous visit some two or three years earlier.[3]

The view that 'Galatia' refers in Acts to the northern territory rather than the Roman province is largely based upon Luke's normal preference for geographical terms,[4] which coheres with the regular use of the term 'Galatians' (cf. Gal. 3:1) to refer to the inhabitants of the original territory. Although Paul's tendency is to use imperial nomenclature,[5] this is by no means an invariable habit.[6]

It is probable that it was on this second visit to North Galatia (Ac. 18:23) that the apostles discovered that false teaching had arisen in the intervening period; the use of ἐπιστηρίζω "presupposes that the Christians who are to be strengthened are under assault and in danger of becoming uncertain or slothful in their faith or walk."[7] Paul is likely, therefore, to have had to contend with his opponents during that visit, and, at the earliest opportunity, possibly on arrival in Ephesus or at some convenient stopping-place *en route*,[8] he writes to the Galatians.

---

[1] So (e.g.) J.G. Machen, *Notes on Galatians* (Presbyterian and Reformed, 1972), p. 208; Kümmel, pp. 296-8; J.C. Beker, *Paul the Apostle* (T. & T. Clark, 1980), p. 41.

[2] So J. Moffatt, *Introduction to the Literature of the New Testament* (Edinburgh: 1911), p. 93.

[3] So Kümmel, p. 296.

[4] Cf (e.g.) D. Guthrie, *Galatians* (Marshall, Morgan and Scott, 1974), p. 17f; *ibid, New Testament Introduction* (IVP, 1970), p. 450f.

[5] Cf (e.g.) W. Hendriksen, *Galatians* (Banner of Truth, 1968), p. 9f; R.H. Gundry, *A Survey of the New Testament* (Paternoster, 1970), p. 262.

[6] Kümmel, p. 297.

[7] G. Harder, 'στηρίζω', in G.Kittel (ed.), Vol. 7, p. 656.

[8] W. Marxsen, *Introduction to the New Testament* (Blackwell, 1968), p. 47.

The major problem with the North Galatian theory is the absence of any mention in the epistle of the Jerusalem decree of Acts 15. It is not necessary to identify Paul's second Jerusalem visit (Gal. 2:1-10) with the famine relief visit of Acts 11:30 and 12:25.[1] It is hard to see how the issue of the law could have arisen as Paul describes it in 2:4 before he had even commenced his apostolic itinerary. Neither is it probable that Galatians 2 refers to a Jerusalem visit much later than Acts 15:[2] this compounds the historical problems. It seems most likely that Galatians 2 is referring to Acts 15.[3] The fact that Acts 15 describes the third Jerusalem visit recorded in Acts is not a serious objection to the historicity of Acts,[4] since the Acts 11-12 visit had nothing to do with theological matters, and may therefore have been passed over by Paul in Galatians 1-2.[5] Galatians 2:1 accords with Acts 15:2, and Galatians 2:4 with Acts 15:1. The differences of detail are no more than might be expected in two independent accounts of the same event, each of which uses different principles of selectivity. The main problem with this identification is posed by the word 'you' in Galatians 2:5, because Paul's first visit to North Galatia (Ac. 16:6) took place after the Jerusalem Conference. However, Paul need not intend to imply in 2:4f that it was into the Churches to which he is now writing that this infiltration took place.[6] Moffatt's claim that 'you' in verse 5 may refer to Gentiles generally as distinct from Jews is dismissed too peremptorily by Guthrie.[7] Alternatively, Paul may mean by 'you' the Galatians specifically, but is discerning in the discussions at Jerusalem, convened to address a particular problem, a significance which transcends that single incident, and which may have relevance to a variety of different, though parallel, situations.[8]

The most likely explanation of the omission of reference to the Jerusalem decree is that from Acts 16:6 Paul begins to break new ground on his second apostolic tour; it was not with reference to the Churches of North

---

[1] So (e.g.) S.J. Mikolaski, 'Galatians', in Guthrie & Motyer (eds), p. 1094; H.D. McDonald, *Freedom in Faith* (Pickering and Inglis, 1973), p. 39; F.F. Bruce, 'Conference in Jerusalem - Galatians 2:1-10', in P.T. O'Brien & D.G. Peterson (eds.), *God Who is Rich in Mercy* (Lancer Books, 1986), p. 209f.

[2] Luther, Vol. 26, p. 79f.

[3] So (e.g.) J. Bligh, *Galatians* (St. Paul Publications, 1969), p. 1; Goulder, pp. 26, 191; P.F. Esler, 'Making and Breaking an Agreement Mediterranean Style: A New Reading of Galatians 2:1-14', in *Bib Interp* 111 (1995), pp. 287, 293.

[4] Against (e.g.) P. Parker, 'Once More, Acts and Galatians', in *J B L* 86 (1967), p. 179f; P.J. Achtemeier, 'An Elusive Unity: Paul, Acts and the Early Church', in *C B Q* 48 (1986), pp. 11-22.

[5] R.A. Cole, *The Epistle of Paul to the Galatians* (IVP, 1965), p. 61.

[6] Against Guthrie, *Galatians,* pp. 11,13, *ibid, Introduction,* p. 456, Goulder, p. 1f.

[7] Guthrie, *Introduction,* p. 456.

[8] Cf. Betz, p. 92.

Galatia that the decree was formulated,[1] as is clear from the terms of address of the decree itself (Ac. 15:23), and, as I shall shortly argue, the divergent teaching at Galatia arose quite independently of the earlier issue. Paul therefore sees the decree as irrelevant to the North Galatian Churches, though discerning the comparability of the situation. He reckons the divine authority which lies behind his gospel a weightier argument against the opponents at Galatia, who were not the same people as the party of Pharisees mentioned in Acts 15:1 and 5.

It is necessary to make a brief comment, in the light of these conclusions, on the place in the chronology of the Antioch incident described in Galatians 2:11ff. I am assuming that it took place after the Jerusalem Conference of Acts 15, and before[2] the Galatian problem had arisen, and that Paul's reference to it here is the only witness to the incident that we have. It is impossible to know either how long after the Conference, or how long before the rise of the Galatian problem, it happened. I take it that Peter, the men who had come from James, and Barnabas, in withdrawing from table-fellowship with Gentile Christians on the grounds that they were uncircumcised, were all acting inconsistently with the decree to which they had already given their assent, and that this accounts to some extent for the vehemence of Paul's response.[3] The rest of the Jews at Antioch were swayed by the inconsistency of their leaders. As to what lay behind the incident we can only speculate. Paul's wording in verse 12 implies that the men who came from James were responsible: perhaps they were some of the party of believing Pharisees and were still finding it hard to accept the conclusion of the Jerusalem Conference. Paul's description of the event need not necessarily be read as implicating James himself.[4] It may be that his moderating influence was restraining the extremists amongst the Jewish Christians at Jerusalem. Now, however, having been sent by James to Antioch on some errand of which we know nothing, his delegates, temporarily outside the scope of his restraining influence, and perhaps for the first time able to see at first hand what the decree really implied in the cities of the Diaspora, begin to baulk and retreat from the position to which they had previously given their assent. From some at Jerusalem, evidently, the decree had received only grudging assent without conviction, and Paul realises at Antioch that he must go on fighting for the true consequences of the principle of justification by faith apart from the works of the law. It is important to emphasize that, as I understand it, there is no historical connection between the Conference of Acts 15 and the Antioch incident on

---

[1] Cf. Machen, p. 219.
[2] Cf. P.F. Esler, *The First Christians in their Social Worlds* (Routledge, 1994), p. 60.
[3] Cf. Lightfoot, *Galatians,* p. 111.
[4] Cf. E.P. Sanders, 'Jewish Association with Gentiles and Galatians 2:11-14', in Fortna & Gaventa (eds.), pp. 170f, 186.

the one hand, and the Galatian situation on the other. The reason for Paul's allusion to Jerusalem and Antioch is only that he can perceive a theological parallel between these earlier events and what is now taking place in Galatia.[1] This will become clear shortly.

There is general agreement that the nature of the Galatian division and the purpose and message of Paul's Epistle are transparent.[2] The source of the problem is less clearcut. It is clear that Paul perceives the Galatians to be in grave danger of apostatizing from the gospel (1:6). This crisis has come about because of the presence within the Church of a group of 'troublers' (1:7; 5:12), apparently with a strong leader-figure (5:10), who are preaching a false Gospel (1:8f), and have bewitched (3:1) and hindered (5:7) the Galatian Christians; some have already been taken in (6:1), though not all as yet - hence the bitter division which has occurred within the fellowship (5:15) - but Paul scents the possibility of a wholesale departure from the truth by the entire Church: he is aware of the pervasive tendency of leaven (5:9). It is not immediately clear whether the troublers are infiltrators or an indigenous group: the reference to 'false brethren secretly brought in' (2:4) is often taken as evidence that the source of the Galatian problem is outside the Church; however, this phrase appears to refer not to the Galatian problem, but to a situation at an earlier date elsewhere (namely in the Churches of Antioch, Iconium, Lystra and Derbe [Ac. 13-14]), which is of relevance because of the similarity of the issues involved. What is clear is that the troublers have questioned Paul's apostolic authority in order to cast doubt upon his message (1:11-24), but, as far as Paul is concerned, their motivation is to build up a personal following (4:17), and to evade the inevitable costliness of true faith (5:11; 6:12).

The message of the troublers evidently centres around circumcision (2:3,7-9; 5:2f,11; 6:12f). This is, however, at least in Paul's view, just the most obvious expression of a total gospel of justification by the works of the law (2:16; 4:10,21; 5:4). Paul's fundamental concern in writing is that the truth of the Gospel might continue amongst the Galatians (2:5), and that they should stand fast in the freedom which Christ has secured, and not impose upon themselves the slavery of a works based religion (5:1), such as they (erroneously, as we shall later see) believed the Old Testament to teach. He shows them that the essence of genuine Christianity is God's new creation in which faith works through love (6:15; 5:6).

That the traditional term 'Judaizers' is an appropriate one to describe such teachers is clear. However, the question of the identity of the Galatian Judaizers is by no means easy to answer. It has normally been understood that these were incoming Jewish Christians, identifiable with, or at least very similar to, the party of believing Pharisees, some of whose members

---

[1] Cf. Esler, *Making*, p. 286.
[2] Cf. D.A. Black, *Paul, Apostle of Weakness* (Peter Lang, 1984), p. 53.

trailed Paul on his first apostolic tour and taught the brethren of Asia Minor that circumcision and obedience to the law of Moses were essential for salvation (Ac. 15:1,5).[1] While it is clear that there are strong points of contact between the two situations, and that the issue is similar, it is not, however, clear that the people involved are to be equated.

While the traditional understanding of the issue at Galatia seems incontrovertible, the traditional identification of Paul's opponents is open to modification at two points. In the first place it is quite possible that a Judaizing party has grown up indigenously within the Churches of Galatia; this could have taken place spontaneously, without any outside influence, perhaps as a result of their own study of the Scriptures. Secondly, it follows from this that the Judaizers at Galatia could have been Gentiles who had come to the conclusion that the Jewish law is binding upon believers.[2] Although both Kümmel[3] and Guthrie[4] dismiss this theory without much consideration, Munck's arguments in its defence are quite compelling.[5] While the resolution of these two issues is not essential to a proper understanding of the Galatian issue, it will become apparent that I am assuming that the Galatian problem is both indigenous and of Gentile origin.

2   Galatians 3:21 and 4:9

Apart from 4:9 the only other place in Galatians where the law is mentioned in conjunction with the vocabulary of weakness or power is 3:21; here Paul, having asked whether the law is against the promises of God, denies that this is so on the grounds that if a law had been given which had the power (δυνάμενος) to give life, then righteousness (which I take to be synonymous with 'justification' in the sense of God's verdict of acquittal[6]) would have been on the basis of the law. Paul, then, sees the law, the rudimentary stage of Jewish religious life as unable to bring life (3:21), and as weak and poor (4:9). But what does he mean in this Epistle by 'law'?

1   The Meaning of 'Law'

It is generally agreed that νόμος generally refers in Galatians to the Mosaic

---

[1] So (e.g.) J.D. Hester, 'The Use and Influence of Rhetoric in Galatians 2:1-14', in *Th Z* 42 (1986), p. 392f.
[2] Cf. J. Munck, *Paul and the Salvation of Mankind* (SCM Press, 1959), p. 132.
[3] Kümmel, p. 299.
[4] Guthrie, *Introduction*, p. 467.
[5] Munck, *Paul*, pp. 87f, 132-4.
[6] So Ridderbos, p. 99, Betz, p. 126, H. Räisänen, 'Galatians 2:16 and Paul's Break with Judaism', in *N T St* 31 (1985), p. 545; against (e.g.) Dunn, *Incident*, p. 40f.

law. This is evident from three factors in Paul's argument. (1) There is the particular emphasis upon circumcision in his response to the Judaizers, which comes to the fore especially in 5:2f. Paul sees circumcision as "the seal of the law",[1] which carried with it the obligation to be ruled in every aspect of life by every detail of the law. (2) The references to the giving of the law 430 years after the Abrahamic covenant (3:17), and the angelic involvement at its delivery (3:19), define the law in view as that conveyed at Sinai. (3) The reference to the birth of Christ 'under law' (4:4) is most likely a statement of his Jewish identity, the law being that which defined Jewish life and marked the parameters of Jewish humanity.

It is sometimes argued that the moral aspects of the law are in the forefront in the Galatian controversy.[2] However, while not denying that the moral law figures in Paul's argument, the centrality given to circumcision, along with the apparent insistence on the part of the Judaizers that the Jewish festivals (4:10) were to be observed, suggest that it was these ceremonial elements in the law which were uppermost in the dispute.

The problem at Galatia was that Gentile Christians had come to the conclusion that it was necessary to live like the Jews, to embrace almost all the prescriptive elements of the Jewish torah, in order to be justified. 'The law', according to the usage of this Epistle, means the total way of life prescribed in the Old Testament; it is the economy introduced at Sinai,[3] which defined, and demarcated the life of the people of God for a period.

It is because of this relevance of the law for a period that Paul sees 'the law' as a definite epoch in the life of the Jewish people.[4] This becomes clear especially in 3:19-25.[5] The epochal status of the law implies that it is a bracketed period within human (and specifically Jewish) history, that the epoch denominated 'the law' is not of unending duration. I shall develop this point later, as it is part of Paul's argument for the weakness of the law. Even where the epochal aspect has disappeared from some of Paul's uses of the word νόμος after 5:4, it still must be referred consistently to the revealed law of God in its prescriptive aspect.[6]

A number of commentators argue very vigorously that 'law' in Galatians must not be restricted to the Jewish law, but that Paul's target is any religion based upon any law, whatever law that may be. It is necessary therefore to consider this interpretation. The main argument used in its support is the fact that νόμος is often employed anarthrously; this is taken as evidence that it refers not to the specific contents of the Mosaic law, but

---

[1] Lightfoot, *Galatians*, p. 203.
[2] Cf. Cole, *Galatians*, p. 157; J.R.W. Stott, *Only One Way* (IVP, 1968), p. 61.
[3] Cf. J. Brown, *Galatians*, pp. 60, 113, 131f.
[4] Cf. Thielman, pp. 59, 65.
[5] Cf. Betz, p. 176, n. 120.
[6] Against J. Brown, *Galatians*, p. 126.

to "the operation of law in general".[1] Some of those who pursue this line of interpretation admit that the law-principle is embodied supremely in the law of Moses, but insist nonetheless that Paul's concern is wider than the Old Testament law merely.[2]

It seems, however, difficult to defend this interpretation: over and above the specific considerations already cited, the overall thrust of the argument in Galatians, couched as it is in confrontation with a Judaizing element within the Gentile Churches, is sufficient to establish that it is the law of God, as revealed in the Hebrew Scriptures, the torah, which is Paul's subject. Furthermore, while Paul would readily have affirmed that the law given as their privilege to the Jews was, in ideal intention at least, applicable to the rest of the world, it is virtually impossible to envisage him, with his Jewish background, allowing that the category 'law' might include more members than the divine revelation in the torah.

The best that can be said for this interpretation is that it represents a legitimate application to other contexts of the principle underlying Paul's words to the Galatians.[3] It is, however, incorrect as an interpretation of the Epistle itself.

Another interpretation which must be considered is that of Burton, who consistently argues that νόμος in Galatians refers to the law understood as a legalistic system without grace, which arises from the detachment of a single element in the divine law from all other aspects of divine revelation. In such detachment, Burton claims, the law actually misrepresents the will of God and his real attitude towards men.[4] Burton goes on to insist that God's actual judgement of men is based on ethical principle.[5] It is hard, however, to sustain a distinction between ethics and law,[6] and Burton's definition of νόμος is in any case inappropriate in the light of Paul's attempt to enable the Gentile Galatians correctly to understand the Old Testament law and its place in God's saving purpose. The meaning of 'law' in Galatians, then, is the torah in its regulative function.

2 The Nature of the Law's Weakness

The statement in 3:21 comes to the heart of Paul's argument about the weakness of the law in this Epistle: his fundamental point is that the law does not have the power to justify, nor to achieve the true life which is the inseparable concomitant of justification. However, Paul does not assert an

---

[1] W.F. Adeney, *Thessalonians and Galatians*, (Caxton, n.d.), p. 286.
[2] So (e.g.) Lightfoot, *Galatians*, pp. 118, 168; Fung, pp. 204, 273.
[3] Cf. Machen, p. 158.
[4] Burton, p. 120, etc.
[5] *Ibid*, p. 452f.
[6] Cf. Machen, p. 156.

unqualified weakness of the law: there are some senses in which he sees the law as possessed of great power.

It used to be taken for granted by Protestant exegetes that integral to Paul's logic is an unstated assumption which must be articulated to clarify his thinking, namely that the law lacks the power to justify because of the power of sin in the lives of those to whom it is directed, the result of which is that there is no-one who keeps the law perfectly. Luther is the archetype of this interpretation: "Anyone who strives to be justified by the Law is trying something that he can never achieve".[1] It is presupposed that, if anyone did in fact obey the law in its entirety, then that person would achieve justification on the basis of the law. However, this is not possible because of sin. This interpretation goes hand-in-hand with an understanding of the power of the law as its function of bringing conviction to the sinner, so impelling him to turn to Christ for a righteousness independent of works of law: the law "was given to cause death and to increase sin, namely, in order that through the Law a man might recognize how sorely he needs the grace of the promise".[2] The weakness of the law is therefore tantamount to the power of sin in human life. This means that the weakness of the law is not intrinsic to the law itself, but is a derivative of the moral weakness of sinful humanity.

However, this explanation of Galatians misses the point. For Paul, the law can be described as weak in respect of justification simply because it was not given by God for the purpose of justification, but rather as an interim provision pointing forward to the Christ, in whom justification would become a reality. To seek justification by the law, therefore, as the Galatians were mistakenly trying to do, is to attempt to direct the law towards an end for which it is essentially unsuited by the purpose of God. The implication of the traditional interpretation is that the law did have the power to give life, but that the moral weakness of human beings made it impossible for them to exploit this life-giving power. Paul says the opposite in 3:21: the law itself had no power to give life. Moreover, the power which the law did possess according to Galatians is not its ability to convict of sin, but its epochal purpose as a pointer to Christ designed to keep God's people hoping for His coming.

The two references to the law as weak occur in the course of a passage which runs from 3:19 to 4:10, beginning with a question, 'Why then the law?', which demands an answer highlighting the law's purpose.[3] The notion of purpose presupposes at least relative power; this passage, with its two references to the weakness of the law, is crucial, therefore, as indicating that this weakness is not absolute.

---

[1] Luther, Vol. 26, p. 406.
[2] *Ibid*, Vol. 27, p. 273.
[3] So Ridderbos, p. 137, n. 15; against Lightfoot, *Galatians,* p. 144, Betz, p. 162.

Before considering this passage in detail it would be well to lay the foundations by examining two verses from the section 2:16-21, in which the word νόμος is used for the first time. This passage is introductory to the whole argument. In it Paul refers to another situation in a different place, which had points of resemblance to the Galatian problem. The address specifically to the Galatian situation begins at 3:1. Our present concern is with verses 16 and 21, in which Paul gives a preliminary indication of the weakness of the law, and expounds the Jewish faith as having always taught that justification is on the basis of the grace of God, and was to be secured by the Messiah. This understanding underlies the whole of the rest of the Epistle.

The fact that justification is not through the law is stated in 2:16: "a man is not justified by the works of the law, but rather[1] through faith in Jesus Christ". This is promptly twice repeated with minor variations. At this point Paul is making a bald assertion of a fact: justification is not by works of the law. Whether it conceivably could be is not here discussed: weakness terminology is not present as yet.[2]

Moreover, in conjunction with the previous verse, Paul's contention is that he and his fellow 'Jews by nature' know that this is so. This raises two questions: how is this known, and what is the range of Jews included in the assertion? The use of φύσει (by nature) suggests that Paul is not thinking only of Jewish Christians. The implication of verse 15f seems to be that the fact that justification is not by the works of the law is a truth known by all Jews (and taught them from birth upwards), and not only by those who have become Christians.[3] It is true that some sects within Judaism at the beginning of the Christian era, particularly the Pharisees, according to Paul's own testimony (Philip. 3:4-9), had fallen into a legalistic form of religion. However, in Galatians, unlike Romans, Paul does not construct his argument in opposition to a Jewish distortion of authentic Biblical faith: here he is at pains to bring his Gentile readers to the correct understanding of the Hebrew Bible.

The context for these words is the dispute between Paul and the Jews at Antioch over circumcision: in the background is the issue raised in Acts 15:1,5, and answered in Acts 15:11. Paul appeals to the strict Jewish believers on the basis of something which they know by virtue of being Jews. His point, then, is that the Old Testament Scriptures have always taught justification by faith,[4] that the Christian Gospel is not a novelty,

---

[1] So (e.g.) J. Ziesler, *The Epistle to the Galatians* (Epworth, 1992), p. 24.
[2] Against (e.g.) J. Brown, *Galatians*, p. 36, Cole, *Galatians*, p. 79, Stott, p. 62.
[3] So J.D.G. Dunn, *Jesus, Paul and the Law* (SPCK, 1990), p. 190; against Räisänen, *Torah*, p. 175.
[4] So Dunn, *Romans*, p. 76; cf. F. Holmgren, *The God Who Cares* (John Knox Press, 1979), pp. 15, 32, 34, 131, etc; H. Maccoby, *Cambridge Commentaries on Writings of*

discontinuous with Jewish faith. The fact that it is said that the Jews by nature know that justification is by faith specifically in Jesus Christ is not an insuperable problem for this interpretation, since Paul understood the Messianic hope to be integral to his ancestral faith,[1] and would have regarded the Old Testament believers as justified through faith in the Christ whom they anticipated, albeit that they could not yet identify Him by the name of Jesus.

This major emphasis in Paul's teaching on the law's weakness becomes apparent again in 2:21. The direction of his argument is in fact the reverse of that which we should expect if the weakness of the law were primarily associated with the moral inability of sinful humanity. He reasons that the doctrine of justification through the law would imply that Christ's death had been unnecessary, superfluous, pointless (δωρεὰν), and the implication of the earlier part of the verse is that to teach righteousness through the law would entail the setting aside of God's grace, and so the giving to God Himself an insulting rebuff.

Paul's argument is that if justification is through the law, then Christ died δωρεὰν. There is a tendency on the part of some commentators to import into this verse the assumption that Paul means that if it were possible for man that righteousness should be by the law, then Christ's death would obviously be unnecessary; the reason why Christ's death was not in vain is that it is not within the power of sinful man to achieve his own justification.[2]

This is, however, to reverse the direction of Paul's logic; his argument is rather that the necessity that the law fails as a method of justification rests on the fact that Christ has died.[3] To import the idea of weakness misses the point. Paul's starting-point is not the weakness of the law, nor the weakness of sinful man, but rather the historical fact of the cross of Christ, which is the supreme demonstration and ultimate locus of the saving grace of God,

---

the Jewish and Christian World 200 BC to AD 200, Vol. 3: *Early Rabbinic Writings* (Cambridge University Press, 1988), p. 205f; D. Cohn-Sherbok, *On Earth as it is in Heaven* (Orbis, 1987), p. 21.

[1] Cf. F.F. Bruce, *Second Thoughts on the Dead Sea Scrolls* (Paternoster, 1956), pp. 76-84; G. Vermes, *The Dead Sea Scrolls in English* (Penguin, 1962), pp. 47-51, 254-7; J.A. Fitzmyer, *Responses to 101 Questions on the Dead Sea Scrolls* (Geoffrey Chapman, 1992), pp. 53-6; J. Klausner, *The Messianic Idea in Israel* (George Allen and Unwin, 1956), pp. 25, 27; L. Jacobs, *A Jewish Theology* (Darton, Longman and Todd, 1973), p. 292; R. Patai, *The Messiah Texts* (Wayne State University Press, 1979), p. xxi; W.S. Green, 'Messiah in Judaism: Rethinking the Question', in J. Neusner, W.S. Green & E.S. Ferichs (eds.), *Judaisms and Their Messiahs at the Turn of the Christian Era* (Cambridge University Press, 1987), *passim*.

[2] Guthrie, *Galatians*, p. 91; cf. J.A.D. Weima, 'Gal 6:11-18: A Hermeneutical Key to the Galatian Letter', in *Cal Th J* 28 (1993), p. 100.

[3] So F.F. Bruce, *Galatians*, p. 147.

so much so that grace and the cross are, in effect, absolutely identified.[1] The question therefore arises how it is that Paul finds in the fact of the crucifixion the evidence that righteousness is not by the law. Guthrie argues that Paul's assumption is that since the cross is a fact there must have been a definite purpose behind it.[2] This, however, reduces Paul's argument to a matter of historical logic, whereas his reasoning is more profoundly Scriptural than that. Bruce finds it sufficient to say that Paul's conclusion that the cross was not in vain was the result of the revelation of Christ which he received on the Damascus Road.[3] While it is certainly true that it was this personal experience which convinced Paul that the grace of God "is to be found definitively in Jesus Christ and in His death",[4] there is more to it than that.

The fact is that, having made the equation between the cross of Christ and the grace of God, Paul was left with no option on purely Biblical grounds but to say that to teach justification through the law is to empty the cross of any purpose. Behind Paul's explicit words lies the implicit assumption that justification is by the grace of God. This is something which, Paul believes (cf. v.15), is known by all Jews, because it is taught in their Scriptures. The doctrine of justification through the law is a snub to God and a rejection of His grace because it flies in the face of His own revelation in the Old Testament. The doctrine of justification through the law inevitably involves setting aside the grace of God, since it contradicts the Hebrew Scriptures, and, inasmuch as that grace has now been enacted in the historical fact of the cross, to set aside God's grace is also to nullify the cross.[5] Here again, Paul is not using the vocabulary of weakness: he is arguing against justification by the works of the law on the simple basis that it is not what the Old Testament teaches. If my reconstruction of the Galatian situation is correct, then it is clearly important that Paul should make an authoritative correction of the misreading of the Old Testament by the Gentile Christians.

This, then, is Paul's preliminary indication of what he means by 'the weakness of the law': it does not have the power to justify because it was never intended by God to serve that purpose: justification has always been by faith in Christ. The law is weak in respect of justification, because justification by faith is the only way of life ever revealed by God, even in the Old Testament.

With this foundation laid, we may now return to the question about the

---

[1] Cf. J. Lambrecht, 'Transgressor by Nullifying God's Grace: A Study of Gal 2:18-21', in *Biblica* 72 (1991), p. 228.
[2] Guthrie, *Galatians*, p. 91.
[3] F.F. Bruce, *Galatians*, p. 147.
[4] Ziesler, *Galatians*, p. 23.
[5] Cf. Lambrecht, p. 228.

purpose of the law in 3:19. The reply reads: "it was added (προσετέθε) because of transgressions, till (ἄχρις οὗ) the Seed should come to whom the promise was made."

The definition of the power of the law depends upon the sense in which the law was added 'because of transgressions'. It must be borne in mind that, throughout this section, Paul is assuming an integrated and epochal view of the law, and it is arguable that the ceremonial aspects of the law are uppermost in his thinking here.[1]

The assumption is often made that Paul is thinking of the function of the law which he expounds in Romans to bring undefined sin to clarity as transgression, to provoke sin, and so to bring the sinner to self-awareness as a transgressor against its own demands. It is doubtful, however, whether this is Paul's meaning here.[2] An alternative interpretation which some have offered understands him to be saying that the law was given to inhibit and restrain transgressions. Ziesler prefers this interpretation because, he argues, it fits better with the following verses, particularly verse 23f.[3] It is, however, debatable whether these verses are referring to such a restraining guardianship: Paul's subject is justification, and it is in the light of that theme that verse 23f must be interpreted.

Some writers try to incorporate both meanings, but Hendriksen appears right to argue that verse 24 'refutes' this alternative interpretation.[4] Moreover, both explanations depend upon a too restrictedly moral understanding of the law. I would therefore reject both.

It is to be noted that this reference to the law's purpose, which implies its power, is sandwiched between two further hints of its weakness. The verb προσετέθε implies that the law is something additional and subsidiary, while the clause beginning ἄχρις οὗ sets a time limit for the powerful purpose of the law which is in view. With the coming of the Seed (identified in verse 16 as the Christ) the law has served its purpose in this respect.

I have already described the law as viewed by Paul in this Epistle, as 'a parenthetic epoch'. Verse 19 makes clear that this is how he views the law in connection with the theme of justification. Since this verse is connected with the passage immediately preceding, it would be well to examine verses 15-18. The parenthetic nature of the law is apparent also in this section, particularly in verse 17, which contains what is arguably the crucial statement in the whole Epistle for understanding the weakness of the law as regards justification.

---

[1] Cf. Bligh, p. 292.
[2] D.J. Lull, 'The Law was our Pedagogue: A Study in Galatians 3:19-25', in *J B L* 105 (1986), p. 481.
[3] Ziesler, *Galatians*, p. 47.
[4] Hendriksen, *Galatians*, p. 140, n. 101.

In this passage the word 'covenant' (διαθήκη) is introduced, Paul's point being that, even in human relationships, a covenant, once confirmed (κεκυρωμένην), can be neither annulled nor supplemented. Verse 16 points out that the promises were made to Abraham and his seed (τῷ σπέρματι). From the singular number, Paul deduces that the true fulfilment of the promises is found in the single Person, Christ. Now comes the crucial sentence: the law, which came in 430 years later, does not 'disconfirm' (ἀκυροῖ) the covenant previously confirmed (προκεκυρωμένην) by God towards Christ so that the promise becomes inoperative. In verse 18 Paul concludes that if the inheritance were on the basis of the law, it would no longer be on the basis of the promise; however, God gave the inheritance to Abraham on the basis of the promise.

The argument here depends upon his understanding of the order of events[1] as an authentic expression of God's intentions in His dealings with His people. There are five points which must be made.

(1) The covenant is fundamental to all God's relating to human beings. It was first declared to Abraham. The temporal priority of the covenant to the law is a symbol of the theological primacy of the covenant over the law.

(2) Having confirmed the covenant and made the promises of which it is composed, neither God nor anyone else will either cancel or supplement the covenant. Paul takes it for granted that God is faithful to His Word; hence subsequent events, such as the giving of the law, must be interpreted within the framework already laid down by the establishment of the covenant: they are not a basis for redefining the framework. The covenant "is made for ever unalterable."[2]

(3) The nature of the covenant is grace. In using the verb κεχάρισται [gave] (v. 18), Paul is assuming that God justifies solely on the basis of His grace, and that the law does not enter into consideration as long as justification, and the fundamental relationship between God and His people, is the subject. The concept 'promise' implies the category 'gift'.[3] Paul understands the doctrine of justification on the basis of grace alone to be the teaching of the Old Testament when accurately understood.

(4) The covenant comes to fulfilment in Christ, because it was originally given to Christ: He is the One who receives the inheritance. Verse 16 does not teach that the covenant with Abraham is superseded by the coming of Christ. Rather, the coming of Christ is the outworking of the covenant with Abraham. Whereas the writer to the Hebrews, as we shall see, distinguishes between the 'old covenant' (by which he means the law) and the 'new covenant', Paul at this point reserves the term 'covenant' for the overarching purpose of God, within which the law amounted to a

---

[1] Cf. Mikolaski, p. 1098.
[2] Adeney, *Thessalonians*, p. 299.
[3] Cf. Betz, p. 160, n. 62.

parenthetic epoch. There is only one covenant of grace: God's method of dealing with His people has always been the same. Whereas a Jew who shared Paul's interpretation of the Bible would have been in total agreement with the first three of the points which I have drawn from Paul's teaching in this passage, the apostle is now breaking new ground from the perspective of Christian faith, in tying the covenant explicitly into Jesus confessed as the Christ. He would no doubt have insisted that even authentic Jewish religion looked forward to the complete realisation of the covenant in the coming of the Christ;[1] to identify Him with Jesus of Nazareth requires Christian commitment. If the longer text of verse 17 is accepted, it means that Paul, in common with authentic Jewish faith, understands that the original confirmation of the covenant was in the Christ, that from the beginning God's grace was located in Him, albeit that many of Paul's Jewish contemporaries have been blind to the fulfilment of their own Messianic hope in Jesus.

(5) It is now possible to spell out the significance of this crucial passage for our subject: the weakness of the law in respect of justification has to do with the place of the law in the divine economy of salvation. Justification through faith is linked inextricably to the grace of God which is declared in the promises of the covenant. The law came in some centuries later, well after the covenant principle of justification through faith by grace had been irreversibly established. The weakness of the law in terms of justification is simply that justification is something with which the law has never had anything to do.[2]

The epoch of law, then, so far as Paul is concerned, is bracketed within the overarching covenant of God which spans the whole of history; within the brackets the law has a powerful role to play, and yet the brackets determine its basic weakness in relation to the justifying grace of the covenant.

The words 'because of transgressions' are Paul's explanation of the reason for this bracketed epoch. The necessity for the law derived from the fact of transgression,[3] in the sense that the law provided provisional atonement for the transgressions of the Jews before Christ, pending His coming in the fullness of time (4:4). The epoch of the law did not itself carry justifying power; within the brackets of its limited epoch, however,

---

[1] Cf. B.A. Demarest, 'sperma', in C. Brown (ed.), Vol. 3, p. 522; J.D.G. Dunn, *New Testament Theology: The Theology of Paul's Letter to the Galatians* (Cambridge University Press, 1993), p. 123.

[2] Cf. A. Barnes, *II Corinthians and Galatians* (Blackie, 1868), p. 339; T.D. Gordon, 'The Problem at Galatia', in *Interp* 41 (1987), p. 41; C.H. Cosgrove, 'Arguing like a Mere Human Being: Galatians 3:15-18 in Rhetorical Perspective', in *N T St* 34 (1988), pp. 539, 541, 549.

[3] Cf. Lull, pp. 483, 487f.

the power which it did possess was that of pointing the people forward and so stimulating hope for the coming of the Messiah, who would enact the ultimate atonement of the cross, so securing their justification with finality.[1] Dunn is therefore close to the truth in interpreting 'because of transgressions' as "to provide through its sacrificial system a means of atoning for transgressions"; however, when he sees this as intended to facilitate daily living within the covenant[2] he surely misses the point: he overlooks the provisionality of the law and its role as anticipatory of Christ.

In this connection it is instructive to note that Paul has already (in 2:19) given a cryptic preview of his understanding of the power of the law. He speaks representatively (ἐγώ) for the Jew who has recognized Jesus to be the Christ,[3] noting that 'through the law' he has 'died to the law'. This appears to mean that the Jewish Christian has died to the law as a stimulator to hope, because the hope is fulfilled: Christ has come. To continue to use circumcision as a dividing line between Jews and 'sinners' amounts to a denial of the fulfilment of the Jewish hope in Christ. This death to the epoch of the law in its hope-stimulating function has come about through the law itself, since it was the law which pointed forward to the Christ, who is its termination.[4]

Nevertheless, lest any of his Galatian readers have still not grasped the point, Paul puts the question even more strongly in 3:20f, in a form which may be in their minds, particularly in view of their commitment to the doctrine of the unity of God: does the fact that the law was only an interim measure mean that the covenant and the law are in fact in fundamental conflict? Are they diametrically opposed to each other? Was the law, as an epoch, at odds with the covenant which spans the history of the world? And therefore, has the one God involved Himself inextricably in a contradiction? This is, in effect, the question which opens verse 21.

After an emphatic denial, Paul begins his explanation of how it is that the law is not opposed to the promises by making the statement which forms one of our key texts: "If there had been a law given which could have offered life, truly righteousness would have been by the law"; he then points out that the Scripture has confined everything under sin in order that (ἵνα) the promise may be given (δοθῇ) through faith in Jesus Christ to those who believe (3:21f).

This reply is, as Calvin notes, indirect,[5] and does not state baldly how the covenant and the law are in harmony. The two parts of Paul's answer taken

---

[1] Cf. J. Brown, *Galatians*, p. 61f.
[2] Dunn, *Galatians*, p. 89.
[3] Cf. F.F. Bruce, *Galatians*, p. 142.
[4] See H.A.W. Meyer, *Handbook to the Epistle to the Galatians* (T. & T. Clark, 1880), p. 123; Bligh, pp. 210-2.
[5] Calvin, *Galatians*, p. 104f.

together amount to the declaration, fundamental to the theology of Galatians, that the law was not given for the purpose of justification, that justification is the province of the covenant, and therefore that there can be no opposition between two phenomena whose roles and intentions are different. Only if the two had been aiming at the same goal would there have been scope for conflict.[1] The first part of the answer takes the form of a 'contrary-to-fact hypothesis',[2] in which Paul admits that justification would indeed have been on the basis of the law if a law with life-giving power had been given. There seems to be little point in enquiring as to what sort of law this would have been. Paul's only point is that there is no such law.[3] The second part of his answer states the reason why there is no such law. It is not, as some commentators assume, because of the sinfulness of those to whom the law is given, which renders them incapable of fulfilling its demands, so that, by derivation, the law becomes powerless to justify them.[4] Paul says that the weakness pertains to the law, not to the recipients of the law. What verse 22 offers is an answer from Scripture: as usual, Paul's argument is based on what is known to be true by those Jews who truly understand the Old Testament. Again, it is important to notice that the point is not, as some would suggest, that justification by faith is on offer because of the moral inability of humanity in respect of the law, that the promise of justification through faith is an alternative to the failed possibility of justification by the works of the law.[5] The only method of justification which God ever revealed is through faith; there is no alternative to the promise of justification through faith, since that is the only way of life that God has ever provided. However, the ἵνα clause affirms that the reason why Scripture has declared[6] universal sinfulness is not with a view to the promise being by faith, but in order that the promise, which is in any case, in its very nature, by faith, may actually be given (δοθῇ). The promise is there, it stands, established in God's grace, but the actual giving of the promised benefit is tied to the instrumentality of faith:[7] the judgement pronounced in Scripture, that all things are confined under sin, enables the bare promise actually to be received in its character as gift, because it demonstrates to sinners how dependent they are upon a salvation of such a character, and so moves the sinner to embrace the promise which is based

---

[1] So *ibid*, p. 105.
[2] So (e.g.) Burton, p. 194; Fung, p. 163; Hansen, p. 104.
[3] Cf. Luther, Vol. 26, p. 330.
[4] Cf. (e.g.) J. Brown, *Galatians*, p. 67; Stott, p. 91; Ridderbos, p. 141; Fung, p. 165f.
[5] Against F.F. Bruce, *Galatians*, p. 180.
[6] Cf. Thayer, p. 593; E.F. Kevan, *The Law of God in Christian Experience* (Pickering and Inglis, 1955), pp. 13, 51.
[7] So Fung, p. 165, n. 72; against G. Howard, *Paul: Crisis in Galatia* (Cambridge University Press, 1979), p. 57f.

on grace. The promise stands independently of the law, but the promised blessing would for ever remain 'ungiven', unless, through the declaration of Scripture, sinners were brought to perceive the hopelessness of any other mistakenly postulated way of justification: without that declaration they would not reach out in faith.

I do not agree with those commentators who take 'the Scripture' to be synonymous here with 'the law'.[1] While the whole Old Testament can indeed be described as the torah, it is significant in the present context that, when Paul wants to highlight the declaration and exposure of sin in the Word of God, the noun which he chooses is not νόμος, since this is not the purpose of the law which is to the fore in this passage. In verse 22 Paul is making a similar point to the emphasis in Romans on the role of the law in the sphere of the flesh; he is affirming that part of the reason why God has spoken His Word is to bring sinners to self-awareness as such. However, given that the main need in Galatians is to portray the law in its role as the stimulator of hope for the coming of Christ, it is important that Paul avoids confusing the issue by speaking of the law in the role of sin-definer, even though we know from his other writings that he might have done so. He realises that the Gentiles of Galatia need to understand the temporary place of the law in the history of the covenant God: it is a proper view of the law as hope-stimulator towards Christ which will help them to abandon their false hope for justification from the law, and lead them to renew their hope in Christ alone. He therefore chooses the term 'the Scripture' when sin-definition is the subject. Paul's avoidance of the word νόμος in verse 22 therefore adds further weight to my argument that sin-definition and exposure is not the meaning of 'because of transgressions' in verse 19.

That this understanding of the powerful purpose of the law as hope-stimulation is correct is borne out by how Paul continues in the next two verses. They concern the time before the coming of this faith (πρὸ τοῦ δὲ ἐλθεῖν τὴν πίστιν), the article having demonstrative force, referring back to the faith mentioned in verse 22, that which finds its object in Jesus Christ.[2] Paul is not implying that faith only came with Christ; that would be quite at odds with his view of Old Testament religion:[3] the word 'faith' is used with objective force, the time note serving to emphasize the fact that Paul is talking here about the law and faith as successive epochs.[4]

The two verses are in clear parallel: 'we were kept unger guard by the law' (v. 23) is the counterpart of 'the law was our tutor [παιδαγωγὸς]' (v. 24). Each of these phrases is followed by an εἰς clause: 'εἰς the faith which

---

[1] E.g. Calvin, *Galatians,* p. 105; Ziesler, *Galatians,* p. 48; Lull, p. 487; E.P. Sanders, *Paul,* pp. 41, 92; *ibid, Paul, the Law,* p. 66.
[2] So (e.g.) Burton, p. 198; Hendriksen, *Galatians,* p. 145, n. 105; Fung, p. 168, n. 6.
[3] So Calvin, *Galatians,* p. 107.
[4] Cf. Burton, p. 200, Fung, p. 169.

would afterwards be revealed' (v. 23), and 'εἰς Christ, that we might be justified by faith' (v. 24).

The first half of each verse is making a statement about the power of the law. Verse 23 depicts the law as a confining power and verse 24 as a disciplining power. The law is often compared by commentators to an imprisoning force,[1] and the echo of verse 22 in the word συγκλειόμενοι is taken to mean that the power of the law is closely associated with the power of sin, and that the phrases 'under sin' and 'under law' are alternative modes of expression for the same experience. The connotation of cruelty associated with the παιδαγωγός in the literature of the day is seen as evidence that Paul intends to portray the law as a harsh, oppressive regime.[2]

This does not seem to me to be correct. The repetition of συγκλείω is better taken as merely verbal, because whereas verse 22 is referring to the declaration by Scripture of confinement under a tyrannical power - sin, the power of the law in verse 23f is a beneficial one.[3] Paul does not appear to intend the verb φρουρέω (to guard) to be read negatively as implying imprisonment, and the alleged severity of the typical Greek παιδαγωγός seems not germane to the discussion, nor necessarily historically true.[4]

The theme of confinement is taken up again in the opening verses of chapter 4 in the picture of slavery, and it is this contextual evidence which must be used to throw light on Paul's meaning in 3:23f. It is important to stress that these verses, like 4:1-5, are concerned with the Jews. Paul is talking about a slavery peculiar to the people of God, and specific to the pre-Christian era, when they were akin to children in their religious life. Moreover, it must be observed that his discussion proceeds from the assumption only that the situation of a child in the home is rather like that of a slave, because of his position under guardians and stewards (4:1f).[5] The statement that the child 'does not differ at all from a slave' is obviously not true absolutely, and it cannot be held that Paul was under any illusion about that: the fact that he immediately describes the child as 'lord of all' proves that he was aware of the vast difference in reality between the slave and the child. The reference in 4:3, therefore, to slavery under τα στοιχεῖα - the law - must be read in the light of this comparison: whatever may have been the position of the Gentile world, Paul's point is that the Jews before Christ were children in the family home, but yet their status was a bit like that of a slave: they were under what might be termed a 'quasi-slavery'. However, it

---

[1] E.g. C.K. Barrett, *Freedom and Obligation* (SPCK, 1985), p. 35.
[2] So (e.g.) Ridderbos, pp. 143-6; Hendriksen, *Galatians,* pp. 145,148.
[3] As Calvin, *Galatians,* p. 107, rightly sees.
[4] Cf. N.H. Young, 'Paidagogos: the Social Setting of a Pauline Metaphor', in *Nov Test* 29 (1987), pp. 165-8.
[5] Cf. G. Braumann & C. Brown, 'Child, Boy, Servant, Son, Adoption' in C. Brown (ed.), Vol. 1, pp. 280, 283.

is obvious that the confinement of the child and his subjection to the guardianship of the παιδαγωγός was not tyrannical nor hostile: it cannot fairly be described as imprisonment, for it was for specific beneficial purposes, and for a limited time only, until the child attained to maturity and to freedom from the oversight of parental delegates.[1]

This leads on to the second part of each of the verses 23 and 24: the word εἰς must, in the light of the foregoing comments be read as both temporal and purposive.[2] Paul's point is that the Jews were subjected by God, the Father of their race, to the oversight of the epoch of the law, only until, and with a view to, the coming of Christ, in whom the faith which had always been their privilege would find its ultimate focus.

It is necessary, therefore, to ask more specifically what the power of the law is in this scheme of things. What is the nature of its confining and disciplining power implied in the two images used in verse 23f?

It is sometimes assumed that Paul is talking of moral restraint.[3] However, given the pervading theme of justification by faith, and the Person of Christ as the fulfilment of the Jews' justifying faith, it seems unlikely that this is the point. These verses rather confirm that the interpretation of 'because of transgressions' offered above is correct: Paul is portraying the epoch of the law (an economy focussed in sacrifice), as a pointer to the fulfilment of the promise on which the Jewish people staked their hope, the various elements included in the provisions of that epoch being designed to stir up longing, to stimulate hope, for the coming of the Messiah, in whom their justification by God's grace revealed in their Scriptures as the only way of justification available in the purpose of God would be finally secured by a conclusive historical atonement. The law therefore, was a power which confined the people of Israel to Him; it was a "protective custody",[4] reserving and preserving the people of God for His coming. The emphasis is not so much restriction FROM, as restriction FOR or UNTO.

This suggests that, when Paul speaks in 4:1-3 of the quasi-slavery of the Jews under the law, during the childhood era of their religious life, he is not thinking primarily of their subjective experience. They were akin to slaves because of the objective incompleteness of their justified standing before God until its securing by the Messiah. Only His cross could finally acquit the Jews of their guilt and complete their justification. Nevertheless, there is a subjective side to these objective realities: the incompleteness of the epoch of the law was designed to stimulate hope by stirring up in the people the longing for the Christ by enabling them powerfully to feel the

---

[1] Cf. T.D. Gordon, 'A Note on the Paidagogos in Galatians 3:24-25', in *N T St* 35 (1989), p. 153.
[2] So Ridderbos, p. 144.
[3] Cf. Ziesler, *Galatians,* p. 47; Lull, p. 482.
[4] Cole, *Galatians,* p. 107; cf. Hays, p. 114.

incompleteness of their present situation. The disciplinary nature of the law was its power to keep the Jewish hope on course towards the Messiah. The epoch of law was thus a parenthesis within the overarching framework of the history of God's grace received through faith, an epoch intended to preserve faith until the fullness of faith should be revealed, to be a signpost sending the people of God to this faith in Christ in whom alone their justification was secured.

This powerful role of the law in Jewish life for a particular epoch, reached its goal, and therefore came to its conclusion "when the fullness of the time had come" (4:4), when the Jewish hope was realised in the sending by God of His Son. In the next verse (4:5) Paul defines the twofold purpose of His coming in true humanity as a member of the Jewish race. The first purpose of His coming was to redeem those who were under the law. This verse echoes 3:13, and must be read in the light of that earlier statement, which indicates that the redemption was from the curse of the law.[1]

It would be well at this point to examine that earlier passage which culminates in the statement of 3:13. Although the chronological schema, in which the law and the faith are treated as successive epochs, comes to clarity only gradually, it does appear to be implicit from the beginning of chapter 3. In verses 2 and 5 Paul reminds his readers that the channel for their own reception of the Spirit and His accompanying powers, subjective experiences associated with their objective justification before God,[2] was not the law, but the faith which they heard. The parallelism between the two phrases ἐξ ἔργων νόμου and ἐξ ἀκοῆς πίστεως (vv. 2,5) suggests that πίστις (faith) is best here given an objective sense (cf. 3:23,25);[3] it is likely that this meaning is present throughout this passage. 'Hearing' is then the response to the faith, and corresponds to 'works' as the response to the law. The faith consists in the preaching of Christ crucified (v. 1). The word πίστις is therefore being employed differently from its use in 2:16, where its juxtaposition with the verb πιστεύω clearly gives it a subjective sense. There is, however, a vital connection between the two uses: it is because justification is secured in the epoch of faith (objective) that justification is by faith (subjective), whether in anticipation during the Jewish dispensation, or by virtue of the fulfilment in Christ.

Paul's main emphasis in this passage is that the Galatians' reception of the Spirit (v. 2) corresponds to God's supply (v. 5). The point is not that the law is weak because of the weakness of sinful man, but that, as a matter of fact, God's chosen and revealed way of dealing with His people is on the

---

[1] Against Cole, *Galatians,* p.116.

[2] Cf. S.K. Williams, 'Justification and the Spirit in Galatians', in *J St N T* 29 (1987), p. 97f.

[3] So Calvin, *Galatians,* p. 81; against (e.g.) Hong In-Gyu, 'Does Paul Misrepresent the Jewish Law? Law and Covenant in Gal. 3:1-14', in *Nov Test* 36 (1994), p. 171.

basis of His own nature as one who freely supplies, that is, as the God of grace. That grace has now reached its conclusive enactment in Christ crucified. The law is simply not God's method for endowing His people with His Spirit at the time of their justification.

At this stage Paul begins to underscore the Biblical theology which he has been expounding by the use of direct Biblical quotations. The word νόμος reappears at verse 10, where Paul argues that to be of the works of the law (ἐξ ἔργων νόμου εἰσίν) is to come under the curse which the law pronounces against all who do not continue in all the things which the law requires to be done. The Biblical support for this is found in Deuteronomy 27:26.

It is usually claimed that to make sense of Galatians 3:10 it is necessary to assume that "a middle term has been omitted."[1] This middle term is that as a matter of fact no-one has ever perfectly kept the law, and that "this argument of Paul would not stand, if we had sufficient strength to fulfil the law."[2]

However, such an interpretation, while certainly *prima facie* defensible, and while possibly consonant with Paul's teaching elsewhere, would not seem to fit with the argument which he is pursuing in this particular Epistle.[3] In the interests of internal consistency, therefore, it is necessary to enquire whether another interpretation is possible. Bruce points out that there is an alternative interpretation which maintains that Paul is arguing that the curse falls on all who seek justification by the works of the law, even if they happen to achieve full marks.[4] This is closer to the truth. However, even this explanation misses Paul's main point, and cannot do justice to verse 13.

If verse 10 is read in its context it becomes apparent how it fits into the apostle's reasoning. The textual underlining of his Biblical theology begins in verse 6 where he quotes Genesis 15:6 to demonstrate that the doctrine of justification by faith is at least as ancient as Abraham. Verse 7 follows as a deduction from verse 6, and makes the point that it is those who find the definition of their being in the faith (οἱ ἐκ πίστεως) who are the true descendants of Abraham, and not, as the Galatians wrongly thought, those who do the works of the ceremonial law. It is worth emphasizing four aspects of this interpretation of verse 7. (1) The present tense is important: Paul is inferring from that which was true of Abraham, something which is true now, that is, since the coming of Christ. (2) The word 'faith' is still to

---

[1] Ziesler, *Galatians*, p. 36.
[2] Calvin, *Galatians,* p. 89; cf. B. Lindars, *New Testament Apologetic* (SCM Press, 1961), p. 229; H.J. Schoeps, *Paul* (Westminster Press, 1961), p. 176f; J.B. Tyson, '"Works of Law" in Galatians', in *J B L* 92 (1973), p. 428.
[3] Cf. Dunn, *Works*, p. 534.
[4] F.F. Bruce, *Galatians,* p. 160f.

be understood objectively. (3) This verse is a direct argument against the Galatians' pursuit of the works of the law, designed to correct their understanding of the way of justification now, in the light of the ancient revelation of justification by faith. (4) Underlying this verse is the view of the law, which Paul will shortly expound in detail, as an interim epoch, incomplete in itself, but set within the overarching framework of the justifying grace of God's covenant as a pointer to the coming of Christ, in whom that justifying grace would attain its historical anchoring. Verse 8 makes the additional point that it had always been God's intention in due course to extend the boundaries of the justified, who are further defined as the blessed, beyond Israel alone, and that this would occur with the coming of the faith, that is to say, with the event of Christ's crucifixion (cf. v. 1). Meanwhile, Abraham received the blessing in the form of a promise. Verse 9 repeats the conclusion succinctly: it is in the epoch of faith that blessing is secured. The Galatians go astray therefore, if they attempt to perpetuate the former epoch.

Verse 10 follows, linked to the preceding passage by γάρ. The import of the conjunction is that the quotation from Deuteronomy is intended to furnish evidence of the fact that it is in the epoch of faith that the promised blessing becomes a reality: to attempt to live, therefore, as if the epoch of the law were still present is to be under the curse, and this is proved by the Scripture which links the curse with failing to do the works of the law.

How this supports the conclusion reached in verse 9 is seen when it is recognized that verse 10 also serves as an introduction to the following verses. Verse 11 points out once more that Scripture opposes the doctrine of justification by the law: Habakkuk 2:4 is evidence of this. Once again, the word 'faith' is probably to be read objectively: it is the faith, the epoch of Christ, which is (and always has been) the life-source of the justified. This is borne out by the use of the phrase ἐν νόμῳ, which implies the epochal view of the law. However, Paul continues in verse 12, the law is not of faith; there is no overlapping of epochal foundations. Rather the law has its own epochal basis, which can be summed up in terms of doing, as Levitcus 18:5 intimates.

It is now possible to see the precise place in the argument of verse 10. Paul has quoted Deuteronomy 27:26 because it clearly associates the concepts of 'law' and 'doing'. The fact that the curse comes as a result of failure to DO makes this connection plain. Whether or not anyone actually does continue in all the things which are written in the book of the law to do them is of secondary importance: the main point is that the law and doing are tied together, and verse 11f proceeds to demonstrate that, as a consequence, justification cannot possibly be on the basis of the works of the law, because the Word of God has already made it transparently clear that justification is through faith, a concept antithetical to doing.

It has sometimes been assumed that the teaching of the Old Testament at this point is that justification and life on the basis of the doing of the works of the law was on offer, at least hypothetically, and that Paul's intention is to demonstrate the impossibility of such a justification, owing to human sin. Calvin, for example, writes: the law "has a method of justifying man which is wholly at variance with faith".[1]

However, once again it has to be said that such an interpretation is out of line with the central emphasis of this Epistle. Moreover, Paul would surely have been quite insistent that such a reading of Leviticus 18:5 is also out of line with the whole tenor of Old Testament faith: the tying together of the law and doing presupposes the covenantal context which is the setting for the entire Old Testament revelation. The offer of life on the basis of doing the works of the law assumes justification by faith as a foregoing fact, and does not amount to the postulation of an alternative route thereto. It is not that the law has a variant and dissonant method of justification, but that in itself it has no method of justification at all, the evidence for this being its link with doing. The law spells out the life of the justifed within the covenant of grace: it was designed to preserve the integrity of relationship between the people and their God. However, it was emphatically not a route to justification and life. The very fact that the law and doing hang together is proof of this, since, as Paul understands all Jews to realize, justification is by faith.

To harmonize Galatians 3:12 with Romans 10:5 is not easy. Paul is addressing different contexts, and uses the same Scripture to different purposes. Romans teaches that the law focussed in moral requirements is the standard of eschatological righteousness and was given to reveal sin. This implies that, if the moral component of the law is isolated, then the law offers life by doing, which entails an impossibility, given the revealed fact of universal failure, Christ excepted. Galatians, on the other hand, views the law as an epoch within the overarching context of the covenant of grace, with justification by faith as its fundamental gift, such that life never was by doing. There is, however, a reciprocal connection between the two emphases. In Romans the presupposition that life never came by doing is tacitly present, for Paul uses Leviticus 18:5 hypothetically, and sees it, as such, as prophetic of Christ alone. Conversely, in Galatians the assumption that universal failure makes justification by the law impossible is tacitly present,[2] because the fact that the overarching covenant is one of grace (undeserved favour) presupposes sin.

Verse 13 decribes the curse referred to in verse 10 as 'the curse of the law', and declares that Christ "has redeemed us from" this curse "having become a curse for us". Biblical support for this assertion is found in

---

[1] Calvin, *Galatians,* p. 90.
[2] Cf. T.L. Donaldson, 'The "Curse of the Law" and the Inclusion of the Gentiles: Galatians 3:13-14', in *N T St* 32 (1986), p. 104.

Deuteronomy 21:23.

The word 'us' here probably refers in the first instance to the Jews as those who were under the law.[1] The universalist language of the parallel statements in v. 10 ('as many', 'everyone') might suggest that Paul sees both the curse and the redemption as in principle susceptible of a wider application. However, the reference to the Gentiles in the next verse suggests that Paul is thinking here only of the Jews. It may seem difficult to gainsay the comment that "it is questionable whether Paul would so have restricted the work of Christ".[2] Nevertheless, in the primary sense the curse of the law can be applicable only to the Jews, since it was only to them that the law was given.

It may now be clarified why it is that Paul finds in the association between the law and doing evidence that those who are of the works of the law are under a curse. It is clear that, if we are right to understand the pronouncement of the curse upon those who are of the works of the law to be linked with the association of the categories of law and doing, then it is inappropriate to jump to the *prima facie* conclusion that the reason why those who are of the works of the law are under the curse is because of their failure in the matter of doing. This verse is often read as indicating the need for an unfailing doing of the works of the law if its curse is to be escaped; however, in verse 11f Paul seems to be tying the curse to the law purely because of the association with doing: the question of success or failure is not here present. The reference in verse 10 to "everyone who does not continue in all things which are written in the book of the law" is more or less incidental. Paul quotes it because it is in his text, but he makes nothing of it in the course of the ensuing discussion. To use those words, therefore, as if they are the key to understanding the curse seems inapposite.[3]

To understand Paul's reasoning it is helpful to refer back to verse 5. It is axiomatic for the apostle that in God's dealings with people everything must be on the basis of grace, since anything else would be incommensurate with the character of the God who has revealed Himself as the One who freely supplies.

The curse is attached to the law, in other words, for the simple reason that the law is associated with doing, and is not, therefore, the method of justification revealed by God.[4] Those who seek justification from the law are therefore placing themselves outside the sphere of God's blessing and bringing upon themselves a curse. Paul simply takes for granted the inappropriateness of justification before God being on the basis of one's

---

[1] Against S.K. Williams, *Justification*, p. 91f, and E.P. Sanders, *Paul, the Law*, p. 68.
[2] Guthrie, *Galatians*, p. 98.
[3] Against Fung, p. 142, n. 28.
[4] Cf. C.D. Stanley, 'Under a Curse: A Fresh Reading of Galatians 3:10-14', in *N T St* 36 (1990), p. 502; Donaldson, p. 103.

own doing. However, his reasoning is not merely philosophical: he knows that the idea of justification by the works of the law is contrary to God's own revealed method of justification through faith.

It must be noted in passing that the word 'curse' (κατάρα and cognates) was the natural one for Paul to choose in this context because it stands as a regular LXX antonym for blessing.[1] According to the Old Testament, the results respectively of the blessing and the curse are life and death.[2] The purpose of verse 10, it must be remembered, is to support the conclusion reached by verse 9, that the blessing comes through faith: the natural way for Paul to prove that truth Biblically by way of contrast was to introduce the concept of the curse.

However, it is necessary to fill out the meaning of the curse as understood by Paul, and in this connection it is helpful to raise the following question: in what sense was it necessary for the Jews to be redeemed from the curse of the law? It has already been noted that true Old Testament religion did not seek justification on the basis of doing the works of the law, but through faith in the anticipated Christ. How can Paul therefore speak of the redemption of the Jews from a curse which pertains to the law because of its association with doing?

It seems that there is in Paul's mind a link between accursedness and incompleteness or unfulfilledness. He regards the law as an epoch which pointed forward to another era as the promise to the fulfilment. The term 'curse' appears to be a description of the law's economic incompleteness.[3] The text quoted in verse 13 (Deut. 21:23) seems to represent a hanging corpse as an uncompleted disposal of a body. Paul speaks of the law's curse as a synonym for the incompleteness of the epoch: there is much to be said for Bligh's suggestion that the genitive in the phrase 'the curse of the law' (ἡ κατάρα τοῦ νόμου) is to be understood as explanatory or defining:[4] the law is itself the curse, just because it contains within itself no fulfilled hope. This explains why Paul can speak in terms of redemption from the curse of the law for the Jews.

The very fact that the law was a matter of doing is evidence that the epoch of the law was an age of unfulfilled hope: the grace of God as yet awaited historical enactment in the cross of Christ. In this constitutional incompleteness lay the curse: the law could not, within the parameters of its own economic arrangements, offer the blessing of justification and life. It always and inevitably pointed onwards and forwards to the Christ who would come.

---

[1] Gen. 27:12; Deut. 11:26,29; 23:5; 30:1,19; Neh. 13:2; Ps. 108:17; Zech. 8:13; Mal. 2:2 (cf. Gen. 27:29; Num. 23:25; Deut. 27:12f; Prov. 3:33; Isa. 65:23).
[2] Deut. 30:19; cf. Deut. 28:45; Jer. 51:12.
[3] Against Hays, p. 203f, n. 24.
[4] Bligh, p. 265.

Redemption from the curse may therefore be quickly defined: essentially it refers to the fulfilment of the Messianic hope of the Jews. It is to be brought into the epoch in which the justifying grace of God has been finally enacted. It is to be delivered from the agony of waiting within an economy which was not designed to justify. It is the transformation of justification from anticipation to full reality.

In what sense, then, did Christ redeem the Jews from the curse of the law by becoming a curse for them? This verse is frequently interpreted as a statement of the truth of substitutionary atonement. However, to interpret in this way is to leave it unrelated to Paul's major emphasis in Galatians (which is that the law is weak as regards justification, because God's chosen way of justification has never been on the basis of the law), and seems not to fit in the immediate passage, where his emphasis is that the curse pertains intrinsically to the law in an epochal sense simply because of its link with doing and its consequent economic incompleteness, and not because of human inability to do the works of the law.

Paul, it appears, is being less ingenious here than his interpreters would allow. It seems that he intends to say nothing more than that the bare fact that Christ hung on the tree is evidence of the fact that He became a curse, because the Scripture says that anyone who thus hangs is accursed.[1] Lying behind this statement is, of course, an elaborate Christological understanding, which makes it legitimate to see the death of Christ in vicarious terms. However, that is not Paul's point just now:[2] he is not explaining the doctrine of the atonement. Matthew Poole suggests that the principal reason why the law appropriated the curse to those who are hanged on a tree was "to foresignify that Christ should undergo this execrable punishment, and be made a curse for us."[3] Perhaps Paul's thinking is similar, and it is his thinking which comes to expression in Poole's theologization of the Deuteronomy text. In other words, the law pointed forward to Christ, and Paul finds in this particular text one of those places where it predicts Him specifically. The Jews' hope centred upon the coming of Messiah, when their redemption from the curse of the anticipatory epoch of the law would take place; Scripture had predicted that this redemption would take place in His crucifixion. The crucifixion of Jesus stands as conclusive evidence of the fact that He is the Christ, and therefore guarantees the redemption of the Jews into the age of hope fulfilled.

Craigie makes the very valid point that the hanged man of Deuteronomy 21:23 was not accursed because he was hanging, but was hanging because he was accursed, and was accursed because of the reason for his death.

---

[1] Cf. McDonald, p. 76.
[2] Against Betz, p. 151.
[3] M. Poole, *Annotations upon the Holy Bible*, Vol. 1 (Turnbull, 1800), p. 463.

Exactly the same is true of Christ; as Craigie puts it: "The manner of His death, crucifixion, symbolized dramatically the meaning of His death."[1] In the present context Paul is concerned with the manner rather than the meaning.[2] However, Craigie's words alert us to the fact that there is more to be said, and more is, of course, said elsewhere. Here, however, it suffices for Paul to draw attention to the manner of Christ's death as evidence of the fact that the epoch of the law is terminated, that redemption has taken place, that the era of fulfilled hope has arrived.

All this does not, of course mean, that Jews who lived during the epoch of the law could not experience justification. The point is that they were justified through faith in the Christ to whom the law was a provisional pointer, and not through the law itself. Paul's purpose at this point is to help the Gentiles at Galatia to see that if they persist in their false gospel of justification by the works of the law, they are in fact bringing themselves under the curse which is linked with the epoch of the law because of the constitutional incompleteness evidenced in its association with doing, which flies in the face of the revelation of the grace of God who alone enacts salvation. He aims to prove to his readers that, in staking all their hope on the provisions of the epoch of the law, they are in effect denying that the hope to which the law pointed forward has been fulfilled in the crucified Christ, and are thereby cutting themselves off from the fulfilment of hope. They are placing themselves in the position where they cannot 'receive the promise of the Spirit through faith' (3:14).

Returning now to 4:5, we find here a reaffirmation of the fact that the economy focussed around the concept of doing and provided to stimulate hope for the coming of the Messiah, was, by definition, terminated by His coming. Hence, by the redemptive work of the Son of God, the Jews were released from a justification uncompleted, in the sense that it awaited its conclusive historical enactment. That took place in Christ's death on the cross, by which, through faith, full justification was finally realized, and their hope fulfilled. This does not mean that there is no place for 'doing' in the new economy; however, its focus is not human doing, but what the Christ has done.

The second purpose of Christ's coming was that the Jews might receive the adoption. The immediate context suggests that this means the complete realisation of everything that being a son implied in terms of justification before God. Primarily Paul is talking about the objective reality of justification fully secured, the fact of a standing before God cleared of guilt; needless to say, however, that objective reality, like the objective reality of an unfinished justification under the law, also has its subjective side: the Jews could now experience the joy of justification completed, whereas

---

[1] P.C. Craigie, *The Book of Deuteronomy* (Eerdmans, 1976), p. 285f.
[2] Cf. D. Luhrmann, *Galatians* (Fortress, 1978, 1988), p. 61.

under the law they had known only the stimulated hope for the securing of their justification, which was still only in prospect. The prospective nature of secured justification for the Jews under the law may be compared, Paul says, with the position of children, who even in the family home have a status little different from that of the slaves. However, just as adulthood brings a new standing within the family home in the realisation of the status of 'lord of all', so the fullness of time brings to the Jews redemption from the curse of the law, the reality of acquittal in the sight of God and the peaceful sense of that reality which follows, because their justification by His grace has now been anchored and secured in the historical event of the cross of Christ, and they can look back to its realisation with joy, their hope, once stimulated by the law, now fulfilled.[1]

Paul next goes on to affirm that this sonship is something in which the Gentiles also share, and which contrasts with their pre-conversion experience, when they really were slaves to those which are not gods (4:6-8). Then comes the devastating challenge. Paul now applies everything which he has so far said by way of exposition of genuine Old Testament religion to the context which he is currently addressing, the heresy which has emerged amongst the Gentiles of Galatia. Given the true purpose of the law as a parenthetic epoch within the framework of the covenant of grace, an epoch designed to stimulate hope for the full and final enactment of grace in the crucifixion of the Christ, for Gentiles to turn, in quest of justification, to the Jewish law as exemplified in its festival regulations, the law which is weak and poor because it was never intended by God as a power for, or provider of, justification, is to seek a resumption of slavery; it is to render vain whatever Christian experience they might have enjoyed, because it is in effect to turn back from the God who has saved them (4:9-11). It constitutes a wholesale retreat from the hoped-for reality. Paul's passionate tone continues as he tries to enable the Galatians to understand the implications of this false Gospel which some of their number are propagating amongst them with such zeal (4:12-20).

He next refers to the law in 4:21, addressing those who desire to be under the law, in the sense of enacting all aspects of the epoch of the law, for the purpose of justification. In 4:22-5:1 Paul explains the allegorization (v. 24) of the story of the two sons of Abraham. I am persuaded by the explanation of this phrase which maintains that Paul means, 'these things are allegorized', namely, in Isaiah 54:1, which he proceeds to quote.[2]

It is sometimes suggested that his opponents may have used this story for their own ends.[3] If the reconstruction assumed in the present study is correct, it would be better to say that it is possible that the Galatians may

---

[1] So Ziesler, *Galatians,* p. 58; against Lightfoot, *Galatians,* p. 168, Hansen, p. 119f.
[2] J. Brown, *Galatians,* p. 99f.
[3] Cf. Hansen, p. 138, n; Dunn, *Galatians,* p. 96.

have come to the view that circumcision and law-observance were necessary for salvation on the basis, in part at least, of their reading of the Genesis account of the life of Abraham and his two sons. Paul is still trying to help Gentiles who have misread the Jewish Scriptures to an informed understanding.

He begins, in verse 22f, by highlighting three contrasts between Ishmael and Isaac. (1) Ishmael was born by a maidservant, Isaac by a free woman; (2) Ishmael was born according to the flesh, whereas Isaac was born through the promise; this is described later (v. 29) in a synonym[1] as 'according to the Spirit'; (3) Ishmael was therefore born into slavery; Isaac on the other hand was born free.

Paul now explains and applies the symbolism (vv. 24-31). This ancient story pictures the two covenants and the two Jerusalems: Hagar represents the Sinaitic covenant of law, which results in slavery, and which corresponds to 'Jerusalem which now is'; that is, it finds all its hopes located on earth, just as the Sinaitic covenant was for the duration of a particular earthly epoch only.[2] Evidence that the covenant of Sinai does not lead to the freedom linked with the promise is found in the geographical location of Sinai in Arabia, outside the promised land, and the later home of the Ishmaelites. Isaac, on the other hand, represents the covenant of promise, which entails freedom, and which has a heavenly origin and orientation: it is associated with the Jerusalem above. Both parts of the picture are elaborated in terms of a mother and her children, the quotation in verse 27 being chosen as Biblical evidence for the requirement that membership of God's people be not by natural descent, but on the basis of the promise whose content is justification through faith in Christ[3] and by the power of the Spirit. The persecution of Isaac by Ishmael is seen as reproduced in the harassment of the Galatians by the false teaching which has sprung up in their midst. This interpretation, which personifies the heresy, seems more likely than those which argue that Paul is referring to Jewish persecution of the Church,[4] or to the Judaizers.[5] Paul insists that he and the Galatians are children of freedom, and that it is their duty to stand against the error which would jeopardize their place as God's sons and heirs. Finally (5:1), he drives home the lesson of his text: the freedom which Christ has achieved for His people is to be prized; all attempts to deprive believers of their liberty resulting from the enslaving tendency, which has arisen among the Gentiles, of seeking justification by the works

---

[1] Cf. S.K. Williams, 'Promise in Galatians: A Reading of Paul's Reading of Scripture', in *J B L* 107 (1988), pp. 712-6.
[2] Cf. H.A.W. Meyer, p. 271.
[3] So Fung, p. 214.
[4] E.g. Luhrmann, p. 92, Betz, p. 250.
[5] E.g. Burton, p. 266, Fung, p. 213.

of the law, must be resisted.

It is necessary now to raise the question as to the nature of both the slavery and the freedom intended in this allegory. The word freedom is newly introduced into the discussion at this point, and this is no doubt significant; moreover the concept of slavery acquires a fresh nuance.[1] In the case of the Jews Paul does not use the word 'freedom', because of his awareness that their confinement during the epoch of the law was not a genuine slavery, but merely resembled slavery in some respects: we have described it as a quasi-slavery, and defined it as a function of the power of the law to stimulate hope for the coming Messiah and so guard them for their release into the full realisation of their privileges as the adopted race, arising from the final securing of their justified standing by the grace of God, as a result of the fulfilment of the sacrificial system in the cross of Christ. Paul does not wish to convey the impression that the race adopted by God's grace as His sons had ever been unfree. I do not therefore agree with Dunn, who believes that Paul, from the eschatological perspective of the gospel, sees his former life in Judaism as slavery.[2] In a sense the Jews had always possessed freedom; during the epoch of the law their freedom simply awaited its full manifestation. Now that the epoch of the law is finished, since Christ has come, the freedom which was always their privilege is realised with finality, in their release into the fullness of sonship.

However, at this point in his letter Paul is addressing his remarks directly to what is a rather different situation: the problem at Galatia was that these Gentile Christians had fallen into the belief that it was necessary to keep the law for justification: this, Paul perceives, could never be a problem for authentic Jewish faith. What then is the relevance of this allegory to the Galatian situation?

Paul's concern hitherto has been to instruct the Gentile Galatians in the true meaning of the Old Testament. He is now attempting to build on that foundation, and is moving on from the exposition of the true meaning of the law, which it was necessary that the Galatians should understand, to an application of the truth by means of a demonstration of the implications of their heretical doctrine of justification by the works of the law.[3] Earlier in the chapter (4:6f; cf. 3:26) Paul has shown that, through the cross, the Gentiles have become partakers in the privileges of Israel, including that of standing before God with the full rights of sons, because they are justified through their faith in Christ. However, in the case of the Gentiles it is possible to express this truth in an additional way in terms of freedom.

It is often assumed that this liberty is to be explained in terms of

---

[1] Cf. Adeney, *Thessalonians*, p. 316.
[2] Dunn, *Galatians*, p. 98.
[3] Cf. Calvin, *Galatians*, p. 138.

subjective experience. Reference is made, for example, to the burdensome nature of the Old Testament ceremonies, and the freedom from that burden which Christ brings,[1] or to liberty from the tyranny of sin.[2] Sometimes the experience of liberty is depicted positively as the ability to delight in God's law.[3]

However, in seeking to understand what Paul means by 'liberty' it is important to keep in mind his fundamental purpose in this Epistle, which is to correct a Gentile misunderstanding of the way of justification revealed in the Old Testament. The Galatians had come to the false conclusion that the Hebrew Scriptures taught that justification had to be achieved through the works of the law. Paul seeks to demonstrate that they have misread the Bible: the law as an epoch within which Jewish life found its ambit, was intended to stimulate hope for the coming of Christ, but He has now come and put the closing bracket around the epoch of the law.

It is sometimes suggested that Paul's reference to freedom means 'freedom from the law';[4] however, it is a pertinent remark by Brown, in view of the fact that Paul is addressing Gentile converts, that "they surely could not with propriety be said to have been made free from that to which they were never subjected."[5]

When Paul speaks of freedom, therefore, essentially he is declaring in an alternative way the fact that the Messiah has come, and consequently that the justification provided by God's grace and embraced by faith has been conclusively secured. It is because Christ is all that the believer needs for justification (which has always been true in anticipation), and because He has now come, that Gentile believers have obtained life by faith in Him: they are justified, they are free. The liberty of which Paul speaks is not primarily a subjective experience: it is the objective position of standing before God justified, which is bound up with the epochal termination of the law.[6]

That Paul is not intending to imply that the Gentiles' liberty involves freedom FROM anything in particular may be inferred from the fact that the counterpart in the allegory is Isaac. He was born free. He was not set free from anything: his freedom was entailed in the objective reality of his being as a result of God's promise. This is likewise the source of the believer's spiritual being as a new creation (6:15), and this is what Paul means by 'freedom'.[7]

---

[1] E.g. Luther, Vol. 27, p. 7.
[2] Calvin, *Galatians*, p. 147.
[3] Hendriksen, *Galatians*, p. 192; Mikolaski, p. 1102.
[4] Cf. Luhrmann, p. 95, Fung, p. 216.
[5] J. Brown, *Galatians*, p. 108.
[6] Cf. Hansen, p. 153.
[7] Against Luhrmann, p. 95.

To describe the Galatians as 'children of promise' (v. 28), and 'children ...of the free' (v. 31) are therefore alternative ways of speaking of the same reality which was previously described as 'adoption' (v. 5). The latter term refers to the fulfilment of Jewish hope, the realisation of everything to which the epoch of the law was a pointer. Gentile freedom is the sharing in that fulfilled hope; it is the objective reality of justification.

However, the term 'slavery' now acquires a meaning different from that earlier in the chapter.[1] Whereas the Jews' quasi-slavery was prospective, preparatory, and hopeful, the Gentiles' slavery is retrograde, and represents the abandonment of hope. In his application of the allegory Paul uses the concept of slavery in a way which views it in the light of the hope already fulfilled: the embracing by the Galatians of the law for justification represents not an anticipation of, but a retreat from, Christ. The misuse of the law by the Galatians is leading them into a self-inflicted slavery which is very real, and is not merely a God-given preparation for the finalized freedom of those whose justification is concluded in Christ. To use the law as a path to righteousness, Paul insists, must lead inevitably to bondage to rules and regulations which, as a matter of fact, were fulfilled in, and therefore terminated by, Christ. Consequently, there is no hope in this slavery.

Hendriksen comments on this part of the allegory that it is when the law is "viewed as a force by which a person achieves deliverance and salvation" that it enslaves.[2] This falls short of the whole of Paul's meaning, although it rightly identifies the Galatian problem. Paul has already stressed the power of the law in the confinement of God's people for the coming of His Son. However, in a case such as that of the Galatians, if the law is misunderstood as a prerequisite for justification, it becomes an enslaving power with no prospect of resolution in a future time of fulfilment; far from being a stimulant to hope, it becomes hopeless: it is a self-inflicted curse.

It is necessary, therefore, Paul insists, that the Galatians reject the law as a way of justification, and conform to the Old Testament Gospel, now fulfilled in Christ, of justification by faith. The point is well made that in the quotation in verse 30 "we find the law itself rejecting the law":[3] Paul uses the law (the very torah, upon which the Galatians have mistakenly erected their hopes) to demonstrate that the proper function of the law (as a parenthetic epoch in Jewish experience) was to lead those under its guardianship to Christ.

The allegory thus serves to highlight the implications of Paul's exposition from Scripture of the proper place of the law in respect of justification by arguing from the opposite end, and demonstrating the

---

[1] Against Burton, p. 263.
[2] Hendriksen, *Galatians*, p. 182.
[3] Stott, p. 127.

consequences of the erroneous doctrine of justification through the law. The law is weak when justification is the theme, because it was not given by God as part of the original covenant of promise. However, in its weakness it also has a positive power, in that it was designed to stimulate hope for the coming of Christ. However, when the proper perspective on the law, as a temporary measure pending the coming of Christ, is lost, the authentic Jewish hope of eventual release in the redemption which would be achieved by the Christ is inevitably absent, and the quasi-slavery of childhood becomes a total slavery to obsolete ceremonies, a slavery, without respite, and without the prospect of deliverance. Nothing remains of the law but its weakness, since its power as a hope-stimulator was inevitably terminated with the fulfilment of the hope in Christ.

In the remaining verses of the passage with which we are presently concerned (5:2-4) Paul seeks to drive home his message by pointing out two things. The first is that the law is a unity, and that to become circumcised (for justification) therefore carries with it the obligation to observe every element in the law (v. 3). It is sometimes alleged that behind these words are two implications: that only such an all-embracing payment of the debt to the law would in fact achieve justification, and that it is manifestly impossible for such a debt to be paid.[1]

However, it is unlikely that Paul, at this late stage in his argument, would introduce a thought which, as we have seen, is at odds with his central teaching, namely that the law was never given as a way of justification, the question of possibility and human potency being strictly irrelevant. Bruce raises the question, in the light of Paul's argument, whether he does mean that everyone is unable to keep the whole law, or whether his point is simply that there is no salvation that way.[2] However, it is hard to see how 5:3 can mean only that there is no salvation by way of the law; there would seem to be no logic behind Paul's brief statement if that is what he meant. It seems more likely, therefore, I would suggest, that Paul is making the point that it is manifestly ludicrous to believe in justification by the works of the law. His argument seems to be as follows: he begins by taking it for granted that even the Judaizing Gentile Galatians are not advocating a return to the Old Testament sacrificial system; hence he deduces that their willingness to stop short at this point of a total commitment to the law, and specifically to omit what any Jew knew were its foundational requirements, is to demonstrate that they do really recognize that the epoch of the law has indeed been fulfilled in, and terminated by, the coming of Christ. The same point is probably being made in 6:13.[3]

It follows from this secondly, Paul insists, that the attempt to be justified

---

[1] So (e.g.) Luther, Vol. 27, pp. 131f, 330f; Barrett, *Freedom*, p. 63.
[2] F.F. Bruce, *Galatians*, p. 231.
[3] Cf. J. Brown, *Galatians*, p. 161, Barrett, *Freedom*, p. 84.

by the law involves estrangement from Christ, such that His redemptive work becomes of no consequence to those who become circumcised with a view to being justified; Paul sums this up as a fall from grace,[1] by which he means that those who seek justification from the law have placed themselves outside the sphere where salvation is exclusively by the grace of God (vv. 2,4). Fung sees 'you have fallen from grace' as explicative of 'you have become estranged from Christ'.[2] Given that Paul now absolutely identifies God's grace with Christ crucified, this is correct.

These two points in effect summarize all that has been said about the law's power and weakness respectively. The first echoes again the truth that the law had the power to stimulate hope for the coming of Christ, but that with His coming its epoch is finished. Then Paul's second point brings him back once more to the heart of his argument about the weakness of the law; again the authentic interpretation of the Hebrew Scriptures is in the background: the law is weak in respect of justification, primarily because it was never given for that purpose. To seek justification by the law, therefore, is to fly in the face of God's revelation throughout history that justification is solely by His grace, now enacted in Christ.

It will now be clear that I am not endorsing the traditional Protestant interpretation of Galatians, and it would be well in concluding this section to spell out where my interpetation differs from the other. The old interpretation of Galatians said that the reason why justification is not by the law is that no one is able to fulfil it, and that the purpose of the law is to demonstrate that fact. I am arguing that the reason why justification is not by the law is that God never intended that it should be, and that the purpose of the law as an epoch was to stimulate hope towards the ultimate securing of justification by the Christ. I do not deny that Paul teaches in Galatians that it is the intention of God's Word as documented in Scripture to drive people to the righteousness of faith by demonstrating their need of justification in the character of gift. This is similar to the way in which the power of the law was understood in the traditional interpretation, except that the word 'law' is (importantly) replaced by the word 'Scripture', because the powerful purpose of the law as defined in this Epistle is rather differently explained as hope-stimulation. Moreover, my understanding of the weakness of the law is significantly different from the traditional: I am suggesting that the weakness of the law for justification is not in any sense linked with the moral weakness of sinful humanity, but rather with the revealed purpose of God in His covenant of grace. The law was intended only for an epoch, bracketed within the overarching saving plan of God in His covenant promise.

Bandstra suggests that the two adjectival clauses qualifying the

---

[1] Cf. Luther, Vol. 27, p. 18; McDonald, p. 124.
[2] Fung, p. 223.

occurrences of τὰ στοιχεῖα in 4:3 and 9 mean the same thing;[1] this is probably so: the law is weak just because it belongs to 'the world', and it seems that κόσμος in Galatians means 'the-world-before-Christ-came'.[2] The significance of the law was, therefore, limited to the duration of a world, the passing away of which was signalled by the coming of Christ. This is why the believer has been crucified to the world (6:14), because the weak epoch of the law has been terminated by the cross of the Messiah.

3   The Ongoing Status of the Law

It is the clear teaching of this Epistle that the law, in some sense at least, has no ongoing place at all in the life of the believer. The issue in dispute at Galatia centred around circumcision, which for Paul is the archetypal symbol of an epoch, an economy, which is now entirely in the past. Both his initial agreement (2:7-9), and his subsequent dispute (2:12-14), with Peter assume that the law as a total religious system is applicable to the Jews alone and quite irrelevant for the Gentile believer, an emphasis which reappears at 5:6 and 6:15. However, underlying this apparently merely ethnic argument is the more important insight that, even for the Jews (and consciously so for the Jewish Christians), the epoch of law is utterly finished: even 'we', the Jews, are no longer under the παιδαγωγὸς of the law (3:25), and the Gentiles must avoid submission to its yoke, which would entail the denial of their justified standing before God. Consequently, Paul can make the general statement about all Christians, "you are not under the law" (5:18b). It is this truth which Paul portrays in terms of sonship [4:5; cf. 3:7,26; 4:6f] and heirdom [3:29; 4:7], and, in the case of the Gentiles, describes as liberty [5:1; cf. 2:4; 4:21-31; 5:13].

However, there is another sense in which, it seems, the law does have an ongoing role in the believing life,[3] and Paul makes it very clear that the liberty to which the believer has been called must not be misconstrued "as an opportunity for the flesh" [5:13a]. Already, in stressing the irrelevance of circumcision, Paul has spoken of the availing strength of faith working through love (5:6): he has expounded the doctrine of justifying faith in the earlier part of the letter; now he goes on to explain that, in the love which binds believers together in mutual slavery all the law is fulfilled; he quotes Leviticus 19:18 [5:13b-14].

That Paul is stressing in these verses that love is the essential evidence of genuine justifying faith is clear.[4] Nevertheless, Dunn is right to say that "what would probably strike his first readers most immediately is that Paul

---

[1] A.J. Bandstra, *The Law and the Elements of the World* (Eerdmans, 1964), p. 55.
[2] Cf. J. Brown, *Galatians*, p. 79.
[3] Cf. Dunn, *Galatians*, p. 92; *ibid, Jesus*, p. 247.
[4] Against Bligh, p. 425f.

here appeals to the law".[1] Furthermore, it is to be noted that there is a sudden switch in Paul's use of νόμος at this point. He is not here using the word in an epochal sense, but rather to denote the moral requirements of the law, which he sees as having a significance transcending their function within the epoch of the law. This use of νόμος is akin to that of the letter to the Romans. However, as in the case of Romans 13:8-10, the relationship between law and love is debated. On the one hand there are those interpreters, such as Ziesler, who argue that Paul is contrasting the law with the love command, and teaching that the love command replaces the law as the standard of the will of God and the Christian life. Ziesler notes that Paul is in line with typical Jewish practice in attempting to give the essence of the law in a nutshell, but seems to claim that, whereas Jewish sources aimed to find one command which implies all the rest, Paul is not saying that the love command leads into all the others, but in effect that it enables the rest of the law to be dispensed with.[2]

Hansen, similarly, believes that Paul means that freedom from the law is not only the way to begin the Christian life, but also the basis for its continuation. He claims that to interpret Paul in these verses as putting Christians under obligation to keep the law would involve him in a major contradiction with everything that he has already said about freedom from the law, and that his intention is simply to describe the life which flows from faith.[3] Meyer, likewise, deeming Paul's spiritual standpoint 'lofty', argues that all the commandments are so subordinate to the command to love that to fulfil this one command is to stand in moral estimation as if one had fulfilled the whole law. He claims that, from this standpoint, everything not connected with the love command falls so completely into the background that it is no longer to be independently fulfilled.[4]

In part these commentators have been led to their conclusion by the obvious necessity of denying that Paul intends to imply that Christians (and particularly Gentile Christians) must obey every detail of the whole law. There can be no argument with the assertion that Paul does not see the command to be circumcised as implicit in the love command.[5] Moreover, their attempt to do justice to Paul's radical emphasis on liberty is to be applauded. However, this interpretation overlooks the fact that the context for Paul's teaching on liberty is specifically the matter of justification.[6]

Moreover, that this interpretation of Paul's words is flawed is evident from the fact that those who endorse it are unable to carry it through to its

---

[1] Dunn, *Galatians*, p. 115.
[2] Ziesler, *Galatians*, pp. 80f, 83f.
[3] Hansen, pp. 27, 165f; cf. p. 99.
[4] H.A.W. Meyer, p. 304.
[5] Ziesler, *Galatians*, p. 81.
[6] See Calvin, *Galatians,* eg., pp. 91, 97, 99-101, 109f, 119, 134, 168.

logical conclusion, and cannot avoid allowing the law to re-enter in some form. Thus Ziesler admits that there is still need for guidance as to how the Christian life is to be lived, and ackowledges that, if the law does not provide that guidance, then something else must take its place. Further, he agrees that to be free from the law is not to be free from the demands of morality, and says that where the law is not the ultimate standard of morality the love command in which the law is summed up assumes that role.[1] Hansen makes the same point when he writes: "the moral standards of the law are not discarded or violated by Christians who are free from the law".[2] However, in that the love command is the epitome of the law, it is hard to see these distinctions as anything more than verbal, and the tendency to separate law and morality seems a very dubious procedure.

It seems necessary to accept that Paul distinguishes, at least in his mind, though he does not spell it out, between the different aspects of the law which have come to be decribed in theological tradition as the moral and the ceremonial law.[3] Christians are not under obligation to fulfil the ceremonial law, since its fulfilment has completely taken place in Christ. However, the alternative interpretation of 5:13f takes Paul to be affirming the continuing binding validity upon Christian believers of the moral law.

Paul's meaning, then, is not that the believer will practise love, and therefore will not need the law, but that the practice of love will inevitably result in obedience to the law, since the law is the articulation of what love means in practice. This interpretation is most clearly expounded by Stott, who notes that Paul

> does not say that if we love one another we can safely break the law in the interests of love, but that if we love one another we shall fulfil the law.... Our Christian freedom from the law...does not mean that we are free to disregard or disobey the law.... Although our justification depends not on the law but on Christ crucified, yet our sanctification consists in the fulfilment of the law.[4]

What this means in practice is that any breach of the second table of the law is an infringement of the law of love: in the end there is no difference between these two concepts. As Kevan writes: "Freedom from the law as a means of earning our acceptance with God still leaves us within the law as a rule of life".[5]

One of the things which influences those who hold to the first of these

---

[1] Ziesler, *Galatians*, p. 80f.
[2] Hansen, p. 166.
[3] Against H.A.W. Meyer, p. 304; Luhrmann, p. 96.
[4] Stott, p. 142f.
[5] Kevan, p. 68.

interpretations is the emphasis on the Spirit in the latter part of Galatians 5. It is argued that for Paul the Spirit replaces the law in the life of the Christian believer, love being the first element in His fruit (5:22). Having defined the love command as the ultimate standard of God's will, Ziesler now describes the Spirit as "the ultimate guide and authority", and argues that in 5:19-24 Paul provides two pictures, the first of life without God at the centre, and the second of the God-centred life, and believes that it is significant that he does not introduce either a modified, or an entirely new, set of commandments.[1] Similarly, Hansen writes: "The command *live by the Spirit* is the central concept in Paul's ethical appeal", and sees the Spirit, in contradistinction to the law, as "the only power to sustain Christian life".[2]

I am not convinced that this is a correct interpretation. However, that Paul puts great stress on the work of the Spirit is clear, and it is therefore necessary now to examine the relationship between the Spirit and the law. Hansen does not absolutely deny that the Christian life will fulfil the law; his point is simply that the law does not in itself possess the power to enable believers to keep it: the power comes from the Spirit.[3] In one sense this is to state the obvious, but the question is, what is the role of the law in relation to the power of the Spirit?

The argument that there is no place for the law in the Christian life proceeds on the basis of the assumption that in 5:16-26 Paul has moved away from consideration of the law to commend the power of the Spirit as the sole factor in Christian living. The two references to the law in these verses may, at first sight, seem to support this reading: in verse 18 Paul says that those who are led by the Spirit are not under the law, and in verse 23 he insists that there is no law against the fruit of the Spirit. However, verse 18 is probably concerned not with the moral law as the timeless revelation of the will of God, but with the totality of the law as an epoch, now superseded by the epoch of the Spirit, and verse 23 may well be an example of litotes, amounting to the affirmation that the fruit of the Spirit is in complete accordance with the law.[4]

Despite Ziesler's description of this passage as two contrasting pictures, it is arguable that Paul does in fact have the law of God in mind as he paints those pictures. Hansen argues that the statement "the works of the flesh are evident" implies that we do not need the Mosaic law to define the nature of evil, since "all of us already know what is evil when we see it".[5] However, this claim is not obviously true, either from Scripture or from experience:

---

[1] Ziesler, *Galatians*, p. 81; cf. p. 86.
[2] Hansen, p. 168.
[3] *Ibid*, p. 169.
[4] Cf. Kevan, p. 73, Burton, p. 318.
[5] Hansen, p. 173.

there is frequent disagreement within human society, and between societies, about right and wrong, and it seems that, unless a relativistic stance be adopted, an objective standard is needed for accurate definition. Underlying both the list of works of the flesh and the summary of the fruit of the Spirit, it would seem, are the requirements of the law.

The longest text contains seventeen works of the flesh. Eleven of them are vices condemned in the torah,[1] while most of the others are synonymous with other terms from the LXX.[2] It seems therefore that Cole is right to suggest that the phrase 'and the like' (v. 21), which clearly indicates that Paul's list is not exhaustive, implies that, if an exhaustive list were produced, "we might find that it corresponded to the Ten Commandments"; he makes the salient point that the similarity of such New Testament lists of vices suggests a common original.[3] Similarly, the fruit of the Spirit is a list of virtues extolled in the Old Testament.[4]

This means that, although Paul can appeal to believers to walk in the Spirit, he also finds it necessary to expound the law as the believer's pattern for that Spirit-led life. In this connection it is instructive to note the different phrases in verse 25: "if we live in the Spirit, let us also walk (στοιχῶμεν) in the Spirit", the latter being apparently an alternative for "walk (περιπατεῖτε) in the Spirit" (v. 16). The Spirit is the sphere of the believer's life, the epoch of which the believer is a part, but it is the responsibility of the believer to walk accordingly. The two pictures are designed to warn the Christian of the things which he must avoid, and to impel him in the direction of the things which he must espouse. As such, they amount to the amplification, first negatively and then positively, of the command to walk by the Spirit; they apply God's law to the beliving life, so that, along with the power of the Spirit, they have an essential guiding role for the believer. It is not strictly true to say that the Spirit replaces the law in the theology of Paul: in epochal terms that is so, but the moral law becomes the pattern through which the Spirit operates in the new epoch.

It is perhaps significant, in the light of our conclusion that τὰ στοιχεῖα refers to the law, that Paul uses the related verb στοιχέω in 5:25. Fung notes that the verb "suggests the picture of believers folllowing a course

---

[1] E.g. (1) μοιχεία - Jer. 13:27; (2) πορνεία - Num. 14:33; (3) ἀκαθαρσία - Lev. 5:3; (4) εἰδωλολατρεία - cf. Ex. 20:4; (5) φαρμακεία - Isa. 47:9,12; (6) ἔχθρα - Jer. 9:8f; (7) ἔρις - cf. 1 Sam. 12:15; (8) ζῆλος – Job 5:2; (9) θυμός - 2 Kgs. 5:12; (10) φόνος - Dt. 22:8; (11) μέθη - Prov. 20:1.

[2] E.g. ἐριθεία - cf. Prov. 16:18; διχοστασία - cf. Num. 12:1-15; αἵρεσις - cf. Dt. 18:20-22; φθόνος - cf. Ex. 20:17; κῶμος - cf. Ex. 32:6,18f.

[3] Cole, *Galatians*, p. 161.

[4] E.g. (1) ἀγάπη - Lev. 19:18; (2) χαρά - Ps. 119(118):passim; (3) εἰρήνη - Ps. 119 (118):165; (4) μακροθυμία - Prov. 14:29; (5) χρηστότης - Ps. 36:3; (6) ἀγαθωσύνη – 2 Chr. 24:16; (7) πίστις - Dt. 32:20; (8) πραΰτης - Ps. 44:4; (9) ἐγκράτεια – cf. Gen. 39:7-12.

with the Spirit as leader".[1] The course along which the Spirit leads believers, we must add, is that laid down in the law.[2]

Ziesler and Hansen are of course right to say that it is from the Spirit that the empowering for the believing life comes: there is no suggestion that the law possesses inherent power independently of the Spirit. The point at issue is whether the Spirit works independently of the law of God, and it seems that Ziesler and Hansen err in separating the two realities of Spirit and law, which Paul appears to hold inextricably together: in the power of the Spirit, the law points the way. It is worth noting that the emphasis here is a little different from that of the Epistle to the Romans, where the law is definitely seen as possessing power in the sphere of the Spirit; in Galatians, on the other hand, Paul reserves the talk of power for his references to the Spirit, but seems to see the law as a pattern during the Spirit's epoch. The Spirit applies the pattern and so empowers the believer to obedience. The teaching of Galatians is not to be construed as different from that of Romans, but the same truth is certainly expressed in different terms.

In 6:2 Paul uses the word νόμος again, when he says, 'Bear one another's burdens, and so fulfil the law of Christ'. It is often alleged that there is a contrast here between the law of Christ and the law of Moses.[3] The law of Christ is then taken to be the whole of Christ's moral teaching as focussed in the command to love. This, however, raises the question of the nature of the contrast, since the moral teaching of Jesus was largely expository of the deepest implications of the Old Testament law, and, as Paul has already indicated, the Old Testament law is also focussed in the command to love.

It seems more probable, therefore, that Paul intends to say that the law with which he has been concerned throughout the Epistle, the law of Moses, has its origin in Christ. Ridderbos rejects the contrast between Christ and Moses, and argues that Paul's point is that the claim of the law continues, but that it accrues to believers from Christ, since Christ stands between believers and the law. The new element, Ridderbos continues, is not the content of the law, although he did modify it, but the fact that the root of the believer's obedience is found in Christ.[4]

While I am in sympathy with Ridderbos' general approach, there are three points at which I am unhappy with his wording. (1) In that I have spoken of the origin of the law with Christ, it would be important to point out that, from the eschatological perspective of Christian faith the law has always come to God's people, even in the old epoch, from Christ: there is nothing new about this. (2) From this it follows that Christ does not stand

---

[1] Fung, p. 275.
[2] cf. Luther, Vol. 27, p. 66.
[3] So (e.g.) Calvin, *Galatians,* p. 173; Lightfoot, *Galatians,* p. 216; Fung, p. 287f.
[4] Ridderbos, p. 213.

between the law and believers, but rather stands over the law for believers; this is consonant with Paul's major emphasis in this Epistle: in its very essence the law is subservient to Christ, in whom God's covenant of promise is confirmed. (3) It is not strictly true to say that Christ modified the law; what He did was to explain it more fully.

To speak of the law as having its origin with Christ, necessitates a brief consideration of one aspect of the Christology of this Epistle. Two texts are relevant. The first to be mentioned is 4:4, where the choice of the verb ἐξαπέστειλεν (sent forth) is a clear indication of the pre-existence of Christ. However, there has already been a hint of Christ's pre-existence in 3:16, where Paul uses an intricate grammatical argument to demonstrate that the authentic recipient of the promises is none other than Christ Himself, the true Seed of Abraham. The use of the verb ἐρρήθησαν (were made) implies that the promises when originally given were given to the Seed of Abraham. Paul is in fact saying more than can be ascertained from the Old Testament alone, where the promises are described as given to Abraham only, but concerning his seed. Paul is arguing on the basis of the assumption that the inspiration of Scripture leaves no place for the merely accidental even down to the level of precise words and word-forms. He therefore perceives that, in making the promises to Abraham, God was ultimately and actually making them to Christ.

Paul's interpretation of Genesis 12:7 is that Abraham received the promise, not on his own behalf, but in the name of Christ, his Seed. Now it could be that this is only a figure of speech, and that Paul sees the promises as made to Christ in anticipation, but his choice of words suggests that he understands God originally to have established covenant with the Christ, the covenant with Abraham being only an earthly reflection of a heavenly transaction between the Father and His pre-existent Son. In 3:16 Paul appears to mean that, when God said to Abraham, "to your seed I will give this land" (Gen. 12:7), He was really referring to the one Seed, Christ, the land of Canaan standing for the entire creation which was to be his inheritance.[1] In His 'will' (διαθήκη), God has bequeathed absolutely everything to Christ. The significance of this for the argument is that there can be no rival claims to the inheritance on the basis of the law; the only way to have a share in the inheritance is to be joined by faith to Christ. For the present purpose, though, the important thing to note is that Paul says that the promises were made to the seed, and not only to Abraham, implying the presence of Christ the true Seed at the time when the covenant was initially established.

In the light of these two Christological texts where Paul indicates the pre-existence of the Son of God, it is worth considering the final words of 3:19. If Christ's pre-existence underlies Paul's teaching, then there is much

---

[1] So S.K. Williams, *Promise*, pp. 717, 719.

to be said for the older interpretation which identifies the Mediator in this passage with the Christ,[1] especially in light of the fact that Paul can elsewhere write that there is "one Mediator between God and men, the man Christ Jesus" (1 Tim. 2:5). Paul is then saying that the law when originally given at Mount Sinai was given mediatorially by Christ. It is 'the law of Christ' because He has always been behind it, since its design was to point His people to Him. He is both the source and the goal of the law; hence it was that believers before the coming of Christ could share in anticipation the blessings of the age of fuliflment, since the Christ to whom they looked forward was the giver of the epoch which pointed to Him: their perspective was wholly eschatological.

However, now, in 6:2, Paul is taking up another theme from the Old Testament perspective on the law: although the law, because of its epochal status, never ever served for justification, nevertheless, there were included within the epoch of the law given by Christ moral requirements which transcended the epoch, and which Paul now also denominates νόμος. The law in this sense did not have justifying power any more than the epoch along with which it was revealed. However, it was always the authentic pattern of life for the redeemed and believing people of God within the covenant which was established with Christ.[2] Now that Christ has come, this particular moral function of the law is not abrogated, even though the law as an epoch has, by definition, fulfilled its purpose as a preparation for His coming. Because He was the Giver of the transcendent element in the law, it follows, Paul argues, that the moral function of the law is still applicable to Christ's people.

In addition to these major passages concerning the ongoing status of the law, there are two further texts which merit brief attention.

(1) In 2:10 Paul mentions the fact that, having agreed with the Jerusalem apostles both on the content of the gospel, and on an ethnic[3] division of labour, their desire was "only that we should remember the poor". Three relevant points may be made. (i)The construction (ἵνα plus subjunctive) is a not uncommon way of expressing command.[4] This is, therefore, more than a vague wish: the Jerusalem apostles are placing upon Paul something of a legal requirement. (ii) The use of the present tense implies that the requirement is continuously and repeatedly binding. The question must be

---

[1] So Calvin, *Galatians,* p. 102, and many patristic commentators (Lightfoot, *Galatians,* p. 146), against the modern commentators who take the mediator to be Moses (cf. T. Callan, 'Pauline Midrash: The Exegetical background of Gal 3:19b', in *J B L* 99 (1980), pp. 555-64).

[2] Cf. T.R. Schreiner, 'Law of Christ', in Hawthorne & Martin (eds.), p. 544.

[3] Cf. D.J. Verseput, 'Paul's Gentile Mission and the Jewish Christian Community: A Study of the Narrative in Galatians 1 and 2', in *N T St* 39 (1993), p. 50.

[4] C.F.D. Moule, pp. 136, 141; F.F. Bruce, *Conference,* p. 206.

raised whether this is a requirement applicable particularly to Paul and his immediate colleagues, or whether it was the expectation of the other apostles that he would generalize it in his preaching to the Gentiles, such that 'we' acquires universal meaning. (iii) The third point may help to answer this question: the requirement of mercy to the poor was one which was enshrined in the Old Testament law,[1] and it may well be that the Jerusalem apostles were in effect reminding Paul that, though it was agreed that the basis for justification was not to be found in the law, nevertheless, the law was not to be ignored altogether in the catechisation of Gentile converts: all those who were justified by faith were expected to give evidence of the reality of their saving experience of the Spirit through a life of obedience to the moral and social requirements of the law. Paul's eagerness to comply is, therefore, explicable in terms of his keenness to obey God's law.[2]

(2) In his parting blessing Paul makes mention of those who "walk according to this rule (τῷ κανόνι τούτῳ στοιχήσουσιν)" [6:16]. The demonstrative pronoun is probably best read as referring back to the previous verse, where Paul has spoken of 'a new creation',[3] a phrase which corresponds with the reference in 5:6 to 'faith working through love' in a verse which is otherwise very similar to 6:15. If what the new creation means in practice is faith working through love, then, as we have seen, it amounts to a life lived in accordance with the moral law of God which had originated from Christ. It is probably correct, therefore to understand Paul to mean by the κανών the law, which is here again therefore portrayed as the pattern for the believing life.[4] Further support for this reading may be found in the fact that the verb used here is the same as that used in 5:25. There Paul stressed that to walk by the Spirit is to live in accordance with the law, and he is now making the same point more explicitly.

Conclusion

The weakness of the law according to this Epistle is, therefore, its inability to justify. This is not however a pejorative comment: unlike the traditional interpretation, I do not understand Paul to reach this conclusion about the weakness of the law on the basis of the weakness of the sinful human material to which the law is directed. It is rather a function of the purpose of God, in which the law never had a justifying role, since justification has always been by grace on the basis of God's covenant promise to Christ. On

---

[1] Hendriksen, *Galatians*, p. 86, cites: Ex. 23:10f; 30:15; Lev. 19:10; Dt. 15:7-11; Jer. 22:16; Dan. 4:27; Amos 2:6f); cf. Dunn, *Galatians*, p. 71.
[2] Cf. Dunn, *Partings*, p. 129.
[3] So Luther, Vol. 27, pp. 141, 406.
[4] Cf. Burton, p. 358f.

the other hand, Paul does not leave the weakness of the law unqualified in this letter: it did, during the epoch which it denominated, possess the power to stimulate and sustain the Jewish hope for the coming of the Messiah, pointing on to Him and His cross as the authentic focus of the grace of God, and the occasion of the final securing of justification by faith. In a paradoxical sense, therefore, the weakness of the law as regards justification is its strength as regards hope-stimulation! With the coming of Christ, this role of the law in respect of justification, therefore, came to an end.

However, this is not the totality of the role of the law, since the word can be used in other than an epochal sense, and, as such, it does have an ongoing status in the believing life. Life in the Spirit entails walking by the rule of the law, and the outworking of this is that, in a life of loving service, the requirements of the law are in fact fulfilled, the law standing as a needed pattern for the redeemed life.

CHAPTER 4

Hebrews

1 Introduction

Hebrews has been called "the riddle of the New Testament."[1] In part this is due to the uncertainty about the location and identity of the recipients and the purpose of the letter. In my judgement it is probable that the original readers were hellenistic[2] Jewish[3] Christians who were in danger of committing apostasy back to Judaism.

That the addressees are Christians who are in danger of apostasy seems clear (2:1,3; 3:6,12; 6:12; 10:35; 12:3,15). That they are Jews, and that their threatened lapse is back into the Jewish faith is more difficult to establish. It seems *prima facie* probable that the method of argument - appeal to the Old Testament, and the substance of the argument - that the old covenant has been superseded, are evidence of this audience. The 'beginning of the word of Christ' (6:1f) could be a reference to Judaism,[4] and the characterisation of the potential apostasy in 13:9f points in the same direction. A hellenistic destination seems likely in that the writer is nowhere concerned with the contemporary Jewish cultus: his argument is centred entirely around the Biblical portrayal of the Levitical tabernacle in the wilderness. The Old Testament quotations are taken invariably from the LXX; if the readers had been Palestinian Jews, they would have been more familiar with the Hebrew Scriptures.

The threat of apostasy appears to have arisen because the readers are suffering persecution, at times severe (10:32-34; 11:13,25f,35-38; 13:13f) from unconverted Jews. It seems that the nature of the Jews' opposition is to ridicule the ritual poverty of Christianity as compared with Old

---

[1] E.F. Scott, *The Epistle to the Hebrews* (Edinburgh, 1922), p. 1.

[2] So (e.g.) T. Hewitt, *The Epistle to the Hebrews* (IVP, 1960), p. 36f; against (e.g.) B.F. Westcott, *The Epistle to the Hebrews* (Macmillan, 1889), p. xl.

[3] Against G. Vos, *The Teaching of the Epistle to the Hebrews* (Eerdmans, 1956), pp. 13f, 20.

[4] So (e.g.) A. Nairne, *The Epistle of Priesthood* (T. & T. Clark, 1913), pp. 15f, 334f, against J. Fischer, 'Covenant, Fulfilment, and Judaism in Hebrews', in *Ev R Th* 13 (1989), p. 183f.

Testament religion. The absence of a priest is their major taunt (4:14; 8:4; 10;10,14).[1] To their perception Christianity lacks the necessary religious rites to effect real forgiveness, and the Jews who have become Christians have thrown away all the means of knowledge of, and access to, God.

The effect of these taunts from their fellow Jews has been to unsettle the Jewish Christians, and to cause them to question the effectiveness of Christianity as a religion. Perhaps they have begun to wonder about the persistence of sin after baptism:[2] if Christ's sacrifice was once-for-all, then where is the ongoing provision for atonement, which was provided for in the repetition of Jewish sacrifices? In the light of their failures, the persecution has led to an accumulated sense of unresolved guilt (2:16,18; 4:16; 10:2). Consequently, the Jewish rituals, the like of which Christianity conspicuously lacks, are beginning to have a strong appeal to them, a return to the faith of their fathers appearing as the possible solution to their spiritual doubts caused by their sufferings,[3] as well as a way of avoiding the suffering itself. The writer aims to avert this disastrous move. He sees that the reason for the basic danger of apostasy is that the Word of God which this congregation is hearing is making no impact upon them because it is not being received with faith (2:1; 3:12f; 4:2,11; 5:11-14). The failure to appropriate the continuing benefits of Christ's death is an expression of unbelief.

The writer's remedy is to send them his word of exhortation (3:14; 4:11,14,16; 6:1,11; 10;22,23), which at times takes on a note of stern warning (4:1; 12:25), so seriously does he regard their thoughts of relapse. He sets out to remind them that suffering is an inescapable part of the Christian life (10:36; 11:25; 13:13). He sees the discouragement which has resulted from his readers' sufferings as pre-eminently a problem of faith, since a true faith is one which will persevere all the way to the end, whatever the trials of the journey (3:6,14; 4:14; 6:11f,15,19; 10:35-39; 11:*passim*; 12:14,27f).[4] Despite the sternness of his tone, the writer nevertheless retains an underlying confidence about his people (6:9f). For their encouragement (13:22) he sets out to expound the great fact of the High Priesthood of Jesus Christ (3:1; 8:1): he aims to demonstrate the objective sufficiency of His sacrifice to deal conclusively and continuously with guilt (2:17; 4:14f; 5:1-10; 7:1-10:18). He shows his readers that, far from having become devoid of the knowledge of God, they have in Christ His final Word (1:1f; 2:3). His method is to elevate Christ in comparison

---

[1] Against R. Dormandy, 'Hebrews 1:1-2 and the Parable of the Wicked Husbandmen" in *Expos T* 100 (1989), p. 372.

[2] Cf. B. Lindars, *New Testament Theoplogy: The Theology of the Letter to the Hebrews* (Cambridge University Press, 1991), p. 12f.

[3] Cf. (e.g.) A.B. Bruce, *The Epistle to the Hebrews* (T. & T. Clark, 1908), p. 11.

[4] Cf. Witherington, p. 149.

with the Jewish rituals after which his readers are presently hankering.

2   Hebrews 7:18f

The writer to the Hebrews sees the weakness and unprofitableness (ἀσθενὲς καὶ ἀνωφελές) of the former commandment (προαγούσης ἐντολῆς) as the reason for its annulment (ἀθέτησις). This is then explained by a parenthetic clause: 'for the law (ὁ νόμος) made nothing perfect'. It is necessary to establish the meaning of 'the former commandment' and its relationship to ὁ νόμος.

1   The Meaning of 'Law'

In the context of the passage beginning from verse 12 the word 'commandment' has already occurred once (v. 16), and the word 'law' twice (vv. 12,16). To understand the significance of the two terms and the relationship between them, it will be helpful to follow through the argument of this passage.

Verse 12 reads: 'For the priesthood being changed, of necessity there is also a change of the law'. Behind this statement lies the teaching of the writer to the Hebrews about the High Priesthood of Jesus Christ according to the order of Melchizedek. The change of priesthood to which he refers is that from the order of Aaron, by which the priesthood passed by hereditary succession down the line of Levi, to that prophesied in Psalm 110:4 and prefigured in Genesis 14:18-20, which now finds its fulfilment in Jesus Christ. The point stressed in verse 12 is that this change of priesthood carries with it, as a matter of necessity, a change of law. The following two verses explain this statement, and clarify the author's process of reasoning: the Lord Jesus Christ, 'of whom these things are spoken', belongs to a different tribe (that of Judah), 'from which no man has officiated at the altar' (v. 13), and the reason why no Judaite has so officiated is that 'Moses spoke nothing concerning priesthood' of this tribe (v. 14). The name of Moses stands for the Law, the point being that there is no commandment in the Law of Moses that a member of the tribe of Judah should be a priest.

According to the Law of Moses, priesthood passed by genetic descent down the generations of the tribe of Levi. Consequently, if the High Priesthood of Christ is not to be invalidated, then the law restricting priesthood to the Levites must of necessity be changed. This implies that 'the law' in verse 12 refers, at least as its primary meaning, to the specific law concerning the Levitical descent of the priesthood.

Verses 15 and 16 make the further point that Jesus, the High Priest in the likeness of Melchizedek, has come 'not according to the law of a fleshly commandment', but according to the power of an endless life. Read in the light of the preceding verses, the 'law of a fleshly commandment' appears here to refer again to the commandment that the Aaronic priesthood be passed on through fleshly descent within the tribe of Levi.[1] When verse 18 speaks of the annulling of the former commandment, it is this commandment which is in view, at least as the primary meaning.

However, at this point in his argument the writer appears to widen the meaning of the terms which he is using. The clarificatory clause which opens verse 19 seems to lack this restriction to the specific commandment. When the weakness and unprofitableness of the commandment is clarified as the failure of the law to make anything perfect, it is most natural to understand this as an allusion to the Law of Moses as a system in its entirety.[2] In that the phrase 'made nothing perfect' is clearly intended to elucidate the twin concepts of weakness and unprofitableness, it may therefore be legitimate to read the idea of the entire system of Mosaic Law backwards, and so to find in the phrase 'the former commandment' an allusion, as yet merely implicit, to the whole Law as weak and unprofitable. The specific commandment is one focus of the Law as a whole, and the weakness and unprofitableness of that one commandment is a reflection upon, and an expression of the character of, the entire Law.

This suggests that it is possible, in the light of the latter part of the argument, to find hints of the entire law-system in the earlier references to the commandment and the law also. Though not as yet spelt out in verses 12 and 16, we may conclude that, in the writer's mind, the specific commandment regarding the genetic descent of the Levitical priesthood is representative of the law as a whole. This means that it is legitimate to reconsider the earlier verses with this in mind. Verse 12 speaks of the necessity of a change of law with the rise of a non-Levitical priesthood. Its primary meaning is that the specific law governing the Levitical descent of the priesthood needed alteration. However, beneath the surface there is present also the thought that the change of priesthood from that of Aaron to that of Christ necessitates also a change of the whole law-based system at the heart of which the Levitical priesthood stood. Verse 12 is in fact to be taken as an absolute statement, albeit that it is couched in terms of the specific legal commandment concerning the tribe of Levi.[3] Similarly, when verse 16 speaks of 'the law of a fleshly commandment', the specific commandment that the priesthood was to be passed on by fleshly descent becomes symbolic of the law as a complete system: the genitive (ἐντολῆς)

---

[1] So (e.g.) H. Montefiore, *A Commentary on the Epistle to the Hebrews* (A. & C. Black, 1964), p. 125; P.E. Hughes, *A Commentary on the Epistle to the Hebrews* (Eerdmans, 1977), p. 264; W.L. Lane, *Hebrews 1-8* (Word, 1991), p. 183.

[2] So A.S. Peake, *The Epistle of Paul the Apostle to the Hebrews* (Caxton, n.d.), p. 160.

[3] Cf. A.B. Bruce, p. 264f.

"expresses that in which the law finds expression."[1] The specific commandment is the particular embodiment of the whole law. In verse 18 also, the specific commandment referred to is that "which constituted the Levitical priesthood: but it is treated as the equivalent to the whole system of sacrifice and propitiation."[2]

In defining the concepts of commandment and law in this passage, it is necessary to note a further aspect of the content of law in the understanding of the writer. The explanatory clause verse 19a is itself an echo of the opening words of verse 11, which may be translated:

Therefore, if perfection were through the Levitical priesthood, for upon it the people were legislated for (νενομοθέτητο), what further need was there that another priest should arise according to the order of Melchizedek, and not be called according to the order of Aaron?"

The first two phrases of this verse need to be examined in the present connection. The denial (implied by the rhetorical question) that perfection is through the Levitical priesthood parallels the statement of verse 19a that the law made nothing perfect, and suggests that for the writer to the Hebrews the terms 'law' and 'Levitical priesthood' are practically equivalent. The next clause, which is clearly a parenthesis, explains how this can be so: the people was furnished with law upon (ἐπί) the Levitical priesthood. The preposition implies that the Levitical priesthood is the foundation upon which the people were given the law, and therefore that Levitical priesthood is the foundation upon which the entire Mosaic law is built.[3]

What, then, is the law which is founded on the Levitical priesthood? It appears that the writer sees the superstructure as the whole Old Testament economy. It includes the specific commandments concerning the priesthood, such as the requirement that priesthood be passed down the genetic tribe of Levi; but it is clear that the implicit reference to the law in verse 11 involves more than just this.[4] The term embraces also the laws governing personal and communal life, summarized in the Ten Commandments, and designed to preserve the distinctiveness of Israel as the covenant community.[5] It is in this sense that the people were legislated for: they were provided with a detailed pattern of individual and social life,

---

[1] Westcott, p. 184.

[2] E.C. Wickham, *The Epistle to the Hebrews, with Introduction and Notes* (Methuen, 1910), p. 51.

[3] Cf. Hewitt, p. 120; against R.C. Stedman, *Hebrews* (IVP, 1992), p. 82.

[4] Against J. Owen, *Calvin's Commentaries on Hebrews, Translated from the Original Latin, and Edited* (Baker, 1853), p. 381, J. Brown, *Hebrews* (Banner of Truth, 1862), p. 338.

[5] Against A.W. Pink, *An Exposition of Hebrews* (Baker, 1954), p. 385f.

appropriate to the covenant people, and rooted in the sacrificial system by which their covenant status was maintained.

It seems probable that the LXX version of Exodus 24 is in our author's mind at this point. Later (9:18-21) he will quote explicitly from that chapter. Exodus 24 has been described as the ratification or the sealing[1] of the covenant. Moses, accompanied by Aaron, Nadab, and Abihu, who will later be set apart as priests (Ex. 28:1), and by seventy of the elders of Israel, is summoned to come up to the LORD. Before their ascent of the mountain, sacrifices are offered on an altar at the foot of the mountain and the Book of the Covenant is read. Although the Levites have not yet been consecrated for their priestly ministry, the sacrificial ceremony involves a priestly function, and it is said that Moses (himself a Levite) built the altar and sprinkled the blood of the sacrifices upon the altar and the people. When Moses and his appointed companions have ascended the mountain, the LORD then calls Moses alone to come into His presence to receive the tables of stone, the law, and the commandments, which He had written in order to legislate for (νομοθετῆσαι) the people. Here, the law was indeed founded upon the priestly ministry of sacrifice, in which the Levite, Moses, was the chief functionary.

For the writer to the Hebrews, therefore, the law which was weak includes the whole Old Testament economy, embracing its specific commandments, which, in their totality, form a coherent Law, which is itself erected upon the essential foundation of priesthood, and that prescribed as Levitical. It is this economy which can be denominated 'the first covenant' (9:15).

It is worth drawing attention also to Hebrews 7:5. This verse occurs in a passage designed to demonstrate the superiority of the Melchizedek priesthood over the Levitical from the fact that Abraham, the ancestor of the Levites gave tithes to Melchizedek, and that therefore Levi, in the loins of his ancestor, acknowledged that Melchizedek was greater than he. The writer notes that the Levitical priests have a commandment (ἐντολὴν ἔχουσιν) to receive tithes from the people of Israel according to the law (κατὰ τὸν νόμον). This whole phrase is sometimes interpreted as denoting simply the legal right that pertained to the Levites to receive the tithes.[2] These interpretations, however, make the words ἐντολὴν ἔχουσιν redundant: the phrase becomes tautologous. It seems better to take ἐντολή as the reference to the specific command that the Levites are to receive the tithe, and κατὰ τὸν νόμον as expressing that it is by the Law, considered as a totality, the entire system of old covenant economy, that this particular

---

[1] H.R. Jones, 'Exodus', in Guthrie & Motyer (eds.), p. 134; R.A. Cole, *Exodus* (IVP, 1973), p. 184; B.S. Childs, *Exodus* (SCM Press, 1974), p. 497.

[2] So A.B. Bruce, p. 257; A.M. Stibbs, 'Hebrews', in Guthrie & Motyer (eds.), p. 1203; D. Guthrie, *The Letter to the Hebrews* (IVP, 1983), p. 158.

commandment, along with all the others, is established. The significance of this, then, is that the payment of tithes by Abraham to Melchizedek is symbolic of the Law (the Old Testament system considered as a whole) deferring to the superior greatness of the economy to come in Christ;[1] this ancient incident is therefore itself a picture of the weakness of the law.

2   The Nature of the Law's Weakness

Reading 'and' epexegetically, verse 18 equates the weakness of the commandment with its unprofitableness (ἀνωφελές). This word has the connotation of something which is unable to make good what it claims to offer. The commandment that Levitical priesthood be laid down as the foundation for the superstructure of the Mosaic economy, the Law, was unprofitable because the promise which that economy offered could not be fulfilled within its own arrangements. The commandment was weak because the Levitical priesthood was ineffective, and so of no real service to the people.

It is important to note that weakness is not an unqualified feature of the law; it is defined by the writer to the Hebrews in a specific way. There is a sense in which he sees the law as powerful. In 2:2 the phrase, 'the word spoken by angels' refers to the law as given to the people of Israel at Sinai, and it is described as βέβαιος, a term with connotations of stability, unshakeable constancy, inviolable validity.[2] These are not symptoms of weakness, but qualities of strength, and the strength of the law was vested in its sanctions: 'every transgression and disobedience received a just reward'.

How, then, was the law weak? It has already been noted that the nature of the commandment's weakness and unprofitableness is defined by the explanatory clause which follows: "for the law made nothing perfect." It was the promise of perfection which the law could not make good. Although it is a single commandment which has been annulled owing to its weakness (v. 18), since this is the fundamental commandment upon which the entire old covenant economy stands, it follows that the law as a total system fails to make anything perfect.

The chief issue which now arises, therefore, is the meaning of 'perfection' (τελειόω/τελείωσις). Hebrews 7:19 contrasts with the law, annulled because too weak to perfect, the 'better hope' which is given in Christ. The benefit of this better hope is that, through it, "we draw near to God." The weakness, the inferior hopefulness, of the law in that it was

---

[1] Cf. Hughes, p. 253f, n. 11, O. Cullmann, *The Christology of the New Testament* (SCM Press, 1963), p. 90; J.A. Fitzmyer, '"Now this Melchizedek ..." (Heb 7,1)', in *C B Q* 25 (1963), p. 319.

[2] Cf. Thayer, pp. 99f.

unable to perfect was, essentially, this failure to create nearness between God and His people. It required a maintained remoteness, and therefore failed to bring perfection: at root 'perfection' means nearness to God.[1]

In this connection it is necessary to examine also Hebrews 9:9 and 10:1. The opening verses of chapter 9 describe the arrangement of 'the earthly sanctuary' (v. 1), with its two sections, into the second of which, 'the holy of holies' (v. 3), only the high priest went but once a year to offer blood for his own sins and those of the people. The reason for this restricted access into the second part of the tabernacle was an indication "that the way into the holy place was not yet made manifest while the first tabernacle was still standing" (v. 8). Verse 9 informs us that this restriction of access into the holy of holies was a symbol for the time then present,[2] during which gifts and sacrifices were offered which lacked the power to perfect those who performed the service. It is clear that the term 'holy place' in verse 8 does not refer to the holy of holies of verse 3, but to that which the latter represented, namely the drawing near to God mentioned in 7:19. Built into the physical arrangements of the tabernacle, therefore, was a symbol of the fact that the old covenant, the law, kept the people at a distance:[3] their exclusion from the holy of holies displayed the absence of perfection.

This inability of the law to bring perfection, to facilitate access to God, is linked in 9:9 with 'the conscience'. This occurrence of συνείδησις is the first of several in chapters 9 and 10. The inability of the law to perfect in regard to the conscience is here connected with 'fleshly ordinances' – probably a reference back to the fleshly commandment of 7:16[4] (v. 10), which serve a merely provisional purpose. According to verse 13, "the blood of bulls and goats and the ashes of a heifer, sprinkling the unclean, sanctifies for the purifying of the flesh". The blood of Christ, by contrast, purifies the conscience from dead works (v. 14).

The writer returns to this theme of the cleansing of the conscience in 10:1-4. In verse 1 the weakness of the law is again stated: it "can never with these same sacrifices, which they offer continually year by year, make those who approach perfect." Evidence of the weakness of the law is found in the very repetitiveness of the sacrifices: "For then [if perfection had been attained] would they not have ceased to be offered?" The need for repeated

---

[1] Cf. G. Vos, 'Hebrews, The Epistle of the Διαθήκη', in *Princeton Theological Review* 13 (1915), p. 623.

[2] So (e.g.) J. Calvin, *Commentaries on the Epistle of Paul the Apostle to the Hebrews* (Geneva, 1549), p. 199; against (e.g.) J. Swetnam, 'On the Imagery and Significance of Hebrews 9,9-10', in *C B Q* 28 (1966), p. 155; J.R. Sharp, 'Typology and the Message of Hebrews', in *East Asia Journal of Theology* 4, No. 2 (1986), p. 100.

[3] Cf. N.H. Young, 'The Gospel According to Hebrews 9', in *N T St* 27 (1981), p. 209.

[4] Cf. Lane, p. 216, Note w.

sacrifices is evidence of their insufficiency, and the absence of perfection is seen in the abiding consciousness of sins on the part of the people. The next phrase is hypothetical; it states what would have been the reality had such perfection been attained that repetition of the sacrifices could have ceased: "For the worshippers, once purified would have had no more consciousness (συνείδησιν) of sins." However, far from that being the case, the annual cycle of repeated sacrifices simply served, by way of constant reminder, to underline the sinfulness of the people (v. 3). Then follows the key statement (v. 4): "For it is not possible that the blood of bulls and goats could take away sins" (cf. 10:11).

The teaching of these passages as regards the weakness of the law is that the law lacked the power to cleanse the conscience by taking away sins. Perfection, which has already been defined as nearness to God, is now linked with a conscience cleansed of sin. For the writer to the Hebrews, indeed, these two concepts are functionally equivalent: it is an uncleansed conscience which is "the really effective barrier to a man's free access to God",[1] and, conversely, when the conscience is cleansed nearness to God is *ipso facto* a reality.

In the present context συνείδησις means the sense of burden derived from the awareness of guilt because of sin.[2] The word 'sin' in Hebrews usually means 'guilt'.[3] Where there is perfection, no consciousness of this guilt remains.

The cleansing of the consciousness is consequent upon the taking away of sins (10:4). This is to be understood primarily in an objective sense, though it has subjective consequences: the blood of Christ removes the sin of which His people are guilty from the sight of God, and it is in knowing by faith that this is so that His people are relieved of their sense of guilt.[4] Corroboration for this objective understanding of the work of Christ is found in the description of His Priesthood as a Godward ministry, defined as "propitiation for the sins of the people" (2:17).[5] The weakness and unprofitableness of the Law was that it had no power to effect this complete, objective removal of sin from the sight of God. Consequently, it was unable to deal radically with the subjective consciousness of guilt on

---

[1] F.F. Bruce, *The Epistle to the Hebrews* (Eerdmans, 1964), p. 196.
[2] Cf. Westcott, p. 293; Lindars, *Hebrews*, p. 88; Hughes, p. 391.
[3] Cf. Vos, *Teaching*, p. 122.
[4] Cf. Vos, *Teaching*, p. 118f, against Westcott, p. 307.
[5] Cf. (e.g.) L. Morris, 'The Use of ἱλάσκεσθαι etc. in Biblical Greek', in *Expos T* 62 (1950), *passim*, G.E. Ladd, *A Theology of the New Testament* (Lutterworth, 1974), p. 407; D. Guthrie, *New Testament Theology* (IVP, 1981), p. 469); against C.H. Dodd, 'ΙΛΆΣΚΕΣΘΑΙ, its Cognates, Derivatives, and Synonyms in the Septuagint', in *J Th St* 32 (1931), *passim*; T.C.G. Thornton, 'Propitiation or Expiation?' in *Expos T* 80 (1968-69), p. 54.

the part of the people. As a result, it could not facilitate the nearness of the people to God: it could not bring perfection.

It is no accident that, while in 9:9f the failure of the law to perfect in regard to the conscience is linked with σάρξ (flesh), in 10:1-4 the link is with the repetitiveness of the old covenant sacrifices. With reference to chapter 9 it is often alleged that there is a contrast between the outwardness of the law, focussed in terms of σάρξ, and the inwardness of the new covenant, focussed in terms of συνείδησις. The weakness of the law, it is claimed, was that its concern was entirely outward: the Levitical sacrifices could restore the worshipper only to "formal communion with God:" the sin-defiled person "was no longer religiously tabu",[1] but there was no inner cleansing from sin, and consequently no enduring freedom from the sense of guilt.[2]

However, it is doubtful whether the intended contrast in Hebrews 7-10 is between outwardness and inwardness. The issue hinges on the meaning of σάρξ. Bruce claims that "'Flesh' in this epistle denotes the outer and physical element in man's make-up in contrast to his inner being, his conscience."[3] However, this does not appear to be correct. Rather, σάρξ in Hebrews refers to the corporate nature of humanity in its earthly, and therefore mortal, existence, and the contrast is not inwardness, but heavenliness and eternality. In 9:12 the fruit of Christ's offering of His own blood, rather than that of bulls and calves, is described as eternal redemption. The similarity of wording with v. 13 suggests a contrast between flesh (v. 13) and eternity. Most commentators discern a contrast in 9:13-14 between flesh and conscience,[4] but I am not persuaded that this is the main point of the passage. The real contrast is between the blood of bulls and goats on the one hand, and the blood of Christ on the other.[5] The former had power only within the (temporal) confines of earthly, mortal human life, whereas the latter removes the consciousness of guilt from the people of God, and therefore enables them to attain access to the heavenly presence of God, and to be caught up into the immortal life of eternity.[6] The emphasis in the final phrase of 9:9 should fall not on 'conscience' but on 'perfect'. The key to understanding the work of Christ is that it perfects, where the law was unable to perfect, and the reason for that perfection is the cleansed consciousness. The weakness of the law was that it was flesh-

---

[1] F.F. Bruce, *Hebrews*, pp. 202, n. 86, 204.
[2] Cf. (e.g.) T.H. Robinson, *The Epistle to the Hebrews* (Hodder & Stoughton, 1933), p. 126f; H.W. Attridge, *A Commentary on the Epistle to the Hebrews* (Fortress Press, 1989), p. 250f; P. Ellingworth, *The Epistle to the Hebrews* (Paternoster, 1993), p. 454.
[3] F.F. Bruce, *Hebrews*, p. 202, n. 87.
[4] So (e.g.) R.McL. Wilson, *Hebrews* (Marshall, Morgan & Scott, 1987), p. 153.
[5] Cf. G.W. Buchanan, *To the Hebrews, Translation* (Doubleday, 1972),p. 148f.
[6] Cf. Lindars, *Hebrews*, p. 88; Wickham, p. 67.

bound, temporary and provisional (cf. v. 10): its efficacy was limited to the duration of earthly, mortal life, but it was inadequate to provide permanent access to the very heavenly presence of God, which is what is intended by 'holy place' in verse 8. The law failed finally to span the distance between God and His people. For that, the blood of Christ was needed, and it is this aspect which is highlighted by the emphasis on the necessary repetitiveness of the Levitical sacrifices in the parallel passage in chapter 10: repetitiveness is an aspect of σάρξ, of mortal, earth-bound life. Only His once-for-all sacrifice could lift God's people into the heavenly realm, that is, could perfect.

All this does not mean that old covenant believers were encumbered permanently with the consciousness of guilt, nor that they were bereft of heavenly experience. There is much in the language of Old Testament worship to indicate that the people experienced great spiritual reality in their relationship with the LORD.[1] However, it was not from the law that such experience came: the law could not bring perfection. Nevertheless, the law anticipated the coming age of fulfilment in Christ, and, as old covenant believers anticipated Him, He brought them the anticipated perfection.[2] However, the full promise (in economic terms) had to await His coming, as the writer indicates in 9:15 and 11:39f.

This leads on to a consideration of the dominant way in which the writer expresses the weakness of the law. In these chapters, the leading motif is the law's provisionality. The weakness of the law is bound up with its status as an intentionally interim measure, pending the coming of Christ, in whom it would be fulfilled, and by whom it would be superseded.

Three different words are used to express the interim nature of the Law. Two of them occur together in 8:5, 'copy' (ὑπόδειγμα) and 'shadow' (σκιά), and both are repeated later, in 9:23 and 10:1 respectively. Then, in 9:24, the word 'figure' (ἀντίτυπον) is used, answering to the word 'pattern' (τύπος), also in 8:5. Taken together these three terms portray the arrangements of the earthly tabernacle as modelled on the heavenly reality. The earthly sanctuary was a copy of the heavenly things; all its provisions were modelled on the true and substantial realities found in heaven.[3] It was "a shadowy outline"[4] of the heavenly arrangements, corresponding to the 'image' (10:1), which here means the thing itself. The reference to the earthly holy places as ἀντίτυπα of the true echoes the words of Exodus 25:40, quoted in 8:5, which defines what Moses was shown on the mountain as the τύπος. Moses was granted to see (in some symbolic

---

[1] See, e.g., Pss. 31:23; 36;10; 116:1; Hos. 6:3; etc.
[2] Cf. Calvin, *Hebrews,* pp. 170f, 200, 224; Vos, Διαθήκη, p. 12.
[3] Cf. Hewitt, p. 131; R.P. Martin, 'Hypodeigma', in C. Brown (ed.), Vol. 2, p. 291.
[4] J. Moffatt, *A Critical and Exegetical Commentary on the Epistle to the Hebrews* (T. & T. Clark, 1924), p. 105.

representation, no doubt) the layout of the heavenly sanctuary; the tabernacle which he proceeded to construct on earth was an exact replica.

It is important to note that, strictly speaking, what the writer says is not that the law IS the shadow, but that it HAS a shadow (σκιὰν γὰρ ἔχων ὁ νόμος), a point overlooked by most commentators. The implication is that it is not the law itself[1] (the Old Testament economy considered as a totality) which is merely an inadequate reproduction of the heavenly realities, but only that part of the law which formed the sacrificial ritual.[2] The law was a larger system which contained at its heart an element of provisionality; this resulted in the law as a whole being weak, unprofitable and provisional. Nevertheless, there were (as we shall later notice) some elements of the law which were certainly not merely provisional.

It is necessary next to notice that the writer elaborates on this teaching concerning the weakness, unprofitableness, and provisionality of the law by pointing to a number of contingencies which epitomize its weakness. Three aspects of this weakness of the law, are brought out in Hebrews 7:20-28 in the course of the detailing of the contrasts between the Levitical and Melchizedek priesthoods.[3] The weakness and unprofitableness of the commandment is in fact a derivative of the limitations of the priesthood which the commandment prescribed.

The first aspect of the weakness of the former commandment is that the priesthood was established without an oath (v. 21). Whereas Psalm 110:4 contains an oath sworn by the LORD in the declaration that the priestly order of Melchizedek is to endure forever, there is no corresponding mention of an oath in the consecration ritual of the Aaronic priesthood. The priesthood was set up by divine command, but the law was not backed up by an oath. The deduction which the writer makes from this observation is that there was no absolute guarantee that the Levitical priesthood would continue for ever. The Old Testament did speak of the perpetuity of its priesthood,[4] but for the writer of Hebrews this stated perpetuity is merely contingent and without the absolute status which only an oath could secure.

The principle underlying these verses is that enunciated in 6:16-18: a divine oath serves as confirmation of immutability. Immutability was never guaranteed in the case of the Levitical priesthood. Lacking this confirmation, the commandment which established that priesthood was inherently weak and unprofitable. Whereas it appeared to promise a perpetual priesthood to meet the spiritual needs of the people, in the event, because it lacked the underpinning of the oath, it was 'repealable'[5] by God

---

[1] Against A. Barnes, *Hebrews*, (Blackie, 1868), p. 220.
[2] Cf. Pink, p. 529f.
[3] Cf. Sharp, p. 98.
[4] Cf. Ex. 29:9; 40:15.
[5] J. Brown, *Hebrews*, p. 350.

at any time, and hence it lacked the power to deliver what it had appeared to promise. Consequently, the entire economy at the base of which was the priesthood was weak.

The second aspect of the weakness of the law is bound up with the mortality of the old covenant priests. This is the theme of verses 23-25, where Jesus' personal "unchangeable priesthood" is contrasted with the "many priests" of the former dispensation. The reason for the difference is that, whereas Jesus "continues forever" and "always lives", the Old Testament priests "were prevented by death from continuing," that is, in office.[1] The commandment was weak, therefore, because it could not secure the unchangeable priesthood which would have the power to "save to the uttermost" The author merely takes it for granted that priesthood which is not eternally vested in a unique individual is weak. He does not give a detailed explanation of why a perpetual priesthood handed down by genetic succession should be inherently unprofitable.

To understand why this is so it is necessary to pick up some clues earlier in this chapter. In verse 8 evidence of the superiority of the Priesthood of Melchizedek is found in the fact that, whereas "here mortal men receive tithes", yet "there he receives them, of whom it is witnessed that he lives." To elucidate this text reference back must be made to verse 3, which includes the statement about Melchizedek that he had "neither beginning of days nor end of life." This is probably an allusion to the tenure of his priestly office as being coterminous with his life.[2] Verse 3 then continues: "but made like the Son of God, remains a priest continually." Although Jesus Christ is said to be a priest 'after the order of Melchizedek', in fact it is Christ and not Melchizedek who is the model or standard.[3] The writer appears to take it as axiomatic that Christ's is the definitive priesthood.[4] Although he is seeking to build up a case for the superiority of Christ's priesthood by working from the commonly held Jewish assumptions about the Levitical priesthood, in his own mind the logical flow of the argument is in the opposite direction. Christ is the true priest, and by reference to Him, the superiority of Melchizedek's priesthood to that of the Levites is apparent, and consequently, the relative weakness of the old covenant economy is evident. Levitical priesthood was of necessity less profitable than that of Melchizedek. The source of this relative superiority is the eternal duration of Jesus Christ as priest. The author sees Christ's priesthood as having precedence because Christ Himself is the eternal Son in whom true priesthood was eternally anticipated.[5] By comparison with

---

[1] So (e.g.) Lane, p. 188; Ellingworth, p. 390; against Westcott, p. 190.
[2] So Barnes, *Hebrews,* p. 153; Pink, p. 366.
[3] So Guthrie, *Hebrews,* p. 157; Hughes, p. 24.
[4] Against D. Gooding, *An Unshakeable Kingdom* IVP, 1989), p. 158.
[5] Against L.D. Hurst, 'The Christology of Hebrews 1 and 2', in L.D. Hurst & N.T.

such a definitive standard, a succession of mortal priests is, essentially, weak and unprofitable. The relative weakness of the old is seen when it is compared with what "came after" (verse 28), which is the temporal manifestation of the eternal standard. Its inferiority relative to the new is associated with the mortality of its priests.

This leads on to a consideration of the contrast in verse 16, where the coming of Christ as priest is said to have been "not acccording to the law of a fleshly commandment" but, in a phrase neatly balanced with the former, "according to the power of an endless life". The authority which legitimated Christ's priesthood was not the law prescribing genetic descent, but the power of His own indestructible life, which is a feature of His eternal being as God.[1] Westcott discerns a double contrast in these parallel phrases between law and power, and between the fleshly commandment and the indissoluble life. The former is the contrast between "outward restraint" and "inward force", and the latter that between change and succession and the state of being "above all change except a change of form." He finds a further two contrasts within the second main contrast. The contrast between commandment and life is that between "external injunction" and "spontaneous energy", while that between flesh and indestructibility is synonymous with that between "that which carries with it the necessity of corruption" and "that which knows no change."[2]

This seems to be an excessively subtle way of reading the text. The writer's point is not that law contrasts inherently with power because it is external, but that this particular law is as a matter of fact weak in comparison with that with which it contrasts.[3] The logical flow of the argument is from the definitive standard of Christ's Melchizedek priesthood to the Levitical priesthood established by a law of genetic descent, which must of necessity be weak just because it is not the unchanging priesthood of the eternal Christ. He is priest by virtue of the powerful indestructible life which is His by dint of His divine essence. Therefore anything which is not that priesthood must, in relative terms at least, be weak.

There is more to be said for Westcott's second contrast. The point of this passage is that one aspect of the weakness of the law is that its priesthood was successive, being vulnerable to the constant interruption of death. This is in contrast with the standard, the authentic priesthood which is Christ's, and His alone, because He ever lives. This links with the contrast noted earlier between the repetitiveness of the sacrifices under the law and the

---

Wright (eds.), *The Glory of Christ in the New Testament* (Clarendon, 1987), p. 163f.

[1] So Westcott, p. 185, against W. Manson, *The Epistle to the Hebrews* (Hodder & Stoughton, 1951), p. 116; see also D. Peterson, *Hebrews and Perfection* (Cambridge University Press, 1982), p. 111.

[2] Westcott, p. 184.

[3] Cf. Hughes, p. 264.

once-for-all sacrifice of Jesus Christ: the logic of the writer's argument is that, just because the old covenant sacrifices are repeated and are not the unique offering of Christ, therefore the law must be weak absolutely as regards perfection.[1]

The third aspect of the weakness of the law is associated with the morality of its priests. According to verse 28 "the law appoints as high priests men who have weakness." The corollary of this has been stated in the previous verse: the Levitical high priests had to offer sacrifices, not only for the sins of the people, but also for their own sins. The same point has already been made in 5:2-3, in more general terms. A priest can empathize with the ignorant and wayward, "since he himself is also beset by weakness." As a result, he is required to offer sacrifices for sins, not only for the people, but also on his own account. The weakness of the law is hence associated with the weakness of its appointed priests. They shared in the ignorant waywardness[2] of the people, and therefore the propitiation which they obtained could never be absolute and final. The very need to offer sacrifices for their own sins also proved the weakness of the system.

The nature of the weakness of the Levitical priests may be inferred from the description of the moral excellence of Jesus Christ given in 7:26. He is extolled as "holy, harmless, undefiled, separate from sinners". These four terms cannot be rigidly distinguished from each other. They amount to a piling up of terms designed emphatically to state that Jesus Christ was pure and undefiled in His innermost nature and His outward life. By contrast the Levitical priests can only be described by the negation of these terms.[3] Jesus is further depicted as having "become higher than the heavens", whereas the Levitical priesthood was earthbound, and could not, if considered in and of itself, enable the people to obtain access to heaven. A final contrast is drawn in verse 28 between the men who have weakness and "the Son who has been perfected forever."

This now leads us back to the clarificatory clause in 7:19 with which we began. "The law [being weak] made nothing perfect", and this is a consequence of the weakness of its priests, but "the Son has been perfected forever". That is, He has obtained complete access to God, and in Him His people have the power to draw near. The weakness of the law was that it could not in and of itself, by any inherent strength of its own, bring the people into the closest of fellowship with God, because of its incompleteness in the light of the eternal standard, which awaited historical manifestation. The entire emphasis of Hebrews is that the law was provisional, temporary, anticipatory of Christ, but apart from this anticipation it was nothing. Christ, though He "came after the law" (cf.

---

[1] Cf. Vos, Διαθήκη, p. 17.
[2] Cf. F.F. Bruce, *Hebrews,* p. 91; against Ellingworth, p. 276.
[3] Against R.McL. Wilson, p. 128.

7:28), is in reality the first thing: He is the definitive standard, and it is by reference to Him that the law is seen to be weak.[1] In reality it was the death of Christ which provided "redemption of the transgressions under the first covenant" (9:15). The cross had retroactive import. It was the true sacrifice, of timeless validity, "the one thing waited for to give validity to all the sacrifices that had been offered through the centuries, and to put the elect people in possession of the 'eternal inheritance' promised to their forefathers, but never given save in type and shadow."[2] In all this the writer is not disparaging and dismissing the institution of Levitical priesthood wholesale. In 9:1 he stresses that the first covenant arrangements were divinely ordained, and proceeds to acknowledge that they had a provisional effectiveness. His way of expressing himself is to say that the new is better. This implies that the old was good up to a point. The good aspect, the relative power, of the law was that, through its sacrifices, it kept the people hoping for that coming great sacrifice.

However, because of the weakness of the provisional economy, the law, the time came inevitably for its ἀθέτησις (7:18). This word reappears in 9:26, where it refers to the putting away of sin. There it means that Christ made a decisive end of sin by His death on the cross: the sin of His people has been removed from the sight of God.[3] Here it is the law which is terminated, decisively and with finality.[4] There is an intrinsic connection between the two things. Because sin has been dealt with absolutely, therefore, the law, which kept alive the sense of sin and was too weak to deal it the decisive death-blow, is no longer necessary. The time of perfection has come with the manifestation of the eternal Christ. The weak, imperfect, provisional law is therefore finished.

3 The Ongoing Status of the Law

It is necessary now to raise the question as to the continuing validity of the law. In that the law, in the sense of the Old Testament economy, founded on the Levitical priesthood, weak, unprofitable, and provisional, has been completely annulled with the coming of Christ, clearly it has no continuing place at all. Nevertheless, the word 'law' may be used in different ways, and shortly before speaking of the its annulment (7:18), the writer has said

---

[1] Cf. Vos, *Teaching*, p. 58, Διαθήκη, p. 13; E. Käsemann, *The Wandering People of God* (Augsburg, 1984), p. 61.
[2] Wickham, p. 70f.
[3] Cf. Wickham, p. 76; Guthrie, *Hebrews*, p. 199.
[4] So W. Klassen, 'To the Hebrews or Against the Hebrews? Anti-Judaism and the Epistle to the Hebrews', in S.G. Wilson (ed.), *Anti-Judaism in Early Christianity*, Vol. 2: *Separation and Polemic* (Wilfrid Laurier University Press, 1986), p. 12; against Fischer, pp. 179f,184, Guthrie, *Hebrews*, p. 164.

that it has been changed (7:12). This implies that the law may continue to function in a modified form. The old economy is completely defunct, but some economical arrangement of divine-human relations is indispensable, and a new 'law', a new economy must supplant the old. The word 'former' (7:18) similarly implies that there is to be a succeeding commandment. The writer does not pursue this line of argument explicitly. Nevertheless, there are hints that he is prepared to consider the new covenant economy in Christ as a new law.[1] The question now, therefore, is whether he uses the word (or at least the concept of) 'law' in any other senses, and whether, according to him, the law, in any sense, has any power at all, which requires that it be seen as having an ongoing place in the lives of the Christians to whom he is writing.

There are several passages in Hebrews which need to be examined in order to answer this question. The first is 8:6, which contrasts with 'the copy and shadow of the heavenly things' (v. 5) the "better covenant, which was established (νενομοθέτηται) on better promises." The verb νομοθετέω can mean simply 'to establish'. However, etymologically it includes the idea that the establishment is on a legal footing, and the perfect tense suggests that this legal basis for the better covenant remains a reality. When compared with the other use of the same verb in Hebrews (7:11), it seems reasonable to suppose that the writer had the legal content of the word in mind, and chose it very deliberately for that reason.[2] This means that Hewitt misses the point when he writes: "The Mosaic covenant was a covenant of law, but the new is a covenant of promise."[3] Both covenants were established upon promises,[4] and the basis of both was a legal one.

But what precisely is the significance of that statement for the new covenant? The implication appears to be that it is always as Lawgiver that God establishes covenant. The covenant may be set up on promises, but the foundation underlying even the promises is the law, for it is against the background of His prerogative as Lawgiver that the LORD establishes covenant with his chosen people. Through the Gospel promises, the people of God under the new covenant are related to God as their Lawgiver. Obedience is required of them.

A few verses later (8:8-12) the writer quotes the passage from Jeremiah 31(LXX38):31-34 pertaining to the new covenant. These are the 'better promises' alluded to in verse 6. Included amongst them are two which are pertinent to the present subject. Verse 10 reads: "This is the covenant that I will make with the house of Israel after those days, says the LORD: I will

---

[1] Cf. Vos, Διαθήκη, p. 591, *Teaching*, p. 28; J. Swetnam, 'A Suggested Interpretation of Hebrews 9, 15-18', in *C B Q* 27 (1965), p. 389.
[2] Cf. Hughes, p. 296f; J. Brown, *Hebrews*, p. 369.
[3] Hewitt, p. 132f.
[4] Against Guthrie, *Hebrews*, p. 174.

put My laws in their mind and write them on their heart." Then verse 12b contains the related promise: "Their sins and their lawless deeds I will remember no more."

That the writer sees these two promises as the epitome of the new covenant may be deduced from the fact that in 10:16-17, when he returns to the Jeremiah extract, it is these promises alone which he repeats, omitting the intervening words.

By reference to the Epistle as a whole, A.B. Bruce sees the central reality in new covenant life as the 'everlasting oblivion' of sin;[1] closely joined to that in the writer's mind is the law indelibly inscribed upon the personality. Commenting on the passage in Jeremiah, J.A. Thompson notes that "there are parallels of a kind" to this emphasis in Deuteronomy.[2] F.F. Bruce's assertion to the effect that there is a great difference between the memorization of the law and the implanting of the law in the heart[3] overlooks the fact that rather more is intended by the Deuteronomy passages than merely memorization. The point is that the people should take the law to heart.

It is often alleged that there is an implicit comparison with the law written, under old covenant arrangements, on tablets of stone. However, this is at most incidental. The real difference between the covenants is not in the location of the law, but in the nature of the heart. Thompson draws attention to the description of the heart as a writing material in relation to sin in Jeremiah 17:1.[4] This verse pictures Judah's sin as engraved upon their heart by an iron tool with a diamond stylus. This is an important verse in the light of the present discussion. It pictures sin as thoroughly written into the national life of Judah; deeply ingrained, it cannot be erased. "Judah's rebellion was deep-rooted and ineradicable."[5] The people are disabled by hearts permanently stamped with sin. The miracle of the new covenant is to erase the ineradicable from the hearts of God's people, and to replace the engraving of sin with the inscription of His law.

What this implies in the end is "the receiving of a new heart by the people."[6] This is, as Peake rightly observes, the Old Testament anticipation of the truth clarified in the New Testament doctrine of the new birth.[7] Within the limits of old covenant arrangements, while "the law could reveal with vivid clearness the ways of good and evil, it failed to give the Israelites

---

[1] A.B. Bruce, p. 298.
[2] J.A. Thompson, *The Book of Jeremiah* (Eerdmans, 1980), p. 581 (Deut. 6:6; 11:18; 30:14).
[3] F.F. Bruce, *Hebrews*, p. 172.
[4] J.A. Thompson, p. 581.
[5] *Ibid*, p. 417.
[6] F.F. Bruce, *Hebrews*, p. 173.
[7] A.S. Peake, *Jeremiah and Lamentations* (Caxton, 1910), Vol. 2, p. 106.

the power which would have enabled them to do the good and resist the evil:" what is promised in the new covenant is the power to obey the law, and this is given in the indwelling Holy Spirit, who is the law inscribed upon the heart.[1]

The contrast between the two covenants, highlighted in the new covenant reality of the law written on the heart, is frequently defined in terms of the externality and internalisation. For example, in his discussion of the quotation in Hebrews 8, Wilson writes: "The point about this new covenant is that it will not be a series of external regulations to be observed; obedience will come from the heart."[2] Similarly, in the introduction to his commentary on Jeremiah, Peake writes: "The law of God and the heart of man no longer stand opposed to each other as external and internal. Man does God's will naturally and spontaneously because it is his own will, it has become an integral part of his personality". Later, commenting on Jeremiah 31:33, Peake suggests that "an external code must always be rigid and inelastic," whereas "the law written on the heart implies an inner principle which can deal with each case of conscience sympathetically as it arises."[3]

However, I am not persuaded that such ways of phrasing the contrast get at what is really intended. This can be illustrated by a closer examination of the words of Wilson and Peake. The presupposition of Wilson's comment is that it is not possible for obedience to external regulations to come from the heart. However, this is a questionable assumption. The heart may be inclined to do the will of an external authority with joy. The fact that 'obedience comes from the heart' in the new covenant does not of necessity imply that there cannot also be 'a series of external regulations to be observed'.

Peake's words also are open to challenge. Four comments seem to be required. (1) It is wrong to see the essence of the opposition between the law of God and the heart of man in 'spatial' categories (external/internal). The problem is, rather, a moral one, and derives from what fallen man is internally, not from the mere fact of the 'otherness' of the God who is his authority. (2) Though the new covenant miracle is that God's will has become an integral part of man's personality, it still remains God's will which has become thus integrated into the human personality.[4] Peake rightly makes this point, but some of his other comments come perilously close to implying that, with the internalization of God's will, that will has altered. (3) To speak of 'instinctive self-adjustment' might convey the false

---

[1] Hewitt, p. 136f.
[2] R.McL. Wilson, p. 139.
[3] Peake, *Jeremiah*, Vol. 1, p. 44f; *ibid*, Vol. 2, p. 106.
[4] Cf. J. Calvin, *Commentaries on the Book of the Prophet Jeremiah and Lamentations* (Baker, 1850), Vol. 4, p. 131f; Lane, p. 209.

impression that in the new covenant man becomes an authority to himself.[1] However, it is not that a new heart discovers the right way from its own instinct; the new heart is God's gift to man, and what is written upon it is God's law. (4) While it is clearly true that there is an element of rigidity and inelasticity about an external code, if, on the other hand, the statement that an inner principle can deal sympathetically with each case of conscience as it arises, be taken to imply that rigidity has been replaced with flexibility, and inelasticity with a capacity for extensive inclusiveness, then we really must ask whether it is still God who is the Lawgiver, or whether man has not rather become a law to himself. If, as God says, it is His own law which He Himself writes upon the hearts of His people, then what rigidity and inelasticity there is about God's law as an external code must remain when that law is internalized; the only alternative is to say that it is not after all God's law which is written upon the heart, but some other undefined and unspecific entity.

The fact of the opposition of the human heart to the law of God in its external form must not be taken as a ground for the dubious suggestion that in internalizing His law in human hearts, God has adapted it to human inability. God's law is a transcription of His own unchanging holiness.[2] It is the heart of man which is renewed and changed, and not the law of God.[3]

These observations lead on to the chief question raised by Hebrews 8:10 in the present context: what is the law which is written on the heart in the new covenant? This question may be answered in three stages. First, what did Jeremiah mean by torah, the Hebrew word which is translated νόμους in Jeremiah 31(LXX38):33? In answering this question I shall trace the use of torah through the book of Jeremiah.

The first reference is 2:8. Here the law is linked with knowledge of the LORD: surprise is expressed at the ignorance of the LORD on the part of those who handle the law. In 6:19 rejection of the law is set in parallel with the failure to heed the word of the LORD, and in 8:8f the parallelism between the law and the word reappears. The fact that the law is the living word of the LORD becomes apparent again through a comparison of the next two occurrences of torah. In 9:13 the two expressions, "they have forsaken My law" and they "have not obeyed My voice" are juxtaposed, while in 16:11 the possibility of interchange of terms is evident: they "have forsaken Me, and not kept My law." The law and the word are again combined in 18:18, while in 26(LXX33):4 to walk in the law of the LORD is to listen to Him. In 32(LXX39):23 and 44(LXX51):10,23 the twin terms the law and the voice of the LORD again coincide.

Thompson suggests that the law referred to by Jeremiah may be the book

---

[1] So W.F. Lofthouse, *Jeremiah and the New Covenant* (SCM Press, 1925), p. 89.
[2] So F. Cawley & A.R. Millard, 'Jeremiah' in Guthrie & Motyer (eds.), p. 645.
[3] Cf. Pink, p. 580.

of Deuteronomy,[1] and Peake interprets torah as "collections of rules" in written form.[2] A.B. Bruce takes it to be the ten commandments.[3] However, in the light of the above survey it seems better to interpret torah more widely as the initiating and sustaining cause of the knowledge of the LORD.[4] The torah is not so much regulation as revelation. To be sure, God's revelation included regulations, but the regulatory aspect of the law was secondary to its revelatory aspect. The torah in its written form was nothing other than the word, the living voice, of God Himself.

The second stage in defining the law written on the heart is to raise the question, what did the LXX translators understand by 'law'? It is necessary to discuss this because of the fact that at this point, uniquely in Jeremiah, the LXX translates torah by the plural νόμους.[5] Guthrie suggests that "it may be that the translator wished to emphasize the separate parts of God's law to distinguish these parts from the law of Moses as a complete unity."[6] However, given the meaning of torah as used by Jeremiah, it is more likely that the translator wishes to emphasize the comprehensiveness of the law rather than to draw attention to its separate parts. He is perhaps stressing the fact that the totality of God's self-revelation is to be written upon His people's heart according to the new covenant promise. The laws written on the heart, therefore, are not the moral laws only, nor even the divine requirements in their diverse aspects, but every element in the divine revelation. The living voice of the living God is to be engraved upon His people's personalities.

The two places where the LXX translates torah in the plural by νόμοι (plural) may be instructive in ascertaining what the translators understood by νόμοι. In Nehemiah 9:13 the laws of truth (νόμους ἀληθείας) were given by God at Sinai; the next verse however, refers to the law (singular) given by the hand of Moses. Both ocurrences of torah are plural, and the context suggests that the same occasion is in view in each case. This implies that the LXX translators may have seen little difference between laws and the law at this point. The phrase 'laws of truth' may express the fact that the various expressions of law are alike expressions of the one truth, which may therefore be an equivalent term to 'law' in the sense of

---

[1] J.A. Thompson, pp. 262, 299.
[2] Peake, *Jeremiah*, Vol. 1, p. 90.
[3] A.B. Bruce, p. 300.
[4] Cf. E. Jacob, *Theology of the Old Testament* (Hodder & Stoughton, 1955), pp. 270-3, following G. Ostborn, *Tora in the Old Testament* (Lund, 1945); H.-H. Esser, 'Law', in C. Brown (ed.), Vol. 2, p. 440; W. Gutbrod, 'The Law in the Old Testament', in Kittel (ed.), Vol. 4, p. 1046; C.H. Dodd, *The Bible and the Greeks* (Hodder & Stoughton, 1935), pp. 32, 40.
[5] Except in some variant MSS [see S.H. Blank, 'The LXX Renderings of Old Testament Terms for Law', *Hebrew Union College Annual*, Vol. 7 (1930), p. 279].
[6] Guthrie, *Hebrews*, p. 176.

'revelation'. In Daniel 9:10 the plural could be read as referring to the words of the prophets in contrast (v. 11) to the normative Law of Moses. Nevertheless, the two are identified, as the verses are linked by the word, 'and'. The words of the prophets were nothing other than the contemporary application of torah. It seems that in the minds of the translators there was little difference between the singular and the plural inasmuch as either could refer to the totality of divine revelation.[1]

Further light may be thrown on this subject by looking at the two places in the LXX of Jeremiah where a word other than torah is translated by νόμος, in one case by the singular and in the other by the plural. In 23:27 the LXX uses νόμος as a translation of שם (name). The prophets are said to be dreaming up their own 'revelation', and are trying to make the people forget the LORD's name/law by their dreams. The fact that the LXX has 'law' at this point may well be significant, in that, wherever else the verb, 'to forget' (שכח) occurs in Jeremiah with the LORD or His name as its object, it is rendered into Greek literally.[2] Assuming, then, that the rendering is deliberate, what would the motivation have been? Accepting that the name of the LORD "refers to the essential character of Yahweh",[3] the use of νόμος is not wholly inappropriate, seeing that the law is the transcript of that essential character. To forget the name, and to forget the law, of the LORD are two ways of speaking of forgetting the covenant God Himself. The translators perhaps wanted to emphasize that it is through His law that His people know the LORD for who He is. His law is indeed His revelation of His name, that is, of Himself. The law written on the heart is nothing other than the holy character of God Himself.

In 31(LXX38):36 νόμοι translates חק, which refers to the 'laws of nature' by which the sun, moon, stars, and sea are kept in their appointed courses. The point of the passage is that the LORD's covenant commitment to Israel is as unchanging as the laws which govern the succession of day and night and the churning of the waves of the sea. The fact that νόμοι is chosen to represent God's providential decree in its unalterable fixedness may imply that the translators found this to be the most suitable term for stressing the irreversible commitment of God to His people. We may then assume that they understood God's laws to be immutable in whatever context the word occurred. The law written on the heart, then, is as immutable as the laws of nature and, even more, as the commitment of God to His people. The possibility that the law written on the heart might be anything other than the law revealed in the Old Testament, which is an expression of the eternal being of God, is inadmissible. A change of the law, in the sense of the covenant arrangements which unite God to His

---

[1] So G.C. Workman, *The Text of Jeremiah* (T. & T. Clark, 1889), p. 146.
[2] Jer. 2:32; 3:21; 13:25; 18:15.
[3] J.A. Thompson, p. 501.

people, cannot include a change in the law, in the sense of the revelation of God to His people.

Furthermore, the fact that the LXX uses the plural here may serve as corroboration that we are right to regard the pluralisation of νόμος in 31:33 as signifying comprehensiveness rather then separateness. The word חק in the Hebrew of 31:36 is singular, whereas the preceding verse uses it in the plural to speak of "the ordinances of the moon and the stars". There is a unity to God's creation decree, but it is possible for it to be analyzed into its constituent parts, not necessarily in order to separate them, but rather to demonstrate how they inevitably hang together. The LXX uses the plural to express the comprehensive decree, rather than the particular elements in it. In the same way, the resolution of the divine self-revelation into its component parts does not in any way detract from their inseparability nor from its integral unity.

The third stage in this enquiry is to ascertain what the writer to the Hebrews understood by 'laws' as he quoted the passage from Jeremiah. Our survey of the meaning of torah as used by Jeremiah and νόμος as used in the LXX points to the conclusion that the word is understood in a broad sense. As has already been established, the writer to the Hebrews so understands it. 'The law', it has already been shown, means in Hebrews 7 the entire old covenant economy founded upon the Levitical priesthood. This was the expression of the eternal being of God: it is because God is who He is that the old covenant economy was established, and in every detail of Old Testament ritual and the life of the old covenant community, the nature of God was being revealed. The Law, in its broadest sense, was His self-revelation to His people, instructing them in the knowledge of the LORD. We may assume that the writer to the Hebrews understood the term 'laws' in the LXX to retain the normal Old Testament content which it would have when used in the singular, and therefore uses the word with that meaning. The laws written on the heart are substantially the same in content as the Old Testament revelation: the phrase represents the personal self-revelation of God in His provision of a way for His people to be in fellowship with Him, founded upon priesthood, and leading fundamentally to the knowledge of the LORD.[1]

The newness of the new covenant, according to our author, is not one of content, but of power, and the power of the new covenant is a function of its finality. The old covenant was provisional: it pointed forward to its fulfilment in Christ. However, the new covenant in Christ is the fulfilment of the old; it is not an entirely new entity. There is continuity[2] as well as newness. To speak of the newness of the new covenant in terms of its power brings us back to the main theme which we are considering. The old

---

[1] Cf. J. Brown, *Hebrews*, p. 373.
[2] So Fischer, p. 176; against Käsemann, *Wandering*, p. 63.

covenant, the law, was weak. The most important thing about the new covenant, the law written on the heart is not its internalisation pure and simple. That is only a means to an end. The end to which the writing of the laws on the heart is directed is to secure the power of God's self-revelation[1] where the former commandment was weak. The weakness of the law was its inability, independently of Christ, to facilitate nearness to God, because of its failure to remove the consciousness of guilt, resulting from the impossibility of its objective removal of sin.

Written upon the heart, the laws do bring knowledge of God: it is most significant that in the Jeremiah quotation the promise following that of the writing of the laws on the heart includes the words, "they all shall know Me" (v. 11). This is the purpose of the heart-inscription; it is not a mode of speaking of obedience "by choice rather than by compulsion",[2] but a declaration of heart-knowledge of the LORD. This is possible because the blood of Christ cleanses the consciousness. It is noteworthy that in 10:22 the writer urges his readers to draw near to God (to enjoy perfection) "with a true heart" and with "hearts sprinkled from an evil conscience." A 'true heart' is usually interpreted to mean a sincere heart. Guthrie points to 8:2 where the same adjective, ἀληθινός, has already occurred; he reads it as referring to "what is real as opposed to what is only apparent."[3]

However, this may not be the best way of taking the expression. The contrast in 8:2 is not between the real and the apparent, but between what is heavenly and final, and what is earthly and provisional.[4] The word ἀληθινός appears again in 9:24: the earthly holy places are differentiated from heaven itself as 'copies of the true'. This is not a declaration of the unreality of the Old Testament tabernacle, but only of its temporary, provisional, typical nature.[5] It may well, therefore, be that by "a true heart", the writer means, not a heart which is subjectively sincere, but one which is focussed on, filled with, the truth of God in all its finality as revealed from heaven as an objective reality.[6] Thus 'a true heart' could well be an alternative expression for a heart with the laws of God inscribed on it, the laws being the embodiment of the truth. The only other place where a cognate of ἀληθινός occurs in Hebrews is in 10:26, which speaks of our having received "the knowledge of the truth". 'The truth' here "amounts to the whole Christian revelation".[7] If we are correct to see 'laws' as

---

[1] Cf. Gooding, p. 174.
[2] R.K. Harrison, *Jeremiah and Lamentations* (IVP, 1973), p. 137.
[3] Guthrie, *Hebrews*, p. 213.
[4] Cf. Lane, p. 205f.
[5] Cf. Vos, Διαθήκν, p. 15.
[6] Cf. D. Hamm, 'Faith in the Epistle to the Hebrews: The Jesus Factor', in *C B Q* 52 (1990), p. 274.
[7] Guthrie, *Hebrews*, p. 217.

synonymous with 'revelation', then 'truth' seems to be a further alternative term for the same divine reality. It is to be noticed further that the noun 'knowledge' is derived from the same root as the verb in 8:11 indicating that in the new covenant it will not be necessary for each to say to his neighbour or his brother, 'Know the LORD.' Because of the laws written on the heart, 'all shall know Me'; to know the LORD is to know the truth. It seems, then, that a true heart is the heart upon which the laws, the self-revelation of God, the truth, has been inscribed. Moreover, a further implication of 10:22 is that 'the laws written on the heart' is an alternative expression for the cleansed consciousness. The reason why the consciousness is cleansed and the laws written on the heart is that the blood of Christ has removed sin totally as an objective barrier between God and man.

If we are correct to interpret the law written upon the heart more broadly than simply God's moral requirements, as the self-revelation of God in His essential being, as the living voice of the eternal God, then it is surely most important to observe that this whole Epistle begins by describing the Son of God Himself as that vital word (1:2). In contrast with the varied nature of God's revelation in times past, His final and absolute revelation took place in His Son. It is the inevitable multiformity of torah which renders it provisional. "In these last days", however, the plurality of Old Testament revelation finds its point of convergence in the one Son.[1] He fulfils in Himself, with complete finality, the Law in its entirety. The law was the transcript of the divine character; because He partakes of the divine nature, He is the law personified. That is why He was able to become greater than the angels (1:4) through whom the law was given at Sinai (2:2) at what was, to the Jew, "the greatest moment of revelation."[2]

Spicq has noted that the prologue 'already contains the entire subject of the epistle, according to the rule of the best ancient rhetoric. It presents the person and work of the Son of God, king and priest, revealer and redeemer, object of faith for Christians'.[3] Wilson comments: "Verses 2 and 3 declare in the clearest possible terms the exalted status of the Son, as heir of all things, agent in creation and sustainer of the universe, sitting on the right hand of the Majesty on high, while the brief reference to the purification of sins in verse 3b already hints at the priestly function which will be more fully developed later."[4] If it is true, as seems likely, that the entire subject of the epistle is contained in the prologue, that subject is probably simpler than the summaries of Spicq and Wilson allow. The main verb in verses 1-4 is

---

[1] Cf. Nairne, p. 302.
[2] Wickham, p. 5.
[3] C. Spicq, *L'épitre aux Hebreux* (Libraire Lecoffre, 1977), p. 34.
[4] R.McL. Wilson, p. 37.

'spoke (ἐλάλησεν) (v. 2).[1] This implies that the chief theme must be God's revelation.[2] Vos says: "The Epistle views religion as a product of revelation."[3] The cultus is itself 'law', and thus revelatory. Even the dominating theme of the central section, the High Priesthood of Christ, is subsidiary to the main theme, which is, 'God spoke'. The major emphasis is the contrast between the old and the new modes of revelation.[4] The contrasts between the other aspects of old and new covenant arrangements are secondary.[5] They are aspects of God's revelation of Himself. The community life of Israel with all its various requirements founded as it was upon the Levitical rituals was 'the Law'; that is, it was God's way of revealing Himself for that time.[6] The variety of methods of past revelation were all aspects of 'the Law', and it was provisional and temporary. The coming of Christ marked the new and final phase in God's self-revelation. The new covenant is likewise fundamentally revelatory: the law is now written on the heart; God spoke once and for all in His Son, in whom He reveals Himself to the hearts of His people. Christ is the Law in its ultimate manifestation. The law written on the heart is nothing other than what Paul calls Christ dwelling in the heart by faith (Eph. 3:17). The 'true heart' of 10:22 is, in the end, the heart filled with Christ. The fulfilment of the provisional covenant embodied in the torah is, then, the Lord Jesus Christ in Person. The weakness of the law was that the One whom it anticipated, the Son of God made man, had not yet come. He is the true Law, the authentic revelation of God. Now He has come, and is the law in the hearts of His people.

With this in mind we may note some other references in Hebrews to this theme of the finality of God's revelation in His Son, the Lord Jesus Christ. If νόμος means God's self-revelation, then lawlessness (ἀνομία) must mean the rejection of that revelation, and the refusal to live commensurately with it.[7] The first reference to ἀνομία in Hebrews comes in 1:9a, quoting Psalm 45(LXX44):7. The line, "You have loved righteousness and hated lawlessness" is interesting in the context of the catena of Old Testament quotations in Hebrews 1:5-13, in that most of the quoted lines serve to back up the author's claim that Jesus Christ is the divine Son. This line is unique in that it depicts the morality of the Son. Nonetheless, it has a vital place in

---

[1] Cf. J.P. Meier, 'Structure and Theology in Heb 1,1-14', in *Biblica* 66 (1985), p. 170.
[2] Cf. Pink, p. 25.
[3] Vos, *Teaching*, p. 68.
[4] Cf. Westcott, p. 3.
[5] Cf. Peake, *Hebrews*, p. 71f.
[6] Cf. J. Swetnam, 'Sacrifice and Revelation in the Epistle to the Hebrews: Observations and Surmises on Hebrews 9,26', in *C B Q* 30 (1968), pp. 227f, 231-3.
[7] Cf. Pink, p. 458.

the author's argument as defining the essential Being of the Son as absolute conformity to the law, and therefore as the unalloyed personification of the law.

In a number of Old Testament contexts there is a close association between righteousness and law.[1] To speak of the Son's love of righteousness, therefore, is to say that He remains ever totally committed to the revelation of God which was embodied in His own Person. Conversely, His hatred of lawlessness represents His refusal to countenance anything which goes counter to God's self-revelation in Himself.

With this in mind, we may note that in 10:5-7 our author applies to Jesus Christ the words of Psalm 40(LXX39):6-8. Interestingly, he omits from his citation the final phrase of the LXX wording, translated literally, "I desired, and Your law is in the midst of my heart." His quotation reads:

Sacrifice and offering You did not desire, But a body You have prepared for Me. In burnt offerings and sacrifices for sin You had no pleasure. Then I said, 'Behold I have come – In the volume of the Book it is written of Me – To do Your will, O God.'

The effect of the omission is to make the infinitive clause, "to do", 'a clause of purpose dependent on "I have come"',[2] and thus to bring Christ's purpose in coming into closer connection with His coming itself.[3]

However, it seems reasonable to assume that the omitted clause is in the back of the writer's mind as he makes this quotation. No doubt the text was called to mind because of the reference to the law in the heart. He has already quoted the Jeremiah passage a couple of chapters earlier, and will quote the key phrase again in just nine verses time, at the conclusion of the passage in which this citation from Psalm 40 appears. To put into the mouth of Christ the words, 'I have come to do Your will, O God', does in any case imply a delight in the doing of that will, which is tantamount to the love of righteousness and the hatred of lawlessness. The omission of 'I desired' is not therefore to be read as indicating that the sentiment of the phrase is alien to the writer's purpose, but rather as the result of the sense that it was superfluous to continue the quotation beyond 'Your will', the willingess of Christ's obedience having been already sufficiently established to serve the present purpose. Similarly, although the phrase 'and Your law is within my heart' is not explicitly quoted, its assonance with Jeremiah 31:33 was, as I have argued, the reason for the inclusion of this quotation at this point. This

---

[1] Cf. Pss. 39(LXX):9-11; 118(LXX):1,7,61f,75,77,105f,109,138,142,144,153,160, 163-5,172,174; Prov. 3:16; Isa. 51:4-8.

[2] F.F. Bruce, *Hebrews*, p. 232, n. 33; Ellingworth, p. 501.

[3] So (e.g.) Buchanan, p. 165; cf. J.C. McCullough, 'The Old Testament Quotations in Hebrews', in *N T St* 26 (1980), p. 369.

means that, although these words are not actually present, they are nevertheless the key to understanding the role of this quotation in the entire argument.

On the significance of the parenthetic clause 'in the volume of the Book it is written of Me' there is general agreement. The 'volume of the Book' means the divine law, embracing "all the written revelations of God's purposes,"[1] and that law is set in the midst of the heart of Jesus Christ. At heart He is the revelation of God, and therefore the body prepared for Him was one in which divine torah was personified and given human embodiment. His life was "the active counterpart of the written law."[2]

The importance of this quotation from Psalm 40 in its context now becomes clearer. In the context of chapters 8-10 the writer is teaching that under new covenant arrangements God's entire self-revelation will be inscribed upon the hearts of His people. The reason why this is possible at all is that that revelation has already been inscribed upon the heart of Jesus Christ, such that He is the divine self-revelation in its final redaction. In its ultimate form divine revelation is personified in human life because it is set at the heart of human personality, and in this last manifestation of torah God's purpose is that the life of Christ should be reproduced in all His people. Christ is the embodiment of the revelation, and His people are to be derived reflections of that revelation, to whom God is known in the heart. Christ is the true Man, the proper Man, the 'real Man',[3] who becomes the forerunner (6:20), in whom all His people know God, because Christ is the law in their hearts.

In the more immediate context of 10:1-17 the quotation from Psalm 40 has a significant place also. Verses 1-4 have described the weakness of the law in that it cannot bring perfection, being unable to take away sins. The coming of Christ into the world therefore marked the taking away of the law (v. 9) - the Levitical sacrificial system, and the merely partial revelation of God which it entailed - and the establishment of the new medium of revelation which finds its focus in the cross, where the Lord Jesus offered the body (v. 10) in which the law was now personified. No longer does the law have a mere shadow of the good things to come (v. 1); the very image (probably an intentional reference to Christ[4]) has been revealed, and the shadow has given place to the reality. Christ, the Law, is in the hearts of His people for ever; they know God, and their lawlessness, their Christlessness, is remembered no more for ever. The theology of Hebrews is characterized by a thoroughgoing Christo-centricity. Christ is the first and the last word of God. The 'law' was an interim revelation pending His coming in the

---

[1] Guthrie, *Hebrews,* p. 205.
[2] F.F. Bruce, *Hebrews,* p. 235.
[3] K.Barth, *Christian Dogmatics,* (T. and T. Clark, 1960), # 44.
[4] So (e.g.) F.D.V. Narborough, *The Epistle to the Hebrews* (Clarendon, 1930), p. 124.

flesh with the law in His heart. Now that He has come knowledge of God is an intimate reality for all His people, because they, like He, have the divine self-revelation inscribed upon their very personalities.

Vos points out that it is just because God's ultimate revelation is in His Son that the new covenant order in Christ results in 'perfection', that is, nearness to God. In emphasing the centrality of the idea of revelation for the theology of Hebrews, Vos notes that this Epistle sounds a complementary note on the subject as compared with the rest of the New Testament. Here revelation is considered as something "natural" for God: it is in His nature to desire personal communion with His own. "Revelation in a sense is the highest that God has to give because in it He gives Himself." The choice of the verb lalein in 1:1f is significant, in that it denotes "speech not primarily for the sake of conveying information but for the purpose of maintaining fellowship." Under old covenant arrangements "there was not that immediateness and directness which the author claims for the self-disclosure of God in Christ." The Word in times past was mediated by Moses and the angels; between God and His new covenant people "stands only The Son." Immediately Vos qualifies this statement: "As regards Christ, no intervention between God and us in the way of revelation can be affirmed. By Christ's activity in this sphere absolutely nothing is detracted from the immediacy of the divine approach to man."[1] In other words, the perfecting of man, in the sense of the effecting of a conscious nearness of man to God, is a function of the self-revelation of God. It was because the older revelation was at a distance, that nearness to God was not achieved. In Christ as His self-revelation, God Himself comes near to man, and that is why man finds himself near to God.

This is why there is so much emphasis in Hebrews on the vital importance that the readers should heed what they have heard. One of these injunctions is of particular importance. In 4:12 the writer portrays 'the Word of God' as 'living and powerful'. The referent of 'the Word of God' here is a matter of debate. Barnes cites four possible interpretations: (1) the particular word from Psalm 95 previously quoted; (2) the Gospel; (3) the whole of God's revelation, as particularly contained in the Scriptures in their entirety; (4) the Son of God, the Lord Jesus Christ.[2] The third of these interpretations could be correct, and is certainly more likely than the first two.[3] However, given that the Son is God's revelation in its final form, it seems impossible to exclude a reference to Him.[4] He is 'living', eternally as

---

[1] Vos, Διαθήκη, pp. 624-30.
[2] Barnes, *Hebrews*, p. 103.
[3] Against J. Brown, *Hebrews*, p. 214, and Lane, p. 103, who prefer (1).
[4] Cf. J. Swetnam, 'Jesus as Logos in Hebrews 4,12-13', in *Biblica* 62 (1981), pp. 214,217f,221f, against G.W. Trompf, 'The Conception of God in Hebrews 4:12-13', in *St Th* 25 (1971), p. 125.

God, and now raised from the dead as Man, and as a result He is a 'powerful' reality, where the law in its merely provisional form was weak. Pink's sumary of verse 12b is excellent: "Christianity consists not so much of external conduct, as the place which the Word of God has within us."[1] It is Christ - the Law – in the heart, as the defining reality of a person's life-commitment, which is the power of the new covenant. Christ is God's final word: if we fail to hear Him, there is no further revelation to follow. As given conclusively in Him, the law operates effectually in the life of the believer.

In the light of the probable *Sitz im Leben* of Hebrews, the writer's strategy is now plain. His purpose is to prevent the disaster of a return to Judaism by Jewish Christians. He has argued vigorously that the provisional arrangements of the old economy of the law have been completely superseded by the final and ultimate arrangements of the new economy in Christ, who is the law personified, and in whom believers attain perfection, that is, nearness to God on the basis of the subjective removal of the consciousness of guilt because of the objective removal of guilt in the eyes of God. He has shown his readers that their unsettledness of mind, resulting from the taunts of their unconverted kinsfolk, regarding the reality of full access to God in Christianity is unfounded, since Christ is the High Priest, and His once-for-all sacrifice has not only retroactive significance, but also prospective significance in His continuing ministry of intercession (7:25). The problem of their guilt in the eyes of God has been decisively dealt with, and the blood of the cross is sufficient to go on clearing them of post-baptismal sin. His solution is to call them to forward-looking faith (ch. 11) in the Word of God, now given absolutely in Christ. Fully to embrace by faith the truth of the finality of Christ is the answer to the potential problem of apostasy. Perseverance to the end (whatever the sufferings of the journey) is the hallmark of genuine faith. It is when discouragement (12:3) gives birth to unbelief that apostasy becomes a threatening possibility. It is when hope is looking onwards and upwards to the eternal Christ that the believer is encouraged and is anchored in his confidence in Jesus the forerunner (6:18-20).

One further cluster of questions must be raised. According to Hebrews does the fact that Christ is the revelation of God in the hearts of His people mean that the law as an external, objective reality (in the narrower sense of regulations) has no ongoing place in the life of the Christian? Is Christ in the heart the totality of the law in new covenant existence? What is the visible form and shaping mould of the life in Christ? Is the Christian life entirely one of direct subjective inspiration by Christ? How does the Christ-centred life function in practice?

The writer to the Hebrews does not appear to draw the conclusion that

---

[1] Pink, p. 216.

the law in the new covenant life is wholly within the believer. He does not perceive it to be a corollary of his teaching that the law as revealed in Scripture, the law as an external authoritative code, is of no value to the Christian and has no place in the believing life. On the contrary, in his final chapter he makes use of the law in instructing his readers about life in Christ. Since true faith is always perseveringly forward-moving, and holiness is the goal of its pursuit (12:14), it is incumbent upon the writer to define holiness for his readers. The key to the definition he finds in the regulatory law of God.

Hebrews 13 is often portrayed as an appendix containing a disconnected collection of various ethical precepts.[1] However, it is striking how many allusions to Old Testament laws there are in this chapter. The unifying factor is that the writer is enjoining upon believers the requirements of God's moral law already revealed prior to the time of Christ. Pink is the commentator who most clearly sees the connection of the final chapter with the rest of Hebrews. He points out that throughout chapters 1-12 not one moral duty enjoined by the second table of the law is inculcated, and finds a close connection between the opening verses of chapter 13 and the immediately preceding verses, for while 12:28 is concerned with the believer's duties Godwards, at 13:1 the writer turns his attention to his duties manwards.[2] In other words, the whole law, in its twofold structure as in the Decalogue, is in view in the second half of chapter 12 and the first six verses of chapter 13. Allusions to the Decalogue are obvious in verses 4 and 5,[3] while verse 2, with its extolling of hospitality to strangers can be read as the application to a different context of an oft-repeated Old Testament duty,[4] and Pink sees verse 3 also as a restatement of the Old Testament requirement of compassion for the afflicted.[5] Kistemaker reads the whole of verses 1-3 as an exhortation to fulfil the summary command of Leviticus 19:18.[6] The point is that "that which was commanded under the old covenant is repeated under the new."[7] The Gospel does not free believers from the demands of the law, and does not shrink from declaring the law openly as the description and prescription of moral duty. This is so, in spite of the fact that the author of Hebrews does not actually use the word νόμος

---

[1] So C.C. Torrey, 'The Authorship and Character of the so-called "Epistle to the Hebrews"', in *J B L* 30 (1911), p. 149. F.V. Filson, *'Yesterday': A Study of Hebrews in the Light of Chapter 13* (SCM Press, 1967), p. 81, sees 13:1-6 as showing how the system of animal sacrifices is replaced by sacrifices of praise, obedience and love.
[2] Pink, pp. 1105-7.
[3] Cf. S.J. Kistemaker, *Exposition of the Epistle to the Hebrews* (Evangelical Press, 1984), p. 409f.
[4] E.g. Dt. 10:18f.
[5] Pink, p. 1121f.
[6] Kistemaker, p. 409.
[7] Pink, p. 1118.

in this connection.

To speak of Christ as the torah written upon the heart must not be read as implying that the law (in the more narrowly defined sense) ceases to have any existence anywhere other than upon the hearts of believers. The written, external law still has a role in the believing life. The new phenomenon is that Christ in the heart by faith is the empowering of the Christian for obedience to the law. This must not be taken to mean that the writer to the Hebrews is preaching an ethic of sinlessness. Buchanan misunderstands him at this point.[1] The Christian is still burdened by weakness (4:15), as long as he lives in the 'not yet' (2:8). The Christian life takes place within the tension between the believer's own weakness on the one hand, and the power of Christ in the heart on the other. The Christian's heart-commitment is to the Word of God embraced by faith; however, when he succumbs to weakness, there is a throne of grace to which he may boldly come for mercy and help (4:16), because eternal satisfaction has been made for his sins. Therefore, guided by the law without and empowered by Christ, the law within, he presses on towards the consummation of perfection.

Conclusion

For the writer to the Hebrews, then, the law which is weak is the Mosaic economy as founded upon the Levitical priesthood and its sacrificial system. Its weakness lay in its restriction of access into God's presence, owing to its inability to bring perfect abolition of guilt. This weakness derived from its nature as a merely temporary, earthly provision pending the coming of Christ's archetypal High Priesthood, morally pure, without mortal succession, and established by God's oath. With His coming the law as a provisional economy was abolished and has no continuing place.

However, the writer is, implicitly, aware of other legitimate uses of the word νόμος, and hints at the possibility of regarding the new covenant as a new 'law'. Part of the newness is that, on the heart of God's people, where once sin was engraved, there is now enshrined His law, His saving self-revelation in Christ.

The believing life in Christ is not, however, divorced from the requirements of God's written law in the Decalogue. Although it is not a major theme of this Epistle, there is nonetheless a brief indication in the final chapter of the ongoing role of the law in Christian experience.

---

[1] Buchanan, pp. 104, 166, etc.

Summary

The studies of these four books have highlighted a basic harmony of teaching, notwithstanding the differences of emphasis between them. This may be demonstrated by drawing together the common threads under our main three headings.

1 The Meaning of 'Law'

In all four books νόμος refers consistently to God's law given by Moses, and all three of our authors view the law as an entire economic system designed to regulate worship of, and relationship with, God; it had sacrificial requirements as its foundation. Luke and Paul depict it further as a total way of life which defined the life of the Jews for the period from Sinai to Christ. In Romans Paul gives particular emphasis to the moral heart of the law. This is the one area of uniqueness in the definition of 'law' in these four books.

2 The Weakness of the Law

All four books are in essential agreement as to that which the law is too weak to accomplish, albeit that the terminology varies. According to Luke it is justification which is outside the power of the law. Paul, writing to the Galatians, links justification with life, and in Romans speaks only of the conferring of life, as that which the law was unable to accomplish. The writer to the Hebrews finds the weakness of the law in its inability to bring perfection, by which he means nearness to God, and which he associates with release from the burdensome consciousness of guilt in God's sight: this is tantamount to justification.

Luke, the writer to the Hebrews, and Paul in Galatians explain this weakness in terms of the law's incompleteness, unfulfilledness, and provisionality: the law is an interim arrangement awaiting the coming of Christ, and provided only provisional atonement. In Galatians and Hebrews, this is linked with the fact that the law pertains only to this world. Paul insists that the law is weak as regards justification because that was not the purpose for which it was given; that purpose is achieved by the covenant of grace. Hebrews expresses the same truth in speaking of the law's cultic foundation as a mere shadow of heavenly reality: its weakness becomes evident in the light of the coming of the eternal Christ.

Where the moral heart of the law is to the fore in addressing the peculiar situation at Rome, Paul makes a different point. The law has been disabled as a result of its seizure by sin's opportunism, which employs the law to arouse covetousness, that condition which pertains in the sphere of the flesh where the creation is accorded the ultimate status which properly belongs to the Creator alone. Consequently, in that sphere the law produces death, the very antithesis of that which it promised to confer.

In none of these books is the law portrayed as weak absolutely. Paul is particularly emphatic on this point. The moral law has the power to define sin, and so to convict the sinner (Romans), and the parenthetic epoch of the law had the power of stimulating hope for the coming of the Messiah (Galatians).

3 The Ongoing Status of the Law

In the three books where the economic definition of the law is uppermost, there is clearly a sense in which the law has no continuing role at all, albeit, as Luke ackowledges, that its requirements may, in certain contexts, linger for a period of transition. Essentially, however, it has been rendered obsolete ('annulled', as Hebrews puts it) by the finality of the ultimate sacrifice offered by Christ on the cross.

Nevertheless, the author of Hebrews depicts the law in its revelatory function as continuing in its very fulfilment in Christ, who is the law personified, and becomes, under new covenant arrangements, the law written on the heart of the believer. His coming gives the law (God's revelation) its power, and this is the newness of the covenant. Paul's equivalent terminology in Galatians is to replace the law in epochal terms by the Spirit.

Additionally, all four books recognize a continuing place for the written law of God as summarized in the Decalogue. In Acts and Hebrews this is only indicated by hints. In Galatians the word νόμος acquires a modified meaning in the last chapter and a half, as the apostle stresses the partnership in the Christian life between the Spirit as power and the law as pattern.

It is, naturally, in Romans that the continuing role of the moral law comes to fullest expression. The believer is no longer under the law as sin-definer, a function which it exercises in the sphere of the flesh. Nevertheless, that there is, in a different sphere, a role for the law in which it is no longer weak is implied by our key text from this Epistle. Comparison with Paul's wider teaching in Romans leads to the conclusion that the law is written on the heart of the believer by the Spirit, and as such acquires both an authority and a power for sanctification in the believing life.

Conclusion

The controversy over the law in the life of the believer within Reformed Evangelical theology is fundamentally a discussion about the interpretation of Scripture. All the parties illustrating the debate in Part One hold in common the assumption that the Bible is the inspired and authoritative Word of God. It is necessary now to assess which of the two broad categories of attitude to the third use has the greater Biblical support, at least as far as the four books studied in Part Two are concerned.

It has become clear that much of the New Testament literature with which we have been occupied is strictly irrelevant to the specific question, because it is not concerned with the moral law. Hence, where it is used in the debate, it is frequently misused. The failure on the part of some Reformed writers to make explicit the various nuances of the word 'law' makes for lack of clarity and misapplication of Scripture. This will become apparent.

Both parties to the debate are agreed that the weakness of the law concerns justification, and that it is derived from the moral weakness of sinful humanity. The reference to justification (allowing for the differences in vocabulary) is a correct interpretation of all four books. The contemporary doctrinal antinomian, Michael Eaton, is wrong to interpret Galatians as the rejection of sanctification through the law. However, the derivation of the law's weakness for justification from human weakness is legitimate for the interpretation of Romans only. In Acts, Galatians and Hebrews the weakness of the law for justification has to do with its God-given purpose as an interim and provisional arrangement pending the coming of Christ. The use of the texts from Acts, Galatians, and Hebrews in this context by some from both sides of the debate (Bonar in defending the third use, and Brine, Fisher, and Macarthur for the doctrinal antinomians) is invalid.

The provisionality of the law understoood as an economy, and its consequent abrogation with the coming of Christ, is recognised by several of those who advocate the third use. This rightly understands the sense of νόμος in Acts, Galatians, and Hebrews. Fletcher attempts, wrongly, to derive this teaching from Romans 7. The doctrinal antinomians, Chafer,

Reisinger and Michael Eaton, err in including in the interpretation of Galatians the idea that the believer is no longer under the ten commandments; Chantry rightly observes that the termination of the Mosaic economy need not carry with it the implication that the moral law is suspended.

Some of our writers express the role of the law as a notional means of justification and life by the phrase 'covenant of works'. Although the idea may have some validity in the case of Romans, the term is not scriptural, and the attempt to support it from Galatians also (Hall for those who advocate the third use, and Chafer for the doctrinal antinomians) is to juxtapose texts which are not using the word νόμος in precisely the same way, and to create confusion by applying to both the moral and the ceremonial law functions which Paul applies distributively to one or the other.

Recognizing the distinctions within the law of God leads on to acknowledging that the power of the law differs according to whether it is understood as the Mosaic dispensation or, more restrictedly, as the moral law. As the latter, the power of the law towards unbelievers is rightly interpreted, from Romans, as the power to condemn. However, those who base this idea on any of the other three books, and who introduce the word 'curse' in this context (John Eaton, Crisp, and Fisher amongst the doctrinal antinomians, and Fletcher from the other party) misread those books.

When νόμος is understood dispensationally its power may be described as 'pedagogical'. Calvin and Hall correctly link the provisionality of the economy with the hope for the Messiah, and define its pedagogical function accordingly. Hall adds to this the insight, which finds support from Hebrews, that the ceremonial law fostered in Israel the sense of guilt: this is not the same as the law's condemning power in Romans, because it is an aspect of the law's shadow-nature. Those who understand the law's pedagogical power in a general sense as the power to drive the sinner to Christ (Bolton and Boston for the third use, and Fisher and Chafer for the antinomians) read into Galatians more than is there, because they fail to pick up the epochal nuance and the reference to Israel specifically.

The doctrinal antinomians sometimes portray a sharp dichotomy between the law and the gospel or grace. This is most evident in John Eaton and in Dispensationalism. Those who advocate the third use (especially Watson, Fletcher, Gerstner, and Chantry), however, reject this disjunction. It is they who appear to have scriptural support. In the three books which use νόμος in the larger sense, there is no suggestion of such a distinction. Acts distinguishes between the law and Christ, but the gospel of grace was proclaimed under the law in the forgiveness of sins. Galatians depicts the law as a parenthesis within the overarching gracious gospel reality of the covenant, where justification has always been by faith alone, the function of the law being that of hope-stimulation for the Messiah. Hebrews distinguishes between the law and the new covenant, but the latter has a legal basis, which indicates that the law is not incompatible with the gospel of grace. Hadow teaches that the law was given by Christ, a view which finds corroboration in Galatians and Hebrews, and is not therefore unconnected with the gospel of grace.

Turning now to the specific issue of the place of the moral law in the believing life, it must be observed that those who interpret Romans 8:4 with reference to sanctification seem to be correct, though the differences of interpretation cut across the main divide. The doctrinal antinomian teaching that sanctification is the direct work of the Spirit alone lacks the support of any of these four New Testament books, as does Cudworth's view that the law and the Spirit must be radically separated. To argue to this conclusion from the premise that the law is weak is to isolate the doctrine of the law's weakness from its true Biblical context, and so to misapply it. Those who insist on the third use of the law have the greater Biblical support. Although it is Romans which most emphatically demonstrates that the law is a powerful instrument for sanctification when employed by the Spirit in the life of the Christian (especially so if my interpretation of 8:3a is correct), an ongoing role for the law is at least hinted at in the other three books also. The doctrinal antinomians typically fail to pick up the shift in meaning of νόμος which occurs in Galatians after 5:4. Calvin rightly interprets Romans 8:3 when he says that the law is weak only in isolation from the Spirit. Shepard has the support of Romans 13:8-10, Galatians 5:14, and Hebrews 13 when he insists that the law within the heart does not mean that there is no need of the law without, and that the love command does not replace the law. Reisinger errs in this respect.

The debate within Reformed Evangelicalism raises a number of other issues too, some of which are of wider interest beyond the particular constituency which has been the concern of this study. The consideration of these is outside the scope of this thesis, but it is worth at least signalling the foremost one. The comments by Jinkins on the American controversy of the 1630's and Gerstner on Dispensationalism indicate that the division over the law may well be linked with a difference in the understanding of human nature. In saving His people does God override the nature which He has created? As early as the Spiritual Libertinism which Calvin confronted there was evidence of a view that 'spirituality' elevated humanity into a sphere above the law; this appears to be the assumption of holiness versions of doctrinal antinomianism also. For the doctrinal antinomians the 'new creation' which is entailed in being a Christian (cf. Gal. 6:15) is not recognized to be 'faith working' (Gal. 5:6), but God at work directly, bypassing the very person whom He has recreated. On the other hand, those who teach the third use recognize that the transforming power of God's grace truly renews the nature which He has created, giving human nature itself a new power to work in obedience to the law.

One observation which was made several times in Part One was that, in the end, it appears to be impossible to sustain a doctrinal antinomian position with absolute consistency. This was demonstrated with reference to John Eaton, Crisp, Dispensationalism, Reisinger, and Michael Eaton. To maintain the position a dubious distinction has to be made between law and morality. However, those who defend the third use speak of the 'moral law', thus evincing an inseparable connection between the two from their perspective. Does this mean that in the end the debate is merely a matter of words, with little real difference of substance between the two categories? I think not. For all that the doctrinal antinomians fail to carry through their position to its logical conclusion, their confidence in the transforming power of God's grace by the Spirit appears to be out of balance with an awareness of the lingering power of sin even in the redeemed human heart.

In terms of pastoral practice, this suggests that Wesley is right to discern effective power in the preaching of the law to believers, and that the doctrinal antinomian claim that such preaching hinders sanctification or breeds legalism is not inevitably true. Fletcher is right to recognize that the bondage to which Paul refers (Gal. 4:9; 5:1) relates not to the moral law, but to the ceremonies.

It has been noted that several of those who defend the third use have argued that it is but a short step from doctrinal antinomianism to practical antinomianism, notwithstanding the intentions of the doctrinal antinomians to the contrary. It is a moot point whether the third use of the law is emphasized purely as correct Biblical doctrine or whether concern with the issue is fuelled by fear of practical antinomianism. In certain cases (for example Luther, Hall, Alderson), advocacy of the third use of the law appears to have been stimulated by outbreaks of moral licence. Nevertheless, it remains the case that the third use is upheld by the evidence of the New Testament texts which we have studied. The onus, it would seem, is on the doctrinal antinomians to provide further evidence that their position really has scriptural warrant, allowing for the different nuances in the word νόμος found in the New Testament. The conclusion to which this study has led is that such a task is in fact impossible. The third use of the law is wholly in tune with the teaching of Acts, Romans, Galatians, and Hebrews.

Bibliography

Abbreviated Journal Titles

Bib Interp	Biblical Interpretation	*Interp*	Interpretation
Bib Sac	Bibliotheca Sacra	*J B L*	Journal of Biblical Literature
Bib Z	Biblische Zeitschrift		
Cal Th J	Calvin Theological Journal	*J St N T*	Journal for the Study of the New Testament
C B Q	Catholic Biblical Quarterly	*Nov Test*	Novum Testamentum
		N T St	New Testament Studies
Ev R Th	Evangelical Review of Theology	*Scot J Th*	Scottish Journal of Theology
Expos T	Expository Times	*St Th*	Studia Theologica
Harv Th R	Harvard Theological Review	*Th*	Theology
		Th Z	Theologische Zeitschrift

1. Historical Sources (Introduction and Part One)

1) Primary Texts

ALDERSON, R., *No Holiness, No Heaven! Antinomianism Today* (Edinburgh: Banner of Truth, 1986)

ALDRICH, R.L., 'Has the Mosaic Law Been Abolished?', in *Bib Sac* (Oct, 1959), pp. 322-35

BAXTER, R., 'A Call to the Unconverted to Turn and Live, and Accept of Mercy while Mercy may be had, as ever they would Find Mercy in the Day of their Extremity; From the Living God', in Jenkyn (ed.), pp. 41-195

BOLTON, S., *The True Bounds of Christian Freedom* (Edinburgh: Banner of Truth, 1645, 1964)

BONAR, H., *God's Way of Holiness* (London: James Nisbet, 1864)

BOSTON, T., *A General Account of My Life, Printed for the First Time from the Original Manuscript* (London: Hodder & Stoughton, 1908)

- 'The Marrow of Modern Divinity', *with Notes* (Falkirk: Patrick Mair, 1789)

BRINE, J., *The Certain Efficacy of the Death of Christ Asserted: Or, The Necessity, Reality, and Perfection of His Satisfaction pleaded for: The Objections of the Socinians and Arminians are answered: The Moral Law proved to be in full Force: And the Inconditional Nature of the New Covenant is demonstrated; in Answer to a Book, called, The Ruin and Recovery of Mankind* (London: Aaron Ward, 1743)

CALVIN, J., *Institues of the Christian Religion*, Books 1-4 [1559] (MacDill: MacDonald, n.d.)

CHAFER, L.S., *Grace* (Chicago: Bible Institute Colportage Association, 1928)

CHANTRY, W.J., *God's Righteous Kingdom: Focussing on the Law's Connection with the Gospel* (Edinburgh: Banner of Truth, 1980)

CRISP, T., *Christ Alone Exalted, in the Perfection and Encouragement of the Saints,*

Notwithstanding Sins and Trials, Being the Complete Works, Containing Fifty-Two Sermons on Several Select Texts of Scripture. A New Edition, Being the Seventh. 2 Vols. (London: John Bennett, 1832)

CUDWORTH, W., *A Dialogue Between a Preacher of Inherent Righteousness, And a Preacher of God's Righteousness, Reveal'd from Faith to Faith: Being an Answer to a Late Dialogue Between an Antinomian and his Friend* (London: J. Hart, 1745)

- *Some Reasons Against making Use of Marks and Evidences In order to attain the Knowledge of our Interest in Christ* (London: J. Hart, 1745)

EATON, J., *The Honey-Combe of Free Justification by Christ Alone, Collected out of the meere Authorities of Scripture, and common and unanimous consent of the faithfull Interpreters and Dispensers of Gods mysteries upon the same, especially as they expresse the excellency of Free Justification* (London: Robert Lancaster, 1642)

EATON, M.A., *How to Live a Godly Life: The Biblical Doctrine of Sanctification* (Tonbridge: Sovereign World, 1993)

FINNEY, G.C., *Views of Sanctification* (London: A.K. Newman, 1843)

FISHER, E., *The Marrow of Modern Divinity: Touching both the Covenant of Works, and the Covenant of Grace: with their use and end, both in the time of the Old Testament, and in the time of the New. Wherein every one may clearly see how far forth he bringeth the LAW into the case of Justification, and so deserveth the name of LEGALIST; And how far forth he rejecteth the LAW in the case of Sanctification, and so deserveth the name of ANTINOMIST. With the middle path betwixt them both, which by JESUS CHRIST leadeth to eternall life* (London: G. Calvert, 1645)

FLETCHER, J., *A Second Check to Antinomianism; occasioned by a late narrative, in three letters to the Hon. and Rev. Author* (London: W. Strahan, 1771)

- *A Vindication of the Rev. Mr. Wesley's Last Minutes: occasioned by A circular, printed Letter, Inviting principal Persons, Both Clergy and Laity, as well of the Dissenters as of the established Church, Who disapprove of those Minutes, To oppose them in a Body, as a dreadful Heresy: and Designed To remove Prejudice, check Rashness, promote Forbearance, defend the Character of an eminent Minister of Christ, and prevent some important Scriptural truths from being hastily branded as heretical. In Five Letters* (Bristol: W. Pine, 1771)

HADOW, J., *The Antinomianism of The Marrow of Modern Divinity Detected. Wherein the Letter to a Private Christian, about Believers Receiving the Law, as the Law of Christ, is specially considered* (Edinburgh: John Mosman, 1721)

- *The Record of God and the Duty of Faith Therein Required* (Edinburgh: John Mosman, 1719)

HALL, R., *Help to Zion's Travellers: Being an Attempt to Remove Various Stumbling Blocks out of the Way Relating to Doctrinal, Experimental, and Practical Religion* (London: Caxton, 1781)

HEIDELBERG CATECHISM [1563], in Schaff (ed.), pp. 307-55

HOPKINS, E.H., *The Law of Liberty in the Spiritual Life* (London: Marshall & Scott, 1952)

JENKYN, T.W. (ed.), *Works of the English Puritan Divines: Baxter* (London: Thomas Nelson, 1846)

LONDON CONFESSION: *The Confession of Faith of those Churches which are commonly (though falsely) called Anabaptists; Presented to the view of all that fear God, to examine by the touchstone of the Word of Truth: As likewise for the taking off those aspersions which are frequently both in Pulpit and Print (although unjustly), cast upon them* (London: Matthew Simmons, 1644); reproduced in Lumpkin, pp. 153-71

MacARTHUR, J.F., *Faith Works: The Gospel According to the Apostles* (Dallas: Word, 1993)

MAHAN, A., *Life Thoughts on the Rest of Faith* (London: F.E. Longley, n.d.)

MESSAGE OF KESWICK AND ITS MEANING, The, [anon] (London: Marshall, Morgan and Scott, 1957)

OSBORNE, S., 'The Christian and the Law', in *Bib Sac* (Jul-Sep, 1952), pp. 239-47

REISINGER, J.G., *Abraham's Four Seeds: An examination of the basic principles of Covenant Theology and Dispensationalism as they each relate to the promise of God to "Abraham and his seed"* (Venetia: Sound of Grace, 1987)
- *Tablets of Stone* (Southbridge: Crowne, 1989)
- *The Law/Grace Controversy: A Defense of the Sword and Trowel and the Council on Baptist Theology* (Sterling: Grace Abounding Ministries, 1982)

REPORT OF THE TRIAL OF MRS. ANNE HUTCHINSON BEFORE THE CHURCH IN BOSTON, in D.D. Hall (ed.),pp. 349-88

SCOFIELD, C.I., 'The Grace of God', in Torrey et al. (eds.), pp. 399-407

SCOTTISH CONFESSION OF FAITH [1560], in Schaff (ed.), pp. 437-79

SECOND HELVETIC CONFESSION [1566], in Schaff (ed.), pp. 233-306

SHEPARD, T., *The Sound Believer, Or A Treatise on Evangelical Conversion: Discovering the Work of God's Spirit in Reconciling a Sinner to God* (Paisley: Stephen and Andrew Young, 1812)

WATSON, T., *The Ten Commandments* (Edinburgh: Banner of Truth, 1692, 1965)

WESLEY, J., *Journal, Enlarged from Original MSS, with Notes From Unpublished Diaries, Annotations, Maps and Illustrations*. 8 Vols. Ed. N. Curnock (London: Charles H. Kelly, n.d.)
- *The Letters*. 8 Vols. Ed. J. Telford (London: Epworth, 1931)
- *A Plain Account of Christian Perfection* (London: Epworth, 1952)

WESTMINSTER CONFESSION OF FAITH [1646], (Glasgow: Free Presbyterian Publications, 1985)

WHEELWRIGHT, J., 'A Fast-Day Sermon', in D.D. Hall (ed.), pp. 152-72

WHITEFIELD, G., *Journals: A new edition containing fuller material than any hitherto published* (Edinburgh: Banner of Truth, 1960)
- *Select Sermons* (London: Banner of Truth, 1958)

WINTHROP, J., 'A Short Story of the Rise, reign, and ruine of the Antinomians, Familists & Libertines', in D.D. Hall (ed.), pp. 199-310

2) Secondary Sources

ABELOVE, H., *The Evangelist of Desire: John Wesley and the Methodists* (Stanford: Stanford University Press, 1990)

d'AUBIGNE, J.H.M., *History of the Reformation in Europe in the Time of Calvin, Vol. III, France, Switzerland, Geneva* (London: Longman, Green, Longman, Roberts and Green, 1864)

AYLING, S., *John Wesley* (London: Collins, 1979)

BARABAS, S., *So Great Salvation: The History and Message of the Keswick Convention* (London: Marshall, Morgan & Scott, 1952)

BARING-GOULD, S., *The Evangelical Revival* (London: Methuen, 1920)
BASS, C.B., *Backgrounds to Dispensationalism: Its Historical Genesis and Ecclesiastical Implications* (Grand Rapids: Baker, 1960)
BATTIS, E., *Saints and Sectaries: Anne Hutchinson and the Antinomian Controversy in the Massachusetts Bay Colony* (Chapel Hill: The University of North Carolina Press, 1962)
BEBBINGTON, D.W., *Evangelicalism in Modern Britain: A History from the 1730's to the 1980's* (London: Unwin Hyman, 1989)
BERGER, P.L., *Invitation to Sociology: A Humanistic Perspective* (Harmondsworth: Penguin 1963)
BERKOUWER, G.C., *Faith and Sanctification* (Grand Rapids: Eerdmans, 1952)
BICKLEY, A.C., 'Tobias Crisp', in Stephen & Lee (eds.), Vol. V, p. 99f
BOLAM, G.C., J. GORING, H.L. SHORT, & R. THOMAS, *The English Presbyterians: From Elizabethan Puritanism to Modern Unitarianism* (London: George Allen & Unwin, 1968)
BROWN, R., *The English Baptists of the Eighteenth Century* (London: Baptist Historical Society, 1986)
BROWN-LAWSON, A., *John Wesley and the Anglican Evangelicals of the Eighteenth Century: A Study in Cooperation and Separation With Special reference to The Calvinistic Controversies* (Durham: Pentland, 1994)
BUGDEN, D. (ed.), *Living the Christian Life* (Huntingdon: Westminster Conference, 1975)
CAMPBELL, K.M., 'Living the Christian Life - The Antinomian Controversies of the 17th Century', in Bugden (ed.), pp. 61-81
CARSON, D., *School of Advanced Learning: Biblical Interpretation*, being four tapes of addresses given at Word Alive, 1994 (Eastbourne: International Christian Communications, 1994)
COAD, F.R., *A History of the Brethren Movement: Its Origins, its Worldwide Development and its Significance for the Present Day* (Exeter: Paternoster, 1968)
COHN, N., *The Pursuit of the Millennium: Revolutionary millenarians and mystical anarchists of the Middle Ages* (London: Paladin, 1970)
DALLIMORE, A., *George Whitefield: The Life and Times of the Great Evangelist of the Eighteenth-Century*. 2 Vols. (Edinburgh: Banner of Truth, 1970, 1980)
DOUMERGUE, E., *Jean Calvin: Les hommes et les choses de son temps*, Quatrieme Partie, Tome Sixieme (Neuilly-sur-Seine: Editions de La Cause, 1926)
ELLIOT, R., 'A Summary of Gospel Doctrine taught by Mr. Whitefield, Recorded in a Funeral Sermon on his Death', in Whitefield, *Select Sermons*, pp. 33-46
FARLEY, B.W., 'The Theology of Calvin's Tract Against the Libertines', in Gamble (ed.), Vol. 5, pp. 206-18
FERGUSON, S., *The Marrow Controversy* [Tape 1. *Historical Background*] (Philadelphia: Westminster Media, 1994)
FOSTER, S., 'New England and the Challenge of Heresy, 1630-1660: The Puritan Crisis in Transantlantic Perspective', in *William and Mary Quarterly* 3rd Series, 38 (1981), pp. 624-60
GAMBLE, R.C. (ed.), *Articles on Calvin and Calvinism*, Vol. 5: *Calvin's Opponents* (New York: Garland, 1992)
GERSTNER, J.H., *Wrongly Dividing the Word of Truth: A Critique of Dispensationalism* (Brentwood: Wolgemuth and Hyatt, 1991)

GILL, J., *Notes Explantory of Several Passages in [the writings of Crisp], with Memoirs of the Doctor's Life*, in Crisp
GUINNESS, O., *Fit Bodies, Fat Minds: Why Evangelicals Don't Think and What to Do About It* (London: Hodder and Stoughton, 1995)
HALL, D.D., 'Introduction', in D.D. Hall (ed.), pp. 3-23
- 'Preface to the Second Edition', in D.D. Hall (ed.), pp. ix-xviii
HALL, D.D. (ed.), *The Antinomian Controversy, 1636-1638: A Documentary History*, Second Edition (Durham: Duke University Press, 1991)
HENDERSON, H.F., *The Religious Controversies of Scotland* (Edinburgh: T. & T. Clark, 1905)
HESSELINK, I.J., *Calvin's Concept of the Law*. Princeton Theological Monograph Series, 30 (Allison Park: Pickwick, 1992)
HOAD, J., *The Baptist: An historical and theological study of the Baptist identity* (London: Grace Publications, 1986)
HOLDEN, J.S. (ed.), *The Keswick Jubilee Souvenir: The Story of the Convention's Fifty years' Ministry and Influence* (London: Marshall Brothers, 1925)
HÖPFL, H., *The Christian Polity of John Calvin* (Cambridge: Cambridge University Press, 1982)
HUEHNS, G., *Antinomianism in English History, With special reference to the period 1640-1660* (London: Cresset, 1960)
HULSE, E., 'What it is to be Under the Law of Christ', in *Reformation Today* (Mar-Apr, 1984), pp. 19-22
JINKINS, M., 'John Cotton and the Antinomian Controversy, 1636-1638: A Profile of Experiential Individualism in American Puritanism', in *Scot J Th* 43 (1990), pp. 321-49
KENDALL, R.T., *Calvin and English Calvinism to 1649* (Oxford: Oxford University Press, 1979)
KEVAN, E.F., *The Grace of Law: A Study in Puritan Theology* (Ligonier: Soli Deo Gloria Publications, 1993 reprint [original edition, London: Carey Kingsgate, 1963])
KIK, J.M., 'Notes', in Bolton
LACHMAN, D.C., T*he Marrow Controversy* (Edinburgh: Rutherford House, 1988)
LAMONT, W.M., *Richard Baxter and the Millennium: Protestant Imperialism and the English Revolution* (London: Croom Helm, 1979)
LECLER, J., *Toleration and the Reformation*. 2 vols (New York: Association Press, 1960)
LEITH, J.H., *An Introduction to the Reformed Tradition: A Way of Being the Christian Community* (Edinburgh: Saint Andrew Press, 1977)
LLOYD-JONES, D.M., *The Puritans: Their Origins and Successors*. Addresses Delivered at the Puritan and Westminster Conferences, 1959-1978 (Edinburgh: Banner of Truth, 1987)
LUMPKIN, W.L., *Baptist Confessions of Faith* (Valley Forge: Judson, 1969)
MACLEOD, J., *Scottish Theology: In relation to Church History since the Reformation* (Edinburgh: Banner of Truth, 1943)
MARSDEN, G.M., *Fundamentalism and American Culture, The Shaping of Twentieth-Century Evangelicalism: 1870-1925* (Oxford: Oxford University Press, 1980)
M'CRIE, T., *The Story of the Scottish Church From the Reformation to the Disruption* (Edinburgh: Free Presbyterian Publications, 1874)
METCALFE, J., *Deliverance from the Law: The Westminster Confession Exploded*

(Tylers Green: John Metcalfe Publishing Trust, 1992)
MILLER, J. (ed.), *Preaching and Revival* (Thornton Heath: Westminster Conference, 1984)
MURRAY, J.J., 'The Marrow Controversy - Thomas Boston and the Free Offer', in Miller (ed.), pp. 34-56
NEAL, D., *History of the Puritans; or, The Rise, Principles and Sufferings of the Protestant Dissenters to the Glorious Era of the Revolution.* Abridged in Two Volumes by Edward Parsons. Vol. II (London: Brown & Robinson, 1811)
NIESEL, W., *Reformed Symbolics: A Comparison of Catholicism, Orthodoxy, and Protestantism* (Edinburgh: Oliver & Boyd, 1962)
NUTTALL, G.F., R. THOMAS, R.D. WHITEHORN, & H.L. SHORT, *The Beginnings of Nonconformity*: The Hibbert Lectures (London: James Clarke, 1962)
OUTLER, A.C. (ed.), *John Wesley* (New York: Oxford University Press, 1964)
PACKER, J.I., *Keep in Step with the Spirit* (Leicester: IVP, 1984)
PAGITT, E., *Heresiography: or, a description of the Heretickes and Sectaries of these latter times* (London, 1645)
PARKER, T.H.L., *John Calvin: A Biography* (London: J.M. Dent, 1975)
RUPP, E.G., *Oxford History of the Christian Church: Religion in England, 1688-1791* (Oxford: Clarendon, 1986)
SANGSTER, W.E., *The Path to Perfection: An Examination and Restatement of John Wesley's Doctrine of Christian Perfection* (London: Hodder & Stoughton, 1943)
SCEATS, D.D., *Perfectionism and the Keswick Convention, 1875-1900* (Unpublished M.A. Dissertation)
SCHAFF, P. (ed.), *The Creeds of the Evangelical Protestant Churches* (London: Hodder and Stoughton, 1877)
SCHMIDT, M., *John Wesley, A Theological Biography.* Vol. II. *John Wesley's Life Mission.* Part II (London: Epworth, 1973)
SMITH, W.M., 'Foreword' to the Second Edition of *Message of Keswick*, pp. vii-viii
SPROUL, R.C., 'Foreword' to Gerstner, pp. v-x.
STEPHEN, L., & S. LEE (eds.), *Dictionary of National Biography* (London: Smith, Elder & Co., 1908)
STOCK, E., 'Fifty Years Ago', in Holden (ed.), pp. 4-15
STOTT, J.R.W., *Men Made New* (London: IVP, 1966)
THOMAS, R., 'Parties in Nonconformity', in Bolam, Goring, Short, & Thomas, pp. 93-112
- 'Presbyterians in Transition', in Bolam, Goring, Short, & Thomas, pp. 113-74
- 'The Break-up of Nonconformity', in Nuttall, Thomas, Whitehorn, & Short, pp. 33-60
THOMSON, A., *Thomas Boston of Ettrick: His Life and Times* (London: Nelson, 1895)
TOON, P., *The Emergence of Hyper-Calvinism in English Nonconformity, 1689-1765* (London: Olive Tree, 1967)
TORREY, R.A., et al. (eds.), updated by C.L. Feinberg, *The Fundamentals: The Famous Sourcebook of Foundational Biblical Truths* (Grand Rapids: Kregel, 1958)
UNDERWOOD, A.C., *A History of the English Baptists* (London: Baptist Union, 1947)
VERHEY, A., 'Calvin's Treatise *"Against the Libertines"*, Introduction', in Gamble (ed.), Vol. 5, pp. 220-35
WALLACE, D.D., *Puritans and Predestination: Grace in English Protestant Theology, 1525-1695* (Chapel Hill: University of North Carolina Press, 1982)

WARFIELD, B.B., *Studies in Perfectionism* (Phillipsburg: Presbyterian & Reformed, 1958)
WATTS, M.R., *The Dissenters: From the Reformation to the French Revolution* (Oxford: Clarendon, 1978)
WENDEL, F., *Calvin. The Origins and Development of his Religious Thought* (New York: Harper, 1963)
WHITLEY, W.T., *A History of British Baptists* (London: Kingsgate, 1932)
WILLIAMS, G.H., *The Radical Reformation* (Philadelphia: Westminster, 1962)
WINSLOW, O., *No Condemnation in Christ Jesus, As unfolded in Romans Chapter 8* (Edinburgh: Banner of Truth, 1853)
WORRALL, B.G., *The Making of the Modern Church: Christianity in England since 1800* (London: SPCK, 1988)

2. Theological and Biblical Works (Part Two)

ACHTEMEIER, P.J., 'An Elusive Unity: Paul, Acts and the Early Church', in *C B Q* 48 (1986), pp. 1-26
ADENEY, W.F., *Luke* (London: Caxton, n.d.)
- *Thessalonians and Galatians* (London: Caxton, n.d.)
ALAND, K., *Komputer Konkordanz zum Neuen Testamentum Graecae*, (Berlin: Walter de Gruyter, 1977)
- *Vollständige Konkordanz zum Griechischen Neuen Testament* (Berlin: Walter de Gruyter, 1983)
ALEXANDER, J.A., *A Commentary on the Acts of the Apostles* (Edinburgh: Banner of Truth, 1857)
ALEXANDER, L., *The Preface to Luke's Gospel: Literary Convention and Social Context in Luke 1:1-4 and Acts 1;1*. SNTS Monograph Series, 78 (Cambridge: Cambridge University Press, 1993)
AMBROSIASTER, 'Commentarius in Epistulas Paulinas, Pars 1: In Epistulam ad Romanos', in *Corpus Scriptorum Ecclesiaticorum Latinorum*, Vol. 81. H.J. Vogels (ed.) (Vindobonae: Hoelder-Pichler-Tempsky, 1966)
ARNDT, W.F., & F.W. GINGRICH, *A Greek-English Lexicon of the New Testament and Other Early Christian Literature* (Cambridge: Cambridge University Press, 1957)
ARNOLD, C.E., 'Returning to the Domain of the Powers: στοιχεῖα as Evil Spirits in Galatians 4:3,9', in *Nov Test* 38 (1996), pp. 55-76
ATTRIDGE, H.W., *A Commentary on the Epistle to the Hebrews* (Philadelphia: Fortress Press, 1989)
AUGUSTINE, 'Against Julian', in *The Fathers of the Chuch, A New Translation*. Vol. 35 (Washington: Catholic University of America Press, 1957).
- 'The Spirit and the Letter', in J. Burnaby (ed.), *The Library of Christian Classics,* Vol. 8. *Augustine: Later Works* (London: SCM Press, 1955)
BADENAS, R., *Christ the End of the Law: Romans 10:4 in Pauline Perspective*. JSNT Supplement Series 10 (Sheffield: JSOT Press, 1985)
BALZ, H., & G. SCHNEIDER (eds.), *Exegetical Dictionary of the New Testament*, Vol. 1 (Grand Rapids: Eerdmans, 1990)
BANDSTRA, A.J., *The Law and the Elements of the World. An Exegetical Study in*

Aspects of Paul's Teaching (Grand Rapids: Eerdmans, 1964)
BARNES, A., *The Acts of the Apostles* (London: Blackie, 1868)
- *II Corinthians and Galatians* (London: Blackie, 1868)
- *Hebrews* (London: Blackie, 1868)
- *Luke and John* (London: Blackie, 1868)
- *Romans* (London: Blackie, 1868)
BARRETT, C.K., *A Commentary on the Epistle to the Romans* (London: A. & C. Black, 1957)
- *Freedom and Obligation: A Study of the Epistle to the Galatians* (London: SPCK, 1985)
BARTH, K., *Christian Dogmatics*, Vol. III, Pt. 2 (Edinburgh: T. and T. Clark, 1960)
- *A Shorter Commentary on Romans* (London: SCM Press, 1959)
BARTH, M., et al., *Foi et Salut selon S. Paul: colloque oecuménique a l'Abbaye de S. Paul hors les murs* (Rome: Institut Biblique Pontifical, 1970)
BARTLET, J.V., *The Acts* (London: Caxton, n.d.)
BECHTLER, S.R., 'Christ the Telos of the Law: The Goal of Romans 10:4', in *C B Q* 56 (1994), pp. 288-308
BEKER, J.C., 'The faithfulness of God and the Priority of Israel in Paul's Letter to the Romans', in *Harv Th R* 79 (1986), pp. 10-16
- *Paul the Apostle: The Triumph of God in Life and Thought* (Edinburgh: T. & T. Clark, 1980)
BELLEVILLE, L.L., 'Under Law: Structural Analysis and the Pauline Concept of Law in Galatians 3:21-4:11', in *J St N T* 26 (1986), pp. 53-78
BEST, E., *The Letter of Paul to the Romans* (Cambridge: Cambridge University Press, 1967)
BETZ, H.D., *Galatians, A Commentary on Paul's Letter to the Churches in Galatia* (Philadelphia: Fortress Press, 1979)
BLACK, D.A., *Paul, Apostle of Weakness: 'Ασθένεια and its Cognates in the Pauline Literature* [American University Studies, Series VII: Theology and Religion, Series 3] (New York, Berne, Frankfort on the Main, Nancy: Peter Lang, 1984)
BLACK, M., *Romans* (London: Oliphants, 1973)
BLAIKLOCK, E.M., *The Acts of the Apostles, An Historical Commentary* (London: Tyndale Press, 1959)
BLANK, S.H., 'The LXX Renderings of Old Testament Terms for Law', *Hebrew Union College Annual*, Vol. 7 (1930)
BLASS, F., *Grammar of New Testament Greek* (London: Macmillan, 1905)
BLIGH, J., *Galatians: A Discussion of Saint Paul's Epistle* (London: St. Paul Publications, 1969)
BLUNT, A.W.F., *The Acts of the Apostles* (Oxford: Clarendon, 1922)
BORNKAMM, g., 'The Missionary Stance of Paul in 1 Corinthians 9 and in Acts', in Keck & Martyn (eds.), pp. 194-207
BOWEN, R., *A Guide to Romans*. TEF Study Guide 11, Published in Association with the USCL for the TEF (London: SPCK, 1975)
BRANICK, v.p., 'The Sinful Flesh of the Son of God (Rom. 8:3): A Key Image of Pauline Theology', in *C B Q* 47 (1985), pp. 246-62
BRAUMANN, g., & C. BROWN, 'Child, Boy, Servant, Son, Adoption' in C. Brown (ed.), Vol. 1, pp. 280-91
BRING, R., 'Paul and the Old Testament: A Study of the Ideas of Election, Faith and

Law in Paul, with special reference to Rom. 9:30-10:30', in *St Th* 25 (1971), pp. 21-60

BROWN, C. (ed.), *New International Dictionary of New Testament Theology* (Exeter: Paternoster, 1975, 1976 & 1978)

BROWN, J., *An Exposition of Galatians* (Grand Rapids: Christian Classics, n.d.)
- *Hebrews* (Edinburgh: Banner of Truth, 1862)

BROWNLEE, W.H., *The Meaning of the Qumran Scrolls for the Bible, with Special Attention to the Book of Isaiah* (New York: Oxford University Press, 1964)

A.B. BRUCE, *The Epistle to the Hebrews, The First Apology for Christianity: An Exegetical Study* (Edinburgh: T. & T. Clark, 1908)

BRUCE, F.F., 'The Acts of the Apostles', in Guthrie & Motyer (eds.), pp. 968-1011
- *The Acts of the Apostles: The Greek Text with Introduction and Commentary* (Leicester: IVP, 1952)
- 'Conference in Jerusalem - Galatians 2:1-10', in O'Brien & Peterson (eds.), pp. 195-212
- *The Epistle to the Galatians, A Commentary on the Greek Text* (Exeter: Paternoster, 1982)
- *The Epistle to the Hebrews, The English Text with Introduction, Exposition and Notes* (Grand Rapids: Eerdmans, 1964)
- *The Epistle of Paul to the Romans, An Introduction and Commentary* (London: Tyndale, 1963)
- *The New London Commentary on the New Testament: Commentary on the Book of Acts* (London: Marshall, Morgan & Scott, 1962)
- *Paul: Apostle of the Free Spirit* (Exeter: Paternoster, 1977)
- 'The Romans Debate - Continued', in Donfried (ed.), pp. 175-94
- *Second Thoughts on the Dead Sea Scrolls* (London: Paternoster, 1956)

BRUNNER, E., *The Letter to the Romans: A Commentary* (London: Lutterworth, 1959)

BUCHANAN, G.W., *To the Hebrews, Translation, Comment and Conclusions* (New York: Doubleday, 1972)

BULTMANN, R., *Theology of the New Testament*, Vol. 1 (London: SCM, 1952)

BURTON, E.E., *A Critical and Exegetical Commentary on the Epistle to the Galatians* (Edinburgh: T. & T. Clark, 1921)

CALLAN, T., 'Pauline Midrash: The Exegetical background of Gal 3:19b', in *J B L* 99 (1980), pp. 549-67
- 'The Background of the Apostolic Decree (Ac. 15:20,29; 21:25)', in *C B Q* 55 (1993), pp. 284-97

CALVIN, J., *Commentary upon the Acts of the Apostles* (Geneva, 1560)
- *Commentaries on the Book of the Prophet Jeremiah and Lamentations* (Grand Rapids: Baker, 1850)
- *Commentaries on the Epistle of Paul the Apostle to the Hebrews* (Geneva, 1549)
- *Commentaries on the Epistle of Paul the Apostle to the Romans* (Geneva, 1539)
- *Commentaries on the Epistles of Paul to the Galatians and Ephesians* (Geneva, 1548)
- *Commentary on a Harmony of the Evangelists, Matthew, Mark, and Luke* (Geneva, 1555)

CAMPBELL, W.S., 'Christ the End of the Law: Romans 10:4', in Livingstone (ed.), pp. 73-81
- 'Did Paul Advocate Separation from the Synagogue? A reaction to Francis Watson:

Paul, Judaism and the Gentiles: A Sociological Approach', in *Scot J Th* 42 (1989), pp. 457-67
CARRAS, G.P., 'Romans 2:1-29: A Dialogue on Jewish Ideals', in *Biblica* 73 (1992), pp. 183-207
CARSON, D.A., D.J. MOO, & L. MORRIS, *An Introduction to the New Testament* (Grand Rapids: Zondervan, 1992)
CAWLEY, F., & A.R. MILLARD, 'Jeremiah' in Guthrie & Motyer (eds.), pp. 626-58.
CHANCE, J.B., *Jerusalem, the Temple, and the New Age in Luke-Acts* (Macon: Mercer University Press, 1988)
CHEYNE, T.K., & J.S. BLACK (eds.), *Encyclopaedia Biblica*, Vol. 2 (London: A. & C. Black, 1901)
CHILDS, B.S., *Exodus, A Commentary* (London: SCM Press, 1974)
- *The New Testament as Canon: An Introduction*, (London: SCM Press, 1984)
CHRYSOSTOM, ST. JOHN, 'Homilies on the Epistle to the Romans', in Schaff (ed.), pp. 566-1016
COHN-SHERBOK, D., *A Dictionary of Judaism and Christianity* (London: SPCK, 1991)
- *On Earth as it is in Heaven: Jews, Christians and Liberation Theology* (New York: Orbis, 1987)
COLE, R.A., *Exodus, An Introduction and Commentary* (Leicester: IVP, 1973)
- *The Epistle of Paul to the Galatians, An Introduction and Commentary* (Leicester: IVP, 1965)
CONZELMANN, H., *Acts of the Apostles* (Philadelphia: Fortress Press, 1987)
COSGROVE, C.H., 'Arguing like a Mere Human Being: Galatians 3:15-18 in Rhetorical Perspective', in *N T St* 34 (1988), pp. 536-49
- 'Justification in Paul: A Linguistic and Theological Reflection', in *J B L* 106 (1987), pp. 653-70
CRAFTON, J.A., 'Paul's Rhetorical Vision and the Purpose of Romans: towards a new understanding', in *Nov Test* 32 (1990), pp. 317-39
CRAIGIE, P.C., *The Book of Deuteronomy* (Grand Rapids: Eerdmans, 1976)
CRANFIELD, C.E.B., *A Critical and Exegetical Commentary on the Epistle to the Romans* [2 Vols.] (Edinburgh: T. & T. Clark Ltd., 1975)
- 'The Works of the Law in the Epistle to the Romans', in *J St N T* 43 (1991), pp. 89-101
CREED, J.M., *The Gospel According to St. Luke, The Greek Text* (London: Macmillan, 1930)
CULLMANN, O., *The Christology of the New Testament* (London: SCM Press, 1963)
DAVIDSON, F., & R.P. MARTIN, 'Romans', in Guthrie & Motyer (eds.), pp. 1012-48
DAVIES, W.D., *Paul and Rabbinic Judaism: Some Rabbinic Elements in Pauline Theology* (Philadelphia: Fortress Press, 1948, 1955, 1980)
DEISSMANN, G.A., 'Elements', in Cheyne & Black (eds.), cols. 1258-61
DELLING, G., 'Στοιχεῖα', in Kittel (ed.), Vol. 7, pp. 684ff
DEMAREST, B.A., 'sperma', in C. Brown (ed.), Vol. 3, pp. 521-3
DIBELIUS, M., *Studies in the Acts of the Apostles* (London: SCM Press, 1956)
DODD, C.H., *The Bible and the Greeks* (London: Hodder & Stoughton, 1935)
- *The Epistle of Paul to the Romans* (London: Hodder & Stoughton, 1932)
- 'ΙΛΑΣΚΕΣΘΑΙ, its Cognates, Derivatives, and Synonyms in the Septuagint', in *J Th St* 32 (1931), pp. 352-60

DONALDSON, T.L., 'The "Curse of the Law" and the Inclusion of the Gentiles: Galatians 3:13-14', in *N T St* 32 (1986), pp. 94-112

DONFRIED, K.P. (ed), *The Romans Debate: Revised and Expanded Edition* (Peabody: Hendrickson, 1977, 1991)

DORMANDY, R., 'Hebrews 1:1-2 and the Parable of the Wicked Husbandmen', in *Expos T* 100 (1989), pp. 371-5

DOUGLAS, J.D., & N. HILLYER (eds.), *Illustrated Bible Dictionary* (Leicester: IVP, 1980)

DUNN, J.D.G., 'Echoes of Intra-Jewish Polemic in Paul's Letter to the Galatians', in *J B L* 112 (1993), pp. 459-77

- 'The Incident at Antioch (Gal. 2:11-18)', in *J St N T* 18 (1983), pp. 3-57
- 'Jesus - Flesh and Spirit: An Exposition of Romans 1:3-4', in *J Th St* ns 24 (1973), pp. 40-68
- *Jesus, Paul and the Law* (London: SPCK, 1990)
- *New Testament Theology: The Theology of Paul's Letter to the Galatians* (Cambridge: Cambridge University Press, 1993)
- *The Partings of the Ways Between Christianity and Judaism and their Significance for the Character of Christianity* (London: SCM Press, 1991)
- '"Righteousness from the Law" and "Righteousness from Faith": Paul's Interpretation of Scripture in Romans 10:1-10', in Hawthorne & Betz (eds.), pp. 216-28
- *Romans* [2 Vols.] (Dallas:Word, 1988)
- 'Works of the Law and the Curse of the Law (Galatians 3:10-14)', in *N T St* 31 (1985), pp. 523-42

EARNSHAW, J.D., 'Reconsidering Paul's Marriage Analogy in Romans 7:1-4', in *N T St* 40 (1994), pp. 68-88

EBELING, G., *Die Wahrheit des Evangeliums: eine Lesehilfe zum Galaterbrief* (Tübingen: J.C.B. Mohr [Paul Siebeck], 1981)

EHRHARDT, A., *The Acts of the Apostles: Ten Lectures* (Manchester: Manchester University Press, 1969)

EISENMAN, R.H., & M. WISE, *The Dead Sea Scrolls Uncovered: The First Complete Translation and Interpretation of 50 Key Documents Withheld for Over 35 Years* (Shaftesbury: Element Books, 1992)

ELLIGER, W., 'εἰς', in Balz & Schneider (eds.), pp. 398-9

ELLINGWORTH, P., *The Epistle to the Hebrews, A Commentary on the Greek Text* (Carlisle: Paternoster, 1993)

EPP, E.J., 'Jewish-Gentile Continuity in Paul: Torah and/or Faith', in Nicklesburg & MacRae (eds.), pp. 80-90

ESLER, P.F., *Community and Gospel in Luke-Acts: The Social and Political Motivations of Lucan Theology* (Cambridge: Cambridge University Press, 1987)

- *The First Christians in their Social Worlds: Social-scientific approaches to New Testament interpretation* (London: Routledge, 1994)
- 'Making and Breaking an Agreement Mediterranean Style: A New Reading of Galatians 2:1-14', in *Bib Interp* 111 (1995), pp. 285-314

ESSER, H.-H., 'Law', in C. Brown (ed.), Vol. 2, pp. 436-51

- 'stoicheia', in C. Brown (ed.), Vol. 2, pp. 451-3

EVANS, C.F., *Saint Luke* (Philadelphia: Trinity Press International, 1990)

FILSON, F.V., *'Yesterday': A Study of Hebrews in the Light of Chapter 13* (London:

SCM Press, 1967)
FISCHER, J., 'Covenant, Fulfilment, and Judaism in Hebrews', in *Ev R Th* 13 (1989), pp. 175-87
FITZMYER, J.A., '"Now this Melchizedek ..." (Heb 7,1)', in *C B Q* 25 (1963), pp. 305-21
- *Responses to 101 Questions on the Dead Sea Scrolls* (London: Geoffrey Chapman, 1992)
- *Romans, A New Translation and Commentary* (London: Geoffrey Chapman, 1993)
FOAKES-JACKSON, F.J., *The Acts of the Apostles* (London: Hodder & Stoughton, 1931)
FORTNA, R.T., & B.R. GAVENTA (eds.), *The Conversation Continues* (Nashville: Abingdon, 1990)
FUNG, R.Y.K., *The Epistle to the Galatians* (Grand Rpaids: Eerdmans, 1988)
FUSCO, V., 'Luke-Acts and the Future of Israel', in *Nov Test* 38 (1996), pp. 1-17
GARVIE, A.E., *Romans* (London: Caxton, n.d.)
GASQUE, W.W., 'A Fruitful Field: Recent Study of the Acts of the Apostles', in *Interp* 42 (1988), pp. 117-31
GASTON, L., 'Angels and Gentiles in Early Judaism and in Paul', in *S R* 11 (1982), pp. 65-75
- 'Paul and the Law in Galatians 2-3', in Richardson & Granskou (eds.), pp. 37-57
GELDENHUYS, N., *The Gospel of Luke* (London: Marshall, Morgan & Scott, 1951)
GOODENOUGH, E.P., 'The Perspective of Acts', in Keck & Martyn (eds.), pp. 51-9
GOODING, D., *An Unshakeable Kingdom, The Letter to the Hebrews for Today* (Leicester: IVP, 1989)
GORDON, T.D., 'A Note on the Paidagogos in Galatians 3:24-25', in *N T St* 35 (1989), pp. 150-4
- 'The Problem at Galatia', in *Interp* 41 (1987), pp. 32-43
GOULDER, M., *A Tale of Two Missions* (London: SCM Press, 1994)
GREEN, W.S., 'Messiah in Judaism: Rethinking the Question', in Neusner, Green & Ferichs (eds.)
GREENE, M.D., 'A Note on Romans 8:3', in *Bib Z* 35 (1991), pp. 103-6
GROH, D., & R. JEWETT (eds.), *The Living Text* (Lenham: University Press of America, 1985)
GUNDRY, R.H., *A Survey of the New Testament* (Exeter: Paternoster, 1970)
GUTBROD, W., 'The Law in the Old Testament', in Kittel (ed.), Vol. 4, pp. 1036-47
GUTHRIE, D., *Galatians* (London: Marshall, Morgan & Scott, 1974)
- *The Letter to the Hebrews, An Introduction and Commentary* (Leicester: IVP, 1983)
- *New Testament Introduction* (Leicester: IVP, 1970)
- *New Testament Theology* (Leicester: IVP, 1981)
GUTHRIE, D., & J.A. MOTYER (eds.), *The New Bible Commentary Revised* (Leicester: IVP, 1970)
HAENCHEN, E., *The Acts of the Apostles, A Commentary* (Oxford: Blackwell, 1971)
HALDANE, R., *An Exposition of the Epistle to the Romans* (Grand Rapids: MacDonald, 1958)
HAMM, D., 'Faith in the Epistle to the Hebrews: The Jesus Factor', in *C B Q* 52 (1990), pp. 270-91
HAMMERTON-KELLY, R.G., 'Sacred Violence and Sinful Desire: Paul's Interpretation of Adam's Sin in the Letter to the Romans', in Fortna & Gaventa

(eds.), pp. 35-54
HANSEN, G.W., *Galatians* (Leicester: IVP, 1994)
HANSON, R.P.C., *The Acts, with Introduction and Commentary* (Oxford: Clarendon, 1967)
HARDER, G., 'στηρίζω', in Kittel (ed.), Vol. 7, pp. 653-7
HARRISON, E.F., *Acts: The Expanding Church* (Chicago: Moody Press, 1975)
HARRISON, R.K., *Jeremiah and Lamentations, An Introduction and Commentary* (Leicester: IVP, 1973),
HATCH, W.H.P., 'Τά στοιχεῖα in Paul and Bardaisan', in *J Th St* 28 (1927), pp. 181-2
HAWTHORNE, G.F., & O. BETZ (eds.), *Tradition and Interpretation in the New Testament* (Grand Rapids: Eerdmans, 1987)
HAWTHORNE, G.F., & R.P. MARTIN (eds.), *Dictionary of Paul and His Letters* (Leicester: IVP, 1993)
HAYS, R.B., *Echoes of Scripture in the Letters of Paul* (New Haven: Yale University Press, 1989)
HEDIN, B.A., 'Romans 8:6-11', in *Interp* 50 (1996), pp. 55-8
HENDRIKSEN, W., *Colossians and Philemon* (Edinburgh: Banner of Truth, 1971)
- *Galatians* (Edinburgh: Banner of Truth, 1968)
- *The Gospel of Luke* (Edinburgh: Banner of Truth, 1978)
- *Romans* [2 Vols.] (Edinburgh: Banner of Truth, 1980, 1981)
HESTER, J.D., 'The Use and Influence of Rhetoric in Galatians 2:1-14', in *Th Z* 42 (1986), pp. 386-408
HEWITT, T., *The Epistle to the Hebrews: An Introduction and Commentary* (Leicester: IVP, 1960)
HILLS, J.V., 'Christ was the Goal of the Law...', in *J Th St* ns 44 (1993), pp. 585-92
HODGE, C., *A Commentary on Romans* (Edinburgh: Banner of Truth, 1835)
HOLMGREN, F., *The God Who Cares: A Christian Looks at Judaism* (Atlanta: John Knox Press, 1979)
HONG IN-GYU, 'Does Paul Misrepresent the Jewish Law? Law and Covenant in Gal. 3:1-14', in *Nov Test* 36 (1994), pp. 164-82
HOWARD, G., 'Christ the End of the Law: the Meaning of Rom. 10:4ff', in *J B L* 88 (1969), pp. 331-7
- *Paul: Crisis in Galatia, A Study in Early Christian Theology*. SNTS Monograph Series, 35 (Cambridge: Cambridge Uinversity Press, 1979)
HÜBNER, H., *Law in Paul's Thought* (Edinburgh: T. & T. Clark, 1984)
HUGHES, P.E., *A Commentary on the Epistle to the Hebrews* (Grand Rapids: Eerdmans, 1977)
HUNTER, A.M., *The Epistle to the Romans, Introduction and Commentary* (London: SCM Press, 1955)
HURST, L.D., 'The Christology of Hebrews 1 and 2', in Hurst & Wright (eds.), pp. 151-64
HURST, L.D., & N.T. Wright (eds.), *The Glory of Christ in the New Testament* (Oxford: Clarendon, 1987)
ITO, A., 'Romans 2: A Deuteronomistic Reading', in *J St N T* 59 (1995), pp. 21-37
JACOB, E., *Theology of the Old Testament* (London: Hodder & Stoughton, 1955)
JACOBS, L., *A Jewish Theology* (London: Darton, Longman & Todd, 1973)
JERVELL, J., 'The Acts of the Apostles and the History of Early Christianity', in *St Th* 37 (1983), pp. 17-32

- 'The Church of Jews and Godfearers', in Tyson (ed.), pp. 11-20.
JEWETT, R., 'The Law and the Coexistence of Jews and Gentiles in Romans', in *Interp* 39 (1985), pp. 341-56
- 'The Redaction and Use of an Early Christian Confession in Romans 1:3-4', in Groh & Jewett (eds.), pp. 99-122
JONES, H.R., 'Exodus', in Guthrie & Motyer (eds.), pp. 115-39
JUEL, D., *Luke-Acts* (London: SCM Press, 1983)
KARRIS, R.J., 'Rom. 14:1-15:13 and the Occasion of Romans', in *C B Q* 35 (1973), pp. 155-78
KÄSEMANN, E., *Commentary on Romans* (London: SCM Press, 1980)
- *The Wandering People of God: An Investigation of the Letter to the Hebrews* (Minneapolis: Augsburg, 1984)
KECK, L.E., & J.L MARTYN (eds.), *Studies in Luke-Acts* (Nashville: Abingdon Press, 1966)
KEVAN, E.F., *The Law of God in Christian Experience: A Study in the Epistle to the Galatians* (London: Pickering & Inglis, 1955)
KILGALLEN, J.J., 'Acts 13:38-39: Culmination of Paul's Speech in Pisidia', in *Biblica* 69 (1988), pp. 480-506
KIRK, K.E., *The Epistle to the Romans in the Revised Version with Introduction and Commentary* (Oxford: Clarendon, 1937)
KISTEMAKER, S.J., *Exposition of the Epistle to the Hebrews* (Welwyn: Evangelical Press, 1984)
KITTEL, G. (ed.), *Theological Dictionary of the New Testament* (Grand Rapids: Eerdmans, 1967)
KLASSEN, W., 'To the Hebrews or Against the Hebrews? Anti-Judaism and the Epistle to the Hebrews', in S.G. Wilson (ed.), pp. 1-16
KLAUSNER, J., *The Messianic Idea in Israel from Its Beginning to the Completion of the Mishnah* (London: George Allen & Unwin, 1956)
KLEIN, G., 'Paul's Purpose in Writing the Epistle to the Romans', in Donfried (ed.), pp. 29-43
KÜMMEL, W.G., *Introduction to the New Testament, Revised Edition* (London: SCM Press, 1975)
LADD, G.E., *A Theology of the New Testament* (Guildford: Lutterworth, 1974)
LAGRANGE, M.-J., *Saint Paul Épitre aux Galates* (Paris: Librairie Lecoffre, 1950)
LAMBRECHT, J., 'Transgressor by Nullifying God's Grace: A Study of Gal 2:18-21', in *Biblica* 72 (1991), pp. 217-36
LAMPE, P., 'The Roman Christians of Romans 16', in Donfried (ed.), pp. 216-30
LANE, W.L., *Hebrews 1-8* (Dallas: Word, 1991)
LARSSON, E., 'Paul: Law and Salvation', in *N T St* 31 (1985), pp. 425-36
LEANEY, A.R.C., *A Commentary on the Gospel According to St. Luke* (London: A. & C. Black, 1958)
LEENHARDT, F.J., *The Epistle to the Romans, A Commentary* (London: Lutterworth, 1961)
LIDDELL, H.G., & R. SCOTT, *A Greek-English Lexicon* (Oxford: Clarendon, 1940)
- *A Lexicon, Abridged from Liddell and Scott's Greek-English Lexicon* (Oxford: Clarendon, 1909)
LIETZMANN, H., *An die Galater* (Tübingen: J.C.B. Mohr [Paul Siebeck], 1971)
LIGHTFOOT, J.B., *The Epistle of St. Paul to the Galatians, with Introduction, Notes*

and Dissertations (Grand Rapids: Zondervan, 1865, 1957)
- *Saint Paul's Epistles to the Colossians and Philemon* (London: Macmillan, 1892)

LINDARS, B., *New Testament Apologetic: The Doctrinal Significance of Old Testament Quotations* (London: SCM Press, 1961)
- *New Testament Theology: The Theology of the Letter to the Hebrews* (Cambridge: Cambridge University Press, 1991)

LIVINGSTONE, E.A. (ed.), *Studia Biblica 1978*, Vol. 3: *Papers on Paul and Other New Testament Authors* (Sheffield: JSOT Press, 1980)

LLOYD-JONES, D.M., *Romans, An Exposition of Chapter 1: The Gospel of God* (Edinburgh: Banner of Truth, 1985)

LOFTHOUSE, W.F., *Jeremiah and the New Covenant* (London: SCM Press, 1925)

LUDEMANN, G., *Early Christianity according to the Traditions in Acts: A Commentary* (Minneapolis: Fortress Press, 1989)

LUHRMANN, D., *Galatians: A Continental Commentary* (Minneapolis: Fortress Press, 1978, 1988)

LULL, D.J., 'The Law was our Pedagogue: A Study in Galatians 3:19-25', in *J B L* 105 (1986), pp. 481-98

LUTHER, M., 'Lectures on Galatians, 1535, Chapters 1-4', in Pelikan (ed.), Vol. 26
- 'Lectures on Galatians, 1535, Chapters 5-6; Lectures on Galatians, 1519, Chapters 1-6', in Pelikan (ed.), Vol. 27
- 'Lectures on Romans', in Oswald (ed.), Vol. 25

McCULLOUGH, J.C., 'The Old Testament Quotations in Hebrews', in *N T St* 26 (1980), pp. 363-79

McDONALD, H.D., *Freedom in Faith: A Commentary on Paul's Epistle to the Galatians* (London: Pickering & Inglis, 1973)

MACCOBY, H., *Cambridge Commentaries on Writings of the Jewish and Christian World 200 BC to AD 200,* Vol. 3: *Early Rabbinic Writings* (Cambridge: Cambridge University Press, 1988)
- *Paul and Hellenism* (London: SCM Press, 1991)

MACHEN, J.G., *Notes on Galatians, and Other Aids to the Interpretation of the Epistle to the Galatians* ed. J.H. Skilton (Philadelphia: Presbyterian and Reformed, 1972)

MANSON, W., *The Epistle to the Hebrews, An Historical and Theological Reconstruction* (London: Hodder & Stoughton, 1951)

MARCUS, J., 'The Circumcision and the Uncircumcision in Rome', in *N T St* 35 (1989), pp. 67-81

MARSHALL, I.H., *The Acts of the Apostles, An Introduction and Commentary* (Leicester: IVP, 1980)
- 'Luke', in Guthrie & Motyer (eds.), pp. 887-925
- *Luke: Historian and Theologian* (Exeter: Paternoster, 1970)

MARTENS, J.W., 'Romans 2:14-16: A Stoic Reading', in *N T ST* 40 (1994), pp. 55-67

MARTIN, R.P., 'Fullness', in Douglas & Hillyer (eds.), Part 1, pp. 529-31
- 'Hypodeigma', in C. Brown (ed.), Vol. 2, p. 290f

MARTIN, T., 'Apostasy to Paganism: The Rhetorical Stasis of the Galatian Controversy', in *J B L* 114 (1995), pp. 437-61

MARXSEN, W., *Introduction to the New Testament* (Oxford: Blackwell, 1968)

MEEKS, W.A., 'Judgement and the Brother: Romans 14:1-15:13', in Hawthorne & Betz (eds.), pp. 290-300

MEIER, J.P., 'Structure and Theology in Heb 1,1-14', in *Biblica* 66 (1985), pp. 168-89

MEYER, H.A.W., *Handbook to the Epistle to the Galatians* (Edinburgh: T. & T. Clark, 1880)
MEYER, P.W., 'The Worm at the Core of the Apple: Exegetical Reflections on Romans 7', in Fortna & Gaventa (eds.), pp. 62-84
MIKOLASKI, S.J., Galatians, in Guthrie & Motyer (eds.), pp. 1089-1104.
MINEAR, P.S., 'Luke's Use of the Birth Stories', in Keck & Martyn (eds.), pp. 111-30
MOESSNER, D.P., '"The Christ Must Suffer": New Light on the Jesus - Peter, Stephen, Paul Parallels in Luke-Acts', in *Nov Test* 28 (1986), pp. 220-56
MOFFATT, J., *A Critical and Exegetical Commentary on the Epistle to the Hebrews* (Edinburgh: T. & T. Clark, 1924)
- *Introduction to the Literature of the New Testament* (Edinburgh: 1911)
MONTEFIORE, H., *A Commentary on the Epistle to the Hebrews* (London: A. & C. Black, 1964)
MOO, D.J., 'Israel and Paul in Romans 7:7-12', in *N T St* 32 (1986), pp. 122-35
MORRIS, L., *The Epistle to the Romans* (Grand Rapids: Eerdmans, 1988)
- *The Gospel According to St. Luke, An Introduction and Commentary* (Leicester: IVP, 1974)
- 'The Use of ἱλάσκεσθαι etc. in Biblical Greek', in *Expos T* 62 (1950), pp. 227-33
MOULE, C.F.D., *An Idiom Book of New Testament Greek* (Cambridge: Cambridge University Press, 1953)
MOULE, H.C.G., *Colossian Studies* (London: HS, 1903)
MOULTON, H.K. (ed), *The Analytical Greek Lexicon Revised* (Grand Rapids: Zondervan, 1978)
MUNCK, J., *The Acts of the Apostles, Introduction, Translation and Notes* (New York: Doubleday, 1967)
- *Paul and the Salvation of Mankind* (London: SCM Press, 1959)
MURRAY, J., *The Epistle to the Romans. The English Text with Introduction, Exposition and Notes* (Grand Rapids: Eerdmans, 1959, 1965)
NAIRNE, A., *The Epistle of Priesthood: Studies in the Epistle to the Hebrews* (Edinburgh: T. & T. Clark, 1913)
NARBOROUGH, F.D.V., *The Epistle to the Hebrews in the Revised Version, with Introduction and Commentary* (Oxford: Clarendon, 1930)
NEIL, W., *The Acts of the Apostles* (London: Marshall, Morgan & Scott, 1973)
NEUSNER, J., W.S. GREEN & E.S. FERICHS (eds.), *Judaisms and Their Messiahs at the Turn of the Christian Era* (Cambridge: Cambridge University Press, 1987)
NICKLESBURG, G., & G. MacRAE (eds.), *Christians Among Jews and Gentiles* (Philadelphia: Fortress, 1986)
NOLLAND, J,. 'A Fresh Look at Acts 15:10', in *N T St* 27 (1981), pp. 105-15
NYGREN, A., *Commentary on Romans* (London: SCM Press, 1952)
O'BRIEN, P.T., & D.G. PETERSON (eds.), *God Who is Rich in Mercy* (Homebush West: Lancer Books, 1986)
O'NEILL, J.C., *Paul's Letter to the Romans* (Harmondsworth: Penguin, 1975)
OLYOTT, S., *The Gospel as it Really is, Paul's Epistle to the Romans Simply Explained* (Welwyn: Evangelical Press, 1979)
ORIGEN, 'Commentary on the Epistle to the Romans', in *J Th St* 14 (1912-13)
OSTBORN, G., *Tora in the Old Testament* (Lund, 1945)
OSWALD, H.C. (ed.), *Luther's Works*, Vol. 25 (St. Louis: Concordia, 1972)
OWEN, J., *Calvin's Commentaries on the Epistle of Paul the Apostle to the Romans,*

Translated and Edited (Grand Rapids: Baker, 1849)
- *Calvin's Commentaries on Hebrews, Translated from the Original Latin, and Edited* (Grand Rapids: Baker, 1853)

PARKER, P., 'Once More, Acts and Galatians', in *J B L* 86 (1967), pp. 175-82

PATAI, R,. *The Messiah Texts: Jewish Legends of Three Thousand Years* (Detroit: Wayne State University Press, 1979)

PEAKE, A.S., *The Epistle of Paul the Apostle to the Hebrews* (London: Caxton, n.d.)
- *Jeremiah and Lamentations* (London: Caxton, 1910)

PELIKAN, J. (ed.) *Luther's Works*, Vol. 26 (St. Louis: Concordia, 1963)
- *Luther's Works*, Vol. 27 (St. Louis: Concordia, 1964)

PETERSON, D., *Hebrews and Perfection: An Examination of the Concept of Perfection in the 'Epistle to the Hebrews'*. SNTS Monograph Series, 47 (Cambridge:Cambridge University Press, 1982)

PETTEM, M., 'Luke's Great Omission and His View of the Law', in *N T St* 42 (1996), pp. 35-54

PHILIP, J., *The Epistle to the Romans: A Commentary* (Aberdeen: Didasko Press, n.d.)

PINK, A.W., *An Exposition of Hebrews* (Grand Rapids: Baker, 1954)

PLUMMER, A., *A Critical and Exegetical Commentary on the Gospel According to S. Luke* (Edinburgh: T. & T. Clark, 1901)

POOLE, M., *Annotations upon the Holy Bible*, Vol. 1 (Edinburgh: Thomas & John Turnbull, 1800)

RACKHAM, R.B., *The Acts of the Apostles, An Exposition* (London: Methuen, 1910)

RÄISÄNEN, H., 'Galatians 2:16 and Paul's Break with Judaism', in *N T St* 31 (1985), pp. 543-53
- 'Paul's Conversion and the Development of his View of the Law', in *N T St* 33 (1987), pp. 404-19
- *The Torah and Christ: Essays in German and English on the Problem of the Law in Early Christianity* (Helsinki: Finnish Exegetical Society, 1986)

REICKE, B., 'The Law and this World according to Paul: some thoughts concerning Gal. 4:1-11', in *J B L* 70 (1951), pp. 259-76

REID, D.G., 'Elements/Elemental Spirits of the World', in Hawthorne & Martin (eds.), pp. 229-33.

RHYNE, C.T., 'Nomos dikaiosunes and the Meaning of Romans 10:4', in *C B Q* 47 (1985), pp. 486-99

RICHARDSON, P. & D. GRANSKOU (eds.), *Anti-Judaism in Early Christianity*. Vol. 1: *Paul and the Gospels* (Waterloo: Wilfrid Laurier University Press, 1986)

RIDDERBOS, H.N., *The Epistle to the Galatians* (London: Marshall, Morgan and Scott, 1961)

ROBINSON, J.A.T., *Wrestling with Romans* (London: SCM Press, 1979)

ROBINSON, T.H., *The Epistle to the Hebrews* (London: Hodder & Stoughton, 1933)

SALMON, M., 'Insider or Outsider? Luke's Relationship with Judaism', in Tyson (ed.), pp. 76-82

SANDAY, W. & A.C. HEADLAM, *A Critical and Exegetical Commentary on the Epistle to the Romans* (Edinburgh: T. & T. Clark, 1902)

SANDERS, E.P., 'Jewish Association with Gentiles and Galatians 2:11-14', in Fortna & Gaventa (eds.), pp. 170-88
- *Paul* (Oxford University Press, 1991)
- *Paul and Palestinian Judaism* (London: SCM Press, 1977)

- *Paul, the Law, and the Jewish People* (Philadelphia: Fortress Press, 1983)
SANDERS, J.T., 'Who is a Jew and Who is a Gentile in the Book of Acts?', in *N T St* 37 (1991), pp. 434-55
SANDMEL, S., *A Jewish Understanding of the New Testament* (London: SPCK, 1974)
SCHAFF, P. (ed.), *The Nicene and Post-Nicene Fathers*, Vol. 11 (New York: Christian Literature Company, 1889)
SCHIPPERS, R., 'Pleroō', in C. Brown (ed.), Vol. 1, pp. 733-41
SCHLIER, H., *Die Brief an die Galater* (Gottingen: Vandenhoeck & Ruprecht, 1962)
SCHOEPS, H.J., *Paul: The Theology of the Apostle in the Light of Jewish Religious History* (Philadelphia: Westminster Press, 1961)
SCHREINER, T.R., 'Law of Christ', in Hawthorne & Martin (eds.), pp. 542-4
SCHWARTZ, D.R., 'The Futility of Preaching Moses (Acts 15,21)', in *Biblica* 67 (1986), pp. 276-81
SCHWEIZER, E., 'Concerning the Speeches in Acts', in Keck & Martyn (eds.), pp. 208-16
- 'Slaves of the Elements and Worshippers of Angels: Gal 4:3,9 and Col 2:8,18,20', in *J B L* 107 (1988), pp. 455-68
SCOTT, E.F., *The Epistle to the Hebrews: Its Doctrine and Significance* (Edinburgh, 1922)
- *Paul's Epistle to the Romans* (London: SCM Press, 1947)
SCROGGS, R., 'Romans 6:7: ὁ γὰρ ἀποθανὼν δεδικαίωται ἀπὸ τῆς ἁμαρτίας', in *N T St* 10 (1963), pp. 104-8
SEIFRID, M.A., 'Jesus and the Law in Acts', in *J St N T* 30 (1987), pp. 39-57
- 'The Subject of Rom. 7:14-25', in *Nov Test* 34 (1992), pp. 313-33
SHARP, J.R.,'Typology and the Message of Hebrews', in *East Asia Journal of Theology* 4, No. 2 (1986), pp. 95-103
SMIGA, g., 'Romans 12:1-2 and 15:30-32 and the Occasion of the Letter to the Romans', in *C B Q* 53 (1991), pp. 257-73
SNODGRASS, K.,'Justification by Grace - to the Doers: An Analysis of the Place of Romans 2 in the Theology of Paul', in *N T St* 32 (1986), pp. 72-93
- 'Spheres of Influence: A Possible Solution to the Problem of Paul and the Law', in *J St N T* 32 (1988), pp. 93-113
SPICQ, C., *L'épitre aux Hebreux* (Paris: Libraire Lecoffre, 1977)
STANLEY, C.D., 'Under a Curse: A Fresh Reading of Galatians 3:10-14', in *N T St* 36 (1990), pp. 481-511
STEDMAN, R.C., *Hebrews* (Leicester: IVP, 1992)
STIBBS, A.M., 'Hebrews', in Guthrie & Motyer (eds.), pp. 1191-1221
STOTT, J.R.W., *Only One Way: The Message of Galatians* (London: IVP, 1968)
SWETNAM, J., 'A Suggested Interpretation of Hebrews 9, 15-18', in *C B Q* 27 (1965), pp. 373-90
- 'Jesus as Logos in Hebrews 4,12-13', in *Biblica* 62 (1981), pp. 214-24
- 'On the Imagery and Significance of Hebrews 9,9-10', in *C B Q* 28 (1966), pp. 155-73
- 'Sacrifice and Revelation in the Epistle to the Hebrews: Observations and Surmises on Hebrews 9,26', in *C B Q* 30 (1968), pp. 227-34
TAYLOR, V,. *The Epistle to the Romans* (London: Epworth Press, 1955)
THAYER, J.H., *A Greek-English Lexicon of the New Testament, being Grimm's Wilke's Clavis Novum Testamenti, Translated, Revised and Enlarged* (Edinburgh: T. & T.

Clark, 1901)
THIELMAN, F., *From Plight to Solution: A Jewish Framework for Understanding Paul's View of the Law in Galatians and Romans.* Supplements to *Novum Testamentum*, Vol. 61 (Leiden, New York, København, Köln: E.J. Brill, 1989)
THOMPSON, J.A., *The Book of Jeremiah* (Grand Rapids: Eerdmans, 1980)
THOMPSON, M.B., 'Strong and Weak', in G.F. Hawthorne & R.P. Martin (eds.), *Dictionary of Paul and His Letters* (Leicester: IVP, 1993), pp. 916-8
THORNTON, T.C.G., 'The Meaning of kai peri hamartias in Romans viii.3', in *J Th St* ns 22 (1971), pp. 515-7
- 'Propitiation or Expiation?' in *Expos T* 80 (1968-69), pp. 53-5
TOBIN, T.H., 'Controversy and Continuity in Romans 1:18-3:20', in *C B Q* 55 (1993), pp. 298-318
TORREY, C.C., 'The Authorship and Character of the so-called "Epistle to the Hebrews"', in *J B L* 30 (1911), pp. 137-56
TROMPF, G.W., 'The Conception of God in Hebrews 4:12-13', in *St Th* 25 (1971), pp. 123-32
TRUDINGER, P., 'An Autobiographical Digression? A Note on Romans 7:7-25', in *Expos T* 107 (1996), pp. 173-4
TURNER, N., 'Syntax'; Vol.3 of J.H. Moulton.
TYSON, J.B., *Images of Judaism in Luke-Acts* (Columbia: University of South Carolina Press, 1992)
- 'Jews and Judaism in Luke-Acts', in *N T St* 41 (1995), pp. 19-38
- '"Works of Law" in Galatians', in *J B L* 92 (1973), pp. 423-31
TYSON, J.B. (ed.), *Luke-Acts and the Jewish People* (Minneapolis: Augsburg, 1988)
VAUGHAN, C.J., *St. Paul's Epistle to the Romans. With Notes* (London: Macmillan, 1885)
VERMES, G., *The Dead Sea Scrolls in English* (Harmondsworth: Penguin, 1962)
VERSEPUT, D.J., 'Paul's Gentile Mission and the Jewish Christian Community: A Study of the Narrative in Galatians 1 and 2', in *N T St* 39 (1993), pp. 36-58
VIELHAUER, P., 'On the "Paulinism" of Acts', in Keck & Martyn (eds.), pp. 33-50
VINE, V.E., 'The Purpose and Date of Acts', in *Expos T* 96 (1984), pp. 45-8
VOS, G., 'Hebrews, The Epistle of the Διαθήκη', in *Princeton Theological Review* 13 (1915), pp. 587-632, and 14 (1916), pp. 1-61.
- *The Teaching of the Epistle to the Hebrews*, Edited and rewritten by J.G. Vos (Grand Rapids: Eerdmans, 1956)
WATSON, F., 'The Two Roman Congregations: Romans 14:1-15:13', in Donfried (ed.), pp. 203-15
WEDDERBURN, A.J.M., *The Reasons for Romans* (Edinburgh: T. & T. Clark, 1988)
WEIMA, J.A.D., 'The Function of the Law in Relation to Sin: an evaluation of the view of H. Räisänen', in *Nov Test* 32 (1990), pp. 219-35
- 'Gal 6:11-18: A Hermeneutical Key to the Galatian Letter', in *Cal Th J* 28 (1993), pp. 90-107
WESTCOTT, B.F., *The Epistle to the Hebrews* (London: Macmillan, 1889)
WHITELEY, D.E.H., 'Hard Sayings [Romans 8:3]' in *Th* 67 (1964), pp. 114-6
WICKHAM, E.C., *The Epistle to the Hebrews, with Introduction and Notes* (London: Methuen, 1910)
WILLIAMS, C.S.C., *A Commentary on the Acts of the Apostles* (London: A. & C. Black, 1964)

WILLIAMS, S.K., 'Justification and the Spirit in Galatians', in *J St N T* 29 (1987), pp. 91-100
- 'Promise in Galatians: A Reading of Paul's Reading of Scripture', in *J B L* 107 (1988), pp. 709-20
WILLS, L.M., 'The Depiction of the Jews in Acts', in *J B L* 110 (1991), pp. 631-54
WILSON, R.McL., *Hebrews* (Basingstoke: Marshall, Morgan & Scott, 1987)
WILSON, S.G. (ed.), *Anti-Judaism in Early Christianity*, Vol. 2: *Separation and Polemic* (Waterloo: Wilfrid Laurier University Press, 1986)
WINER, G.B., *A Treatise on the Grammar of New Testament Greek* (Edinburgh: T. & T. Clark, 1882)
WITHERINGTON, B., 'The Influence of Galatians on Hebrews', in *N T St* 37 (1991), pp. 146-52
WORKMAN, G.C., *The Text of Jeremiah* (Edinburgh: T. & T. Clark, 1889)
YOUNG, N.H., 'The Gospel According to Hebrews 9', in *N T St* 27 (1981), pp. 198-210
- 'Paidagogos: the Social Setting of a Pauline Metaphor', in *Nov Test* 29 (1987), pp. 150-76
ZIESLER, J., *Paul's Letter to the Romans* (Philadelphia: Trinity Press International, 1989)
- *The Epistle to the Galatians* (London: Epworth Press, 1992)
- 'The Role of the Tenth Commandment in Romans 7', in *J St N T* 33 (1988), pp. 42-56.

Index

1. Scripture References

Genesis
12:7 *171*
14:18-20 *177*
15:6 *63, 151*
27:12 *155*
27:29 *155*
39:7-12 *169*
46:4 *120*

Exodus
12:49f *77*
13:10 *77*
17:2 *78*
17:7 *78*
18:20 *77*
20:4 *169*
20:17 *98, 169*
22:1 *78*
23:11 *78*
24 *180*
25:40 *185*
28:1 *180*
32:6 *169*
32:18f *169*

Leviticus
4:2 *79*
4:20 *63*
4:26 *63*
4:31 *63*
4:35 *63*
5:3 *169*
5:10 *63*
5:13 *63*
5:16 *63*
5:18 *63*
6:2f *78*
6:7 *63*
18 *70*
18:5 *152f*
19:9f *78*
19:11 *78*
19:18 *165, 169, 205*

19:37 *77*
23:22 *78*
25:35 *79*
27:23 *120*

Numbers
5:30 *77*
9:3 *77*
9:12 *77*
9:14 *77*
12:1-15 *169*
14:22 *78*
14:33 *169*
17:13 *120*
23:25 *155*

Deuteronomy
5:21 *98*
10:18f *205*
11:26 *155*
11:29 *155*
17:10f *77*
18:20-22 *169*
21:23 *154-6*
22:8 *169*
23:5 *155*
24:10 *77*
24:21 *78*
27:12f *155*
27:26 *77, 151f*
28:45 *155*
28:58 *77*
29:29 *77*
30:1 *155*
30:10 *77*
30:19 *155*
31:12 *77*
31:24 *120*
32:1 *120*
32:20 *169*
32:46 *77*
33:8 *78*

Joshua
3:16 *120*
8:24 *120*
10:13 *120*
10:20 *120*
24:27 *78*

Judges
11:39 *120*

Ruth
4:5 *79*

First Samuel
2:4 *100*
12:15 *169*
15:22 *69*

Second Samuel
12:6 *78*
15:7 *120*
24:8 *120*

Second Kings
5:12 *169*
8:3 *120*
18:10 *120*

First Chronicles
28:9 *120*
29:19 *120*

Second Chronicles
12:12 *120*
18:2 *120*
24:16 *169*
28:15 *100*
31:1 *120*

Nehemiah
9:13 *195*
13:2 *155*
13:6 *120*

Job
4:4 *100*
5:2 *169*
6:9 *120*
14:20 *120*
20:7 *120*
23:3 *120*
23:7 *120*
29:12 *78*

Psalms
9:3 *100*
9:7 *120*
9:18 *120*
9:31 *120*
12:2 *120*
15:11 *120*
17:35 *120*
27:2 *100*
31:10 *100*
33:11 *106*
36:3 *169*
37:7 *120*
39:9-11 *201*
40:6-8 *69, 201f*
43:23 *120*
44:4 *169*
45:7 *200*
48:9 *120*
51:5 *120*
51:16f *69*
67:16 *120*
72 *78*
73:1 *120*
73:3 *120*
73:10f *120*
73:19 *120*
76:8 *120*
78:5 *120*
78:41 *78*
78:56 *78*
88:46 *120*
95 *203*
95:9 *78*
102:9 *120*
105:37 *100*
106:14 *78*
107:12 *100*
108:17 *155*
109:24 *100*
110:4 *177, 186*
119 *169, 201*
131:2 *79*

Proverbs
3:16 *79, 201*
3:19 *78*
3:23 *79*
3:33 *155*
4:19 *79*
14:29 *169*
15:8 *69*
16:18 *169*
16:19 *79*
20:1 *169*
22:14 *79*
24:16 *100*

Ecclesiastes
3:11 *120*
7:3 *120*
12:13 *120*

Isaiah
1:11-17 *69*
9:15 *120*
47:9 *169*
47:12 *169*
51:4-8 *201*
54:1 *158*
58:7 *78*
62:6 *120*
65:23 *155*
66:3f *69*

Jeremiah
2:8 *194*
2:32 *196*
3:21 *196*
5:24 *112*
6:19f *69*
6:19 *194*
6:21 *100*
8:8f *194*
9:8f *169*
9:13 *194*
10:15 *100*
13:25 *196*
13:27 *169*
14:10-12 *69*
16:11 *194*
17:1 *192*
18:11 *106*
18:15 *196*
18:18 *194*
23:27 *196*
26:4 *194*
27:45 *106*
28:29 *106*
31:31-34 *191*
31:33f *105*
31:33 *193f, 197, 201*
31:36 *196f*
32:23 *194*
36:11 *106*
44:10 *194*
44:23 *194*
46:6 *100*
46:12 *100*
46:16 *100*
50:32 *100*
51:12 *155*

Lamentations
1:14 *100*
5:13 *100*

Ezekiel
15:4f *120*
20:40 *120*
21:15 *100*
22:30 *120*
36:10 *120*

Daniel
1:15 *120*
1:18 *120*
2:34 *120*
3:19 *120*
4:31 *120*
6:26 *120*
7:26 *120*
9:10f *196*
9:26 *120*

Index

11:13 *120*
11:14 *100*
11:19 *100*
11:33-35 *100*
11:41 *100*

Hosea
4:5 *100*
5:5 *100*
6:6 *69*
14:1 *100*
14:9 *100*

Amos
5:22-24 *69*
9:8 *120*

Micah
4:12 *106*
6:6-8 *69*

Nahum
2:5 *100*
3:3 *100*

Hababkkuk
1:4 *120*
2:4 *152*

Zephaniah
1:3 *100*

Zechariah
7:10 *78*
8:13 *155*
12:8 *100*

Malachi
2:2 *155*
2:8 *100*

Matthew
5:17-20 *77*
5:20 *78*
10:22 *120*
24:6 *120*
24:13f *120*
26:58 *120*

Mark
2:19 *86*
3:26 *120*
13:7 *120*
13:13 *120*

Luke
1-2 *72, 75*
1:1-4 *56*
1:33 *120*
5:34 *86*
6:20-49 *77*
8:21 *77*
9:20 *72*
9:22 *72*
10:26 *72*
11:28 *77*
11:46 *72*
11:52 *72*
16:16f *72*
16:17 *77*
17:10 *78*
18:5 *120*
18:9-14 *62*
19:8f *78*
21:9 *120*
22:37 *72, 120*
24:44 *72, 74*
24:47 *74*
24:53 *74*

John
13:1 *120*

Acts
1:2-4 *78*
1:6f *56*
1:8 *57*
2:17 *57*
2:23 *72*
2:36 *72*
2:44f *78*
3:25 *57*
4:34f *78*
5:3f *78*
5:9 *78*
5:42 *72*
6 *73*

6:7 *58*
6:13f *64*
9:22 *72*
10 *73*
10:34f *57*
11:18 *66*
11:30 *132*
12:24 *58*
12:25 *132*
13-14 *134*
13:15-35 *60*
13:38-42 *11*
13:38-40 *10*
13:38f *4*
13:38 *62, 63*
13:39 *21, 51, 59, 63*
13:47 *57*
13:49 *58*
15 *69, 75, 132f*
15:1 *61, 64, 135, 139*
15:5 *61, 135, 139*
15:8-21 *67f*
15:11 *66, 139*
15:16f *57*
15:19 *73*
15:20 *65*
15:21 *58*
15:24 *61*
15:28 *70*
15:28f *68*
16:6 *131f*
17:3 *72*
18:5 *72*
18:13 *60*
18:15 *60*
18:23 *131*
18:28 *72*
19:20 *58*
19:39 *60*
20:17-38 *79*
21 *71*
21:20 *61, 65*
21:21 *66f*
21:23f *61*
21:24 *66*
21:25 *68f*
21:28 *60*
22:3 *64*

22:12 *66*
22:15 *57*
22:21 *57*
23:29 *60*
24:6 *60*
24:14 *66*
24:16 *79*
25:8 *60, 66*
26:17f *57*
26:20 *57*
26:22 *64*
26:23 *57*
28:20 *72*
28:23 *64, 73*
28:28 *57*

Romans
1:3 *96*
1:6 *83*
1:13 *81*
1:10-12 *81*
1:15f *81*
1:16-15:16 *81*
1:17 *100*
1:18-32 *88, 104, 106*
1:18 *91, 100*
1:25 *96, 99*
1:32 *106*
2:1-23 *88f*
2:7 *100*
2:12-29 *91, 116*
2:12 *92*
2:13-16 *103-7*
2:13 *100*
2:14-29 *83*
2:15 *109*
2:16 *108*
2:20 *122*
2:25-29 *107-109*
2:28 *96*
2:29 *119*
3-4 *110*
3 *89, 90*
3:1-20 *83*
3:9-19 *106*
3:19-31 *116*
3:19-21 *89*
3:20 *91f, 96, 100*

3:21ff *109*
3:21f *9*
3:21 *91, 101*
3:27-4:25 *83*
3:27 *88, 109-111*
3:28 *91, 101, 109*
3:31 *109-111*
4 *90*
4:1 *96*
4:2ff *63*
4:2 *101*
4:5 *122*
4:6 *101*
4:13-16 *116*
4:15 *92*
5 *90*
5:13 *92, 116*
5:17f *100*
5:20 *92, 116*
5:21 *100*
6-8 *41, 91*
6:1-23 *83*
6:7 *62*
6:14f *115-7*
6:14 *94, 117*
6:19 *111f, 117*
6:21f *120*
7 *88, 210*
7-8 *35*
7:1-8:4 *39*
7:1-25 *83*
7:4 *117f*
7:5f *94*
7:5 *92, 94, 96f, 101, 118*
7:6 *117-9*
7:7-8:3 *94f*
7:7-11 *97, 118*
7:7 *92, 98*
7:8-14 *112*
7:8f *92*
7:10-13 *92*
7:13 *118*
7:14 *96, 99, 118*
7:18 *96*
7:21 *93*
7:22 *88*
7:23 *93*
7:25 *88, 93, 96, 99*

8 *10*
8:1-4 *45*
8:1-3 *18*
8:1f *85*
8:1 *101*
8:2-9 *101-3*
8:2-4 *43*
8:2f *15, 97*
8:2 *88, 93, 109*
8:3f *4, 10, 31, 36, 51, 84-7, 212*
8:3 *6, 13, 20f, 25, 29, 41, 46, 88, 92, 118*
8:4f *96*
8:4 *13, 25, 34, 37, 40, 46f, 48, 50, 52, 98, 109*
8:5-13 *98f*
8:5 *96*
8:6f *96*
8:6 *96*
8:7f *96*
8:7 *88*
8:8f *96, 109*
8:10 *100*
9-11 *83, 121*
9:3 *96*
9:4 *90*
9:5 *96*
9:8 *96*
9:30-10:9 *120f*
9:31 *88*
10:4 *119-24*
10:5f *101*
10:5 *153*
11:13 *107*
11:14 *96*
13:8-10 *112-5, 166, 212*
14-15 *83f*
14:1-15:13 *83*
15:9 *107*
15:20-31 *81*
15:27 *96*

First Corinthians
1:8 *120*
7:19 *67, 69*
10:11 *120*
10:25 *67*

Index 239

15:24 *120*

Second Corinthians
1:13 *120*
3:13 *120*
11:15 *120*

Galatians
1:6-9 *134*
1:11-24 *134*
1:14 *65*
2:1-10 *132*
2:3-5 *134*
2:4 *165*
2:7-9 *134, 165*
2:10 *172*
2:11-21 *133*
2:12-14 *165*
2:16-21 *139-41*
2:16 *134, 150*
2:19 *145*
3-4 *10, 44*
3:1-14 *150-7*
3:1 *131, 134, 139*
3:6ff *63*
3:7 *165*
3:10-14 *7*
3:15-4:11 *47*
3:15-18 *142-4*
3:16 *171*
3:17-24 *5*
3:17 *136*
3:19-4:11 *138, 142, 145-50, 157f*
3:19-25 *136*
3:19 *15, 126, 136, 142, 171*
3:21 *4, 25, 28f, 37, 43, 52, 135, 137f*
3:23-4:10 *126-31*
3:23 *150*
3:25 *150, 165*
3:26 *160, 165*
3:29 *165*
4 *11*
4-5 *41*
4:3 *125, 165*
4:4 *136, 144, 171*

4:5-7 *165*
4:6f *160*
4:8 *126*
4:9 *4, 35, 41, 47, 52, 125, 135, 165, 213*
4:10 *134, 136*
4:12-20 *158*
4:13 *131*
4:17 *134*
4:21-5:4 *158-64*
4:21-31 *165*
4:21 *134*
5:1 *67, 134, 165, 213*
5:2-4 *134*
5:2f *136*
5:4 *136, 212*
5:6 *134, 165, 173, 212*
5:7 *134*
5:9-12 *134*
5:13f *165-7*
5:14 *212*
5:15 *134*
5:16-26 *168f*
5:18 *165*
5:25 *173*
6:1 *134*
6:2 *170, 172*
6:12f *134*
6:13 *163*
6:14 *130, 165*
6:15f *173*
6:15 *134, 161, 165, 212*

Ephesians
3:17 *200*
5:5 *99*

Philippians
3:4-9 *116, 139*
3:8f *65*
3:19 *120*

Colossians
2:8 *125*
2:11 *67*
2:14 *67*
2:16 *67*
2:20 *125*

3:5 *99*

First Thessalonians
2:16 *120*

First Timothy
1:5 *120*
2:5 *172*

Hebrews
1-12 *205*
1:1-4 *199f*
1:1f *176, 203*
1:5-13 *200*
2:1 *175f*
2:2 *181, 199*
2:3 *175f*
2:8 *206*
2:16-18 *176*
2:17 *183*
3:1 *176*
3:6 *120, 175f*
3:12f *175f*
3:14 *120, 176*
4:1f *176*
4:11 *176*
4:12 *203*
4:14f *176*
4:15 *206*
4:16 *176, 206*
5:1-10 *176*
5:2-3 *189*
5:11-14 *176*
5:12 *126*
6:1f *175f*
6:8 *120*
6:9f *176*
6:11f *176*
6:11 *120, 176*
6:12 *175*
6:15 *176*
6:16-18 *186f*
6:18-20 *204*
6:19 *176*
6:20 *202*
7-10 *5, 184*
7 *197*
7:1-10:18 *176*

7:3 *120, 187*
7:5 *180*
7:8 *187*
7:11-19 *177-80*
7:11 *191*
7:12 *191*
7:16 *182, 188*
7:18f *4, 21, 52, 177, 181*
7:18 *29, 190f*
7:19 *10, 189*
7:20-28 *186-90*
7:25 *204*
8-10 *202*
8:1 *176*
8:2 *198*
8:4 *176*
8:5f *191*
8:5 *185*
8:8-12 *191-4*
8:11 *198f*
9:1-14 *182*
9:1 *190*
9:8 *185*
9:9f *184f*
9:12-14 *184*
9:15 *180, 185, 190*

9:18-21 *180*
9:23f *185*
9:24 *198*
9:26 *190*
10:1-17 *202*
10:1-4 *182-5*
10:1 *185*
10:2 *176*
10:5-7 *201*
10:10 *176*
10:11 *182*
10:14 *176*
10:16f *192*
10:22f *176*
10:22 *198-200*
10:26 *198*
10:32-34 *175*
10:35-39 *176*
10:35 *175*
10:36 *176*
11 *176, 204*
11:13 *175*
11:25f *175f*
11:35-38 *175*
11:39f *185*
12:3 *175, 204*

12:14 *176, 205*
12:15 *175*
12:25 *176*
12:27f *176*
12:28 *205*
13 *205, 212*
13:9f *175*
13:13f *175f*
13:22 *176*

James
5:11 *120*

First Peter
1:9 *120*
3:8 *120*
4:7 *120*
4:17 *120*

Revelation
1:8 *120*
2:26 *120*
21:6 *120*
22:13 *120*

2. Main Subjects

Abraham 63, 90, 130, 136, 143, 151f, 158f, 171, 180f
Adoption [see Sonship]
Antinomianism / antinomians 13, 16f, 19-21, 23, 29f, 32, 35f, 47, 77, 83, 110, 124
    doctrinal 4, 8-11, 14f, 18, 22, 24, 26-28, 31, 33, 37, 39, 41-3, 44-6, 49-52, 210-13
    practical 4, 15, 18f, 22, 24f, 33, 39, 41-3, 45, 48, 50f, 213
Atonement
    in Christ [see Christ, death of]
    before Christ 144, 176, 207

Blood of Christ [see Christ, death of]

Calvinism [see Reformed Evangelicalism]

Christ
    death of 10f, 23, 27, 33f, 38f, 41, 44-6, 61, 64, 71-4, 101, 110, 116f, 130, 140f, 145, 149-52, 155-8, 160, 164f, 167, 174, 176, 182-5, 189f, 198f, 202, 204, 208
    pre-existence / eternity of 171, 187-90, 203f, 208
Christ, the [see Messiah / Messianic hope]
Church, unity of [see Unity of Church]
Circumcision 61, 63, 67-70, 95, 107-9, 133-6, 139, 145, 159, 163-6
Commandments, ten [see Decalogue]
Continuity between Israel and Church [see Covenants – unity / continuity of]
'Covenantal nomism' 115
Covenants
    Abrahamic covenant 136, 143, 171

Index 241

covenant of grace / promise 6, 18, 21, 26, 34, 44, 46, 50, 90, 116, 135, 138, 142-7, 149, 152f, 157-9, 161-4, 171, 191, 208
  differences between the covenants 11, 36, 47, 57-9, 63, 64, 71, 75-7, 80, 90, 118, 159, 175, 181, 187, 191-3, 196f, 200, 202, 206, 208, 211f
  new covenant 20, 24, 34, 36, 45-8, 50, 143, 184, 191-5, 197-200, 202-6, 208, 212
  old covenant 36, 44, 47, 143, 145, 153, 155, 159, 175, 180-2, 184f, 187, 189-92, 196-8, 200, 203, 205
  overarching purpose of God 126, 143, 145f, 147, 152, 172, 211
  promise fulfilled in Christ 32, 60, 62-5, 67, 70, 71-4, 76f, 80, 115, 119, 143-5, 149-51, 155-8, 160, 162f, 167, 171-3, 185, 197, 199f, 204, 208
  unity / continuity of 21, 42, 46, 57f, 63f, 73, 75-7, 108, 115, 117, 126, 139f, 143f, 191f, 197, 200, 205, 211f
Covetousness 94f, 98-100, 118, 208
Cross [see Christ, death of]
Crucifixion [see Christ, death of]

Death of Christ [see Christ, death of]
Decalogue 12, 14-16, 19, 21-4, 26, 37, 41, 43-5, 47f, 50, 78f, 91, 94f, 98, 102, 112-5, 118, 166f, 169, 179f, 195, 205f, 208, 211

Election 8, 60, 65, 190
Eternity of Christ [see Christ- pre-existence / eternity of]

Flesh 6, 13, 28, 32f, 39, 41, 46, 57, 84f, 87, 95-103, 108f, 111f, 116-9, 123f, 147, 159, 165, 168f, 177f, 182, 184f, 188, 203, 208
Forgiveness of sins 15, 23, 62f, 116, 176, 211
Fulfilment in Jesus Christ [see Covenant – promise fulfilled in Christ]

Gentile mission 73-6
Gentiles 56-8, 60, 63, 65, 67-71, 75-7, 79f, 83, 100, 104-9, 127-30, 133, 135-7, 139, 141, 148, 160-3, 165f, 173
Gospel 4, 10f, 13, 15f, 20, 22, 24f, 28f, 30f, 35, 41f, 44-6, 48, 50, 56, 58, 64, 71-5, 78, 81-3, 110f, 114, 121, 133f, 139, 157f, 160, 162, 172, 191, 203, 205, 211f
Grace 3f, 6, 11, 13-15, 17-19, 21-4, 26-8, 30, 34, 36f, 40-4, 46, 51f, 60, 62f, 65, 67, 72, 90f, 100, 104, 111, 114-6, 122, 137-41, 143f, 146f, 149-58, 160f, 164, 173f, 206, 208, 211-13

Holiness [see Sanctification]
Holy Spirit 4, 6f, 12-20, 22, 24, 26, 28f, 31-43, 45-51, 57, 67, 71, 78, 84, 93f, 96, 98, 101-3, 106, 108-12, 114, 116-9, 124, 128, 150f, 157, 159, 168-70, 173, 174, 193, 208, 212f

Imputed righteousness [see Justification - by faith / apart from law]
Israel [see Jews]

Jerusalem Conference 63, 67f, 132f
Jerusalem decree 58, 65, 68-71, 75, 132f
Jews 5, 21, 29, 44f, 57-61, 63-77, 79f, 81-3, 88-91, 94f, 99f, 103-9, 110, 115, 118, 120-4, 127-30, 132-7, 139-41, 144-6, 148-50, 152-63, 165f, 174-7, 179-81, 187, 191f, 196, 199f, 204, 207, 211
Judaism 60, 65f, 72, 74-6, 115, 121, 127f, 139, 160, 175, 204
Judaizers / Judaizing 58, 83, 134f, 136f, 159, 163
Justification
  by faith / apart from law 3f, 6-15, 17, 19-25, 28, 32f, 35-43, 45-9, 51f, 59-67, 89-91, 100-4, 109-11, 115-7, 120-3, 133-67, 172-4, 207, 210f
  eschatological 91, 100, 103f, 109, 116, 123, 153

Law
  abrogation of 7, 17, 20, 29, 31, 41, 47, 52, 58f, 65, 70-4, 76f, 80, 119f, 145, 157, 160-5, 168, 172, 174, 177f, 181,

185, 190f, 202, 204, 206, 208, 210f
believers and 3f, 6-8, 10, 12, 16, 17,
19, 21f, 24, 26, 28, 30f, 34f, 37, 39, 42-
4, 47, 51f, 58, 65, 67, 71, 75, 77, 83f,
101-3, 107, 111f, 115-7, 119, 123f,
135, 165, 168-74, 191, 204-6, 208f,
210-13
ceremonial 10, 17, 25, 29, 35, 47, 50,
52, 60f, 63, 65-74, 76f, 79f, 136, 142,
151, 161, 163, 167, 211, 213
Christ as termination of [see Law –
abrogation of]
'covenant of works' 8, 17, 21, 25f, 28-
30, 44f, 51f, 211
curse of 7, 13f, 16, 28, 35, 40, 49f, 115,
150-8, 211
death to [see Law – freedom from]
definition of holiness 117
deliverance from [see Law – freedom
from]
dispensation / epoch 90, 92, 136, 138,
142, 144f, 147, 149f, 152f, 155-66,
168, 170, 172, 174, 207f, 211
epoch [see Law- dispensation / epoch]
founded on priesthood and sacrifice
179f, 181, 187, 190, 197, 200, 206, 207
freedom from 13, 19, 24f, 28, 30-3, 35,
39, 41, 52, 67, 83, 102, 117f, 134, 145,
166f
good in itself 94, 112f, 130
Hebrew Bible 89
hope-stimulator 145, 147, 149f, 157f,
160-4, 174, 190, 208, 211
Jewish 58, 65, 88f, 94, 124, 127-9,
135, 136, 158
letter 7, 105, 108, 118f
liberty in 38
moral 3-5, 8, 10-12, 16-18, 22, 24, 29,
31, 35, 43, 45, 47, 50f, 65, 68f, 76f,
79f, 83, 90-3, 105, 107, 110, 112f, 115,
123, 136, 142, 153, 166-9, 172f, 195,
199, 205, 207f, 210-13
Mosaic economy 5, 31, 35, 47, 52, 60f,
63, 67, 70-2, 79f, 136, 155-7, 165, 179-
81, 186f, 190f, 197, 204, 206, 208,
210f
of Christ 21f, 24f, 31, 35, 43, 50, 170,
172

of faith 21, 31, 109-11
of God 7-9, 18, 24, 28, 31, 35f, 38, 43,
45, 50, 73, 77-80, 83, 88, 93, 96, 98f,
102-5, 108, 111f, 114, 121, 127, 129,
131, 136f, 161, 168-70, 173, 193-9,
205, 207f, 211
of love 31, 49, 114, 176
of Moses 41, 48f, 59f, 88, 113, 118,
135-7, 170, 177f, 195f
of righteousness 121f
of sin (and death) 93-5, 99, 101, 118
of the Spirit of life 93, 101
of works 21f, 24, 25, 109
Old Testament economy [see Law –
Mosaic economy]
pattern / standard of righteousness 7, 9,
22, 25f, 28f, 35, 100, 103, 111, 116,
122f, 153, 201
pedagogue 11, 21, 25, 41, 45, 47, 51,
126, 130, 147-9, 165, 211
Pentateuch 60, 64
power of 4, 6f, 9, 11, 13f, 16f, 19, 24-
7, 30f, 44, 46-51, 64, 85, 101f, 108-12,
117, 119, 124, 138, 142, 144f, 147-50,
160, 162-4, 168, 170, 174, 181, 190f,
197f, 204, 208f, 211f
preparatory for Christ 5, 44, 52, 63, 76,
119-21, 123, 130, 138, 145, 149f, 152,
155-7, 162f, 172, 185, 189, 197, 200,
206f, 210
provisionality of 5, 7, 52, 63f, 73f, 76,
126, 138, 144f, 147, 149, 152, 155-7,
163, 185f, 189f, 197-200, 204, 206f,
210f
purpose of 12, 67, 95, 99, 113f, 138,
141f, 146f, 149, 162, 164, 172f, 208,
210
revelation 47, 89, 91, 115, 123, 130,
136f, 168, 195-203, 206, 208
rule of life 7f, 12, 16-18, 21f, 24, 28,
30, 32, 37, 40f, 45, 51f, 111, 167, 169f,
172-4, 208
sin defined by 90-2, 94f, 100, 116f,
123, 142, 147, 208
sin-exposed by 38, 92, 94, 123, 147
sin stimulated by 92, 94f, 97, 118, 123,
142
slavery to 127f, 130, 134, 148f, 158-

60, 162f
standard of righteousness [see Law – pattern / standard of righteousness]
third use of 3-8, 14, 17-20, 24, 40, 44, 48, 51f, 210-13
threefold division of 3, 5, 31
torah 61, 66, 68, 70, 74f, 89-95, 104, 107, 128, 136f, 147, 162, 169, 195-7, 199f, 202, 206
transcript of God's character 194, 196f, 199
weakness of 4-6, 9, 12-14, 17, 21, 25, 28f, 37, 39, 44, 46, 48f, 51f, 59, 61, 63f, 84-7, 92-5, 98-101, 108f, 112, 119, 124, 135-42, 144, 146, 150, 156, 158, 163-5, 173f, 177f, 180-90, 198, 200, 202, 204, 206-8, 210, 212
will of God and 37, 61, 168
worship and 60f, 71, 207
written on heart 19, 22, 34, 45f, 50, 103, 105, 107-9, 111, 192-204, 206, 208, 212
Lawlessness 72, 111, 200-2
Legalism 20f, 23f, 39, 41, 44, 46, 48, 137, 139, 213
Liberty 159-62, 165f

Messiah / Messianic hope 10, 29, 52, 61, 63, 71-3, 77, 123, 130, 138-40, 142, 144f, 147, 149f, 155-8, 160f, 163-5, 171f, 174, 185, 190, 208, 211

Neonomianism 20f, 23, 25, 27
New covenant [see Covenants – new covenant]

Obedience 6-8, 11, 17-21, 25f, 30, 33f, 37-9, 45, 48, 50, 52, 59, 69, 73, 78-80, 91, 99f, 103, 107-13, 116, 119, 122, 135, 166f, 170, 173, 191, 193, 198, 201, 206, 212
Old covenant [see Covenants – old covenant]
Old Testament gospel 60, 64-7, 115, 120, 134, 139-41, 143f, 146f, 152f, 155, 158, 160-2, 164

Perfection 177-9, 181-5, 189f, 198, 202-4, 206, 207
Pharisees 33, 61f, 66, 78, 116, 122, 133f, 139
Pre-existence of Christ [see Christ – pre-existence / eternity of]
Priesthood 176-80, 181, 186-90, 197, 206
of Christ 176-8, 183, 187f, 199f, 204, 206

Reformed Evangelicalism 3f, 8, 20f, 28, 30, 33-8, 40, 42-4, 210, 212
Righteousness
eschatological [see Justification – eschatological]
imputed [see Justification - by faith / apart from law]
law and [see Justification – by faith / apart from law]
practical 13, 37, 39f, 47, 78, 115

Sacrifice of Christ [see Christ, death of]
Sanctification 4, 6, 8, 10f, 13-16, 18, 22-4, 26, 28-38, 40, 42-52, 102, 109-12, 115, 117, 124, 167, 205, 209, 210, 212f
Seed, Christ as 142f, 171
Sermon on the Mount 77f
Sonship 130, 157-60, 162, 165
Sovereignty of God 50, 60, 65, 67, 72, 114
Stephen 64f, 73f

Temple 60f, 71, 74, 76
Ten commandments [see Decalogue]

Union with Christ 17, 26, 39, 48
Unity of Church 57f, 69f, 73, 83, 128, 130
Unity of covenants [see Covenants – unity / continuity of]
Universality
of grace 90, 116
of law 29, 110
of sin 41, 88f, 98, 100, 104, 146, 153

Works of the law 3, 32, 49, 91, 100f, 109, 111, 120, 122f, 133f, 138f, 141, 146, 151-7, 160f, 163

Paternoster Biblical Monographs
(All titles uniform with this volume)
Dates in bold are of projected publication

Joseph Abraham
Eve: Accused or Acquitted?
A Reconsideration of Feminist Readings of the Creation Narrative Texts in Genesis 1–3
Two contrary views dominate contemporary feminist biblical scholarship. One finds in the Bible an unequivocal equality between the sexes from the very creation of humanity, whilst the other sees the biblical text as irredeemably patriarchal and androcentric. Dr Abraham enters into dialogue with both camps as well as introducing his own method of approach. An invaluable tool for any one who is interested in this contemporary debate.
2002 / 0-85364-971-5 / xxiv + 272pp

Octavian D. Baban
Mimesis and Luke's on the Road Encounters in Luke-Acts
Luke's Theology of the Way and its Literary Representation
The book argues on theological and literary (mimetic) grounds that Luke's on-the-road encounters, especially those belonging to the post-Easter period, are part of his complex theology of the Way. Jesus' teaching and that of the apostles is presented by Luke as a challenging answer to the Hellenistic reader's thirst for adventure, good literature, and existential paradigms.
***2005** / 1-84227-253-5 / approx. 374pp*

Paul Barker
The Triumph of Grace in Deuteronomy
This book is a textual and theological analysis of the interaction between the sin and faithlessness of Israel and the grace of Yahweh in response, looking especially at Deuteronomy chapters 1–3, 8–10 and 29–30. The author argues that the grace of Yahweh is determinative for the ongoing relationship between Yahweh and Israel and that Deuteronomy anticipates and fully expects Israel to be faithless.
2004 / 1-84227-226-8 / xxii + 270pp

Jonathan F. Bayes
The Weakness of the Law
God's Law and the Christian in New Testament Perspective
A study of the four New Testament books which refer to the law as weak (Acts, Romans, Galatians, Hebrews) leads to a defence of the third use in the Reformed debate about the law in the life of the believer.
2000 / 0-85364-957-X / xii + 244pp

Mark Bonnington
The Antioch Episode of Galatians 2:11-14 in Historical and Cultural Context

The Galatians 2 'incident' in Antioch over table-fellowship suggests significant disagreement between the leading apostles. This book analyses the background to the disagreement by locating the incident within the dynamics of social interaction between Jews and Gentiles. It proposes a new way of understanding the relationship between the individuals and issues involved.

2005 / 1-84227-050-8 / approx. 350pp

David Bostock
A Portrayal of Trust
The Theme of Faith in the Hezekiah Narratives

This study provides detailed and sensitive readings of the Hezekiah narratives (2 Kings 18–20 and Isaiah 36–39) from a theological perspective. It concentrates on the theme of faith, using narrative criticism as its methodology. Attention is paid especially to setting, plot, point of view and characterization within the narratives. A largely positive portrayal of Hezekiah emerges that underlines the importance and relevance of scripture.

2005 / 1-84227-314-0 / approx. 300pp

Mark Bredin
Jesus, Revolutionary of Peace
A Non-violent Christology in the Book of Revelation

This book aims to demonstrate that the figure of Jesus in the Book of Revelation can best be understood as an active non-violent revolutionary.

2003 / 1-84227-153-9 / xviii + 262pp

Robinson Butarbutar
Paul and Conflict Resolution
An Exegetical Study of Paul's Apostolic Paradigm in 1 Corinthians 9

The author sees the apostolic paradigm in 1 Corinthians 9 as part of Paul's unified arguments in 1 Corinthians 8–10 in which he seeks to mediate in the dispute over the issue of food offered to idols. The book also sees its relevance for dispute-resolution today, taking the conflict within the author's church as an example.

2006 / 1-84227-315-9 / approx. 280pp

Daniel J-S Chae
Paul as Apostle to the Gentiles
His Apostolic Self-awareness and its Influence on the Soteriological Argument in Romans
Opposing 'the post-Holocaust interpretation of Romans', Daniel Chae competently demonstrates that Paul argues for the equality of Jew and Gentile in Romans. Chae's fresh exegetical interpretation is academically outstanding and spiritually encouraging.
1997 / 0-85364-829-8 / xiv + 378pp

Luke L. Cheung
The Genre, Composition and Hermeneutics of the Epistle of James
The present work examines the employment of the wisdom genre with a certain compositional structure and the interpretation of the law through the Jesus tradition of the double love command by the author of the Epistle of James to serve his purpose in promoting perfection and warning against doubleness among the eschatologically renewed people of God in the Diaspora.
2003 / 1-84227-062-1 / xvi + 372pp

Youngmo Cho
Spirit and Kingdom in the Writings of Luke and Paul
The relationship between Spirit and Kingdom is a relatively unexplored area in Lukan and Pauline studies. This book offers a fresh perspective of two biblical writers on the subject. It explores the difference between Luke's and Paul's understanding of the Spirit by examining the specific question of the relationship of the concept of the Spirit to the concept of the Kingdom of God in each writer.
2005 / 1-84227-316-7 / approx. 270pp

Andrew C. Clark
Parallel Lives
The Relation of Paul to the Apostles in the Lucan Perspective
This study of the Peter-Paul parallels in Acts argues that their purpose was to emphasize the themes of continuity in salvation history and the unity of the Jewish and Gentile missions. New light is shed on Luke's literary techniques, partly through a comparison with Plutarch.
2001 / 1-84227-035-4 / xviii + 386pp

Andrew D. Clarke
Secular and Christian Leadership in Corinth
A Socio-Historical and Exegetical Study of 1 Corinthians 1–6

This volume is an investigation into the leadership structures and dynamics of first-century Roman Corinth. These are compared with the practice of leadership in the Corinthian Christian community which are reflected in 1 Corinthians 1–6, and contrasted with Paul's own principles of Christian leadership.

2005 / 1-84227-229-2 / 200pp

Stephen Finamore
God, Order and Chaos
René Girard and the Apocalypse

Readers are often disturbed by the images of destruction in the book of Revelation and unsure why they are unleashed after the exaltation of Jesus. This book examines past approaches to these texts and uses René Girard's theories to revive some old ideas and propose some new ones.

2005 / 1-84227-197-0 / approx. 344pp

David G. Firth
Surrendering Retribution in the Psalms
Responses to Violence in the Individual Complaints

In *Surrendering Retribution in the Psalms*, David Firth examines the ways in which the book of Psalms inculcates a model response to violence through the repetition of standard patterns of prayer. Rather than seeking justification for retributive violence, Psalms encourages not only a surrender of the right of retribution to Yahweh, but also sets limits on the retribution that can be sought in imprecations. Arising initially from the author's experience in South Africa, the possibilities of this model to a particular context of violence is then briefly explored.

2005 / 1-84227-337-X / xviii + 154pp

Scott J. Hafemann
Suffering and Ministry in the Spirit
Paul's Defence of His Ministry in II Corinthians 2:14–3:3

Shedding new light on the way Paul defended his apostleship, the author offers a careful, detailed study of 2 Corinthians 2:14–3:3 linked with other key passages throughout 1 and 2 Corinthians. Demonstrating the unity and coherence of Paul's argument in this passage, the author shows that Paul's suffering served as the vehicle for revealing God's power and glory through the Spirit.

2000 / 0-85364-967-7 / xiv + 262pp

Scott J. Hafemann
Paul, Moses and the History of Israel
The Letter/Spirit Contrast and the Argument from Scripture in 2 Corinthians 3
An exegetical study of the call of Moses, the second giving of the Law (Exodus 32–34), the new covenant, and the prophetic understanding of the history of Israel in 2 Corinthians 3. Hafemann's work demonstrates Paul's contextual use of the Old Testament and the essential unity between the Law and the Gospel within the context of the distinctive ministries of Moses and Paul.
2005 / 1-84227-317-5 / xii + 498pp

Douglas S. McComiskey
Lukan Theology in the Light of the Gospel's Literary Structure
Luke's Gospel was purposefully written with theology embedded in its patterned literary structure. A critical analysis of this cyclical structure provides new windows into Luke's interpretation of the individual pericopes comprising the Gospel and illuminates several of his theological interests.
2004 / 1-84227-148-2 / xviii + 388pp

Stephen Motyer
Your Father the Devil?
A New Approach to John and 'The Jews'
Who are 'the Jews' in John's Gospel? Defending John against the charge of antisemitism, Motyer argues that, far from demonising the Jews, the Gospel seeks to present Jesus as 'Good News for Jews' in a late first century setting.
1997 / 0-85364-832-8 / xiv + 260pp

Esther Ng
Reconstructing Christian Origins?
The Feminist Theology of Elizabeth Schüssler Fiorenza: An Evaluation
In a detailed evaluation, the author challenges Elizabeth Schüssler Fiorenza's reconstruction of early Christian origins and her underlying presuppositions. The author also presents her own views on women's roles both then and now.
2002 / 1-84227-055-9 / xxiv + 468pp

Robin Parry
Old Testament Story and Christian Ethics
The Rape of Dinah as a Case Study

What is the role of story in ethics and, more particularly, what is the role of Old Testament story in Christian ethics? This book, drawing on the work of contemporary philosophers, argues that narrative is crucial in the ethical shaping of people and, drawing on the work of contemporary Old Testament scholars, that story plays a key role in Old Testament ethics. Parry then argues that when situated in canonical context Old Testament stories can be reappropriated by Christian readers in their own ethical formation. The shocking story of the rape of Dinah and the massacre of the Shechemites provides a fascinating case study for exploring the parameters within which Christian ethical appropriations of Old Testament stories can live.

2004 / 1-84227-210-1 / xx + 350pp

Ian Paul
Power to See the World Anew
The Value of Paul Ricoeur's Hermeneutic of Metaphor in Interpreting the Symbolism of Revelation 12 and 13

This book is a study of the hermeneutics of metaphor of Paul Ricoeur, one of the most important writers on hermeneutics and metaphor of the last century. It sets out the key points of his theory, important criticisms of his work, and how his approach, modified in the light of these criticisms, offers a methodological framework for reading apocalyptic texts.

2006 / 1-84227-056-7 / approx. 350pp

Robert L. Plummer
Paul's Understanding of the Church's Mission
Did the Apostle Paul Expect the Early Christian Communities to Evangelize?

This book engages in a careful study of Paul's letters to determine if the apostle expected the communities to which he wrote to engage in missionary activity. It helpfully summarizes the discussion on this debated issue, judiciously handling contested texts, and provides a way forward in addressing this critical question. While admitting that Paul rarely explicitly commands the communities he founded to evangelize, Plummer amasses significant incidental data to provide a convincing case that Paul did indeed expect his churches to engage in mission activity. Throughout the study, Plummer progressively builds a theological basis for the church's mission that is both distinctively Pauline and compelling.

2006 / 1-84227-333-7 / approx. 324pp

David Powys
'Hell': A Hard Look at a Hard Question
The Fate of the Unrighteous in New Testament Thought
This comprehensive treatment seeks to unlock the original meaning of terms and phrases long thought to support the traditional doctrine of hell. It concludes that there is an alternative—one which is more biblical, and which can positively revive the rationale for Christian mission.

1997 / 0-85364-831-X / xxii + 478pp

Sorin Sabou
Between Horror and Hope
Paul's Metaphorical Language of Death in Romans 6.1-11
This book argues that Paul's metaphorical language of death in Romans 6.1-11 conveys two aspects: horror and hope. The 'horror' aspect is conveyed by the 'crucifixion' language, and the 'hope' aspect by 'burial' language. The life of the Christian believer is understood, as relationship with sin is concerned ('death to sin'), between these two realities: horror and hope.

2005 / 1-84227-322-1 / approx. 224pp

Rosalind Selby
The Comical Doctrine
The Epistemology of New Testament Hermeneutics
This book argues that the gospel breaks through postmodernity's critique of truth and the referential possibilities of textuality with its gift of grace. With a rigorous, philosophical challenge to modernist and postmodernist assumptions, Selby offers an alternative epistemology to all who would still read with faith *and* with academic credibility.

2005 / 1-84227-212-8 / approx. 350pp

Kiwoong Son
Zion Symbolism in Hebrews
Hebrews 12.18-24 as a Hermeneutical Key to the Epistle
This book challenges the general tendency of understanding the Epistle to the Hebrews against a Hellenistic background and suggests that the Epistle should be understood in the light of the Jewish apocalyptic tradition. The author especially argues for the importance of the theological symbolism of Sinai and Zion (Heb. 12:18-24) as it provides the Epistle's theological background as well as the rhetorical basis of the superiority motif of Jesus throughout the Epistle.

2005 / 1-84227-368-X / approx. 280pp

Kevin Walton
Thou Traveller Unknown
The Presence and Absence of God in the Jacob Narrative
The author offers a fresh reading of the story of Jacob in the book of Genesis through the paradox of divine presence and absence. The work also seeks to make a contribution to Pentateuchal studies by bringing together a close reading of the final text with historical critical insights, doing justice to the text's historical depth, final form and canonical status.
2003 / 1-84227-059-1 / xvi + 238pp

George M. Wieland
The Significance of Salvation
A Study of Salvation Language in the Pastoral Epistles
The language and ideas of salvation pervade the three Pastoral Epistles. This study offers a close examination of their soteriological statements. In all three letters the idea of salvation is found to play a vital paraenetic role, but each also exhibits distinctive soteriological emphases. The results challenge common assumptions about the Pastoral Epistles as a corpus.
2005 / 1-84227-257-8 / approx. 324pp

Alistair Wilson
When Will These Things Happen?
A Study of Jesus as Judge in Matthew 21–25
This study seeks to allow Matthew's carefully constructed presentation of Jesus to be given full weight in the modern evaluation of Jesus' eschatology. Careful analysis of the text of Matthew 21–25 reveals Jesus to be standing firmly in the Jewish prophetic and wisdom traditions as he proclaims and enacts imminent judgement on the Jewish authorities then boldly claims the central role in the final and universal judgement.
2004 / 1-84227-146-6 / xxii + 272pp

Lindsay Wilson
Joseph Wise and Otherwise
The Intersection of Covenant and Wisdom in Genesis 37–50
This book offers a careful literary reading of Genesis 37–50 that argues that the Joseph story contains both strong covenant themes and many wisdom-like elements. The connections between the two helps to explore how covenant and wisdom might intersect in an integrated biblical theology.
2004 / 1-84227-140-7 / xvi + 340pp

Stephen I. Wright
The Voice of Jesus
Studies in the Interpretation of Six Gospel Parables
This literary study considers how the 'voice' of Jesus has been heard in different periods of parable interpretation, and how the categories of figure and trope may help us towards a sensitive reading of the parables today.
2000 / 0-85364-975-8 / xiv + 280pp

Paternoster
9 Holdom Avenue,
Bletchley,
Milton Keynes MK1 1QR,
United Kingdom
Web: www.authenticmedia.co.uk/paternoster

Paternoster Theological Monographs
(All titles uniform with this volume)
Dates in bold are of projected publication

Emil Bartos
Deification in Eastern Orthodox Theology
An Evaluation and Critique of the Theology of Dumitru Staniloae

Bartos studies a fundamental yet neglected aspect of Orthodox theology: deification. By examining the doctrines of anthropology, christology, soteriology and ecclesiology as they relate to deification, he provides an important contribution to contemporary dialogue between Eastern and Western theologians.

1999 / 0-85364-956-1 / xii + 370pp

Graham Buxton
The Trinity, Creation and Pastoral Ministry
Imaging the Perichoretic God

In this book the author proposes a three-way conversation between theology, science and pastoral ministry. His approach draws on a Trinitarian understanding of God as a relational being of love, whose life 'spills over' into all created reality, human and non-human. By locating human meaning and purpose within God's 'creation-community' this book offers the possibility of a transforming engagement between those in pastoral ministry and the scientific community.

***2005** / 1-84227-369-8 / approx. 380 pp*

Iain D. Campbell
Fixing the Indemnity
The Life and Work of George Adam Smith

When Old Testament scholar George Adam Smith (1856–1942) delivered the Lyman Beecher lectures at Yale University in 1899, he confidently declared that 'modern criticism has won its war against traditional theories. It only remains to fix the amount of the indemnity.' In this biography, Iain D. Campbell assesses Smith's critical approach to the Old Testament and evaluates its consequences, showing that Smith's life and work still raises questions about the relationship between biblical scholarship and evangelical faith.

2004 / 1-84227-228-4 / xx + 256pp

Tim Chester
Mission and the Coming of God
Eschatology, the Trinity and Mission in the Theology of Jürgen Moltmann
This book explores the theology and missiology of the influential contemporary theologian, Jürgen Moltmann. It highlights the important contribution Moltmann has made while offering a critique of his thought from an evangelical perspective. In so doing, it touches on pertinent issues for evangelical missiology. The conclusion takes Calvin as a starting point, proposing 'an eschatology of the cross' which offers a critique of the over-realised eschatologies in liberation theology and certain forms of evangelicalism.
2006 / 1-84227-320-5 / approx. 224pp

Sylvia Wilkey Collinson
Making Disciples
The Significance of Jesus' Educational Strategy for Today's Church
This study examines the biblical practice of discipling, formulates a definition, and makes comparisons with modern models of education. A recommendation is made for greater attention to its practice today.
2004 / 1-84227-116-4 / xiv + 278pp

Darrell Cosden
A Theology of Work
Work and the New Creation
Through dialogue with Moltmann, Pope John Paul II and others, this book develops a genitive 'theology of work', presenting a theological definition of work and a model for a theological ethics of work that shows work's nature, value and meaning now and eschatologically. Work is shown to be a transformative activity consisting of three dynamically inter-related dimensions: the instrumental, relational and ontological.
2005 / 1-84227-332-9 / xvi + 208pp

Stephen M. Dunning
The Crisis and the Quest
A Kierkegaardian Reading of Charles Williams
Employing Kierkegaardian categories and analysis, this study investigates both the central crisis in Charles Williams's authorship between hermetism and Christianity (Kierkegaard's Religions A and B), and the quest to resolve this crisis, a quest that ultimately presses the bounds of orthodoxy.
2000 / 0-85364-985-5 / xxiv + 254pp

Keith Ferdinando
The Triumph of Christ in African Perspective
A Study of Demonology and Redemption in the African Context
The book explores the implications of the gospel for traditional African fears of occult aggression. It analyses such traditional approaches to suffering and biblical responses to fears of demonic evil, concluding with an evaluation of African beliefs from the perspective of the gospel.
1999 / 0-85364-830-1 / xviii + 450pp

Andrew Goddard
Living the Word, Resisting the World
The Life and Thought of Jacques Ellul
This work offers a definitive study of both the life and thought of the French Reformed thinker Jacques Ellul (1912-1994). It will prove an indispensable resource for those interested in this influential theologian and sociologist and for Christian ethics and political thought generally.
2002 / 1-84227-053-2 / xxiv + 378pp

David Hilborn
The Words of our Lips
Language-Use in Free Church Worship
Studies of liturgical language have tended to focus on the written canons of Roman Catholic and Anglican communities. By contrast, David Hilborn analyses the more extemporary approach of English Nonconformity. Drawing on recent developments in linguistic pragmatics, he explores similarities and differences between 'fixed' and 'free' worship, and argues for the interdependence of each.
2006 / 0-85364-977-4 / approx. 350pp

Roger Hitching
The Church and Deaf People
A Study of Identity, Communication and Relationships with Special Reference to the Ecclesiology of Jürgen Moltmann
In *The Church and Deaf People* Roger Hitching sensitively examines the history and present experience of deaf people and finds similarities between aspects of sign language and Moltmann's theological method that 'open up' new ways of understanding theological concepts.
2003 / 1-84227-222-5 / xxii + 236pp

John G. Kelly
One God, One People
The Differentiated Unity of the People of God in the Theology of Jürgen Moltmann

The author expounds and critiques Moltmann's doctrine of God and highlights the systematic connections between it and Moltmann's influential discussion of Israel. He then proposes a fresh approach to Jewish–Christian relations building on Moltmann's work using insights from Habermas and Rawls.

2005 / 0-85346-969-3 / approx. 350pp

Mark F.W. Lovatt
Confronting the Will-to-Power
A Reconsideration of the Theology of Reinhold Niebuhr

Confronting the Will-to-Power is an analysis of the theology of Reinhold Niebuhr, arguing that his work is an attempt to identify, and provide a practical theological answer to, the existence and nature of human evil.

2001 / 1-84227-054-0 / xviii + 216pp

Neil B. MacDonald
Karl Barth and the Strange New World within the Bible
Barth, Wittgenstein, and the Metadilemmas of the Enlightenment

Barth's discovery of the strange new world within the Bible is examined in the context of Kant, Hume, Overbeck, and, most importantly, Wittgenstein. MacDonald covers some fundamental issues in theology today: epistemology, the final form of the text and biblical truth-claims.

2000 / 0-85364-970-7 / xxvi + 374pp

Keith A. Mascord
Alvin Plantinga and Christian Apologetics

This book draws together the contributions of the philosopher Alvin Plantinga to the major contemporary challenges to Christian belief, highlighting in particular his ground-breaking work in epistemology and the problem of evil. Plantinga's theory that both theistic and Christian belief is warrantedly basic is explored and critiqued, and an assessment offered as to the significance of his work for apologetic theory and practice.

2005 / 1-84227-256-X / approx. 304pp

Gillian McCulloch
The Deconstruction of Dualism in Theology
With Reference to Ecofeminist Theology and New Age Spirituality
This book challenges eco-theological anti-dualism in Christian theology, arguing that dualism has a twofold function in Christian religious discourse. Firstly, it enables us to express the discontinuities and divisions that are part of the process of reality. Secondly, dualistic language allows us to express the mysteries of divine transcendence/immanence and the survival of the soul without collapsing into monism and materialism, both of which are problematic for Christian epistemology.

2002 / 1-84227-044-3 / xii + 282pp

Leslie McCurdy
Attributes and Atonement
The Holy Love of God in the Theology of P.T. Forsyth
Attributes and Atonement is an intriguing full-length study of P.T. Forsyth's doctrine of the cross as it relates particularly to God's holy love. It includes an unparalleled bibliography of both primary and secondary material relating to Forsyth.

1999 / 0-85364-833-6 / xiv + 328pp

Nozomu Miyahira
Towards a Theology of the Concord of God
A Japanese Perspective on the Trinity
This book introduces a new Japanese theology and a unique Trinitarian formula based on the Japanese intellectual climate: three betweennesses and one concord. It also presents a new interpretation of the Trinity, a co-subordinationism, which is in line with orthodox Trinitarianism; each single person of the Trinity is eternally and equally subordinate (or serviceable) to the other persons, so that they retain the mutual dynamic equality.

2000 / 0-85364-863-8 / xiv + 256pp

Eddy José Muskus
The Origins and Early Development of Liberation Theology in Latin America
With Particular Reference to Gustavo Gutiérrez
This work challenges the fundamental premise of Liberation Theology, 'opting for the poor', and its claim that Christ is found in them. It also argues that Liberation Theology emerged as a direct result of the failure of the Roman Catholic Church in Latin America.

2002 / 0-85364-974-X / xiv + 296pp

Jim Purves
The Triune God and the Charismatic Movement
A Critical Appraisal from a Scottish Perspective
All emotion and no theology? Or a fundamental challenge to reappraise and realign our trinitarian theology in the light of Christian experience? This study of charismatic renewal as it found expression within Scotland at the end of the twentieth century evaluates the use of Patristic, Reformed and contemporary models of the Trinity in explaining the workings of the Holy Spirit.
2004 / 1-84227-321-3 / xxiv + 246pp

Anna Robbins
Methods in the Madness
Diversity in Twentieth-Century Christian Social Ethics
The author compares the ethical methods of Walter Rauschenbusch, Reinhold Niebuhr and others. She argues that unless Christians are clear about the ways that theology and philosophy are expressed practically they may lose the ability to discuss social ethics across contexts, let alone reach effective agreements.
2004 / 1-84227-211-X / xx + 294pp

Ed Rybarczyk
Beyond Salvation
Eastern Orthodoxy and Classical Pentecostalism on Becoming Like Christ
At first glance eastern Orthodoxy and classical Pentecostalism seem quite distinct. This ground-breaking study shows they share much in common, especially as it concerns the experiential elements of following Christ. Both traditions assert that authentic Christianity transcends the wooden categories of modernism.
2004 / 1-84227-144-X / xii + 356pp

Signe Sandsmark
Is World View Neutral Education Possible and Desirable?
A Christian Response to Liberal Arguments
(Published jointly with The Stapleford Centre)
This book discusses reasons for belief in world view neutrality, and argues that 'neutral' education will have a hidden, but strong world view influence. It discusses the place for Christian education in the common school.
2000 / 0-85364-973-1 / xiv + 182pp

Hazel Sherman
Reading Zechariah
The Allegorical Tradition of Biblical Interpretation through the Commentary of Didymus the Blind and Theodore of Mopsuestia
A close reading of the commentary on Zechariah by Didymus the Blind alongside that of Theodore of Mopsuestia suggests that popular categorising of Antiochene and Alexandrian biblical exegesis as 'historical' or 'allegorical' is inadequate and misleading.
2005 / 1-84227-213-6 / approx. 280pp

Andrew Sloane
On Being a Christian in the Academy
Nicholas Wolterstorff and the Practice of Christian Scholarship
An exposition and critical appraisal of Nicholas Wolterstorff's epistemology in the light of the philosophy of science, and an application of his thought to the practice of Christian scholarship.
2003 / 1-84227-058-3 / xvi + 274pp

Damon W.K. So
Jesus' Revelation of His Father
A Narrative-Conceptual Study of the Trinity with Special Reference to Karl Barth
This book explores the trinitarian dynamics in the context of Jesus' revelation of his Father in his earthly ministry with references to key passages in Matthew's Gospel. It develops from the exegeses of these passages a non-linear concept of revelation which links Jesus' communion with his Father to his revelatory words and actions through a nuanced understanding of the Holy Spirit, with references to K. Barth, G.W.H. Lampe, J.D.G. Dunn and E. Irving.
2005 / 1-84227-323-X / approx. 380pp

Daniel Strange
The Possibility of Salvation Among the Unevangelised
An Analysis of Inclusivism in Recent Evangelical Theology
For evangelical theologians the 'fate of the unevangelised' impinges upon fundamental tenets of evangelical identity. The position known as 'inclusivism', defined by the belief that the unevangelised can be ontologically saved by Christ whilst being epistemologically unaware of him, has been defended most vigorously by the Canadian evangelical Clark H. Pinnock. Through a detailed analysis and critique of Pinnock's work, this book examines a cluster of issues surrounding the unevangelised and its implications for christology, soteriology and the doctrine of revelation.
2002 / 1-84227-047-8 / xviii + 362pp

Scott Swain
God According to the Gospel
Biblical Narrative and the Identity of God in the Theology of Robert W. Jenson
Robert W. Jenson is one of the leading voices in contemporary Trinitarian theology. His boldest contribution in this area concerns his use of biblical narrative both to ground and explicate the Christian doctrine of God. *God According to the Gospel* critically examines Jenson's proposal and suggests an alternative way of reading the biblical portrayal of the triune God.
2006 / 1-84227-258-6 / approx. 180pp

Justyn Terry
The Justifying Judgement of God
A Reassessment of the Place of Judgement in the Saving Work of Christ
The argument of this book is that judgement, understood as the whole process of bringing justice, is the primary metaphor of atonement, with others, such as victory, redemption and sacrifice, subordinate to it. Judgement also provides the proper context for understanding penal substitution and the call to repentance, baptism, eucharist and holiness.
2005 / 1-84227-370-1 / approx. 274 pp

Graham Tomlin
The Power of the Cross
Theology and the Death of Christ in Paul, Luther and Pascal
This book explores the theology of the cross in St Paul, Luther and Pascal. It offers new perspectives on the theology of each, and some implications for the nature of power, apologetics, theology and church life in a postmodern context.
1999 / 0-85364-984-7 / xiv + 344pp

Adonis Vidu
Postliberal Theological Method
A Critical Study
The postliberal theology of Hans Frei, George Lindbeck, Ronald Thiemann, John Milbank and others is one of the more influential contemporary options. This book focuses on several aspects pertaining to its theological method, specifically its understanding of background, hermeneutics, epistemic justification, ontology, the nature of doctrine and, finally, Christological method.
2005 / 1-84227-395-7 / approx. 324pp

Graham J. Watts
Revelation and the Spirit
A Comparative Study of the Relationship between the Doctrine of Revelation and Pneumatology in the Theology of Eberhard Jüngel and of Wolfhart Pannenberg

The relationship between revelation and pneumatology is relatively unexplored. This approach offers a fresh angle on two important twentieth century theologians and raises pneumatological questions which are theologically crucial and relevant to mission in a postmodern culture.

2005 / 1-84227-104-0 / xxii + 232pp

Nigel G. Wright
Disavowing Constantine
Mission, Church and the Social Order in the Theologies of John Howard Yoder and Jürgen Moltmann

This book is a timely restatement of a radical theology of church and state in the Anabaptist and Baptist tradition. Dr Wright constructs his argument in dialogue and debate with Yoder and Moltmann, major contributors to a free church perspective.

2000 / 0-85364-978-2 / xvi + 252pp

Paternoster
9 Holdom Avenue,
Bletchley,
Milton Keynes MK1 1QR,
United Kingdom
Web: www.authenticmedia.co.uk/paternoster

www.ingramcontent.com/pod-product-compliance
Lightning Source LLC
Chambersburg PA
CBHW051632230426
43669CB00013B/2273